SO-AEY-164

1975

Al Beitzinger

The GREEKS and the IRRATIONAL

The GREEKS
and the
IRRATIONAL

By E. R. DODDS

UNIVERSITY OF CALIFORNIA PRESS

Berkeley, Los Angeles, London

University of California Press
Berkeley and Los Angeles
California

University of California Press, Ltd.
London, England

Copyright, 1951, by
The Regents of the University of California

Originally published as Volume Twenty-five
of the Sather Classical Lectures
Eighth printing, 1973

ISBN: 0-520-00327-6

Manufactured in the United States of America

To GILBERT MURRAY

τροφεῖα

PREFACE

THIS BOOK is based on a course of lectures which I had the honour of giving at Berkeley in the autumn of 1949. They are reproduced here substantially as they were composed, though in a form slightly fuller than that in which they were delivered. Their original audience included many anthropologists and other scholars who had no specialist knowledge of ancient Greece, and it is my hope that in their present shape they may interest a similar audience of readers. I have therefore translated virtually all Greek quotations occurring in the text, and have transliterated the more important of those Greek terms which have no true English equivalent. I have also abstained as far as possible from encumbering the text with controversial arguments on points of detail, which could mean little to readers unfamiliar with the views controverted, and from complicating my main theme by pursuing the numerous side-issues which tempt the professional scholar. A selection of such matter will be found in the notes, in which I have tried to indicate briefly, where possible by reference to ancient sources or modern discussions, and where necessary by argument, the grounds for the opinions advanced in the text.

To the nonclassical reader I should like to offer a warning against treating the book as if it were a history of Greek religion, or even of Greek religious ideas or feelings. If he does, he will be gravely misled. It is a study of the successive interpretations which Greek minds placed on one particular type of human experience—a sort of experience in which nineteenth-century rationalism took little interest, but whose cultural significance is now widely recognised. The evidence which is here brought together

vii

illustrates an important, and relatively unfamiliar, aspect of the mental world of ancient Greece. But an aspect must not be mistaken for the whole.

To my fellow-professionals I perhaps owe some defence of the use which I have made in several places of recent anthropological and psychological observations and theories. In a world of specialists, such borrowings from unfamiliar disciplines are, I know, generally received by the learned with apprehension and often with active distaste. I expect to be reminded, in the first place, that "the Greeks were not savages," and secondly, that in these relatively new studies the accepted truths of to-day are apt to become the discarded errors of to-morrow. Both statements are correct. But in reply to the first it is perhaps sufficient to quote the opinion of Lévy-Bruhl, that "dans tout esprit humain, quel qu'en soît le développement intellectuel, subsiste un fond indéracinable de mentalité primitive"; or, if nonclassical anthropologists are suspect, the opinion of Nilsson, that "primitive mentality is a fairly good description of the mental behaviour of most people to-day except in their technical or consciously intellectual activities." Why should we attribute to the ancient Greeks an immunity from "primitive" modes of thought which we do not find in any society open to our direct observation?

As to the second point, many of the theories to which I have referred are admittedly provisional and uncertain. But if we are trying to reach some understanding of Greek minds, and are not content with describing external behaviour or drawing up a list of recorded "beliefs," we must work by what light we can get, and an uncertain light is better than none. Tylor's animism, Mannhardt's vegetation-magic, Frazer's year-spirits, Codrington's mana, have all in their day helped to illuminate dark places in the ancient record. They have also encouraged many rash guesses. But time and the critics can be trusted to deal with the guesses; the illumination remains. I see here good reason to be cautious in applying to the Greeks generalisations based on non-Greek evidence, but none for the withdrawal of Greek scholarship into a self-imposed isolation. Still less are classical scholars justified in continuing to operate—as many of them do—with obsolete anthropological concepts, ignoring the new directions which these studies have taken in the last thirty years, such as the promising recent alliance between social anthropology and social psychology. If the truth is beyond our grasp, the errors of to-morrow are still to be preferred to the errors of yesterday; for error in the sciences is only another name for the progressive approximation to truth.

It remains to express my gratitude to those who have helped in the production of this book: in the first place to the University of California, for causing me to write it; then to Ludwig Edelstein, W. K. C. Guthrie, I. M. Linforth, and A. D. Nock, all of whom read the whole or a part in typescript and made valuable suggestions; and finally to Harold A. Small, W. H. Alexander, and others at the University of California Press, who took great and uncomplaining trouble in preparing the text for the printer. I must also thank Professor Nock and the Council of the Roman Society for permission to reprint as appendices two articles which appeared respectively in the *Harvard Theological Review* and the *Journal of Roman Studies;* and the Council of the Hellenic Society for permission to reproduce some pages from an article published in the *Journal of Hellenic Studies.*

E. R. D.

OXFORD
August 1950

CONTENTS

I   Agamemnon's Apology   1

II   From Shame-Culture to Guilt-Culture   28

III   The Blessings of Madness   64

IV   Dream-Pattern and Culture-Pattern   102

V   The Greek Shamans and the Origin of Puritanism   135

VI   Rationalism and Reaction in the Classical Age   179

VII   Plato, the Irrational Soul, and the Inherited Conglomerate   207

VIII   The Fear of Freedom   236

Appendix I   Maenadism   270

Appendix II   Theurgy   283

Index   315

I

Agamemnon's Apology

The recesses of feeling, the darker, blinder strata of character, are the only places in the world in which we catch real fact in the making.

WILLIAM JAMES

SOME YEARS ago I was in the British Museum looking at the Parthenon sculptures when a young man came up to me and said with a worried air, "I know it's an awful thing to confess, but this Greek stuff doesn't move me one bit." I said that was very interesting: could he define at all the reasons for his lack of response? He reflected for a minute or two. Then he said, "Well, it's all so terribly *rational*, if you know what I mean." I thought I did know. The young man was only saying what has been said more articulately by Roger Fry[1] and others. To a generation whose sensibilities have been trained on African and Aztec art, and on the work of such men as Modigliani and Henry Moore, the art of the Greeks, and Greek culture in general, is apt to appear lacking in the awareness of mystery and in the ability to penetrate to the deeper, less conscious levels of human experience.

This fragment of conversation stuck in my head and set me thinking. Were the Greeks in fact quite so blind to the importance of nonrational factors in man's experience and behaviour as is commonly assumed both by their apologists and by their critics? That is the question out of which this book grew. To answer it completely would evidently involve a survey of the whole cultural achievement of ancient Greece. But what I propose attempting is something much more modest: I shall

[1] For notes to chapter i see pages 18–27.

merely try to throw some light on the problem by examining afresh certain relevant aspects of Greek religious experience. I hope that the result may have a certain interest not only for Greek scholars but for some anthropologists and social psychologists, indeed for anyone who is concerned to understand the springs of human behaviour. I shall therefore try as far as possible to present the evidence in terms intelligible to the non-specialist.

I shall begin by considering a particular aspect of Homeric religion. To some classical scholars the Homeric poems will seem a bad place to look for any sort of religious experience. "The truth is," says Professor Mazon in a recent book, "that there was never a poem less religious than the *Iliad*."[2] This may be thought a little sweeping; but it reflects an opinion which seems to be widely accepted. Professor Murray thinks that the so-called Homeric religion "was not really religion at all"; for in his view "the real worship of Greece before the fourth century almost never attached itself to those luminous Olympian forms."[3] Similarly Dr. Bowra observes that "this complete anthropomorphic system has *of course* no relation to real religion or to morality. These gods are a delightful, gay invention of poets."[4]

Of course—if the expression "real religion" means the kind of thing that enlightened Europeans or Americans of to-day recognise as being religion. But if we restrict the meaning of the word in this way, are we not in danger of undervaluing, or even of overlooking altogether, certain types of experience which we no longer interpret in a religious sense, but which may nevertheless in their time have been quite heavily charged with religious significance? My purpose in the present chapter is not to quarrel with the distinguished scholars I have quoted over their use of terms, but to call attention to one kind of experience in Homer which is *prima facie* religious and to examine its psychology.

Let us start from that experience of divine temptation or infatuation (*atē*) which led Agamemnon to compensate himself

for the loss of his own mistress by robbing Achilles of his.
"Not I," he declared afterwards, "not I was the cause of this
act, but Zeus and my portion and the Erinys who walks in
darkness: they it was who in the assembly put wild *ate* in my
understanding, on that day when I arbitrarily took Achilles'
prize from him. So what could I do? Deity will always have its
way."[5] By impatient modern readers these words of Agamemnon's have sometimes been dismissed as a weak excuse or
evasion of responsibility. But not, I think, by those who read
carefully. An evasion of responsibility in the juridical sense
the words certainly are not; for at the end of his speech Agamemnon offers compensation precisely on this ground—"But
since I was blinded by *ate* and Zeus took away my understanding, I am willing to make my peace and give abundant
compensation."[6] Had he acted of his own volition, he could
not so easily admit himself in the wrong; as it is, he will pay
for his acts. Juridically, his position would be the same in
either case; for early Greek justice cared nothing for intent—
it was the act that mattered. Nor is he dishonestly inventing a
moral alibi; for the victim of his action takes the same view of
it as he does. "Father Zeus, great indeed are the *atai* thou givest
to men. Else the son of Atreus would never have persisted in
rousing the *thūmos* in my chest, nor obstinately taken the girl
against my will."[7] You may think that Achilles is here politely
accepting a fiction, in order to save the High King's face? But
no: for already in Book 1, when Achilles is explaining the situation to Thetis, he speaks of Agamemnon's behaviour as his *ate*;[8]
and in Book 9 he exclaims, "Let the son of Atreus go to his
doom and not disturb me, for Zeus the counsellor took away
his understanding."[9] It is Achilles' view of the matter as much
as Agamemnon's; and in the famous words which introduce the
story of the Wrath—"The plan of Zeus was fulfilled"[10]—we
have a strong hint that it is also the poet's view.

If this were the only incident which Homer's characters
interpreted in this peculiar way, we might hesitate as to the
poet's motive: we might guess, for example, that he wished

to avoid alienating the hearers' sympathy too completely from Agamemnon, or again that he was trying to impart a deeper significance to the rather undignified quarrel of the two chiefs by representing it as a step in the fulfilment of a divine plan. But these explanations do not apply to other passages where "the gods" or "some god" or Zeus are said to have momentarily "taken away" or "destroyed" or "ensorcelled" a human being's understanding. Either of them might indeed be applied to the case of Helen, who ends a deeply moving and evidently sincere speech by saying that Zeus has laid on her and Alexandros an evil doom, "that we may be hereafter a theme of song for men to come."[11] But when we are simply told that Zeus "ensorcelled the mind of the Achaeans," so that they fought badly, no consideration of persons comes into play; still less in the general statement that "the gods can make the most sensible man senseless and bring the feeble-minded to good sense."[12] And what, for example, of Glaucus, whose understanding Zeus took away, so that he did what Greeks almost never do—accepted a bad bargain, by swopping gold armour for bronze?[13] Or what of Automedon, whose folly in attempting to double the parts of charioteer and spearman led a friend to ask him "which of the gods had put an unprofitable plan in his breast and taken away his excellent understanding?"[14] These two cases clearly have no connection with any deeper divine purpose; nor can there be any question of retaining the hearers' sympathy, since no moral slur is involved.

At this point, however, the reader may naturally ask whether we are dealing with anything more than a *façon de parler*. Does the poet mean anything more than that Glaucus was a fool to make the bargain he did? Did Automedon's friend mean anything more than "What the dickens prompted you to behave like that?" Perhaps not. The hexameter formulae which were the stock-in-trade of the old poets lent themselves easily to the sort of semasiological degeneration which ends by creating a *façon de parler*. And we may note that neither the Glaucus episode nor the futile *aristeia* of Automedon is integral to the plot even of an "expanded" *Iliad:* they may well be additions by a later hand.[15] Our aim, however, is to understand the original experience which lies at the root of such stereo-typed formulae—for even a *façon de parler* must have an origin. It may help us to do so if we look a little more closely at the nature of *ate* and of the agencies to which Agamemnon ascribes it, and then glance at some other sorts of statement which the epic poets make about the sources of human behaviour.

There are a number of passages in Homer in which unwise and unaccountable conduct is attributed to *ate*, or described by the cognate verb *aasasthai*, without explicit reference to divine intervention. But *ate* in Homer[16] is not itself a personal agent: the two passages which speak of *ate* in personal terms, *Il.* 9.505 ff. and 19.91 ff., are transparent pieces of allegory. Nor does the word ever, at any rate in the *Iliad*, mean objective disaster,[17] as it so commonly does in tragedy. Always, or prac-tically always,[18] *ate* is a state of mind—a temporary clouding or bewildering of the normal consciousness. It is, in fact, a partial and temporary insanity; and, like all insanity, it is ascribed, not to physiological or psychological causes, but to an external "daemonic" agency. In the *Odyssey*,[19] it is true, excessive consumption of wine is said to cause *ate;* the implica-tion, however, is probably not that *ate* can be produced "natu-rally," but rather that wine has something supernatural or daemonic about it. Apart from this special case, the agents pro-ductive of *ate*, where they are specified, seem always to be supernatural beings;[20] so we may class all instances of nonalco-holic *ate* in Homer under the head of what I propose to call "psychic intervention."

If we review them, we shall observe that *ate* is by no means necessarily either a synonym for, or a result of, wickedness. The assertion of Liddell and Scott that *ate* is "mostly sent as the punishment of guilty rashness" is quite untrue of Homer. The *ate* (here a sort of stunned bewilderment) which overtook Patroclus after Apollo had struck him[21] might possibly be claimed as an instance, since Patroclus had rashly routed the

Trojans ὑπὲρ αἶσαν;²² but earlier in the scene this rashness is itself ascribed to the will of Zeus and characterised by the verb ἀάσθη.²³ Again, the *ate* of one Agastrophus²⁴ in straying too far from his chariot, and so getting himself killed, is not a "punishment" for rashness; the rashness is itself the *ate*, or a result of the *ate*, and it involves no discernible moral guilt—it is just an unaccountable error, like the bad bargain which Glaucus made. Again, Odysseus was neither guilty nor rash when he took a nap at an unfortunate moment, thus giving his companions a chance to slaughter the tabooed oxen. It was what we should call an accident; but for Homer, as for early thought in general,²⁵ there is no such thing as accident—Odysseus knows that his nap was sent by the gods εἰς ἄτην, "to fool him."²⁶ Such passages suggest that *ate* had originally no connection with guilt. The notion of *ate* as a punishment seems to be either a late development in Ionia or a late importation from outside: the only place in Homer where it is explicitly asserted is the unique Λιταί passage in *Iliad* 9,²⁷ which suggests that it may possibly be a Mainland idea, taken over along with the Meleager story from an epic composed in the mother country.

A word next about the agencies to which *ate* is ascribed. Agamemnon cites, not one such agency, but three: Zeus and *moira* and the Erinys who walks in darkness (or, according to another and perhaps older reading, the Erinys who sucks blood). Of these, Zeus is the mythological agent whom the poet conceives as the prime mover in the affair: "the plan of Zeus was fulfilled." It is perhaps significant that (unless we make Apollo responsible for the *ate* of Patroclus) Zeus is the only individual Olympian who is credited with causing *ate* in the *Iliad* (hence *ate* is allegorically described as his eldest daughter).²⁸ *Moira*, I think, is brought in because people spoke of any unaccountable personal disaster as part of their "portion" or "lot," meaning simply that they cannot understand why it happened, but since it has happened, evidently "it had to be." People still speak in that way, more especially of death, for which μῖρα has in fact become a synonym in modern Greek, like μόρος in classical Greek.

I am sure it is quite wrong to write *Moira* with a capital "M" here, as if it signified either a personal goddess who dictates to Zeus or a Cosmic Destiny like the Hellenistic *Heimarmenē*. As goddesses, *Moirai* are always plural, both in cult and in early literature, and with one doubtful exception[29] they do not figure at all in the *Iliad*. The most we can say is that by treating his "portion" as an agent—by making it *do* something—Agamemnon is taking a first step towards personification.[30] Again, by blaming his *moira* Agamemnon no more declares himself a systematic determinist than does the modern Greek peasant when he uses similar language. To ask whether Homer's people are determinists or libertarians is a fantastic anachronism: the question has never occurred to them, and if it were put to them it would be very difficult to make them understand what it meant.[31] What they do recognize is the distinction between normal actions and actions performed in a state of *ate*. Actions of the latter sort they can trace indifferently either to their *moira* or to the will of a god, according as they look at the matter from a subjective or an objective point of view. In the same way Patroclus attributes his death directly to the immediate agent, the man Euphorbus, and indirectly to the mythological agent, Apollo, but from a subjective standpoint to his bad *moira*. It is, as the psychologists say, "overdetermined."[32]

On this analogy, the Erinys should be the immediate agent in Agamemnon's case. That she should figure at all in this context may well surprise those who think of an Erinys as essentially a spirit of vengeance, still more those who believe, with Rohde,[33] that the Erinyes were originally the vengeful dead. But the passage does not stand alone. We read also in the *Odyssey*[34] of "the heavy *ate* which the hard-hitting goddess Erinys laid on the understanding of Melampus." In neither place is there any question of revenge or punishment. The explanation is perhaps that the Erinys is the personal agent who ensures the fulfilment of a *moira*. That is why the Erinyes cut short the speech of Achilles' horses: it is not "according to *moira*" for horses to talk.[35] That is why they would punish the sun, according to Heraclitus,[36] if the sun should "transgress his measures" by exceeding the task assigned to him. Most probably, I think, the moral function of the Erinyes as ministers of vengeance derives from this primitive task of enforcing a *moira* which was at first morally neutral, or rather, contained by implication both an "ought" and a "must" which early thought did not clearly distinguish. So in Homer we find them enforcing the claims to status which arise from family or social relationship and are felt to be part of a person's *moira:*[37] a parent,[38] an elder brother,[39] even a beggar,[40] has something due to him as such, and can invoke "his" Erinyes to protect it. So too they are called upon to witness oaths; for the oath creates an assignment, a *moira.* The connection of Erinys with *moira* is still attested by Aeschylus,[41] though the *moirai* have now become quasi-personal; and the Erinyes are still for Aeschylus dispensers of *ate*,[42] although both they and it have been moralised. It rather looks as if the complex *moira*-Erinys-*ate* had deep roots, and might well be older than the ascription of *ate* to the agency of Zeus.[43] In that connection it is worth recalling that Erinys and *aisa* (which is synonymous with *moira*) go back to what is perhaps the oldest known form of Hellenic speech, the Arcado-Cypriot dialect.[44]

Here, for the present, let us leave *ate* and its associates, and consider briefly another kind of "psychic intervention" which is no less frequent in Homer, namely, the communication of power from god to man. In the *Iliad*, the typical case is the communication of *měnos*[45] during a battle, as when Athena puts a triple portion of *menos* into the chest of her protégé Diomede, or Apollo puts *menos* into the *thumos* of the wounded Glaucus.[46] This *menos* is not primarily physical strength; nor is it a permanent organ of mental life[47] like *thumos* or *nŏŏs*. Rather it is, like *ate*, a state of mind. When a man feels *menos* in his chest, or "thrusting up pungently into his nostrils,"[48] he is conscious of a mysterious access of energy; the life in him is strong, and he is filled with a new confidence and eagerness. The connection of *menos* with the sphere of volition comes out clearly in the related words μενοινᾶν, "to be eager," and δυσμενής, "wishing ill." It is significant that often, though not always, a communication of *menos* comes as a response to prayer. But it is something much more spontaneous and instinctive than what we call "resolution"; animals can have it,[49] and it is used by analogy to describe the devouring energy of fire.[50] In man it is the vital energy, the "spunk," which is not always there at call, but comes and goes mysteriously and (as we should say) capriciously. But to Homer it is not caprice: it is the act of a god, who "increases or diminishes at will a man's *arĕtē* (that is to say, his potency as a fighter)."[51] Sometimes, indeed, the *menos* can be roused by verbal exhortation; at other times its onset can only be explained by saying that a god has "breathed it into" the hero, or "put it in his chest," or, as we read in one place, transmitted it by contact, through a staff.[52]

I think we should not dismiss these statements as "poetic invention" or "divine machinery." No doubt the particular instances are often invented by the poet for the convenience of his plot; and certainly the psychic intervention is sometimes linked with a physical one, or with a scene on Olympus. But we can be pretty sure that the underlying idea was not invented by any poet, and that it is older than the conception of anthropomorphic gods physically and visibly taking part in a battle. The temporary possession of a heightened *menos* is, like *ate*, an abnormal state which demands a supernormal explanation. Homer's men can recognise its onset, which is marked by a peculiar sensation in the limbs. "My feet beneath and hands above feel eager (μαιμώωσι)," says one recipient of the power: that is because, as the poet tells us, the god has made them nimble (ἐλαφρά).[53] This sensation, which is here shared by a second recipient, confirms for them the divine origin of the *menos*.[54] It is an abnormal experience. And men in a condition of divinely heightened *menos* behave to some extent abnormally. They can perform the most difficult feats with ease (ῥέα):[55] that is a traditional mark of divine power.[56] They can even, like Diomede, fight with impunity against gods[57]—an action which to men in their normal state is excessively dangerous.[58] They are in fact for the time being rather more, or perhaps rather less, than human. Men who have received a communication of *menos* are several times compared to ravening lions;[59] but the most striking description of the state is in Book 15, where Hector goes berserk (μαίνεται), he foams at the mouth, and his eyes glow.[60] From such cases it is only a step to the idea of actual possession (δαιμονᾶν); but it is a step which Homer does not take. He does say of Hector that after he had put on Achilles' armour "Ares entered into him and his limbs were filled with courage and strength";[61] but Ares here is hardly more than a synonym for the martial spirit, and the communication of power is produced by the will of Zeus, assisted perhaps by the divine armour. Gods do of course for purposes of disguise assume the shape and appearance of individual human beings; but that is a different belief. Gods may appear at times in human form, men may share at times in the divine attribute of power, but in Homer there is nevertheless no real blurring of the sharp line which separates humanity from deity.

In the *Odyssey*, which is less exclusively concerned with fighting, the communication of power takes other forms. The poet of the "Telemachy" imitates the *Iliad* by making Athena put *menos* into Telemachus;[62] but here the *menos* is the *moral* courage which will enable the boy to face the overbearing suitors. That is literary adaptation. Older and more authentic is the repeated claim that minstrels derive their creative power from God. "I am self-taught," says Phemius; "it was a god who implanted all sorts of lays in my mind."[63] The two parts of his statement are not felt as contradictory: he means, I think, that he has not memorised the lays of other minstrels, but is a creative poet who relies on the hexameter phrases welling up spontaneously as he needs them out of some unknown and uncontrollable depth; he sings "out of the gods," as the best minstrels always do.[64] I shall come back to that in the latter part of chapter iii, "The Blessings of Madness."

But the most characteristic feature of the *Odyssey* is the way in which its personages ascribe all sorts of mental (as well as physical) events to the intervention of a nameless and indeterminate daemon[65] or "god" or "gods."[66] These vaguely conceived beings can inspire courage at a crisis[67] or take away a man's understanding,[68] just as gods do in the *Iliad*. But they are also credited with a wide range of what may be called loosely "monitions." Whenever someone has a particularly brilliant[69] or a particularly foolish[70] idea; when he suddenly recognises another person's identity[71] or sees in a flash the meaning of an omen;[72] when he remembers what he might well have forgotten[73] or forgets what he should have remembered,[74] he or someone else will see in it, if we are to take the words literally, a psychic intervention by one of these anonymous supernatural beings.[75] Doubtless they do not always expect to be taken literally: Odysseus, for example, is hardly serious in ascribing to the machinations of a daemon the fact that he went out without his cloak on a cold night. But we are not dealing simply with an "epic convention." For it is the poet's characters who talk like this, and not the poet:[76] his own convention is quite other—he operates, like the author of the *Iliad*, with clear-cut anthropomorphic gods such as Athena and Poseidon, not with anonymous daemons. If he has made his characters employ a different convention, he has presumably done so because that is how people did in fact talk: he is being "realistic."

And indeed that is how we should expect people to talk who believed (or whose ancestors had believed) in daily and hourly monitions. The recognition, the insight, the memory, the brilliant or perverse idea, have this in common, that they come suddenly, as we say, "into a man's head." Often he is conscious of no observation or reasoning which has led up to them. But in that case, how can he call them "his"? A moment ago they were not in his mind; now they are there. Something has put them there, and that something is other than himself. More than this he does not know. So he speaks of it noncommittally as "the gods" or "some god," or more often (especially when its prompting has turned out to be bad) as a daemon.[77] And by analogy he applies the same explanation to the ideas and actions of other people when he finds them difficult to understand or out of character. A good example is Antinous' speech in *Odyssey* 2, where, after praising Penelope's exceptional intelligence and propriety, he goes on to say that her idea of refusing to remarry is not at all proper, and concludes that "the gods are putting it into her chest."[78] Similarly, when Telemachus for the first time speaks out boldly against the suitors, Antinous infers, not without irony, that "the gods are teaching him to talk big."[79] His teacher is in fact Athena, as the poet and the reader know;[80] but Antinous is not to know that, so he says "the gods."

A similar distinction between what the speaker knows and what the poet knows may be observed in some places in the *Iliad*. When Teucer's bowstring breaks, he cries out with a shudder of fear that a daemon is thwarting him; but it was in fact Zeus who broke it, as the poet has just told us.[81] It has been suggested that in such passages the poet's point of view is the older: that he still makes use of the "Mycenaean" divine machinery, while his characters ignore it and use vaguer language like the poet's Ionian contemporaries, who (it is asserted) were losing their faith in the old anthropomorphic gods.[82] In my view, as we shall see in a moment, this is almost an exact reversal of the real relationship. And it is anyhow clear that Teucer's vagueness has nothing to do with scepticism: it is the simple result of ignorance. By using the word *daemon* he "expresses the fact that a higher power has made something happen,"[83] and this fact is all he knows. As Ehnmark has pointed out,[84] similar vague language in reference to the supernatural was commonly used by Greeks at all periods, not out of scepticism, but simply because they could not identify the particular god concerned. It is also commonly used by primitive peoples, whether for the same reason or because they lack the idea of personal gods.[85] That its use by the Greeks is very old is shown by the high antiquity of the adjective *daemŏnios*. That word must originally have meant "acting at the monition of a daemon"; but already in the *Iliad* its primitive sense has so far faded that Zeus can apply it to Hera.[86] A verbal coinage so defaced has clearly been in circulation for a long time.

We have now surveyed, in such a cursory manner as time permits, the commonest types of psychic intervention in Homer. We may sum up the result by saying that all departures from normal human behaviour whose causes are not immediately perceived,[87] whether by the subjects' own consciousness or by the observation of others, are ascribed to a supernatural agency, just as is any departure from the normal behaviour of the weather or the normal behaviour of a bowstring. This finding will not surprise the nonclassical anthropologist: he will at once produce copious parallels from Borneo or Central Africa. But it is surely odd to find this belief, this sense of constant daily dependence on the supernatural, firmly embedded in poems supposedly so "irreligious" as the *Iliad* and the *Odyssey*. And we may also ask ourselves why a people so civilised, clearheaded, and rational as the Ionians did not eliminate from their national epics these links with Borneo and the primitive past, just as they eliminated fear of the dead, fear of pollution, and other primitive terrors which must originally have played a part in the saga. I doubt if the early literature of any other European people—even my own superstitious countrymen, the Irish—postulates supernatural interference in human behaviour with such frequency or over so wide a field.[88]

Nilsson is, I think, the first scholar who has seriously tried to find an explanation of all this in terms of psychology. In a paper published in 1924,[89] which has now become classical, he contended that Homeric heroes are peculiarly subject to rapid and violent changes of mood: they suffer, he says, from mental instability (*psychische Labilität*). And he goes on to point out that even to-day a person of this temperament is apt, when his mood changes, to look back with horror on what he has just done, and exclaim, "I didn't really mean to do that!"—from which it is a short step to saying, "It wasn't really I who did it." "His own behaviour," says Nilsson, "has become alien to him. He cannot understand it. It is for him no part of his Ego." This is a perfectly true observation, and its relevance to some of the phenomena we have been considering cannot, I think, be doubted. Nilsson is also, I believe, right in holding that experiences of this sort played a part—along with other elements, such as the Minoan tradition of protecting goddesses—in building up that machinery of *physical* intervention to which Homer resorts so constantly and, to our thinking, often so superfluously. We find it superfluous because the divine machinery seems to us in many cases to do no more than duplicate a natural psychological causation.[90] But ought we not perhaps to say rather that the divine machinery "duplicates" a psychic intervention—that is, presents it in a concrete pictorial form? This was not superfluous; for only in this way could it be made vivid to the imagination of the hearers. The Homeric poets were without the refinements of language which would have been needed to "put across" adequately a purely psychological miracle. What more natural than that they should first supplement, and later replace, an old unexciting threadbare formula like μένος ἔμβαλε θυμῷ by making the god appear as a physical presence and exhort his favourite with the spoken word?[91] How much more vivid than a mere inward monition is the famous scene in *Iliad* 1 where Athena plucks Achilles by the hair and warns him not to strike Agamemnon! But she is visible to Achilles alone: "none of the others saw her."[92] That is a plain hint that she is the projection, the pictorial expression, of an inward monition[93]—a monition which Achilles might have described by such a vague phrase as ἐνέπνευσε φρεσὶ δαίμων. And I suggest that in general the inward monition, or the sudden unaccountable feeling of power, or the sudden unaccountable loss of judgement, is the germ out of which the divine machinery developed.

One result of transposing the event from the interior to the external world is that the vagueness is eliminated: the indeterminate daemon has to be made concrete as some particular personal god. In *Iliad* 1 he becomes Athena, the goddess of good counsel. But that was a matter for the poet's choice. And through a multitude of such choices the poets must gradually have built up the personalities of their gods, "distinguishing," as Herodotus says,[94] "their offices and skills, and fixing their physical appearance." The poets did not, of course, invent the gods (nor does Herodotus say so): Athena, for example, had been, as we now have reason to believe, a Minoan house-goddess. But the poets bestowed upon them personality—and thereby, as Nilsson says, made it impossible for Greece to lapse into the magical type of religion which prevailed among her Oriental neighbours.

Some, however, may be disposed to challenge the assertion on which, for Nilsson, all this construction rests. *Are* Homer's people exceptionally unstable, as compared with the characters in other early epics? The evidence adduced by Nilsson is rather slight. They come to blows on small provocation; but so do Norse and Irish heroes. Hector on one occasion goes berserk; but Norse heroes do so much oftener. Homeric men weep in a more uninhibited manner than Swedes or Englishmen; but so do all the Mediterranean peoples to this day. We may grant that Agamemnon and Achilles are passionate, excitable men (the story requires that they should be). But are not Odysseus and Ajax in their several ways proverbial types of steady endurance, as is Penelope of female constancy? Yet these stable characters are not more exempt than others from psychic intervention. I should hesitate on the whole to press this point of Nilsson's, and should prefer instead to connect Homeric man's belief in psychic intervention with two other peculiarities which do unquestionably belong to the culture described by Homer.

The first is a negative peculiarity: Homeric man has no unified concept of what we call "soul" or "personality" (a fact to whose implications Bruno Snell[95] has lately called particular attention). It is well known that Homer appears to credit man with a *psyche* only after death, or when he is in the act of fainting or dying or is threatened with death: the only recorded function of the *psyche* in relation to the living man is to leave him. Nor has Homer any other word for the living personality. The *thumos* may once have been a primitive "breath-soul" or "life-soul"; but in Homer it is neither the soul nor (as in Plato) a "part of the soul." It may be defined, roughly and generally, as the organ of feeling. But it enjoys an independence which the word "organ" does not suggest to us, influenced as we are by the later concepts of "organism" and "organic unity." A man's *thumos* tells him that he must now eat or drink or slay an enemy, it advises him on his course of action, it puts words into his mouth: θυμὸς ἀνώγει, he says, or κέλεται δέ με θυμός. He can converse with it, or with his "heart" or his "belly," almost as man to man. Sometimes he scolds these detached entities (κραδίην ἠνίπαπε μύθῳ);[96] usually he takes their advice, but he may also reject it and act, as Zeus does on one occasion, "without the consent of his *thumos*."[97] In the latter case, we should say, like Plato, that the man was κρείττων ἑαυτοῦ, he had controlled *himself*. But for Homeric man the *thumos* tends not to be felt as part of the self: it commonly appears as an independent inner voice. A man may even hear two such voices, as when Odysseus "plans in his *thumos*" to kill the Cyclops forthwith, but a second voice (ἕτερος θυμός) restrains him.[98] This habit of (as we should say) "objectifying emotional drives," treating them as not-self, must have opened the door wide to the religious idea of psychic intervention, which is often said to operate, not directly on the man himself, but on his *thumos*[99] or on its physical seat, his chest or midriff.[100] We see the connection very clearly in Diomede's remark that Achilles will fight "when the *thumos* in his chest tells him to *and* a god rouses him"[101] (overdetermination again).

A second peculiarity, which seems to be closely related to the first, must have worked in the same direction. This is the habit of explaining character or behaviour in terms of knowledge.[102] The most familiar instance is the very wide use of the verb οἶδα, "I know," with a neuter plural object to express not only the possession of technical skill (οἶδεν πολεμήια ἔργα and the like) but also what we should call moral character or personal feelings: Achilles "knows wild things, like a lion," Polyphemus "knows lawless things," Nestor and Agamemnon "know friendly things to each other."[103] This is not merely a Homeric "idiom": a similar transposition of feeling into intellectual terms is implied when we are told that Achilles has "a merciless *understanding* (νόος)," or that the Trojans "*remembered* flight and *forgot* resistance."[104] This intellectualist approach to the explanation of behaviour set a lasting stamp on the Greek mind: the so-called Socratic paradoxes, that "virtue is knowledge," and that "no one does wrong on purpose," were no novelties, but an explicit generalised formulation of what had long been an ingrained habit of thought.[105] Such a habit of thought must have encouraged the belief in psychic intervention. If character is knowledge, what is not knowledge is not part of the character, but comes to a man from outside. When he acts in a manner contrary to the system of conscious dispositions which he is said to "know," his action is not properly his own, but has been dictated to him. In other words, unsystematised, nonrational impulses, and the acts resulting from them, tend to be excluded from the self and ascribed to an alien origin.

Evidently this is especially likely to happen when the acts in question are such as to cause acute shame to their author. We know how in our own society unbearable feelings of guilt are got rid of by "projecting" them in phantasy on to someone else. And we may guess that the notion of *ate* served a similar purpose for Homeric man by enabling him in all good faith to project on to an external power his unbearable feelings of shame. I say "shame" and not "guilt," for certain American anthropologists have lately taught us to distinguish "shame-cultures" from "guilt-cultures,"[106] and the society described by Homer clearly falls into the former class. Homeric man's highest good is not the enjoyment of a quiet conscience, but the enjoyment of *tīmē*, public esteem: "Why should I fight," asks Achilles, "if

the good fighter receives no more τιμή than the bad?"[107] And
the strongest moral force which Homeric man knows is not the
fear of god,[108] but respect for public opinion, *aidōs: αἰδέομαι
Τρῶας*, says Hector at the crisis of his fate, and goes with open
eyes to his death.[109] The situation to which the notion of *ate*
is a response arose not merely from the impulsiveness of Homeric man, but from the tension between individual impulse and
the pressure of social conformity characteristic of a shame-
culture.[110] In such a society, anything which exposes a man to
the contempt or ridicule of his fellows, which causes him to
"lose face," is felt as unbearable.[111] That perhaps explains
how not only cases of moral failure, like Agamemnon's loss of
self-control, but such things as the bad bargain of Glaucus, or
Automedon's disregard of proper tactics, came to be "projected" on to a divine agency. On the other hand, it was the
gradually growing sense of guilt, characteristic of a later age,
which transformed *ate* into a punishment, the Erinyes into
ministers of vengeance, and Zeus into an embodiment of cosmic
justice. With that development I shall deal in my next chapter.

What I have thus far tried to do is to show, by examining one
particular type of religious experience, that behind the term
"Homeric religion" there lies something more than an artificial
machinery of serio-comic gods and goddesses, and that we shall
do it less than justice if we dismiss it as an agreeable interlude
of lighthearted buffoonery between the presumed profundities of
an Aegean Earth-religion about which we know little, and those
of an "early Orphic movement" about which we know even less.

NOTES TO CHAPTER I

[1] *Last Lectures*, 182 ff.
[2] *Introduction à l'Iliade*, 294.
[3] *Rise of the Greek Epic*[4], 265.
[4] *Tradition and Design in the Iliad*, 222. The italics are mine.
Similarly Wilhelm Schmid thinks that Homer's conception of the

gods "cannot be called religious." (*Gr. Literaturgeschichte*, I.i.112 f.)

5 *Il.* 19.86 ff.

6 137 ff. Cf. 9.119 f.

7 19.270 ff.

8 1.412.

9 9.376.

10 1.5.

11 *Il.* 6.357. Cf. 3.164, where Priam says that not Helen but the gods are to blame (αἴτιοι) for the war; and *Od.* 4.261, where she speaks of her ἄτη.

12 *Il.* 12.254 f.; *Od.* 23.11 ff.

13 *Il.* 6.234 ff.

14 *Il.* 17.469 f.

15 Cf. Wilamowitz, *Die Ilias und Homer*, 304 f., 145.

16 For this account of ἄτη cf. W. Havers, "Zur Semasiologie von griech. ἄτη," *Ztschr. f. vgl. Sprachforschung*, 43 (1910) 225 ff.

17 The transition to this sense may be seen at *Od.* 10.68, 12.372, and 21.302. Otherwise it seems to be post-Homeric. L.-S. still cites for it *Il.* 24.480, but I think wrongly: see Leaf and Ameis-Hentze *ad loc.*

18 The plural seems to be twice used of actions symptomatic of the state of mind, at *Il.* 9.115 and (if the view taken in n. 20 is right) at *Il.* 10.391. This is an easy and natural extension of the original sense.

19 11.61; 21.297 ff.

20 *Il.* 10.391 is commonly quoted as a solitary exception. The meaning, however, may be, not that Hector's unwise advice produced ἄτη in Dolon, but that it was a symptom of Hector's own condition of (divinely inspired) ἄτη. ἄται will then be used in the same sense as at 9.115, whereas the common view postulates not only a unique psychology but a unique use of ἄται as "acts productive of infatuation." At *Od.* 10.68 Odysseus' companions are named as subordinate agents along with ὕπνος σχέτλιος.

21 *Il.* 16.805.

22 *Ibid.*, 780.

23 *Ibid.*, 684–691.

24 *Il.* 11.340.

25 Cf. L. Lévy-Bruhl, *Primitive Mentality*, 43 ff.; *Primitives and the Supernatural*, 57 f. (Eng. trans.).

26 *Od.* 12.371 f. Cf. 10.68.

27 *Il.* 9.512: τῷ ἄτην ἅμ' ἕπεσθαι, ἵνα βλαφθεὶς ἀποτίσῃ.

[28] *Il.* 19.91. At *Il.* 18.311 Athena, in her capacity as Goddess of Counsel, takes away the understanding of the Trojans, so that they applaud Hector's bad advice. This is not, however, called an ἄτη. But in the "Telemachy" Helen ascribes her ἄτη to Aphrodite (*Od.* 4.261).

[29] *Il.* 24.49, where the plural may refer merely to the "portions" of different individuals (Wilamowitz, *Glaube*, I.360). But the "mighty Spinners" of *Od.* 7.197 seem to be a kind of personal fates, akin to the Norns of Teutonic myth (cf. Chadwick, *Growth of Literature*, I.646).

[30] Cf. Nilsson, *History of Greek Religion*, 169. Cornford's view, that μοῖρα "stands for the provincial ordering of the world," and that "the notion of the individual lot or fate comes last, not first, in the order of development" (*From Religion to Philosophy*, 15 ff.), seems to me intrinsically unlikely, and is certainly not supported by the evidence of Homer, where μοῖρα is still quite concretely used for, e.g., a "helping" of meat (*Od.* 20.260). Nor does George Thomson convince me that the Μοῖραι originated "as symbols of the economic and social functions of primitive communism," or that "they grew out of the neolithic mother-goddesses" (*The Prehistoric Aegean*, 339).

[31] Snell, *Philol.* 85 (1929–1930) 141 ff., and (more elaborately) Chr. Voigt, *Ueberlegung u. Entscheidung . . . bei Homer*, have pointed out that Homer has no word for an act of choice or decision. But the conclusion that in Homer "man still possesses no consciousness of personal freedom and of deciding for himself" (Voigt, *op. cit.*, 103) seems to me misleadingly expressed. I should rather say that Homeric man does not possess the concept of will (which developed curiously late in Greece), and therefore cannot possess the concept of "free will." That does not prevent him from distinguishing in practice between actions originated by the ego and those which he attributes to psychic intervention: Agamemnon can say ἐγὼ δ' οὐκ αἴτιός εἰμι, ἀλλὰ Ζεύς. And it seems a little artificial to deny that what is described in passages like *Il.* 11.403 ff. or *Od.* 5.355 ff. is in effect a reasoned decision taken after consideration of possible alternatives.

[32] *Il.* 16.849 f. Cf. 18.119, 19.410, 21.82 ff., 22.297–303; and on "overdetermination" chap. ii, pp. 30 f.

[33] *Rh. Mus.* 50 (1895) 6 ff. (= *Kl. Schriften*, II.229). Cf. Nilsson, *Gesch. d. gr. Rel.* I.91 f.; and, *contra*, Wilamowitz in the introduction to his translation of the *Eumenides*, and Rose, *Handbook of Greek Mythology*, 84.

34 15.233 f.

35 *Il.* 19.418. Cf. Σ B *ad loc.*, ἐπίσκοποι γάρ εἰσιν τῶν παρὰ φύσιν.

36 Fr. 94 Diels.

37 In all cases but one (*Od.* 11.279 f.) the claims are those of *living* persons. This seems to tell heavily against the theory (invented in the confident heyday of animism) that the ἐρινύες are the vengeful dead. So do (*a*) the fact that in Homer they never punish murder; (*b*) the fact that gods as well as men have "their" ἐρινύες. The ἐρινύες of Hera (*Il.* 21.412) have exactly the same function as those of Penelope (*Od.* 2.135)—to protect the status of a mother by punishing an unfilial son. We can say that they are the maternal anger projected as a personal being. The θεῶν ἐρινύς who in the *Thebais* (fr. 2 Kinkel) heard the curse of the (living) Oedipus embodies in personal form the anger of the gods invoked in the curse: hence ἐρινύς and curse can be equated (Aesch. *Sept.* 70, *Eum.* 417). On this view Sophocles was not innovating, but using the traditional language, when he made Teiresias threaten Creon with Ἅιδου καὶ θεῶν ἐρινύες (*Ant.* 1075); their function is to punish Creon's violation of the μοῖρα, the natural apportionment, by which the dead Polyneices belongs to Hades, the living Antigone to the ἄνω θεοί (1068–1073). For μοῖρα as status cf. Poseidon's claim to be ἰσόμορος καὶ ὁμῇ πεπρωμένος αἴσῃ with Zeus, *Il.* 15.209. Since writing this, I find the intimate connection of ἐρινύς with μοῖρα also stressed by George Thomson (*The Prehistoric Aegean,* 345) and by Eduard Fraenkel on *Agam.* 1535 f.

38 *Il.* 9.454, 571; 21.412; *Od.* 2.135.

39 *Il.* 15.204.

40 *Od.* 17.475.

41 *P.V.* 516, Μοῖραι τρίμορφοι μνήμονές τ' Ἐρινύες, also *Eum.* 333 ff. and 961, Μοῖραι ματρικασιγνῆται. Euripides in a lost play made an ἐρινύς declare that her other names are τύχη, νέμεσις, μοῖρα, ἀνάγκη (fr. 1022). Cf. also Aeschylus, *Sept.* 975–977.

42 *Eum.* 372 ff., etc.

43 On the long-standing problem of the relation of the gods to μοῖρα (which cannot be solved in logical terms), see especially E. Leitzke, *Moira u. Gottheit im alten griech. Epos,* which sets out the material in full; E. Ehnmark, *The Idea of God in Homer,* 74 ff.; Nilsson, *Gesch. d. gr. Rel.* I.338 ff.; W. C. Greene, *Moira,* 22 ff.

44 Demeter Ἐρινύς and verb ἐρινύειν in Arcadia, Paus. 8.25.4 ff. αἶσα in Arcadian, *IG* V.2.265, 269; in Cypriot, *GDI* I.73.

45 Cf. E. Ehnmark, *The Idea of God in Homer,* 6 ff.; and on the mean-

ing of the word μένος, J. Böhme, *Die Seele u. das Ich im Homerischen Epos*, 11 ff., 84 f.

[46] *Il.* 5.125 f., 136; 16.529.

[47] That kings were once thought of as possessing a special μένος which was communicated to them in virtue of their office seems to be implied by the usage of the phrase ἱερὸν μένος (cf. ἱερὴ ἲς), although its application in Homer (to Alcinous, *Od.* 7.167 etc., to Antinous, *Od.* 18.34) is governed merely by metrical convenience. Cf. Pfister, P.-W., s.v. "Kultus," 2125 ff.; Snell, *Die Entdeckung des Geistes*, 35 f.

[48] *Od.* 24.318.

[49] Horses, *Il.* 23.468; βοὸς μένος, *Od.* 3.450. At *Il.* 17.456 Achilles' horses receive a communication of μένος.

[50] *Il.* 6.182, 17.565. So the medical writers speak of the μένος of wine (Hipp. *acut.* 63), and even the μένος of famine (*vet. med.* 9), meaning the immanent power shown by their effects on the human organism.

[51] *Il.* 20.242. Cf. the "Spirit of the Lord" which "came mightily upon" Samson, enabling him to do superhuman feats (Judges 14: 6, 15: 14).

[52] *Il.* 13.59 ff. The physical transmission of power by contact is, however, rare in Homer, and in Greek belief generally, in contrast with the importance which has been attached in Christianity (and in many primitive cultures) to the "laying on of hands."

[53] *Il.* 13.61, 75. γυῖα δ' ἔθηκεν ἐλαφρά is a recurrent formula in descriptions of communicated μένος (5.122, 23.772); cf. also 17.211 f.

[54] Cf. Leaf's note on 13.73. At *Od.* 1.323 Telemachus recognises a communication of power, we are not told exactly how.

[55] *Il.* 12.449. Cf. *Od.* 13.387–391.

[56] *Il.* 3.381: ῥεῖα μάλ', ὥστε θεός, Aesch. *Supp.* 100: πᾶν ἄπονον δαιμονίων, etc.

[57] *Il.* 5.330 ff., 850 ff.

[58] *Il.* 6.128 ff.

[59] *Il.* 5.136; 10.485; 15.592.

[60] *Il.* 15.605 ff.

[61] *Il.* 17.210.

[62] *Od.* 1.89, 320 f.; cf. 3.75 f.; 6.139 f.

[63] *Od.* 22.347 f. Cf. Demodocus, 8.44, 498; and Pindar, *Nem.* 3.9, where the poet begs the Muse to grant him "an abundant flow of song welling from *my own* thought." As MacKay has put it, "The Muse is the source of the poet's originality, rather than his conventionality" (*The Wrath of Homer*, 50). Chadwick, *Growth of*

Literature, III.182, quotes from Radloff a curiously exact primitive parallel, the Kirghiz minstrel who declared, "I can sing any song whatever, for God has implanted this gift of song in my heart. He gives the words on my tongue without my having to seek them. I have learned none of my songs. All springs from my inner self."

⁶⁴ *Od*. 17.518 f., Hes. *Theog*. 94 f. (= *H. Hymn* 25.2 f.). Cf. chap. iii, pp. 80 ff.

⁶⁵ On Homer's use of the term δαίμων and its relationship to θεός (which cannot be discussed here), see Nilsson in *Arch. f. Rel.* 22 (1924) 363 ff., and *Gesch. d. gr. Rel.* I.201 ff.; Wilamowitz, *Glaube*, I.362 ff.; E. Leitzke, *op. cit.*, 42 ff. According to Nilsson the δαίμων was originally not only indeterminate but impersonal, a mere "manifestation of power (*orenda*)"; but about this I am inclined to share the doubts expressed by Rose, *Harv. Theol. Rev.* 28 (1935) 243 ff. Such evidence as we have suggests rather that while μοῖρα developed from an impersonal "portion" into a personal Fate, δαίμων evolved in the opposite direction, from a personal "Apportioner" (cf. δαίω, δαιμόνη) to an impersonal "luck." There is a point where the two developments cross and the words are virtually synonymous.

⁶⁶ Occasionally also to Zeus (14.273, etc.), who in such phrases is perhaps not so much an individual god as the representative of a generalised divine will (Nilsson, *Greek Piety*, 59).

⁶⁷ 9.381.

⁶⁸ 14.178; cf. 23.11.

⁶⁹ 19.10; 19.138 f.; 9.339.

⁷⁰ 2.124 f.; 4.274 f.; 12.295.

⁷¹ 19.485. Cf. 23.11, where a *mistake* in identification is similarly explained.

⁷² 15.172.

⁷³ 12.38.

⁷⁴ 14.488.

⁷⁵ If his intervention is harmful, he is usually called δαίμων, not θεός.

⁷⁶ This distinction was first pointed out by O. Jørgensen, *Hermes*, 39 (1904) 357 ff. On exceptions to Jørgensen's rule see Calhoun, *AJP* 61 (1940) 270 ff.

⁷⁷ Cf. the δαίμων who brings unlucky or unwelcome visitors, 10.64, 24.149, 4.274 f., 17.446, and is called κακός in the first two of these places; and the στυγερὸς δαίμων who causes sickness, 5.396. These passages at least are surely exceptions to Ehnmark's generalisation (*Anthropomorphism and Miracle*, 64) that the δαίμονες of the *Odyssey* are simply unidentified Olympians.

[78] 2.122 ff.

[79] 1.384 f.

[80] 1.320 ff.

[81] *Il.* 15.461 ff.

[82] E. Hedén, *Homerische Götterstudien*.

[83] Nilsson, *Arch. f. Rel.* 22.379.

[84] *The Idea of God in Homer*, chap. v. Cf. also Linforth, "Named and Unnamed Gods in Herodotus," *Univ. of California Publications in Classical Philology*, IX.7 (1928).

[85] Cf., e.g., the passages quoted by Lévy-Bruhl, *Primitives and the Supernatural*, 22 f.

[86] *Il.* 4.31. Cf. P. Cauer, *Kunst der Uebersetzung*², 27.

[87] A particularly good, because particularly trivial, example of the significance attached to the unexplained is the fact that sneezing—that seemingly causeless and pointless convulsion—is taken as an omen by so many peoples, including the Homeric Greeks (*Od.* 17.541), as well as those of the Classical Age (Xen. *Anab.* 3.3.9) and of Roman times (Plut. *gen. Socr.* 581 F). Cf. Halliday, *Greek Divination*, 174 ff., and Tylor, *Primitive Culture*, I.97 ff.

[88] Something analogous to ἄτη is perhaps to be seen in the state called "fey" or "fairy-struck," which in Celtic belief comes on people suddenly and "makes them do somewhat verie unlike their former practice" (Robert Kirk, *The Secret Commonwealth*).

[89] "Götter und Psychologie bei Homer," *Arch. f. Rel.* 22.363 ff. Its conclusions are summarised in his *History of Greek Religion*, 122 ff.

[90] As Snell points out (*Die Entdeckung des Geistes*, 45), the "superfluous" character of so many divine interventions shows that they were *not* invented simply to get the poet out of a difficulty (since the course of events would be the same without them), but rest on some older foundation of belief. Cauer thought (*Grundfragen*, I.401) that the "naturalness" of many Homeric miracles was an unconscious refinement dating from an age when the poets were ceasing to believe in miracles. But the unnecessary miracle is in fact typically primitive. Cf., e.g., E. E. Evans-Pritchard, *Witchcraft, Oracles and Magic among the Azande*, 77, 508; and for a criticism of Cauer, Ehnmark, *Anthropomorphism and Miracle*, chap. iv.

[91] E.g., *Il.* 16.712 ff., and often. At *Il.* 13.43 ff., the physical and (60) the psychic intervention stand side by side. No doubt epiphanies of gods in battle had also some basis in popular belief (the same belief which created the Angels at Mons), though, as Nilsson observes, in later times it is usually heroes, not gods, who appear in this way.

⁹² *Il.* 1.198.

⁹³ Cf. Voigt, *Ueberlegung u. Entscheidung . . . bei Homer*, 54 ff. More often the warning is given by the god "disguised' as a human personage; this may derive from an older form in which the advice was given, at the monition of a god or δαίμων, by the personage himself (Voigt, *ibid.*, 63).

⁹⁴ Hdt. 2.53. Lowie has observed that the primitive artist, following his aesthetic impulse, "may come to create a type that at once synthesises the essentials of current belief, without contravening them in any particular, and yet at the same time adds a series of strokes that may not merely shade but materially alter the pre-existing picture. So long as things go no further, the new image is no more than an individual version of the general norm. But as soon as that variant . . . is elevated to the position of a standard representation, it becomes itself thenceforward a determinant of the popular conception." (*Primitive Religion*, 267 f.) This refers to the visual arts, but it affords an exact description of the manner in which I conceive the Greek epic to have influenced Greek religion.

⁹⁵ Snell, *Die Entdeckung des Geistes*, chap. i. Cf. also Böhme, *op. cit.*, 76 ff., and W. Marg, *Der Charakter i. d. Sprache der frühgriechischen Dichtung*, 43 ff.

⁹⁶ *Od.* 22.17.

⁹⁷ *Il.* 4.43: ἐκὼν ἀέκοντί γε θυμῷ. As Pfister has pointed out (P.-W. XI.2117 ff.), this relative independence of the affective element is common among primitive peoples (cf., e.g., Warneck, *Religion der Batak*, 8). On the weakness of the "ego-consciousness" among primitives see also Hans Kelsen, *Society and Nature* (Chicago, 1943), 8 ff.

⁹⁸ *Od.* 9.299 ff. Here the "ego" identifies itself originally with the first voice, but accepts the warning of the second. A similar plurality of voices, and a similar shift of self-identification, seems to be implicit in the curious passage *Il.* 11.403–410 (cf. Voigt, *op. cit.*, 87 ff.). One of Dostoievsky's characters, in *A Raw Youth*, describes this fluctuating relation of self and not-self very nicely. "It's just as though one's second self were standing beside one; one is sensible and rational oneself, but the other self is impelled to do something perfectly senseless, and sometimes very funny; and suddenly you notice that you are longing to do that amusing thing, goodness knows why; that is, you want to, as it were, against your will; though you fight against it with all your might, you want to."

⁹⁹ E.g., *Il.* 5.676: τράπε θυμὸν Ἀθήνη ; 16.691: (Ζεὺς) θυμὸν ἐνὶ στήθεσ-
σιν ἀνῆκε ; *Od.* 15.172: ἐνὶ θυμῷ ἀθάνατοι βάλλουσι. Hence the
θυμός is the organ of seership, *Il.* 7.44, 12.228. (Cf. Aesch. *Pers.* 10:
κακόμαντις . . . θυμός ; 224: θυμόμαντις. Also Eur. *Andr.* 1073:
πρόμαντις θυμός, and *Trag. Adesp.* fr. 176: πηδῶν δ' ὁ θυμὸς ἔνδοθεν
μαντεύεται.)

¹⁰⁰ E.g., *Il.* 16.805: ἄτη φρένας εἷλε ; *Il.* 5.125: ἐν γάρ τοι στήθεσσι μένος
. . . ἧκα.

¹⁰¹ *Il.* 9.702 f. Cf. *Od.* 8.44: "a god" has given Demodocus the gift of
singing as his θυμός prompts him.

¹⁰² Cf. W. Marg, *op. cit.*, 69 ff.; W. Nestle, *Vom Mythos zum Logos*,
33 ff.

¹⁰³ *Il.* 24.41; *Od.* 9.189; *Od.* 3.277.

¹⁰⁴ *Il.* 16.35, 356 f.

¹⁰⁵ The same point has been made by W. Nestle, *NJbb* 1922, 137 ff.,
who finds the Socratic paradoxes "echt griechisch," and remarks
that they are already implicit in the naïve psychology of Homer.
But we should beware of regarding this habitual "intellectualism"
as an attitude consciously adopted by the spokesmen of an "intellectual" people; it is merely the inevitable result of the absence
of the concept of will (cf. L. Gernet, *Pensée juridique et morale*,
312).

¹⁰⁶ A simple explanation of these terms will be found in Ruth Benedict, *The Chrysanthemum and the Sword*, 222 ff. We are ourselves
the heirs of an ancient and powerful (though now declining) guilt-
culture, a fact which may perhaps explain why so many scholars
have difficulty in recognising that Homeric religion is "religion"
at all.

¹⁰⁷ *Il.* 9.315 ff. On the importance of τιμή in Homer see W. Jaeger,
Paideia, I.7 ff.

¹⁰⁸ Cf. chap. ii, pp. 29 ff.

¹⁰⁹ *Il.* 22.105. Cf. 6.442, 15.561 ff., 17.91 ff.; *Od.* 16.75, 21.323 ff.;
Wilamowitz, *Glaube*, I.353 ff.; W. J. Verdenius, *Mnem.* 12 (1944)
47 ff. The sanction of αἰδώς is νέμεσις, public disapproval: cf.
Il. 6.351, 13.121 f.; and *Od.* 2.136 f. The application to conduct
of the terms καλόν and αἰσχρόν seems also to be typical of a shame-
culture. These words denote, not that the act is beneficial or hurt-
ful to the agent, or that it is right or wrong in the eyes of a deity,
but that it looks "handsome" or "ugly" in the eyes of public opinion.

¹¹⁰ Once the idea of psychic intervention had taken root, it would, of
course, encourage impulsive behaviour. Just as recent anthropologists, instead of saying, with Frazer, that primitives believe in

magic because they reason faultily, are inclined to say that they reason faultily because they are socially conditioned to believe in magic, so, instead of saying with Nilsson that Homeric man believes in psychic intervention because he is impulsive, we should perhaps say rather that he gives way to his impulses because he is socially conditioned to believe in psychic intervention.

[111] On the importance of the fear of ridicule as a social motive see Paul Radin, *Primitive Man as Philosopher*, 50.

II
From Shame-Culture to
Guilt-Culture

*It is a fearful thing to fall into the hands of the living
God.*

HEBREWS 10:31

IN MY first chapter I discussed Homer's interpretation of the irrational elements in human behaviour as
"psychic intervention"—an interference with human life by
nonhuman agencies which put something into a man and thereby influence his thought and conduct. In this one I shall deal
with some of the new forms which these Homeric ideas assumed
in the course of the Archaic Age. But if what I have to say
is to be intelligible to the nonspecialist, I must first attempt
to make plain, at least in rough outline, certain of the general
differences which separate the religious attitude of the Archaic
Age from that presupposed in Homer. At the end of my first
chapter I used the expressions "shame-culture" and "guilt-
culture" as descriptive labels for the two attitudes in question.
I am aware that these terms are not self-explanatory, that they
are probably new to most classical scholars, and that they lend
themselves easily to misconception. What I intend by them
will, I hope, emerge as we proceed. But I should like to make
two things clear at once. First, I use them only as descriptions,
without assuming any particular theory of cultural change. And
secondly, I recognise that the distinction is only relative, since
in fact many modes of behaviour characteristic of shame-cultures
persisted throughout the archaic and classical periods. There is
a transition, but it is gradual and incomplete.

When we turn from Homer to the fragmentary literature of the Archaic Age, and to those writers of the Classical Age who still preserve the archaic outlook[1]—as do Pindar and Sophocles, and to a great extent Herodotus—one of the first things that strikes us is the deepened awareness of human insecurity and human helplessness (ἀμηχανία),[2] which has its religious correlate in the feeling of divine hostility—not in the sense that Deity is thought of as evil, but in the sense that an overmastering Power and Wisdom forever holds Man down, keeps him from rising above his station. It is the feeling which Herodotus expresses by saying that Deity is always φθονερόν τε καὶ ταραχῶδες.[3] "Jealous and interfering," we translate it; but the translation is not very good—how should that overmastering Power be jealous of so poor a thing as Man? The thought is rather that the gods resent any success, any happiness, which might for a moment lift our mortality above its mortal status, and so encroach on their prerogative.

Such ideas were of course not entirely new. In *Iliad* 24 Achilles, moved at last by the spectacle of his broken enemy Priam, pronounces the tragic moral of the whole poem: "For so the gods have spun the thread for pitiful humanity, that the life of Man should be sorrow, while themselves are exempt from care." And he goes on to the famous image of the two jars, from which Zeus draws forth his good and evil gifts. To some men he gives a mixed assortment, to others, unmixed evil, so that they wander tormented over the face of the earth, "unregarded by gods or men."[4] As for unmixed good, that, we are to assume, is a portion reserved for gods. The jars have nothing to do with justice: else the moral would be false. For in the *Iliad* heroism does not bring happiness; its sole, and sufficient, reward is fame. Yet for all that, Homer's princes bestride their world boldly; they fear the gods only as they fear their human overlords; nor are they oppressed by the future even when, like Achilles, they know that it holds an approaching doom.

[1] For notes to chapter ii see pages 50–63.

So far, what we meet in the Archaic Age is not a different belief but a different emotional reaction to the old belief. Listen, for example, to Semonides of Amorgos: "Zeus controls the fulfilment of all that is, and disposes as he will. But insight does not belong to men: we live like beasts, always at the mercy of what the day may bring, knowing nothing of the outcome that God will impose upon our acts."[5] Or listen to Theognis: "No man, Cyrnus, is responsible for his own ruin or his own success: of both these things the gods are the givers. No man can perform an action and know whether its outcome will be good or bad. . . . Humanity in utter blindness follows its futile usages; but the gods bring all to the fulfilment that they have planned."[6] The doctrine of man's helpless dependence on an arbitrary Power is not new; but there is a new accent of despair, a new and bitter emphasis on the futility of human purposes. We are nearer to the world of the *Oedipus Rex* than to the world of the *Iliad*.

It is much the same with the idea of divine *phthŏnos* or jealousy. Aeschylus was right when he called it "a venerable doctrine uttered long ago."[7] The notion that too much success incurs a supernatural danger, especially if one brags about it, has appeared independently in many different cultures[8] and has deep roots in human nature (we subscribe to it ourselves when we "touch wood"). The *Iliad* ignores it, as it ignores other popular superstitions; but the poet of the *Odyssey* —always more tolerant of contemporary ways of thought— permits Calypso to exclaim in a temper that the gods are the most jealous beings in the world—they grudge one a little happiness.[9] It is plain, however, from the uninhibited boasting in which Homeric man indulges that he does not take the dangers of *phthonos* very seriously: such scruples are foreign to a shame-culture. It is only in the Late Archaic and Early Classical time that the *phthonos* idea becomes an oppressive menace, a source—or expression—of religious anxiety. Such it is in Solon, in Aeschylus, above all in Herodotus. For Herodotus, history is overdetermined: while it is overtly the outcome of human purposes, the penetrating eye can detect everywhere the covert working of *phthonos*. In the same spirit the Messenger in the *Persae* attributes Xerxes' unwise tactics at Salamis to the cunning Greek who deceived him, and simultaneously to the *phthonos* of the gods working through an *alastor* or evil dae-mon:[10] the event is doubly determined, on the natural and on the supernatural plane.

By the writers of this age divine *phthonos* is sometimes,[11] though not always,[12] moralised as *nemesis*, "righteous indig-nation." Between the primitive offence of too much success and its punishment by jealous Deity, a moral link is inserted: success is said to produce *kŏros*—the complacency of the man who has done too well—which in turn generates *hubris*, arro-gance in word or deed or even thought. Thus interpreted, the old belief appeared more rational, but it was not the less oppressive on that account. We see from the carpet scene in the *Agamemnon* how every manifestation of triumph arouses anxious feelings of guilt: *hubris* has become the "primal evil," the sin whose wages is death, which is yet so universal that a Homeric hymn calls it the *thĕmis* or established usage of man-kind, and Archilochus attributes it even to animals. Men knew that it was dangerous to be happy.[13] But the restraint had no doubt its wholesome side. It is significant that when Euripides, writing in the new age of scepticism, makes his chorus lament the collapse of all moral standards, they see the culminating proof of that collapse in the fact that "it is no longer the com-mon aim of men to escape the *phthonos* of the gods."[14]

The moralisation of *phthonos* introduces us to a second characteristic feature of archaic religious thought—the tend-ency to transform the supernatural in general, and Zeus in particular, into an agent of justice. I need hardly say that re-ligion and morals were not initially interdependent, in Greece or elsewhere; they had their separate roots. I suppose that, broadly speaking, religion grows out of man's relationship to his total environment, morals out of his relation to his fellow-men. But sooner or later in most cultures there comes a time of suffering when most people refuse to be content with Achilles' view, the view that "God's in his Heaven, all's wrong with the world." Man projects into the cosmos his own nascent demand for social justice; and when from the outer spaces the magnified echo of his own voice returns to him, promising punishment for the guilty, he draws from it courage and reassurance.

In the Greek epic this stage has not yet been reached, but we can observe increasing signs of its approach. The gods of the *Iliad* are primarily concerned with their own honour (τιμή). To speak lightly of a god, to neglect his cult, to maltreat his priest, all these understandably make him angry; in a shame-culture gods, like men, are quick to resent a slight. Perjury comes under the same rubric: the gods have nothing against straight-forward lying, but they do object to their names being taken in vain. Here and there, however, we get a hint of something more. Offences against parents constitute so monstrous a crime as to demand special treatment: the underworld Powers are constrained to take up the case.[15] (I shall come back to that later on.) And once we are told that Zeus is angry with men who judge crooked judgements.[16] But that I take to be a reflex of later conditions which, by an inadvertence common in Homer, has been allowed to slip into a simile.[17] For I find no indication in the narrative of the *Iliad* that Zeus is concerned with justice as such.[18]

In the *Odyssey* his interests are distinctly wider: not only does he protect suppliants[19] (who in the *Iliad* enjoy no such security), but "all strangers and beggars are from Zeus";[20] in fact, the Hesiodic avenger of the poor and oppressed begins to come in sight. The Zeus of the *Odyssey* is, moreover, becoming sensitive to moral criticism: men, he complains, are always finding fault with the gods, "for they say that their troubles come from us; whereas it is they who by their own wicked acts incur more trouble than they need."[21] Placed where it is, at the very be-ginning of the poem, the remark sounds, as the Germans say, "programmatic." And the programme is carried out. The suitors by their own wicked acts incur destruction,[22] while

Odysseus, heedful of divine monitions, triumphs against the odds: divine justice is vindicated.

The later stages of the moral education of Zeus may be studied in Hesiod, in Solon, in Aeschylus; but I cannot here follow this progress in detail. I must, however, mention one complication which had far-reaching historical consequences. The Greeks were not so unrealistic as to hide from themselves the plain fact that the wicked flourished like a green bay-tree. Hesiod, Solon, Pindar, are deeply troubled by it, and Theognis finds it necessary to give Zeus a straight talk on the subject.[23] It was easy enough to vindicate divine justice in a work of fiction like the *Odyssey:* as Aristotle observed, "poets tell this kind of story to gratify the desires of their audience."[24] It was not so easy in real life. In the Archaic Age the mills of God ground so slowly that their movement was practically imperceptible save to the eye of faith. In order to sustain the belief that they moved at all, it was necessary to get rid of the natural time-limit set by death. If you looked beyond that limit, you could say one (or both) of two things: you could say that the successful sinner would be punished in his descendants, or you could say that he would pay his debt personally in another life.

The second of these solutions emerged, as a doctrine of general application, only late in the Archaic Age, and was possibly confined to fairly limited circles; I shall postpone its consideration to a later chapter. The other is the characteristic archaic doctrine: it is the teaching of Hesiod, of Solon and Theognis, of Aeschylus and Herodotus. That it involved the suffering of the morally innocent was not overlooked: Solon speaks of the hereditary victims of *nemesis* as ἀναίτιοι, "not responsible"; Theognis complains of the unfairness of a system by which "the criminal gets away with it, while someone else takes the punishment later"; Aeschylus, if I understand him rightly, would mitigate the unfairness by recognising that an inherited curse may be broken.[25] That these men nevertheless accepted the idea of inherited guilt and deferred punishment is due to that belief in family solidarity which Archaic Greece

shared with other early societies[26] and with many primitive
cultures to-day.[27] Unfair it might be, but to them it appeared
as a law of nature, which must be accepted: for the family was
a moral unit, the son's life was a prolongation of his father's,[28]
and he inherited his father's moral debts exactly as he inherited
his commercial ones. Sooner or later, the debt *exacted its own
payment:* as the Pythia told Croesus, the causal nexus of crime
and punishment was *moira*, something that even a god could not
break; Croesus had to complete or fulfil (ἐκπλῆσαι) what was
begun by the crime of an ancestor five generations back.[29]

It was a misfortune for the Greeks that the idea of cosmic
justice, which represented an advance on the old notion of
purely arbitrary divine Powers, and provided a sanction for
the new civic morality, should have been thus associated with
a primitive conception of the family. For it meant that the
weight of religious feeling and religious law was thrown against
the emergence of a true view of the individual as a person, with
personal rights and personal responsibilities. Such a view did
eventually emerge in Attic secular law. As Glotz showed in his
great book, *La Solidarité de la famille en Grèce*,[30] the liberation
of the individual from the bonds of clan and family is one of
the major achievements of Greek rationalism, and one for
which the credit must go to Athenian democracy. But long
after that liberation was complete in law, religious minds were
still haunted by the ghost of the old solidarity. It appears from
Plato that in the fourth century fingers were still pointed at
the man shadowed by hereditary guilt, and he would still pay
a *cathartes* to be given ritual relief from it.[31] And Plato himself,
though he accepted the revolution in secular law, admits inherited religious guilt in certain cases.[32] A century later, Bion
of Borysthenes still found it necessary to point out that in
punishing the son for the father's offence God behaved like a
physician who should dose the child to cure the father; and the
devout Plutarch, who quotes this witticism, tries nevertheless to
find a defence for the old doctrine in an appeal to the observed
facts of heredity.[33]

To return to the Archaic Age, it was also a misfortune that the functions assigned to the moralised Supernatural were predominantly, if not exclusively, penal. We hear much about inherited guilt, little about inherited innocence; much about the sufferings of the sinner in Hell or Purgatory, relatively little about the deferred rewards of virtue; the stress is always on sanctions. That no doubt reflects the juridical ideas of the time; criminal law preceded civil law, and the primary function of the state was coercive. Moreover, divine law, like early human law, takes no account of motive and makes no allowance for human weakness; it is devoid of that humane quality which the Greeks called ἐπιείκεια or φιλανθρωπία. The proverbial saying popular in that age, that "all virtue is comprehended in justice,"[34] applies no less to gods than to men: there was little room for pity in either. That was not so in the *Iliad:* there Zeus pities the doomed Hector and the doomed Sarpedon; he pities Achilles mourning for his lost Patroclus, and even Achilles' horses mourning for their charioteer.[35] μέλουσί μοι, ὀλλύμενοί περ, he says in *Iliad* 21: "I care about them, though they perish." But in becoming the embodiment of cosmic justice Zeus lost his humanity. Hence Olympianism in its moralised form tended to become a religion of fear, a tendency which is reflected in the religious vocabulary. There is no word for "god-fearing" in the *Iliad;* but in the *Odyssey* to be θεουδής is already an important virtue, and the prose equivalent, δεισιδαίμων, was used as a term of praise right down to Aristotle's time.[36] The love of god, on the other hand, is missing from the older Greek vocabulary:[37] φιλόθεος appears first in Aristotle. And in fact, of the major Olympians, perhaps only Athena inspired an emotion that could reasonably be described as love. "It would be eccentric," says the *Magna Moralia*, "for anyone to claim that he loved Zeus."[38]

And that brings me to the last general trait which I want to stress—the universal fear of pollution (*miasma*), and its correlate, the universal craving for ritual purification (*catharsis*). Here once again the difference between Homer and the Archaic

Age is relative, not absolute; for it is a mistake to deny that a certain minimum of catharsis is practised in both epics.[39] But from the simple Homeric purifications, performed by laymen, it is a long step to the professional *cathartai* of the Archaic Age with their elaborate and messy rituals. And it is a longer step still from Telemachus' casual acceptance of a self-confessed murderer as a shipmate to the assumptions which enabled the defendant in a late fifth-century murder trial to draw presumptive proof of his innocence from the fact that the ship on which he travelled had reached port in safety.[40] We get a further measure of the gap if we compare Homer's version of the Oedipus saga with that familiar to us from Sophocles. In the latter, Oedipus becomes a polluted outcast, crushed under the burden of a guilt "which neither the earth nor the holy rain nor the sunlight can accept." But in the story Homer knew he continues to reign in Thebes after his guilt is discovered, and is eventually killed in battle and buried with royal honours.[41] It was apparently a later Mainland epic, the *Thebais*, that created the Sophoclean "man of sorrows."[42]

There is no trace in Homer of the belief that pollution was either infectious or hereditary. In the archaic view it was both,[43] and therein lay its terror: for how could any man be sure that he had not contracted the evil thing from a chance contact, or else inherited it from the forgotten offence of some remote ancestor? Such anxieties were the more distressing for their very vagueness—the impossibility of attaching them to a cause which could be recognised and dealt with. To see in these beliefs the *origin* of the archaic sense of guilt is probably an oversimplification; but they certainly expressed it, as a Christian's sense of guilt may express itself in the haunting fear of falling into mortal sin. The distinction between the two situations is of course that sin is a condition of the will, a disease of man's inner consciousness, whereas pollution is the automatic consequence of an action, belongs to the world of external events, and operates with the same ruthless indifference to motive as a typhoid germ.[44] Strictly speaking, the archaic sense of guilt becomes a sense of sin only as a result of what Kardiner[45] calls the "internalising" of conscience—a phenomenon which appears late and uncertainly in the Hellenic world, and does not become common until long after secular law had begun to recognise the importance of motive.[46] The transference of the notion of purity from the magical to the moral sphere was a similarly late development: not until the closing years of the fifth century do we encounter explicit statements that clean hands are not enough—the heart must be clean also.[47]

Nevertheless, we should, I think, be hesitant about drawing hard chronological lines: an idea is often obscurely at work in religious behaviour long before it reaches the point of explicit formulation. I think Pfister is probably right when he observes that in the old Greek word ἄγos (the term which describes the worst kind of *miasma*) the ideas of pollution, curse, and sin were already fused together at an early date.[48] And while *catharsis* in the Archaic Age was doubtless often no more than the mechanical fulfilment of a ritual obligation, the notion of an automatic, quasi-physical cleansing could pass by imperceptible gradations into the deeper idea of atonement for sin.[49] There are some recorded instances where it is hardly possible to doubt that this latter thought was involved, e.g., in the extraordinary case of the Locrian Tribute.[50] The people who in compensation for the crime of a remote ancestor were willing year after year, century after century, to send two daughters of their noblest families to be murdered in a distant country, or at best to survive there as temple slaves—these people, one would suppose, must have laboured not only under the fear of a dangerous pollution, but under the profound sense of an inherited sin which must be thus horribly atoned.

I shall come back to the subject of *catharsis* in a later chapter. But it is time now to return to the notion of psychic intervention which we have already studied in Homer, and to ask what part it played in the very different religious context of the Archaic Age. The simplest way to answer this is to look at some post-Homeric usages of the word *ate* (or its prose equiva-

lent θεοβλάβεια) and of the word *daemon*. If we do so, we shall
find that in some respects the epic tradition is reproduced with
remarkable fidelity. *Ate* still stands for irrational as distinct
from rationally purposive behaviour: e.g., on hearing that
Phaedra won't eat, the Chorus enquires whether this is due to
ate or to a suicidal purpose.[51] Its seat is still the *thumos* or the
phrĕnes,[52] and the agencies that cause it are much the same as
in Homer: mostly an unidentified daemon or god or gods; much
more rarely a specific Olympian;[53] occasionally, as in Homer,
Erinys[54] or *moira*;[55] once, as in the *Odyssey*, wine.[56]

But there are also important developments. In the first
place, *ate* is often, though not always, moralised, by being represented as a punishment; this appears once only in Homer—
in *Iliad* 9—and next in Hesiod, who makes *ate* the penalty of
hubris and observes with relish that "not even a nobleman" can
escape it.[57] Like other supernatural punishments, it will fall on
the sinner's descendants if the "evil debt" is not paid in his
lifetime.[58] Out of this conception of *ate* as punishment grows a
wide extension of the word's meaning. It is applied not only to
the sinner's state of mind, but to the objective disasters resulting from it: thus the Persians at Salamis experience "marine
atai," and the slaughtered sheep are the *ate* of Ajax.[59] *Ate* thus
acquires the general sense of "ruin," in contrast with κέρδος
or σωτηρία,[60] though in literature it always, I think, retains
the implication that the ruin is supernaturally determined.
And by a still further extension it is sometimes applied also
to the instruments or embodiments of the divine anger: thus
the Trojan Horse is an *ate*, and Antigone and Ismene are to
Creon "a pair of *atai*."[61] Such usages are rooted in feeling
rather than in logic: what is expressed in them is the consciousness of a mysterious dynamic nexus, the μένος ἄτης, as
Aeschylus calls it, binding together crime and punishment;
all the elements of that sinister unity are in a wide sense *ate*.[62]

Distinct from this vaguer development is the precise theological interpretation which makes of *ate* not merely a punishment leading to physical disasters, but a deliberate deception

which draws the victim on to fresh error, intellectual or moral, whereby he hastens his own ruin—the grim doctrine that *quem deus vult perdere, prius dementat.* There is a hint of this in *Iliad* 9, where Agamemnon calls his *ate* an evil deception (ἀπάτη) contrived by Zeus (l. 21); but there is no general statement of the doctrine in Homer or Hesiod. The orator Lycurgus[63] attributes it to "certain old poets" unspecified and quotes from one of them a passage in iambics: "when the anger of the daemons is injuring a man, the first thing is that it takes the good understanding out of his mind and turns him to the worse judgement, so that he may not be aware of his own errors." Similarly Theognis[64] declares that many a man who is pursuing "virtue" and "profit" is deliberately misled by a daemon, who causes him to mistake evil for good and the profitable for the bad. Here the action of the daemon is not moralised in any way: he seems to be simply an evil spirit, tempting man to his damnation.

That such evil spirits were really feared in the Archaic Age is also attested by the words of the Messenger in the *Persae* which I have already quoted in another connection: Xerxes was tempted by an "*alastor* or evil daemon." But Aeschylus himself knows better: as Darius' ghost explains later, the temptation was the punishment of *hubris;*[65] what to the partial vision of the living appears as the act of a fiend, is perceived by the wider insight of the dead to be an aspect of cosmic justice. In the *Agamemnon* we meet again the same interpretation on two levels. Where the poet, speaking through his Chorus, is able to detect the overmastering will of Zeus (παναιτίου, πανεργέτα)[66] working itself out through an inexorable moral law, his characters see only a daemonic world, haunted by malignant forces. We are reminded of the distinction we observed in the epic between the poet's point of view and that of his characters. Cassandra sees the Erinyes as a band of daemons, drunken with human blood; to Clytemnestra's excited imagination, not only the Erinyes but *ate* itself are personal fiends to whom she has offered her husband as a human sacrifice; there is even a moment when she feels her human personality lost and submerged in that of the *alastor* whose agent and instrument she was.[67] This last I take to be an instance, not exactly of "possession" in the ordinary sense, but rather of what Lévy-Bruhl calls "participation," the feeling that in a certain situation a person or thing is not only itself but also something else: I should compare the "cunning Greek" of the *Persae* who was also an *alastor*, and the priestess Timo in Herodotus, the woman who tempted Miltiades to sacrilege, concerning whom Apollo declared that "not Timo was the cause of these things, but because Miltiades was destined to end ill, one appeared to him to lead him into evil"[68]—she had acted, not as a human person, but as the agent of a supernatural purpose.

This haunted, oppressive atmosphere in which Aeschylus' characters move seems to us infinitely older than the clear air breathed by the men and gods of the *Iliad*. That is why Glotz called Aeschylus "ce revenant de Mycènes" (though he added that he was also a man of his own time); that is why a recent German writer asserts that he "revived the world of the daemons, and especially the evil daemons."[69] But to speak thus is in my view completely to misapprehend both Aeschylus' purpose and the religious climate of the age in which he lived. Aeschylus did not have to revive the world of the daemons: it is the world into which he was born. And his purpose is not to lead his fellow-countrymen back into that world, but, on the contrary, to lead them through it and out of it. This he sought to do, not like Euripides by casting doubt on its reality through intellectual and moral argument, but by showing it to be capable of a higher interpretation, and, in the *Eumenides*, by showing it transformed through Athena's agency into the new world of rational justice.

The daemonic, as distinct from the divine, has at all periods played a large part in Greek popular belief (and still does). People in the *Odyssey*, as we saw in chapter i, attribute many events in their lives, both mental and physical, to the agency of anonymous daemons; we get the impression, however, that they do not always mean it very seriously. But in the age that lies between the *Odyssey* and the *Oresteia*, the daemons seem to draw closer: they grow more persistent, more insidious, more sinister. Theognis and his contemporaries did take seriously the daemon who tempts man to *ate*, as appears from the passages I quoted just now. And the belief lived on in the popular mind long after Aeschylus' day. The Nurse in the *Medea* knows that *ate* is the work of an angry daemon, and she links it up with the old idea of *phthonos:* the greater the household, the greater the *ate;* only the obscure are safe from it.[70] And as late as the year 330 the orator Aeschines could suggest, though with a cautious "perhaps," that a certain rude fellow who interrupted his speech at the Amphictyonic Council may have been led on to this unseemly behaviour by "something daemonic" (δαιμονίου τινὸς παραγομένου).[71]

Closely akin to this agent of *ate* are those irrational impulses which arise in a man against his will to tempt him. When Theognis calls hope and fear "dangerous daemons," or when Sophocles speaks of Eros as a power that "warps to wrong the righteous mind, for its destruction,"[72] we should not dismiss this as "personification": behind it lies the old Homeric feeling that these things are not truly part of the self, since they are not within man's conscious control; they are endowed with a life and energy of their own, and so can force a man, as it were from the outside, into conduct foreign to him. We shall see in later chapters that strong traces of this way of interpreting the passions survive even in writers like Euripides and Plato.

To a different type belong the daemons projected by a particular human situation. As Professor Frankfort has said with reference to other ancient peoples, "evil spirits are often no more than the evil itself conceived as substantial and equipped with power."[73] It is thus that the Greeks spoke of famine and pestilence as "gods,"[74] and that the modern Athenian believes a certain cleft in the Hill of the Nymphs to be inhabited by three demons whose names are Cholera, Smallpox, and

Plague. These are powerful forces in whose grip mankind is helpless; and deity is power. It is thus that the persistent power and pressure of a hereditary pollution can take shape as the Aeschylean δαίμων γέννης, and that, more specifically, the blood-guilt situation is projected as an Erinys.[75] Such beings, as we have seen, are not wholly external to their human agents and victims: Sophocles can speak of "an Erinys in the brain."[76] Yet they are objective, since they stand for the objective rule that blood must be atoned; it is only Euripides[77] and Mr. T. S. Eliot who psychologise them as the pangs of conscience.

A third type of daemon, who makes his first appearance in the Archaic Age, is attached to a particular individual, usually from birth, and determines, wholly or in part, his individual destiny. We meet him first in Hesiod and Phocylides.[78] He represents the individual *moira* or "portion" of which Homer speaks,[79] but in the personal form which appealed to the imagination of the time. Often he seems to be no more than a man's "luck" or fortune;[80] but this luck is not conceived as an extraneous accident—it is as much part of a man's natal endowment as beauty or talent. Theognis laments that more depends on one's daemon than on one's character: if your daemon is of poor quality, mere good judgement is of no avail—your enterprises come to nothing.[81] In vain did Heraclitus protest that "character *is* destiny" (ἦθος ἀνθρώπῳ δαίμων); he failed to kill the superstition. The words κακοδαίμων and δυσδαίμων seem in fact to be fifth-century coinages (εὐδαίμων is as old as Hesiod). In the fate which overtook great kings and generals—a Candaules or a Miltiades—Herodotus sees neither external accident nor the consequence of character, but "what had to be"—χρῆν γὰρ Κανδαύλῃ γενέσθαι κακῶς.[82] Pindar piously reconciles this popular fatalism with the will of God: "the great purpose of Zeus *directs* the daemon of the men he loves."[83] Eventually Plato picked up and completely transformed the idea, as he did with so many elements of popular belief: the daemon becomes a sort of lofty spirit-guide, or Freudian Superego,[84] who in the *Timaeus* is identified with the element of pure reason in man.[85] In that glorified dress, made morally and philosophically respectable, he enjoyed a renewed lease of life in the pages of Stoics and Neoplatonists, and even of mediaeval Christian writers.[86]

Such, then, were some of the daemons who formed part of the religious inheritance of the fifth century B.C. I have not attempted to draw anything like a complete picture of that inheritance. Certain other aspects of it will emerge in later chapters. But we cannot go further without pausing to ask ourselves a question, one which must already have formed itself in the mind of the reader. How are we to conceive the relationship between the "guilt-culture" I have been describing in these last pages and the "shame-culture" with which I dealt in the first chapter? What historical forces determined the differences between them? I have tried to indicate that the contrast is less absolute than some scholars have assumed. We have followed various threads that lead from Homer down into the imperfectly mapped jungle of the Archaic Age, and out beyond it into the fifth century. The discontinuity is not complete. Nevertheless, a real difference of religious outlook separates Homer's world even from that of Sophocles, who has been called the most Homeric of poets. Is it possible to make any guess at the underlying causes of that difference?

To such a question we cannot hope to find any single, simple answer. For one thing, we are not dealing with a continuous historical evolution, by which one type of religious outlook was gradually transformed into another. We need not, indeed, adopt the extreme view that Homeric religion is nothing but a poetic invention, "as remote from reality and life as the artificial Homeric language."[87] But there is good reason to suppose that the epic poets ignored or minimised many beliefs and practices which existed in their day but did not commend themselves to their patrons. For example, the old cathartic scapegoat-magic was practised in Ionia in the sixth century, and had presumably been brought there by the first colonists, since the same ritual was observed in Attica.[88] The poets of the

Iliad and the *Odyssey* must have seen it done often enough. But they excluded it from their poems, as they excluded much else that seemed barbarous to them and to their upper-class audience. They give us, not something completely unrelated to traditional belief, but a *selection* from traditional belief—the selection that suited an aristocratic military culture, as Hesiod gives us the selection proper to a peasant culture. Unless we allow for this, comparison of the two will produce an exaggerated impression of historical discontinuity.

Nevertheless, when all such allowances have been made, there is an important residue of differences which seem to represent, not different selections from a common culture, but genuine cultural changes. The development of some of these we can trace—scanty though our evidence is—within the limits of the Archaic Age itself. Even Pfister, for example, recognises "an undeniable growth of anxiety and dread in the evolution of Greek religion."[89] It is true that the notions of pollution, of purification, of divine *phthonos*, may well be part of the original Indo-European inheritance. But it was the Archaic Age that recast the tales of Oedipus and Orestes as horror-stories of bloodguilt; that made purification a main concern of its greatest religious institution, the Oracle of Delphi; that magnified the importance of *phthonos* until it became for Herodotus the underlying pattern of all history. This is the sort of fact that we have to explain.

I may as well confess at once that I have no complete explanation to give; I can only guess at some partial answers. No doubt general social conditions account for a good deal.[90] In Mainland Greece (and we are concerned here with Mainland tradition) the Archaic Age was a time of extreme personal insecurity. The tiny overpopulated states were just beginning to struggle up out of the misery and impoverishment left behind by the Dorian invasions, when fresh trouble arose: whole classes were ruined by the great economic crisis of the seventh century, and this in turn was followed by the great political conflicts of the sixth, which translated the economic crisis into

terms of murderous class warfare. It is very possible that the
resulting upheaval of social strata, by bringing into prominence
submerged elements of the mixed population, encouraged the
reappearance of old culture-patterns which the common folk
had never wholly forgotten.[91] Moreover, insecure conditions of
life might in themselves favour the development of a belief in
daemons, based on the sense of man's helpless dependence upon
capricious Power; and this in turn might encourage an increased resort to magical procedures, if Malinowski[92] was right
in holding that the biological function of magic is to relieve
pent-up and frustrated feelings which can find no rational outlet. It is also likely, as I suggested earlier, that in minds of a
different type prolonged experience of human injustice might
give rise to the compensatory belief that there is justice in
Heaven. It is doubtless no accident that the first Greek to
preach divine justice was Hesiod—"the helots' poet," as King
Cleomenes called him,[93] and a man who had himself smarted
under "crooked judgements." Nor is it accidental that in this
age the doom overhanging the rich and powerful becomes so
popular a theme with poets[94]—in striking contrast to Homer,
for whom, as Murray has observed, the rich men are apt to be
specially virtuous.[95]

With these safe generalities scholars more prudent than
I am will rest content. So far as they go, I think they are
valid. But as an explanation of the more specific developments
in archaic religious feeling—particularly that growing sense of
guilt—I cannot convince myself that they go the whole way.
And I will risk the suggestion that they should be supplemented
(but not replaced) by another sort of approach, which would
start not from society at large but from the family. The family
was the keystone of the archaic social structure, the first
organised unit, the first domain of law. Its organisation, as in
all Indo-European societies, was patriarchal; its law was *patria
potestas*.[96] The head of a household is its king, οἴκοιο ἄναξ; and
his position is still described by Aristotle as analogous to that
of a king.[97] Over his children his authority is in early times un-

limited: he is free to expose them in infancy, and in manhood
to expel an erring or rebellious son from the community, as
Theseus expelled Hippolytus, as Oeneus expelled Tydeus, as
Strophios expelled Pylades, as Zeus himself cast out Hephaestos
from Olympus for siding with his mother.[98] In relation to his
father, the son had duties but no rights; while his father lived,
he was a perpetual minor—a state of affairs which lasted at
Athens down to the sixth century, when Solon introduced certain safeguards.[99] And indeed more than two centuries after
Solon the tradition of family jurisdiction was still so strong
that even Plato—who was certainly no admirer of the family—
had to give it a place in his legislation.[100]

So long as the old sense of family solidarity was unshaken,
the system presumably worked. The son gave the father the
same unquestioning obedience which in due course he would
receive from his own children. But with the relaxation of the
family bond, with the growing claim of the individual to personal rights and personal responsibility, we should expect
those internal tensions to develop which have so long characterised family life in Western societies. That they had in
fact begun to show themselves overtly in the sixth century, we
may infer from Solon's legislative intervention. But there is
also a good deal of indirect testimony to their covert influence.
The peculiar horror with which the Greeks viewed offences
against a father, and the peculiar religious sanctions to which
the offender was thought to be exposed, are in themselves
suggestive of strong repressions.[101] So are the many stories in
which a father's curse produces terrible consequences—stories
like those of Phoenix, of Hippolytus, of Pelops and his sons,
of Oedipus and his sons—all of them, it would seem, products
of a relatively late period,[102] when the position of the father was
no longer entirely secure. Suggestive in a different way is the
barbarous tale of Kronos and Ouranos, which Archaic Greece
may have borrowed from a Hittite source. There the mythological projection of unconscious desires is surely transparent—
as Plato perhaps felt when he declared that this story was fit to

be communicated only to a very few in some exceptional μυστήριον and should at all costs be kept from the young.[103] But to the eye of the psychologist the most significant evidence is that afforded by certain passages in writers of the Classical Age. The typical example by which Aristophanes illustrates the pleasures of life in Cloudcuckooland, that dream-country of wish-fulfilment, is that if you up and thrash your father, people will admire you for it: it is καλόν instead of being αἰσχρόν.[104] And when Plato wants to illustrate what happens when rational controls are not functioning, his typical example is the Oedipus dream. His testimony is confirmed by Sophocles, who makes Jocasta declare that such dreams are common; and by Herodotus, who quotes one.[105] It seems not unreasonable to argue from identical symptoms to some similarity in the cause, and conclude that the family situation in ancient Greece, like the family situation to-day, gave rise to infantile conflicts whose echoes lingered in the unconscious mind of the adult. With the rise of the Sophistic Movement, the conflict became in many households a fully conscious one: young men began to claim that they had a "natural right" to disobey their fathers.[106] But it is a fair guess that such conflicts already existed at the unconscious level from a very much earlier date—that in fact they go back to the earliest unconfessed stirrings of individualism in a society where family solidarity was still universally taken for granted.

You see perhaps where all this is tending. The psychologists have taught us how potent a source of guilt-feelings is the pressure of unacknowledged desires, desires which are excluded from consciousness save in dreams or daydreams, yet are able to produce in the self a deep sense of moral uneasiness. This uneasiness often takes a religious form to-day; and if a similar feeling existed in Archaic Greece, this would be the natural form for it to take. For, to begin with, the human father had from the earliest times his heavenly counterpart: Zeus *pater* belongs to the Indo-European inheritance, as his Latin and Sanskrit equivalents indicate; and Calhoun has shown how closely the status and conduct of the Homeric Zeus is modelled on that of the Homeric paterfamilias,[107] the οἴκοιο ἄναξ. In cult also Zeus appears as a supernatural Head of the Household: as Patroos he protects the family, as Herkeios its dwelling, as Ktesios its property. It was natural to project on to the heavenly Father those curious mixed feelings about the human one which the child dared not acknowledge even to himself. That would explain very nicely why in the Archaic Age Zeus appears by turns as the inscrutable source of good and evil gifts alike; as the jealous god who grudges his children their heart's desire;[108] and finally as the awful judge, just but stern, who punishes inexorably the capital sin of self-assertion, the sin of *hubris*. (This last aspect corresponds to that phase in the development of family relations when the authority of the father is felt to need the support of a moral sanction; when "You will do it because I say so" gives place to "You will do it because it is right.") And secondly, the cultural inheritance which Archaic Greece shared with Italy and India[109] included a set of ideas about ritual impurity which provided a natural explanation for guilt-feelings generated by repressed desires. An archaic Greek who suffered from such feelings was able to give them concrete form by telling himself that he must have been in contact with *miasma*, or that his burden was inherited from the religious offence of an ancestor. And, more important, he was able to relieve them by undergoing a cathartic ritual. Have we not here a possible clue to the part played in Greek culture by the idea of *catharsis*, and the gradual development from it, on the one hand of the notions of sin and atonement, on the other of Aristotle's psychological purgation, which relieves us of unwanted feelings through contemplating their projection in a work of art?[110]

I will not pursue these speculations further. They are clearly incapable of direct proof. At best, they may receive indirect confirmation if social psychology succeeds in establishing analogous developments in cultures more accessible to detailed study. Work on those lines is now being done,[111] but it would be

premature to generalise its results. In the meantime, I shall
not complain if classical scholars shake their heads over the
foregoing remarks. And, to avoid misunderstanding, I would
in conclusion emphasise two things. First, I do not expect
this particular key, or any key, to open all the doors. The
evolution of a culture is too complex a thing to be explained
without residue in terms of any simple formula, whether economic or psychological, begotten of Marx or begotten of Freud.
We must resist the temptation to simplify what is not simple.
And secondly, to explain origins is not to explain away values.
We should beware of underrating the religious significance
of the ideas I have discussed to-day, even where, like the
doctrine of divine temptation, they are repugnant to our
moral sense.[112] Nor should we forget that out of this archaic
guilt-culture there arose some of the profoundest tragic poetry
that man has produced. It was above all Sophocles, the last
great exponent of the archaic world-view, who expressed the
full tragic significance of the old religious themes in their un-
softened, unmoralised forms—the overwhelming sense of human helplessness in face of the divine mystery, and of the *ate*
that waits on all human achievement—and who made these
thoughts part of the cultural inheritance of Western Man. Let
me end this chapter by quoting a lyric from the *Antigone*
which conveys far better than I could convey it the beauty and
terror of the old beliefs.[113]

> Blessed is he whose life has not tasted of evil.
> When God has shaken a house, the winds of madness
> Lash its breed till the breed is done:
> Even so the deep-sea swell
> Raked by wicked Thracian winds
> Scours in its running the subaqueous darkness,
> Churns the silt black from sea-bottom;
> And the windy cliffs roar as they take its shock.

> Here on the Labdacid house long we watched it piling,
> Trouble on dead men's trouble: no generation
> Frees the next from the stroke of God:
> Deliverance does not come.

The final branch of Oedipus
Grew in his house, and a lightness hung above it:
To-day they reap it with Death's red sickle,
The unwise mouth and the tempter who sits in the brain.

The power of God man's arrogance shall not limit:
Sleep who takes all in his net takes not this,
Nor the unflagging months of Heaven—ageless the Master
Holds for ever the shimmering courts of Olympus.
    For time approaching, and time hereafter,
    And time forgotten, one rule stands:
    That greatness never
Shall touch the life of man without destruction.

Hope goes fast and far: to many it carries comfort,
To many it is but the trick of light-witted desire—
Blind we walk, till the unseen flame has trapped our footsteps.
For old anonymous wisdom has left us a saying
    "Of a mind that God leads to destruction
    The sign is this—that in the end
    Its good is evil."
Not long shall that mind evade destruction.

NOTES TO CHAPTER II

[1] The Archaic Age is usually made to end with the Persian Wars, and for the purposes of political history this is the obvious dividing line. But for the history of thought the true cleavage falls later, with the rise of the Sophistic Movement. And even then the line of demarcation is chronologically ragged. In his thought, though not in his literary technique, Sophocles (save perhaps in his latest plays) still belongs entirely to the older world; so, in most respects, does his friend Herodotus (cf. Wilamowitz, *Hermes*, 34 [1899]; E. Meyer, *Forschungen z. alt. Gesch.* II.252 ff.; F. Jacoby, P.-W., Supp.-Band II, 479 ff.). Aeschylus, on the other hand, struggling as he does to interpret and rationalise the legacy of the Archaic Age, is in many ways prophetic of the new time.

[2] The feeling of ἀμηχανία is well illustrated from the early lyric poets by Snell, *Die Entdeckung des Geistes*, 68 ff. In the following pages I am especially indebted to Latte's brilliant paper, "Schuld u. Sünde i. d. gr. Religion," *Arch. f. Rel.* 20 (1920–1921) 254 ff.

3 All Herodotus' wise men know this: Solon, 1.32; Amasis, 3.40; Artabanus, 7.10ε. On the meaning of the word φθόνος cf. Snell, *Aischylos u. das Handeln im Drama*, 72, n. 108; Cornford, *From Religion to Philosophy*, 118; and for its association with ταραχή Pind. *Isthm*. 7.39: ὁ δ'ἀθανάτων μὴ θρασσέτω φθόνος. Ταράσσειν is regularly used of supernatural interference, e.g., Aesch. *Cho*. 289; Plato, *Laws* 865ε.

4 *Il*. 24.525–533.

5 Semonides of Amorgos, 1.1 ff. Bergk. On the meaning of ἐφήμεροι see H. Fränkel, *TAPA* 77 (1946) 131 ff.; on that of τέλος F. Wehrli, Λάθε βιώσας, 8, n. 4.

6 Theognis, 133–136, 141–142. For man's lack of insight into his own situation cf. also Heraclitus, fr. 78 Diels: ἦθος γὰρ ἀνθρώπειον μὲν οὐκ ἔχει γνώμας, θεῖον δὲ ἔχει, and for his lack of control over it, *H. Apoll*. 192 f., Simonides, frs. 61, 62 Bergk; for both, Solon, 13.63 ff. This is also the teaching of Sophocles, for whom all men's generations are a nothingness—ἴσα καὶ τὸ μηδὲν ζώσας, *O.T.* 1186— when we see their life as time and the gods see it; viewed thus, men are but phantoms or shadows (*Ajax* 125).

7 *Agam*. 750.

8 The unmoralised belief is common among primitive peoples to-day (Lévy-Bruhl, *Primitives and the Supernatural*, 45). In its moralised form it appears in classical China: "If you are rich and of exalted station," says the *Tao Te Ching* (? fourth century B.C.), "you become proud, and thus abandon yourself to unavoidable ruin. When everything goes well, it is wise to put yourself in the background." It has left its mark also on the Old Testament: e.g., Isaiah 10: 12 ff., "I will punish . . . the glory of his high looks. For he saith, By the strength of my hand I have done it, and by my wisdom. . . . Shall the ax boast itself against him that heweth therewith?" For the notion of κόρος, cf. Proverbs 30: 8 f., "Give me neither poverty nor riches; feed me with food convenient for me: Lest I be full, and deny thee, and say, Who is the Lord?"

9 *Od*. 5.118 ff. Cf. 4.181 f.; 8.565 f. = 13.173 f.; 23.210 ff. All these are in speeches. The instances which some claim to find in the *Iliad*, e.g., 17.71, are of a different type, and hardly true cases of φθόνος.

10 *Pers*. 353 f., 362. This is not, strictly speaking, a new development. We have noticed a similar "overdetermination" in Homer (chap. i, pp. 7, 16). It is common among present-day primitives: e.g., Evans-Pritchard tells us that among the Azande "belief in death

from natural causes and belief in death from witchcraft are not mutually exclusive" (*Witchcraft, Oracles and Magic*, 73).

11 Solon, fr. 13 Bergk (cf. Wilamowitz, *Sappho u. Sim.* 257 ff., Wehrli, *op. cit. supra*, 11 ff., and R. Lattimore, *AJP* 68 [1947] 161 ff.); Aesch. *Agam.* 751 ff., where it is contrasted with the common view; Hdt. 1.34.1.

12 E.g., Hdt. 7.10. Sophocles seems nowhere to moralise the idea, which appears at *El.* 1466, *Phil.* 776, and is stated as a general doctrine (if πάμπολύ γ' is right) at *Ant.* 613 ff. And cf. Aristophanes, *Plut.* 87–92, where it is argued that Zeus must have a special grudge against the χρηστοί.

13 For ὕβρις as the πρῶτον κακόν see Theognis, 151 f.; for its universality, *H. Apoll.* 541: ὕβρις θ', ἥ θέμις ἐστὶ καταθνητῶν ἀνθρώπων, and Archilochus, fr. 88: ὦ Ζεῦ ... σοὶ δὲ θηρίων ὕβρις τε καὶ δίκη μέλει. Cf. also Heraclitus, fr. 43 D.: ὕβριν χρὴ σβεννύναι μᾶλλον ἢ πυρκαϊήν. For the dangers of happiness cf. Murray's remark that "It is a bad look-out for any one in Greek poetry when he is called 'a happy man'" (*Aeschylus*, 193).

14 *I.A.* 1089–1097.

15 *Il.* 9.456 f., 571 f.; cf. *Od.* 2.134 f., 11.280. It is worth noticing that three of these passages occur in narratives which we may suppose to be borrowed from Mainland epics, while the fourth belongs to the "Telemachy."

16 *Il.* 16.385 ff. On the Hesiodic character of 387–388 see Leaf *ad loc.*; but we need not call the lines an "interpolation" (cf. Latte, *Arch. f. Rel.* 20.259).

17 See Arthur Platt, "Homer's Similes," *J. Phil.* 24 (1896) 28 ff.

18 Those who argue otherwise seem to me to confuse the punishment of perjury as an offence against the divine τιμή (4.158 ff.), and the punishment of offences against hospitality by Zeus Xeinios (13.623 ff.), with a concern for justice as such.

19 *Od.* 7.164 f.; 9.270 f.; 14.283 f. Contrast the fate of Lycaon, *Il.* 21.74 ff.

20 *Od.* 6.207 f.

21 *Od.* 1.32 ff. On the significance of this much-discussed passage see most recently K. Deichgräber, *Gött. Nachr.* 1940, and W. Nestle, *Vom Mythos zum Logos*, 24. Even if the καί in 1.33 is to be taken as "also," I cannot agree with Wilamowitz (*Glaube*, II.118) that "der Dichter des α hat nichts neues gesagt."

22 *Od.* 23.67: δι' ἀτασθαλίας ἔπαθον κακόν, the same word that Zeus uses at 1.34. We must, of course, remember that the *Odyssey*, unlike the *Iliad*, has a large fairy-tale element, and that the hero of

a fairy-tale is bound to win in the end. But the poet who gave the story its final shape seems to have taken the opportunity to emphasise the lesson of divine justice.

[23] Theognis, 373–380, 733 ff. Cf. Hesiod, *Erga* 270 ff., Solon, 13.25 ff., Pindar, fr. 201 B. (213 S.). The authenticity of the Theognis passages has been denied, but on no very strong grounds (cf. W. C. Greene, *Moira*, App. 8, and Pfeiffer, *Philol.* 84 [1929] 149).

[24] *Poetics* 1453ª 34.

[25] Solon, 13.31; Theognis, 731–742. Cf. also Sophocles, *O.C.* 964 ff. (where Webster, *Introduction to Sophocles*, 31, is surely mistaken in saying that Oedipus *rejects* the explanation by inherited guilt). For Aeschylus' attitude, see later in the present chapter, pp. 39 ff. Herodotus sees such deferred punishment as peculiarly θεῖον, and contrasts it with human justice (τὸ δίκαιον), 7.137.2.

[26] Cf., e.g., the case of Achan, in which an entire household, including even the animals, is destroyed on account of a minor religious offence committed by one of its members (Joshua 7: 24 ff.). But such mass executions were later forbidden, and the doctrine of inherited guilt is explicitly condemned by Jeremiah (31: 29 f.) and by Ezekiel (18: 20, "The son shall not bear the iniquity of the father," and the whole chapter). It appears nevertheless as a popular belief in John 9: 2, where the disciples ask, "Who did sin, this man *or his parents*, that he was born blind?"

[27] Some examples will be found in Lévy-Bruhl, *The "Soul" of the Primitive*, chap. ii, and *Primitives and the Supernatural*, 212 ff.

[28] Cf. Kaibel, *Epigr. graec.* 402; Antiphon, *Tetral.* II.2.10; Plutarch, *ser. vind.* 16, 559D.

[29] Hdt. 1.91: cf. Gernet, *Recherches sur le développement de la pensée juridique et morale en Grèce*, 313, who coins the word "chosisme" to describe this conception of ἁμαρτία.

[30] See esp. pp. 403 ff., 604 ff.

[31] *Theaet.* 173D, *Rep.* 364BC. Cf. also [Lys.] 6.20; Dem. 57.27; and the implied criticism in Isocrates, *Busiris* 25.

[32] *Laws* 856C, πατρὸς ὀνείδη καὶ τιμωρίας παίδων μηδενὶ συνέπεσθαι. This, however, is subject to exception (856D); and the heritability of *religious* guilt is recognised in connection with the appointment of priests (759C), and with sacrilege (854B, where I take the guilt to be that of the Titans, cf. *infra*, chap. v, n. 133).

[33] Plut. *ser. vind.* 19, 561C ff. If we can believe Diog. Laertius (4.46), Bion had every reason to be bitter about the doctrine of inherited guilt: he and his whole family had been sold into slavery on account of an offence committed by his father. His *reductio ad ab-*

surdum of family solidarity has its parallels in actual practice: see Lévy-Bruhl, *The "Soul" of the Primitive*, 87, and *Primitive Mentality*, 417.

34 Theognis, 147; Phocyl. 17. Justice is the daughter of Zeus (Hesiod, *Erga* 256; Aesch. *Sept.* 662) or his πάρεδρος (Pindar, *Ol.* 8.21; Soph. *O.C.* 1382). Cf. the Presocratic interpretation of natural law as δίκη, which has been studied by H. Kelsen, *Society and Nature*, chap. v, and by G. Vlastos in a penetrating paper, *CP* 42 (1947) 156 ff. This emphasis on justice, human, natural, or supernatural, seems to be a distinctive mark of guilt-cultures. The nature of the psychological connection was indicated by Margaret Mead in an address to the International Congress on Mental Health in 1948: "Criminal law which metes out due punishment for proved crimes is the governmental counterpart of the type of parental authority which develops the sort of internalised parent image conducive to a sense of guilt." It is probably significant that in the *Iliad* δίκαιος occurs only thrice, and perhaps only once means "just."

35 *Il.* 15.12; 16.431 ff.; 19.340 ff.; 17.441 ff.

36 Cf. Rohde, *Kl. Schriften*, II.324; P. J. Koets, Δεισιδαιμονία, 6 ff. Δεισίθεος occurs in Attica as a proper name from the sixth century onwards (Kirchner, *Prosopographia Attica*, s.v.). Φιλόθεος is not attested until the fourth (*Hesperia* 9 [1940] 62).

37 L.-S. (and Campbell Bonner, *Harv. Theol. Rev.* 30 [1937] 122) are mistaken in attributing an active sense to θεοφιλῶς at Isocrates 4.29. The context shows that the reference is to Demeter's love of Athens, πρὸς τοὺς προγόνους ἡμῶν εὐμενῶς διατεθείσης (28).

38 *M.M.* 1208ᵇ 30: ἄτοπον γὰρ ἂν εἴη εἴ τις φαίη φιλεῖν τὸν Δία. The possibility of φιλία between man and God was denied also by Aristotle, *E.N.* 1159ᵃ 5 ff. But we can hardly doubt that the Athenians loved their goddess: cf. Aesch. *Eum.* 999: παρθένου φίλας φίλοι and Solon 4.3 f. The same relationship of absolute trust exists in the *Odyssey* between Athena and Odysseus (see esp. *Od.* 13.287 ff.). No doubt it derives ultimately from her original function as a protectress of Mycenaean kings (Nilsson, *Minoan-Mycenaean Religion*², 491 ff.).

39 That Homer knows anything of magical κάθαρσις is denied by Stengel (*Hermes*, 41.241) and others. But that the purifications described at *Il.* 1.314 and at *Od.* 22.480 ff. are thought of as cathartic in the magical sense seems fairly clear, in the one case from the disposal of the λύματα, in the other from the description of the brimstone as κακῶν ἄκος. Cf. Nilsson, *Gesch.* I.82 f.

From Shame-Culture to Guilt-Culture   55

40 *Od.* 15.256 ff.; Antiphon, *de caede Herodis* 82 f. For the older attitude cf. also Hesiod, fr. 144.

41 *Od.* 11.275 f.; *Il.* 23.679 f. Cf. Aristarchus, ΣA on *Iliad* 13.426 and 16.822; Hesiod, *Erga* 161 ff.; Robert, *Oidipus*, I.115.

42 Cf. L. Deubner, "Oedipusprobleme," *Abh. Akad. Berl.* 1942, No. 4.

43 The infectious character of μίασμα is first attested by Hesiod, *Erga* 240. The *leges sacrae* of Cyrene (Solmsen, *Inscr. Gr. dial.*⁴ No. 39) include detailed prescriptions about its extent in individual cases; for the Attic law cf. *Dem.* 20.158. That it was still commonly accepted in the Classical Age appears from such passages as Aesch. *Sept.* 597 ff., Soph. *O.C.* 1482 f., Eur. *I.T.* 1229, Antiph. *Tetr.* 1.1.3, Lys. 13.79. Euripides protested against it, *Her.* 1233 f., *I.T.* 380 ff.; but Plato would still debar from all religious or civic activities all individuals who have had *voluntary* contact, however slight, with a polluted person, until they have been purified (*Laws* 881 DE).

44 The distinction was first clearly stated by Rohde, *Psyche* (Eng. trans.), 294 ff. The mechanical nature of μίασμα is evident not only from its infectiousness but from the puerile devices by which it could be avoided: cf. Soph. *Ant.* 773 ff., with Jebb's note, and the Athenian practice of putting criminals to death by *self-administered* hemlock.

45 *The Psychological Frontiers of Society*, 439.

46 See F. Zucker's interesting lecture, *Syneidesis-Conscientia* (Jenaer Akademische Reden, Heft 6, 1928). It is, I think, significant that side by side with the old objective words for religious guilt (ἄγος, μίασμα) we meet for the first time in the later years of the fifth century a term for the *consciousness* of such guilt (whether as a scruple about incurring it or as remorse for guilt already incurred). This term is ἐνθύμιον (or ἐνθυμία, Thuc. 5.16.1), a word long in use to describe anything "weighing on one's spirits," but used by Herodotus, Thucydides, Antiphon, Sophocles, and Euripides with specific reference to the sense of religious guilt (Wilamowitz on *Heracles* 722; Hatch, *Harv. Stud. in Class. Phil.* 19.172 ff.). Democritus has ἐγκάρδιον in the same sense (fr. 262). The specific usage is practically confined to this particular period; it vanished, as Wilamowitz says, with the decline of the old beliefs, whose psychological correlate it was.

47 Eur. *Or.* 1602–1604, Ar. *Ran.* 355, and the well-known Epidaurian inscription (early fourth century?) quoted by Theophrastus, *apud* Porph. *abst.* 2.19, which defines ἁγνεία as φρονεῖν ὅσια. (I neglect Epicharmus, fr. 26 Diels, which I cannot believe to be genuine.)

56 The Greeks and the Irrational

As Rohde pointed out (*Psyche*, ix, n. 80), the shift of standpoint is well illustrated by Eur. *Hipp.* 316–318, where by μίασμα φρενός Phaedra means impure thoughts, but the Nurse understands the phrase as referring to magical attack (μίασμα can be imposed by cursing, e.g., Solmsen, *Inscr. Gr. dial.*⁴ 6.29). The antithesis between hand and heart may in fact have involved at first merely the contrast between an external and an internal physical organ, but since the latter was a vehicle of consciousness its physical pollution became *also* a moral pollution (Festugière, *La Sainteté*, 19 f.).

⁴⁸ Art. κάθαρσις, P.-W., Supp.-Band VI (this article provides the best analysis I have seen of the religious ideas associated with purification). On the original fusion of "objective" and "subjective" aspects, and the eventual distinction of the latter from the former, see also Gernet, *Pensée juridique et morale*, 323 f.

⁴⁹ Cf. for example the cathartic sacrifice to Zeus Meilichios at the Diasia, which we are told was offered μετά τινος στυγνότητος (Σ Lucian, *Icaromen.* 24)—not exactly "in a spirit of contrition," but "in an atmosphere of gloom" created by the sense of divine hostility.

⁵⁰ The evidence about the Locrian Tribute, and references to earlier discussions of it, will be found in Farnell, *Hero Cults*, 294 ff. Cf. also Parke, *Hist. of the Delphic Oracle*, 331 ff. To a similar context of ideas belongs the practice of "dedicating" (δεκατεύειν) a guilty people to Apollo. This meant enslaving them and pastoralising their land; it was carried out in the case of Crisa in the sixth century, and was threatened against the Medizers in 479 and against Athens in 404. (Cf. Parke, *Hermathena*, 72 [1948] 82 ff.)

⁵¹ Eur. *Hipp.* 276.

⁵² θυμός, Aesch. *Sept.* 686, Soph. *Ant.* 1097; φρήν, φρένες, Aesch. *Supp.* 850, Soph. *Ant.* 623.

⁵³ Aesch. *Cho.* 382 f. (Zeus); Soph. *Aj.* 363, 976 (the madness sent by Athena is called an ἄτη).

⁵⁴ Aesch. *Eum.* 372 ff. Cf. Soph. *Ant.* 603, and Ἐρινύες ἠλιθιῶναι (i.e., ἠλιθίους ποιοῦσαι) in an Attic *defixio* (Wünsch, *Defix. Tab. Att.* 108).

⁵⁵ So perhaps Soph. *Trach.* 849 f. And cf. Herodotus' conception of disastrous decisions as predetermined by the destiny of the person who takes them: 9.109.2: τῇ δὲ κακῶς γὰρ ἔδει πανοικίῃ γενέσθαι, πρὸς ταῦτα εἶπε Ξέρξῃ κτλ.; 1.8.2, 2.161.3, 6.135.3.

⁵⁶ Panyassis, fr. 13.8 Kinkel.

⁵⁷ *Erga* 214 ff.

58 Theognis, 205 f.

59 Aesch. *Pers.* 1037, Soph. *Aj.* 307.

60 Theognis, 133, Aesch. *Cho.* 825 f., Soph. *O.C.* 92; Soph. *Ant.* 185 f. In Dorian law ἄτη seems to have become completely secularized as a term for any legal penalty: *leg. Gortyn.* 11.34 (*GDI* 4991).

61 Eur. *Tro.* 530 (cf. Theognis, 119); Soph. *Ant.* 533. Soph. *O.C.* 532 is different; there Oedipus calls his daughters ἄται as being the fruits of his own γάμων ἄτα (526).

62 Compare the extension of usage by which the words ἀλιτήριος, παλαμναῖος, προστρόπαιος, were applied not only to the guilty man but to the supernatural being who punishes him. (Cf. W. H. P. Hatch, *Harv. Stud. in Class. Phil.* 19 [1908] 157 ff.)—μένος ἄτης, Aesch. *Cho.* 1076.

63 *In Leocratem* 92. Cf. the similar anonymous γνώμη quoted by Sophocles, *Ant.* 620 ff.

64 Theognis, 402 ff.

65 Aesch. *Pers.* 354 (cf. 472, 724 f.); contrast 808, 821 f. The divine ἀπάτη is thus for Aeschylus δικαία (fr. 301). In his condemnation of those who make gods the cause of evil Plato included Aeschylus, on the strength of Niobe's words: θεὸς μὲν αἰτίαν φύει βροτοῖς, ὅταν κακῶσαι δῶμα παμπήδην θέλῃ (fr. 156, *apud* Pl. *Rep.* 380A). But he omitted to quote the δέ clause, which contained—as we now know from the *Niobe* papyrus, D. L. Page, *Greek Literary Papyri*, I.1, p. 8—a warning against ὕβρις, μὴ θρασυστομεῖν. Here, as elsewhere, Aeschylus carefully recognised man's contribution to his own fate.

66 Aesch. *Agam.* 1486; cf. 160 ff., 1563 f.

67 *Ibid.*, 1188 ff., 1433, 1497 ff.

68 Hdt. 6.135.3.

69 Glotz, *Solidarité*, 408; K. Deichgräber, *Gött. Nachr.* 1940.

70 Eur. *Med.* 122–130. Phaedra too ascribes her state to δαίμονος ἄτη, *Hipp.* 241. And we know from a treatise in the Hippocratic corpus (*Virg.* I, VIII.466 L.), that mental disturbance often showed itself in dreams or visions of angry daemons.

71 Aeschin. *in Ctes.* 117. Aeschines knew that he was living in a strange, revolutionary time, when the old centres of power were giving place to new ones (*ibid.*, 132), and this inclined him, like Herodotus, to see the hand of God everywhere. Thus he speaks of the Thebans as τήν γε θεοβλάβειαν καὶ τὴν ἀφροσύνην οὐκ ἀνθρωπίνως ἀλλὰ δαιμονίως κτησάμενοι (*ibid.*, 133).

72 Theognis, 637 f.; Soph. *Ant.* 791 f. On Ἐλπίς see Wehrli, Λάθε βιώσας, 6 ff.

73 H. and H. A. Frankfort, *The Intellectual Adventure of Ancient Man*, 17.

74 Sem. Amorg. 7.102; Soph. *O.T.* 28. Cf. also chap. iii, n. 14, and on similar Indian beliefs Keith, *Rel. and Phil. of Veda and Upanishads*, 240.

75 For the view of the modern Athenian see Lawson, *Modern Greek Folklore and Ancient Greek Religion*, 21 ff. For bloodguilt projected as an Erinys cf. Aesch. *Cho.* 283: προσβολὰς Ἐρινύων ἐκ τῶν πατρῴων αἱμάτων τελουμένας, with Verrall *ad loc.*; *ibid.*, 402; Antiphon, *Tetral.* 3.1.4.

76 Soph. *Ant.* 603. Cf. the verb δαιμονᾶν, used both of "haunted" places (*Cho.* 566) and of "possessed" persons (*Sept.* 1001, *Phoen.* 888).

77 Eur. *Or.* 395 ff. If letters VII and VIII are genuine, even Plato believed in objective beings who punish bloodguilt: VII.336B: ἤ πού τις δαίμων ἤ τις ἀλιτήριος ἐμπεσών (cf. 326E); VIII.357A: ξενικαὶ ἐρινύες ἐκώλυσαν.

78 Hesiod, *Erga* 314: δαίμονι δ' οἷος ἔησθα, τὸ ἐργάζεσθαι ἄμεινον, and Phocylides, fr. 15.

79 See chap. i, p. 6. Side by side with the more personal δαίμων, the Homeric notion of an individual μοῖρα also lived on, and is common in tragedy. Cf. Archilochus, fr. 16: πάντα τύχη καὶ μοῖρα, Περίκλεες, ἀνδρὶ δίδωσιν, Aesch. *Agam.* 1025 ff., *Cho.* 103 f., etc.; Soph. *O.T.* 376, 713 etc.; Pind. *Nem.* 5.40: πότμος δὲ κρίνει συγγενὴς ἔργων περὶ πάντων, and Plato, *Gorg.* 512E: πιστεύσαντα ταῖς γυναιξὶν ὅτι τὴν εἱμαρμένην οὐδ' ἂν εἷς ἐκφύγοι. The Homeric phrase θανάτου (-οιο) μοῖρα reappears in Aeschylus, *Pers.* 917, *Agam.* 1462. Sometimes μοῖρα and δαίμων are combined: Ar. *Thesm.* 1047: μοίρας ἄτεγκτε δαίμων (tragic parody); Lys. 2.78: ὁ δαίμων ὁ τὴν ἡμετέραν μοῖραν εἰληχώς.

80 δαίμων (the religious interpretation) and τύχη (the profane or noncommittal view) are not felt to be mutually exclusive, and are in fact often coupled: Ar. *Av.* 544: κατὰ δαίμονα καί ⟨τινα⟩ συντυχίαν ἀγαθήν, Lys. 13.63: τύχη καὶ ὁ δαίμων, [Dem.] 48.24, Aeschin. *in Ctes.* 115, Aristotle, fr. 44. Eur., however, distinguishes them as alternatives (fr. 901.2). In the concept of θεία τύχη (Soph. *Phil.* 1326, and often in Plato) chance regains the religious value which primitive thought assigns to it (chap. i, n. 25).

81 Theognis, 161–166.

82 Hdt. 1.8.2. Cf. n. 55 above.

83 Pindar, *Pyth.* 5.122 f. But he does not always thus moralise the

popular belief. Cf. *Ol.* 13.105, where the "luck" of the γένος is projected as a δαίμων.

⁸⁴ The Stoic δαίμων comes even closer to Freud's conception than the Platonic: he is, as Bonhöffer put it (*Epiktet*, 84), "the ideal as contrasted with the empirical personality"; and one of his principal functions is to punish the ego for its carnal sins (cf. Heinze, *Xenokrates*, 130 f.; Norden, *Virgil's Aeneid VI*, pp. 32 f.). Apuleius, *d. Socr.* 16, makes the daemon reside in ipsis penitissimis mentibus *vice conscientiae.*

⁸⁵ *Phaedo* 107D; *Rep.* 617DE, 620DE (where Plato avoids the fatalism of the popular view by making the soul choose its own guide); *Tim.* 90A–C (discussed below, chap. vii, pp. 213 f.).

⁸⁶ Cf. M. Ant. 2.13, with Farquharson's note; Plut. *gen. Socr.* 592BC; Plot. 2.4; Rohde, *Psyche*, XIV, n. 44; J. Kroll, *Lehren des Hermes Trismegistos*, 82 ff. Norden, *loc. cit.*, shows how the idea was taken over by Christian writers.

⁸⁷ Fr. Pfister, P.-W., Supp.-Band VI, 159 f. Cf. his *Religion d. Griechen u. Römer* (Bursian's Jahresbericht, 229 [1930]), 219.

⁸⁸ The evidence about the φαρμακοί is conveniently assembled in Murray's *Rise of the Greek Epic*, App. A. In regarding the rite as primarily cathartic I follow Deubner, *Attische Feste*, 193 ff., and the Greeks themselves. For a summary of other opinions see Nilsson, *Gesch.* I.98 f.

⁸⁹ P.-W., Supp.-Band VI, 162.

⁹⁰ Cf. Nilsson, *Gesch.* I.570 ff., and Diels, "Epimenides von Kreta," *Berl. Sitzb.* 1891, 387 ff.

⁹¹ Some scholars would attribute the peculiarities of archaic as compared with Homeric religion to the resurgence of pre-Greek "Minoan" ideas. This may well prove to be true in certain cases. But most of the traits which I have stressed in this chapter seem to have Indo-European roots, and we should therefore hesitate, I think, to invoke "Minoan religion" in this context.

⁹² As Malinowski puts it, when a man feels himself impotent in a practical situation, "whether he be savage or civilised, whether in possession of magic or entirely ignorant of its existence, passive inaction, the only thing dictated by reason, is the last thing in which he can acquiesce. His nervous system and his whole organism drive him to some substitute activity. . . . The substitute action in which the passion finds its vent, and which is due to impotence, has subjectively all the virtue of a real action, to which emotion would, if not impeded, naturally have led" (*Magic, Science and Religion*). There is some evidence that the same principle

holds good for societies: e.g., Linton (in A. Kardiner, *The Individu-al and His Society*, 287 ff.) reports that among the effects produced by a grave economic crisis among certain of the Tanala tribes in Madagascar were a great increase in superstitious fears and the emergence of a belief in evil spirits, which had previously been lacking.

93 Plut. *Apophth. Lac.* 223A.

94 E.g., Hesiod, *Erga* 5 f.; Archilochus, fr. 56; Solon, frs. 8, 13.75; Aesch. *Sept.* 769 ff., *Agam.* 462 ff.; etc.

95 Murray, *Rise of the Greek Epic*⁴, 90; cf. *Il.* 5.9, 6.14, 13.664, and *Od.* 18.126 f. This is the attitude to be expected in a shame-culture; wealth brings τιμή (*Od.* 1.392, 14.205 f.). It was still so in Hesiod's day, and (conscious though he was of the attendant dangers) he used the fact to reinforce his gospel of work: *Erga* 313: πλούτῳ δ' ἀρετὴ καὶ κῦδος ὀπηδεῖ.

96 For the evidence see Glotz, *Solidarité*, 31 ff.

97 Arist. *Pol.* 1.2, 1252ᵇ 20: πᾶσα γὰρ οἰκία βασιλεύεται ὑπὸ τοῦ πρεσβυτάτου. Cf. *E.N.* 1161ᵃ 18: φύσει ἀρχικὸν πατὴρ υἱῶν ... καὶ βασιλεὺς βασιλευομένων. Plato uses stronger terms; he speaks of the proper status of the young as πατρὸς καὶ μητρὸς καὶ πρεσβυτέρων δουλείαν (*Laws* 701B).

98 Eur. *Hipp.* 971 ff., 1042 ff. (Hippolytus expects death rather than banishment); *Alcmaeonis*, fr. 4 Kinkel (apud [Apollod.] *Bibl.* 1.8.5); Eur. *Or.* 765 ff.; *Il.* 1.590 ff. The myths suggest that in early times banishment was the necessary consequence of ἀποκήρυξις, a rule which Plato proposed to restore (*Laws* 928E).

99 Cf. Glotz, *op. cit.*, 350 ff.

100 Plato, *Laws* 878DE, 929A–C.

101 Honouring one's parents comes next in the scale of duties after fearing the gods: Pind. *Pyth.* 6.23 ff. and Σ *ad loc.*; Eur. fr. 853; Isocr. 1.16; Xen. *Mem.* 4.4.19 f., etc. For the special supernatural sanctions attaching to offences against parents see *Il.* 9.456 f.; Aesch. *Eum.* 269 ff.; Eur. frs. 82, 852; Xen. *Mem.* 4.4.21; Plato, *Euthyphro* 15D; *Phaedo* 114A; *Rep.* 615C; *Laws* 872E and esp. 880E ff.; also Paus. 10.28.4; Orph. fr. 337 Kern. For the feelings of the involuntary parricide cf. the story of Althaimenes, Diod. 5.59 (but it should be noticed that, like Oedipus, he is eventually heroised).

102 The story of Phoenix, like the rest of his speech in *Il.* 9 (432–605), seems to reflect rather late Mainland conditions: cf. chap. i, p. 6. The other stories are post-Homeric (Oedipus' curse first in the

Thebais, frs. 2 and 3 K.; cf. Robert, *Oidipus*, I.169 ff.). Plato still professes belief in the efficacy of a parent's curse, *Laws* 931C, E.

103 Plato, *Rep.* 377E-378B. The Kronos myth has, as we should expect, parallels of a sort in many cultures; but one parallel, with the Hurrian-Hittite Epic of Kumarbi, is so close and detailed as strongly to suggest borrowing (E. Forrer, *Mél. Cumont*, 690 ff.; R. D. Barnett, *JHS* 65 [1945] 100 f.; H. G. Güterbock, *Kumarbi* [Zurich, 1946], 100 ff.). This does not diminish its significance: we have to ask in that case what feelings induced the Greeks to give this monstrous Oriental phantasy a central place in their divine mythology. It is often—and perhaps rightly—thought that the "separation" of Ouranos from Gaia mythologises an imagined physical separation of sky from earth which was originally one with it (cf. Nilsson, *Hist. of Greek Religion*, 73). But the father-castration motive is hardly a natural, and certainly not a necessary, element in such a myth. I find its presence in the Hittite and Greek theogonies difficult to explain otherwise than as a reflex of unconscious human desires. Confirmation of this view may perhaps be seen in the birth of Aphrodite from the severed member of the old god (Hesiod, *Theog.* 188 ff.), which can be read as symbolising the son's attainment of sexual freedom through removal of his father-rival. What is certain is that in the Classical Age the Kronos stories were frequently appealed to as a precedent for unfilial conduct: cf. Aesch. *Eum.* 640 ff.; Ar. *Nub.* 904 ff., *Av.* 755 ff.; Plato, *Euthyphro* 5E-6A.

104 The figure of the πατραλοίας seems to have fascinated the imagination of the Classical Age: Aristophanes brings him on the stage in person, *Av.* 1337 ff., and shows him arguing his case, *Nub.* 1399 ff.; for Plato he is the stock example of wickedness (*Gorg.* 456D, *Phd.* 113E *fin.*, etc.). It is tempting to see in this something more than a reflex of sophistic controversies, or of a particular "conflict of generations" in the late fifth century, though these no doubt helped to throw the πατραλοίας into prominence.

105 Plato, *Rep.* 571C; Soph. *O.T.* 981 f.; Hdt. 6.107.1. That undisguised Oedipus dreams were likewise common in later antiquity, and that their significance was much debated by the ὀνειροκριτικοί, appears from the unpleasantly detailed discussion of them in Artemidorus, 1.79. It may be thought that this implies a less deep and rigorous repression of incestuous desires than is usual in our own society. Plato, however, specifically testifies, not only that incest was universally regarded as αἰσχρῶν αἴσχιστον, but that most people were completely unconscious of any impulse towards

it (*Laws* 838B). It seems that we ought rather to say that the necessary disguising of the forbidden impulse was accomplished, not within the dream itself, but by a subsequent process of interpretation, which gave it an innocuous symbolic meaning. Ancient writers do, however, also mention what would now be called disguised Oedipus dreams, e.g., the dream of plunging into water (Hipp. περὶ διαίτης 4.90, VI.658 Littré).

[106] Cf. S. Luria, "Väter und Söhne in den neuen literarischen Papyri," *Aegyptus*, 7 (1926) 243 ff., a paper which contains an interesting collection of evidence on family relations in the Classical Age, but seems to me to exaggerate the importance of intellectual influences, and in particular that of the sophist Antiphon.

[107] G. M. Calhoun, "Zeus the Father in Homer," *TAPA* 66 (1935) 1 ff. Conversely, later Greeks thought it right to treat one's parent "like a god": θεὸς μέγιστος τοῖς φρονοῦσιν οἱ γονεῖς (Dicaeogenes, fr. 5 Nauck); νόμος γονεῦσιν ἰσοθέους τιμὰς νέμειν (Menander, fr. 805 K.).

[108] The doctrine of divine φθόνος has often been regarded as a simple projection of the resentment felt by the unsuccessful against the eminent (cf. the elaborate but monomaniac book of Ranulf). There is no doubt a measure of truth in this theory. Certainly divine and human φθόνος have much in common, e.g., both work through the Evil Eye. But passages like Hdt. 7.46.4: ὁ δὲ θεὸς γλυκὺν γεύσας τὸν αἰῶνα φθονερὸς ἐν αὐτῷ εὑρίσκεται ἐών to my mind point in a different direction. They recall rather Piaget's observation that "children sometimes think the opposite from what they want, *as if reality made a point of failing their desires*" (quoted by A. R. Burn, *The World of Hesiod*, 93, who confirms the statement from his own experience). Such a state of mind is a typical by-product of a guilt-culture in which domestic discipline is severe and repressive. It may easily persist in adult life and find expression in quasi-religious terms.

[109] Rohde called attention to the similarity between Greek ideas about pollution and purification and those of early India (*Psyche*, chap. ix, n. 78). Cf. Keith, *Religion and Philosophy of Veda and Upanishads*, 382 ff., 419 f.; and for Italy, H. J. Rose, *Primitive Culture in Italy*, 96 ff., 111 ff., and H. Wagenvoort, *Roman Dynamism* (Eng. trans., 1947), chap. v.

[110] I am tempted also to suggest that Aristotle's preference among tragic subjects for deeds of horror committed ἐν ταῖς φιλίαις (*Poet.* 1453[b] 19), and among these for stories where the criminal act is prevented at the last moment by an ἀναγνώρισις (1454[a] 4),

is unconsciously determined by their greater effectiveness as an abreaction of guilt-feelings—especially as the second of these preferences stands in flat contradiction to his general view of tragedy. On catharsis as abreaction see below, chap. iii, pp. 76, 78.

111 See especially Kardiner's books, *The Individual and His Society* and *The Psychological Frontiers of Society;* also Clyde Kluckhohn, "Myths and Rituals: A General Theory," *Harv. Theol. Rev.* 35 (1942) 74 ff., and S. de Grazia, *The Political Community* (Chicago, 1948).

112 See Latte's excellent remarks, *Arch. f. Rel.* 20.275 ff. As he points out, the religious consciousness is not only patient of moral paradoxes, but often perceives in them the deepest revelation of the tragic meaning of life. And we may remind ourselves that this particular paradox has played an important part in Christianity: Paul believed that "whom He will He hardeneth" (Rom. 9: 18), and the Lord's Prayer includes the petition "Lead us not into temptation" (μὴ εἰσενέγκῃς ἡμᾶς εἰς πειρασμόν). Cf. Rudolph Otto's remark that "to the religious men of the Old Covenant the Wrath of God, so far from being a diminution of his Godhead, appears as a natural expression of it, an element of 'holiness' itself, and a quite indispensable one" (*The Idea of the Holy*, 18). I believe this to be equally true of men like Sophocles. And the same formidable "holiness" can be seen in the gods of archaic and early classical art. As Professor C. M. Robertson has said in his recent inaugural lecture (London, 1949), "they are conceived indeed in human form, but their divinity is humanity with a terrible difference. To these ageless, deathless creatures ordinary humans are as flies to wanton boys, and this quality is conveyed in their statues, at any rate far down into the fifth century."

113 Soph. *Ant.* 583 ff. The version which follows attempts to reproduce the significant placing of the recurrent key word ἄτη, and also some of the metrical effects, but cannot reproduce the sombre magnificence of the original. For several turns of phrase I am indebted to a gifted pupil, Miss R. C. Collingwood.

III
The Blessings of Madness

In the creative state a man is taken out of himself.
He lets down as it were a bucket into his subconscious,
and draws up something which is normally beyond his
reach.

E. M. FORSTER

"OUR greatest blessings," says Socrates in the *Phaedrus*, "come to us by way of madness": τὰ μέγιστα τῶν ἀγαθῶν ἡμῖν γίγνεται διὰ μανίας.[1] That is, of course, a conscious paradox. No doubt it startled the fourth-century Athenian reader hardly less than it startles us; for it is implied a little further on that most people in Plato's time regarded madness as something discreditable, an ὄνειδος.[2] But the father of Western rationalism is not represented as maintaining the general proposition that it is better to be mad than sane, sick than sound. He qualifies his paradox with the words θείᾳ μέντοι δόσει διδομένης, "provided the madness is given us by divine gift." And he proceeds to distinguish four types of this "divine madness," which are produced, he says, "by a divinely wrought change in our customary social norms" (ὑπὸ θείας ἐξαλλαγῆς τῶν εἰωθότων νομίμων).[3] The four types are:

1) Prophetic madness, whose patron god is Apollo.
2) Telestic or ritual madness, whose patron is Dionysus.
3) Poetic madness, inspired by the Muses.
4) Erotic madness, inspired by Aphrodite and Eros.[4]

About the last of these I shall have something to say in a later chapter;[5] I do not propose to discuss it here. But it may be worth while to look afresh at the first three, not attempting

[1] For notes to chapter iii see pages 82–101.

64

any exhaustive survey of the evidence, but concentrating on what may help us to find answers to two specific questions. One is the historical question: how did the Greeks come by the beliefs which underlie Plato's classification, and how far did they modify them under the influence of advancing rationalism? The other question is psychological: how far can the mental states denoted by Plato's "prophetic" and "ritual" madness be recognised as identical with any states known to modern psychology and anthropology? Both questions are difficult, and on many points we may have to be content with a verdict of *non liquet*. But I think they are worth asking. In attempting to deal with them I shall of course be standing, as we all stand, on the shoulders of Rohde, who traversed most of this ground very thoroughly in his great book *Psyche*. Since that book is readily available, both in German and in English, I shall not recapitulate its arguments; I shall, however, indicate one or two points of disagreement.

Before approaching Plato's four "divine" types, I must first say something about his general distinction between "divine" madness and the ordinary kind which is caused by disease. The distinction is of course older than Plato. From Herodotus we learn that the madness of Cleomenes, in which most people saw the godsent punishment of sacrilege, was put down by his own countrymen to the effects of heavy drinking.[6] And although Herodotus refuses to accept this prosaic explanation in Cleomenes' case, he is inclined to explain the madness of Cambyses as due to congenital epilepsy, and adds the very sensible remark that when the body is seriously deranged it is not surprising that the mind should be affected also.[7] So that he recognises at least two types of madness, one which is supernatural in origin (though not beneficent) and another which is due to natural causes. Empedocles and his school are also said to have distinguished madness arising *ex purgamento animae* from the madness due to bodily ailments.[8]

This, however, is relatively advanced thinking. We may doubt if any such distinction was drawn in earlier times. It is

the common belief of primitive peoples throughout the world
that *all* types of mental disturbance are caused by supernatural
interference. Nor is the universality of the belief very surprising.
I suppose it to have originated in, and to be maintained by, the
statements of the sufferers themselves. Among the commonest
symptoms of delusional insanity to-day is the patient's belief
that he is in contact with, or even identified with, supernatural
beings or forces, and we may presume that it was not otherwise
in antiquity; indeed, one such case, that of the fourth-century
physician Menecrates, who thought he was Zeus, has been
recorded in some detail, and forms the subject of a brilliant
study by Otto Weinreich.[9] Epileptics, again, often have the
sensation of being beaten with a cudgel by some invisible
being; and the startling phenomena of the epileptic fit, the
sudden falling down, the muscular contortions, the gnashing
teeth and projecting tongue, have certainly played a part in
forming the popular idea of possession.[10] It is not surprising
that to the Greeks epilepsy was *the* "sacred disease" *par excellence*, or that they called it ἐπίληψις, which—like our words
"stroke," "seizure," "attack"—suggests the intervention of a
daemon.[11] I should guess, however, that the idea of true possession, as distinct from mere psychic interference, derived
ultimately from cases of secondary or alternating personality,
like the famous Miss Beauchamp whom Morton Prince studied.[12] For here a new personality, usually differing widely from
the old one in character, in range of knowledge, and even in
voice and facial expression, appears suddenly to take possession
of the organism, speaking of itself in the first person and of the
old personality in the third. Such cases, relatively rare in
modern Europe and America, seem to be found more often
among the less advanced peoples,[13] and may well have been
commoner in antiquity than they are to-day; I shall return to
them later. From these cases the notion of possession would
easily be extended to epileptics and paranoiacs; and eventually
all types of mental disturbance, including such things as sleepwalking and the delirium of high fever,[14] would be put down

to daemonic agencies. And the belief, once accepted, naturally created fresh evidence in its own support by the operation of autosuggestion.[15]

It has long been observed that the idea of possession is absent from Homer, and the inference is sometimes drawn that it was foreign to the oldest Greek culture. We can, however, find in the *Odyssey* traces of the vaguer belief that mental disease is of supernatural origin. The poet himself makes no reference to it, but he once or twice allows his characters to use language which betrays its existence. When Melantho jeeringly calls the disguised Odysseus ἐκπεπαταγμένος,[16] "knocked out of his senses," i.e., crazy, she is using a phrase which in origin probably implied daemonic intervention, though on her lips it may mean no more than we mean when we describe someone as "a bit touched." A little later, one of the suitors is jeering at Odysseus, and calls him ἐπίμαστον ἀλήτην. ἐπίμαστος (from ἐπιμαίομαι) is not found elsewhere, and its meaning is disputed; but the sense "touched," i.e., crazy, given by some ancient scholars, is the most natural, and the one best suited to the context.[17] Here again a supernatural "touch" is, I think, implied. And finally, when Polyphemus starts screaming, and the other Cyclopes, on asking what is the matter, are informed that "No-man is trying to kill him," they observe in response that "the sickness from great Zeus cannot be avoided," and piously recommend prayer.[18] They have concluded, I think, that he is mad: that is why they abandon him to his fate. In the light of these passages it seems fairly safe to say that the supernatural origin of mental disease was a commonplace of popular thought in Homer's time, and probably long before, though the epic poets had no particular interest in it and did not choose to commit themselves to its correctness; and one may add that it has remained a commonplace of popular thought in Greece down to our own day.[19] In the Classical Age, intellectuals might limit the range of "divine madness" to certain specific types. A few, like the author of the late-fifth-century treatise *de morbo sacro*, might even go the length of denying that any sickness is more "divine" than any other, holding that every disease is "divine" as being part of the divine order, but every disease has also natural causes which human reason can discover—πάντα θεῖα καὶ πάντα ἀνθρώπινα.[20] But it is unlikely that popular belief was much affected by all this, at any rate outside a few great cultural centres.[21] Even at Athens, the mentally afflicted were still shunned by many, as being persons subject to a divine curse, contact with whom was dangerous: you threw stones at them to keep them away, or at least took the minimum precaution of spitting.[22]

Yet if the insane were shunned, they were also regarded (as indeed they still are in Greece)[23] with a respect amounting to awe; for they were in contact with the supernatural world, and could on occasion display powers denied to common men. Ajax in his madness talks a sinister language "which no mortal taught him, but a daemon";[24] Oedipus in a state of frenzy is guided by a daemon to the place where Jocasta's corpse awaits him.[25] We see why Plato in the *Timaeus* mentions disease as one of the conditions which favour the emergence of supernatural powers.[26] The dividing line between common insanity and prophetic madness is in fact hard to draw. And to prophetic madness we must now turn.

Plato (and Greek tradition in general) makes Apollo its patron; and out of the three examples which he gives, the inspiration of two—the Pythia and the Sibyl—was Apolline,[27] the third instance being the priestesses of Zeus at Dodona. But if we are to believe Rohde[28] in this matter—and many people still do[29]—Plato was entirely mistaken: prophetic madness was unknown in Greece before the coming of Dionysus, who forced the Pythia on Delphi; until then, Apolline religion had been, according to Rohde, "hostile to anything in the nature of ecstasy." Rohde had two reasons for thus rejecting the Greek tradition. One was the absence from Homer of any reference to inspired prophecy; the other was the impressive antithesis which his friend Nietzsche had drawn between the "rational" religion of Apollo and the "irrational" religion of Dionysus. But I think Rohde was wrong.

In the first place, he confused two things that Plato carefully distinguished—the Apolline mediumship which aims at knowledge, whether of the future or of the hidden present, and the Dionysiac experience which is pursued either for its own sake or as a means of mental healing, the mantic or mediumistic element being absent or quite subordinate.[30] Mediumship is the rare gift of chosen individuals; Dionysiac experience is essentially collective or congregational—θιασεύεται ψυχάν—and is so far from being a rare gift that it is highly infectious. And their methods are as different as their aims: the two great Dionysiac techniques—the use of wine and the use of the religious dance—have no part whatever in the induction of Apolline ecstasy. The two things are so distinct that the one seems most unlikely to be derived from the other.

Furthermore, we know that ecstatic prophecy was practised from an early date in western Asia. Its occurrence in Phoenicia is attested by an Egyptian document of the eleventh century; and three centuries earlier still we find the Hittite king Mursili II praying for a "divine man" to do what Delphi was so often asked to do—to reveal for what sins the people were afflicted with a plague.[31] The latter example would become especially significant if we could accept, as Nilsson inclines to do, the guess of Hrozný that Apollo, the sender and the healer of plague, is none other than a Hittite god Apulunas.[32] But in any case it seems to me reasonably certain, from the evidence afforded by the *Iliad*, that Apollo was originally an Asiatic of some sort.[33] And in Asia, no less than in Mainland Greece, we find ecstatic prophecy associated with his cult. His oracles at Claros near Colophon and at Branchidae outside Miletus are said to have existed before the colonisation of Ionia,[34] and at both ecstatic prophecy appears to have been practised.[35] It is true that our evidence on the latter point comes from late authors; but at Patara in Lycia—which is thought by some to be Apollo's original homeland, and was certainly an early centre of his cult—at Patara we know from Herodotus that the prophetess was locked into the temple at night, with a view to mystic union with the god. Apparently she was thought to be at once his medium and his bride, as Cassandra should have been, and as Cook and Latte conjecture the Pythia to have been originally.[36] That points fairly plainly to ecstatic prophecy at Patara, and Delphic influence is here very unlikely.

I conclude that the prophetic madness is at least as old in Greece as the religion of Apollo. And it may well be older still. If the Greeks were right in connecting μάντις with μαίνομαι— and most philologists think they were[37]—the association of prophecy and madness belongs to the Indo-European stock of ideas. Homer's silence affords no sound argument to the contrary; we have seen before that Homer could keep his mouth shut when he chose. We may notice, moreover, that in this matter as in others the *Odyssey* has a somewhat less exacting standard of seemliness, of epic dignity, than has the *Iliad*. The *Iliad* admits only inductive divination from omens, but the *Odyssey*-poet cannot resist introducing something more sensational—an example of what the Scots call second-sight.[38] The symbolic vision of the Apolline hereditary seer Theoclymenus in Book 20 belongs to the same psychological category as the symbolic visions of Cassandra in the *Agamemnon*, and the vision of that Argive prophetess of Apollo who, as Plutarch tells, rushed one day into the streets, crying out that she saw the city filled with corpses and blood.[39] This is one ancient type of prophetic madness. But it is not the usual oracular type; for its occurrence is spontaneous and incalculable.[40]

At Delphi, and apparently at most of his oracles, Apollo relied, not on visions like those of Theoclymenus, but on "enthusiasm" in its original and literal sense. The Pythia became *entheos, plena deo*:[41] the god entered into her and used her vocal organs as if they were his own, exactly as the so-called "control" does in modern spirit-mediumship; that is why Apollo's Delphic utterances are always couched in the first person, never

in the third. There were, indeed, in later times, those who held
that it was beneath the dignity of a divine being to enter into a
mortal body, and preferred to believe—like many psychical re-
searchers in our own day—that all prophetic madness was due
to an innate faculty of the soul itself, which it could exercise
in certain conditions, when liberated by sleep, trance, or religious ritual both from bodily interference and from rational
control. This opinion is found in Aristotle, Cicero, and Plutarch;[42] and we shall see in the next chapter that it was used in
the fifth century to account for prophetic dreams. Like the other,
it has abundant savage parallels; we may call it the "shamanistic" view, in contrast with the doctrine of possession.[43] But as
an explanation of the Pythia's powers it appears only as a
learned theory, the product of philosophical or theological
reflection; there can be little doubt that her gifts were originally
attributed to possession, and that this remained the usual view
throughout antiquity—it did not occur even to the Christian
Fathers to question it.[44]

Nor was prophetic possession confined to official oracles.
Not only were legendary figures like Cassandra, Bakis, and the
Sibyl believed to have prophesied in a state of possession,[45]
but Plato refers frequently to inspired prophets as a familiar
contemporary type.[46] In particular, some sort of private mediumship was practised in the Classical Age, and for long afterwards, by the persons known as "belly-talkers," and later as
"pythons."[47] I should like to know more about these "belly-
talkers," one of whom, a certain Eurycles, was famous enough
to be mentioned both by Aristophanes and by Plato.[48] But our
direct information amounts only to this, that they had a second
voice inside them which carried on a dialogue with them,[49]
predicted the future, and was believed to belong to a daemon.
They were certainly not ventriloquists in the modern sense of
the term, as is often assumed.[50] A reference in Plutarch seems
to imply that the voice of the daemon—presumably a hoarse
"belly-voice"—was heard speaking through their lips; on the
other hand, a scholiast on Plato writes as if the voice were

merely an inward monition.[51] Scholars have overlooked, however, one piece of evidence which not only excludes ventriloquism but strongly suggests trance: an old Hippocratic casebook, the *Epidemiae*, compares the noisy breathing of a heart patient to that of "the women called belly-talkers." Ventriloquists do not breathe stertorously; modern "trance mediums" often do.[52]

Even on the psychological state of the Pythia our information is pretty scanty. One would like to be told how she was chosen in the first instance, and how prepared for her high office; but practically all we know with certainty is that the Pythia of Plutarch's day was the daughter of a poor farmer, a woman of honest upbringing and respectable life, but with little education or experience of the world.[53] One would like, again, to know whether on coming out of trance she remembered what she had said in the trance state, in other words, whether her "possession" was of the somnambulistic or the lucid type.[54] Of the priestesses of Zeus at Dodona it is definitely reported that they did not remember; but for the Pythia we have no decisive statement.[55] We know, however, from Plutarch that she was not always affected in the same manner,[56] and that occasionally things went badly wrong, as they have been known to do at modern seances. He reports the case of a recent Pythia who had gone into trance reluctantly and in a state of depression, the omens being unfavourable. From the outset she spoke in a hoarse voice, as if distressed, and appeared to be filled with "a dumb and evil spirit";[57] finally she rushed screaming towards the door and fell to the ground, whereupon all those present, and even the *Prophetes*, fled in terror. When they came back to pick her up, they found her senses restored;[58] but she died within a few days. There is no reason to doubt the substantial truth of this story, which has parallels in other cultures.[59] Plutarch probably had it at first hand from the *Prophetes* Nicander, a personal friend of his, who was actually present at the horrid scene. It is important as showing both that the trance was still genuine in Plutarch's day, and that it could be witnessed not only by the *Prophetes* and some of the *Hosioi*, but by the enquirers.[60] Incidentally, the change of voice is mentioned by Plutarch elsewhere as a common feature of "enthusiasm." It is no less common in later accounts of possession, and in modern spirit mediums.[61]

I take it as fairly certain that the Pythia's trance was auto-suggestively induced, like mediumistic trance to-day. It was preceded by a series of ritual acts: she bathed, probably in Castalia, and perhaps drank from a sacred spring; she established contact with the god through his sacred tree, the laurel, either by holding a laurel branch, as her predecessor Themis does in a fifth-century vase painting, or by fumigating herself with burnt laurel leaves, as Plutarch says she did, or perhaps sometimes by chewing the leaves, as Lucian asserts; and finally she seated herself on the tripod, thus creating a further contact with the god by occupying his ritual seat.[62] All these are familiar magical procedures, and might well assist the autosuggestion; but none of them could have any physiological effect—Professor Oesterreich once chewed a large quantity of laurel leaves in the interests of science, and was disappointed to find himself no more inspired than usual.[63] The same applies to what is known of the procedure at other Apolline oracles—drinking from a sacred spring at Claros and possibly at Branchidae, drinking the blood of the victim at Argos.[64] As for the famous "vapours" to which the Pythia's inspiration was once confidently ascribed, they are a Hellenistic invention, as Wilamowitz was, I think, the first to point out.[65] Plutarch, who knew the facts, saw the difficulties of the vapour theory, and seems finally to have rejected it altogether; but like the Stoic philosophers, nineteenth-century scholars seized with relief on a nice solid materialist explanation. Less has been heard of this theory since the French excavations showed that there are to-day no vapours, and no "chasm" from which vapours could once have come.[66] Explanations of this type are really quite needless; if one or two living scholars still cling to them,[67] it is only because they ignore the evidence of anthropology and abnormal psychology.

Scholars who attributed the Pythia's trance to inhaling mephitic gases naturally concluded that her "ravings" bore little relation to the response eventually presented to the enquirer; the responses must on this view be products of conscious and deliberate fraud, and the reputation of the Oracle must have rested partly on an excellent intelligence service, partly on the wholesale forgery of oracles *post eventum*. There is one piece of evidence, however, which suggests, for what it is worth, that in early times the responses were really based on the Pythia's words: when Cleomenes suborned the Oracle to give the reply he wanted, the person whom his agent approached was, if we can trust Herodotus, not the *Prophetes* or one of the *Hosioi*, but the Pythia herself; and the desired result followed.[68] And if in later days, as Plutarch implies, the enquirers were, on some occasions at least, able to hear the actual words of the entranced Pythia, her utterances could scarcely on such occasions be radically falsified by the *Prophetes*. Nevertheless, one cannot but agree with Professor Parke that "the history of Delphi shows sufficient traces of a consistent policy to convince one that human intelligence at some point could play a deciding part in the process."[69] And the necessity of reducing the Pythia's words to order, relating them to the enquiry, and— sometimes, but not always[70]—putting them into verse, clearly did offer considerable scope for the intervention of human intelligence. We cannot see into the minds of the Delphic priesthood, but to ascribe such manipulations in general to conscious and cynical fraud is, I suspect, to oversimplify the picture. Anyone familiar with the history of modern spiritualism will realise what an amazing amount of virtual cheating can be done in perfectly good faith by convinced believers.

Be that as it may, the rarity of open scepticism about Delphi before the Roman period is very striking.[71] The prestige of the Oracle must have been pretty deeply rooted to survive its scandalous behaviour during the Persian Wars. Apollo on that occasion showed neither prescience nor patriotism, yet his people did not turn away from him in disgust; on the contrary, his clumsy attempts to cover his tracks and eat his words appear to have been accepted without question.[72] The explanation must, I think, be sought in the social and religious conditions described in the preceding chapter. In a guilt-culture, the need for supernatural assurance, for an authority transcending man's, appears to be overwhelmingly strong. But Greece had neither a Bible nor a Church;[73] that is why Apollo, vicar on earth of the heavenly Father,[74] came to fill the gap. Without Delphi, Greek society could scarcely have endured the tensions to which it was subjected in the Archaic Age. The crushing sense of human ignorance and human insecurity, the dread of divine *phthonos*, the dread of *miasma*—the accumulated burden of these things would have been unendurable without the assurance which such an omniscient divine counsellor could give, the assurance that behind the seeming chaos there was knowledge and purpose. "I know the count of the sand grains and the measures of the sea"; or, as another god said to another people, "the very hairs of your head are all numbered." Out of his divine knowledge, Apollo would tell you what to do when you felt anxious or frightened; he knew the rules of the complicated game that the gods play with humanity; he was the supreme ἀλεξίκακος, "Averter of Evil." The Greeks believed in their Oracle, not because they were superstitious fools, but because they could not do without believing in it. And when the importance of Delphi declined, as it did in Hellenistic times, the main reason was not, I suspect, that men had grown (as Cicero thought) more sceptical,[75] but rather that other forms of religious reassurance were now available.

So much for prophetic madness. With Plato's other types I can deal more briefly. On what Plato meant by "telestic" or ritual madness, much light has recently been thrown in two important papers by Professor Linforth;[76]and I need not repeat things which he has already said better than I could say them. Nor shall I repeat here what I have myself said in print[77] about what I take to be the prototype of ritual madness, the Dionysiac ὀρειβασία or mountain dancing. I should like, however, to make some remarks of a more general character.

If I understand early Dionysiac ritual aright, its social function was essentially cathartic,[78] in the psychological sense: it purged the individual of those infectious irrational impulses which, when dammed up, had given rise, as they have done in other cultures, to outbreaks of dancing mania and similar manifestations of collective hysteria; it relieved them by providing them with a ritual outlet. If that is so, Dionysus was in the Archaic Age as much a social necessity as Apollo; each ministered in his own way to the anxieties characteristic of a guilt-culture. Apollo promised security: "Understand your station as man; do as the Father tells you; and you will be safe to-morrow." Dionysus offered freedom: "Forget the difference, and you will find the identity; join the θίασος, and you will be happy to-day." He was essentially a god of joy, πολυγηθής, as Hesiod calls him; χάρμα βροτοῖσιν, as Homer says.[79] And his joys were accessible to all, including even slaves, as well as those freemen who were shut out from the old gentile cults.[80] Apollo moved only in the best society, from the days when he was Hector's patron to the days when he canonised aristocratic athletes; but Dionysus was at all periods δημοτικός, a god of the people.

The joys of Dionysus had an extremely wide range, from the simple pleasures of the country bumpkin, dancing a jig on greased wineskins, to the ὠμοφάγος χάρις of the ecstatic bacchanal. At both levels, and at all the levels between, he is Lusios, "the Liberator"—the god who by very simple means, or by other means not so simple, enables you for a short time to *stop being yourself*, and thereby sets you free. That was, I think, the main secret of his appeal to the Archaic Age: not only because life in that age was often a thing to escape from, but more specifically because the individual, as the modern world knows him, began in that age to emerge for the first time from the old solidarity of the family,[81] and found the unfamiliar

burden of individual responsibility hard to bear. Dionysus
could lift it from him. For Dionysus was the Master of Magical
Illusions, who could make a vine grow out of a ship's plank, and
in general enable his votaries to see the world as the world's
not.[82] As the Scythians in Herodotus put it, "Dionysus leads
people on to behave madly"—which could mean anything from
"letting yourself go" to becoming "possessed."[83] The aim of his
cult was *ecstasis*—which again could mean anything from
"taking you out of yourself" to a profound alteration of personality.[84] And its psychological function was to satisfy and
relieve the impulse to reject responsibility, an impulse which
exists in all of us and can become under certain social conditions
an irresistible craving. We may see the mythical prototype of
this homoeopathic cure in the story of Melampus, who healed
the Dionysiac madness of the Argive women "with the help
of ritual cries and a sort of possessed dancing."[85]

With the incorporation of the Dionysiac cult in the civic
religion, this function was gradually overlaid by others.[86] The
cathartic tradition seems to have been carried on to some extent
by private Dionysiac associations.[87] But in the main the cure
of the afflicted had in the Classical Age passed into the hands of
other cults. We have two lists of the Powers whom popular
thought in the later fifth century associated with mental or
psycho-physical disturbances, and it is significant that Dionysus does not figure in either. One occurs in the *Hippolytus*, the
other in the *de morbo sacro*.[88] Both lists include Hecate and the
"Mother of the Gods" or "Mountain Mother" (Cybele);
Euripides adds Pan[89] and the Corybantes; Hippocrates adds
Poseidon, Apollo Nomios, and Ares, as well as the "heroes,"
who are here simply the unquiet dead associated with Hecate.
All these are mentioned as deities who *cause* mental trouble.
Presumably all could cure what they had caused, if their anger
were suitably appeased. But by the fifth century the Corybantes at any rate had developed a special ritual for the treatment of madness. The Mother, it would appear, had done likewise (if indeed her cult was at that time distinct from that of

the Corybantes);[90] and possibly Hecate also.[91] But about these we have no detailed information. About the Corybantic treatment we do know something, and Linforth's patient examination has dissipated much of the fog that surrounded the subject. I shall content myself with stressing a few points which are relevant to the particular questions I have in mind.

1) We may note first the essential similarity of the Corybantic to the old Dionysiac cure: both claimed to operate a catharsis by means of an infectious "orgiastic" dance accompanied by the same kind of "orgiastic" music—tunes in the Phrygian mode played on the flute and the kettledrum.[92] It seems safe to infer that the two cults appealed to similar psychological types and produced similar psychological reactions. Of these reactions we have, unhappily, no precise description, but they were evidently striking. On Plato's testimony, the physical symptoms of οἱ κορυβαντιῶντες included fits of weeping and violent beating of the heart,[93] and these were accompanied by mental disturbance; the dancers were "out of their minds," like the dancers of Dionysus, and apparently fell into a kind of trance.[94] In that connection we should remember Theophrastus' remark that hearing is the most emotive (παθητικωτάτην) of all the senses, as well as the singular moral effects which Plato attributes to music.[95]

2) The malady which the Corybantes professed to cure is said by Plato to consist in "phobies or anxiety-feelings (δείματα) arising from some morbid mental condition."[96] The description is fairly vague, and Linforth is doubtless right in saying that antiquity knew no specific disease of "Corybantism."[97] If we can trust Aristides Quintilianus, or his Peripatetic source, the symptoms which found relief in Dionysiac ritual were of much the same nature.[98] It is true that certain people did try to distinguish different types of "possession" by their outward manifestations, as appears from the passage in de morbo sacro.[99] But the real test seems to have been the patient's response to a particular ritual: if the rites of a god X stimulated him and produced a catharsis, that showed that his trouble was due to

$X;^{100}$ if he failed to react, the cause must lie elsewhere. Like the old gentleman in Aristophanes' parody, if he did not respond to the Corybantes, he might then perhaps try Hecate, or fall back on the general practitioner Asclepius.[101] Plato tells us in the *Ion* that οἱ κορυβαντιῶντες "have a sharp ear for one tune only, the one which belongs to the god by whom they are possessed, and to that tune they respond freely with gesture and speech, while they ignore all others." I am not sure whether οἱ κορυβαντιῶντες is here used loosely as a general term for "people in an anxiety-state," who try one ritual after another, or whether it means "those who take part in the Corybantic ritual"; on the second view, the Corybantic performance must have included different types of religious music, introduced for a diagnostic purpose.[102] But in any case the passage shows that the diagnosis was based on the patient's response to music. And diagnosis was the essential problem, as it was in all cases of "possession": once the patient knew what god was causing his trouble, he could appease him by the appropriate sacrifices.[103]

3) The whole proceeding, and the presuppositions on which it rested, are highly primitive. But we cannot dismiss it—and this is the final point I want to stress—either as a piece of back-street atavism or as the morbid vagary of a few neurotics. A casual phrase of Plato's[104] appears to imply that Socrates had personally taken part in the Corybantic rites; it certainly shows, as Linforth has pointed out, that intelligent young men of good family might take part in them. Whether Plato himself accepted all the religious implications of such ritual is an open question, to be considered later;[105] but both he and Aristotle evidently regard it as at least a useful organ of social hygiene—they believe that it *works*, and works for the good of the participants.[106] And in fact analogous methods appear to have been used by laymen in Hellenistic and Roman times for the treatment of certain mental disorders. Some form of musical catharsis had been practised by Pythagoreans in the fourth century, and perhaps earlier;[107] but the Peripatetic school seems to have been the first who studied it in the light of physiology

and the psychology of the emotions.[108] Theophrastus, like Plato, believed that music was good for anxiety-states.[109] In the first century B.C. we find Asclepiades, a fashionable physician at Rome, treating mental patients by means of "symphonia"; and in the Antonine Age Soranus mentions flute music among the methods used in his day for the treatment either of depression or of what we should call hysteria.[110] Thus the old magico-religious catharsis was eventually detached from its religious context and applied in the field of lay psychiatry, to supplement the purely physical treatment which the Hippocratic doctors had used.

There remains Plato's third type of "divine" madness, the type which he defines as "possession (κατοκωχή) by the Muses" and declares to be indispensable to the production of the best poetry. How old is this notion, and what was the original connection between poets and Muses?

A connection of some sort goes back, as we all know, to epic tradition. It was a Muse who took from Demodocus his bodily vision, and gave him something better, the gift of song, because she loved him.[111] By grace of the Muses, says Hesiod, some men are poets, as others are kings by grace of Zeus.[112] We may safely assume that this is not yet the empty language of formal compliment which it was later to become; it has religious meaning. And up to a point the meaning is plain enough: like all achievements which are not wholly dependent on the human will, poetic creation contains an element which is not "chosen," but "given";[113] and to old Greek piety "given" signifies "divinely given."[114] It is not quite so clear in what this "given" element consists; but if we consider the occasions on which the *Iliad*-poet himself appeals to the Muses for help, we shall see that it falls on the side of content and not of form. Always he asks the Muses what he is to say, never how he is to say it; and the matter he asks for is always factual. Several times he requests information about important battles;[115] once, in his most elaborate invocation, he begs to be inspired with an Army List—"for you are goddesses, watching all things, knowing all things; but we have only hearsay and not knowledge."[116] These wistful words have the ring of sincerity; the man who first used them knew the fallibility of tradition and was troubled by it; he wanted first-hand evidence. But in an age which possessed no written documents, where should first-hand evidence be found? Just as the truth about the future would be attained only if man were in touch with a knowledge wider than his own, so the truth about the past could be preserved only on a like condition. Its human repositories, the poets, had (like the seers) their technical resources, their professional training; but vision of the past, like insight into the future, remained a mysterious faculty, only partially under its owner's control, and dependent in the last resort on divine grace. By that grace poet and seer alike enjoyed a knowledge[117] denied to other men. In Homer the two professions are quite distinct; but we have good reason to believe that they had once been united,[118] and the analogy between them was still felt.

The gift, then, of the Muses, or one of their gifts, is the power of true speech. And that is just what they told Hesiod when he heard their voice on Helicon, though they confessed that they could also on occasion tell a pack of lies that counterfeited truth.[119] What particular lies they had in mind we do not know; possibly they meant to hint that the true inspiration of saga was petering out in mere invention, the sort of invention we can observe in the more recent portions of the *Odyssey*. Be that as it may, it was detailed factual truth that Hesiod sought from them, but facts of a new kind, which would enable him to piece together the traditions about the gods and fill the story out with all the necessary names and relationships. Hesiod had a passion for names, and when he thought of a new one, he did not regard it as something he had just invented; he heard it, I think, as something the Muse had given him, and he knew or hoped that it was "true." He in fact interpreted in terms of a traditional belief-pattern a feeling which has been shared by many later writers[120]—the feeling that creative thinking is not the work of the *ego*.

It was truth, again, that Pindar asked of the Muse. "Give me an oracle," he says, "and I will be your spokesman (προφατεύ-σω)."[121] The words he uses are the technical terms of Delphi; implicit in them is the old analogy between poetry and divination. But observe that it is the Muse, and not the poet, who plays the part of the Pythia; the poet does not ask to be himself "possessed," but only to act as interpreter for the entranced Muse.[122] And that seems to be the original relationship. Epic tradition represented the poet as deriving supernormal knowledge from the Muses, but not as falling into ecstasy or being possessed by them.

The notion of the "frenzied" poet composing in a state of ecstasy appears not to be traceable further back than the fifth century. It may of course be older than that; Plato calls it an old story, παλαιὸς μῦθος.[123] I should myself guess it to be a by-product of the Dionysiac movement with its emphasis on the value of abnormal mental states, not merely as avenues to knowledge, but for their own sake.[124] But the first writer whom we know to have talked about poetic ecstasy is Democritus, who held that the finest poems were those composed μετ' ἐνθουσιασμοῦ καὶ ἱεροῦ πνεύματος, "with inspiration and a holy breath," and denied that anyone could be a great poet *sine furore*.[125] As recent scholars have emphasised,[126] it is to Democritus, rather than to Plato, that we must assign the doubtful credit of having introduced into literary theory this conception of the poet as a man set apart from common humanity[127] by an abnormal inner experience, and of poetry as a revelation apart from reason and above reason. Plato's attitude to these claims was in fact a decidedly critical one—but that is matter for a later chapter.

NOTES TO CHAPTER III

[1] Plato, *Phaedrus* 244A.

[2] *Ibid.*, 244B: τῶν παλαιῶν οἱ τὰ ὀνόματα τιθέμενοι οὐκ αἰσχρὸν ἡγοῦντο οὐδὲ ὄνειδος μανίαν, which implies that people nowadays do

think it αἰσχρόν. Hippocrates, *morb. sacr.* 12, speaks of the αἰσχύνη felt by epileptics.

3 *Ibid.*, 265A.

4 *Ibid.*, 265B. Cf. the fuller description of the first three types, 244A–245A.

5 See below, chap. vii, p. 218.

6 Hdt. 6.84 (cf. 6.75.3).

7 Hdt. 3.33. Cf. also Xen. *Mem.* 3.12.6.

8 Caelius Aurelianus, *de morbis chronicis*, 1.5 = Diels, *Vorsokr.* 31 A 98. Cf. A. Delatte, *Les Conceptions de l'enthousiasme chez les philosophes présocratiques*, 21 ff. But it is impossible to be sure that the doctrine goes back to Empedocles himself.

9 O. Weinreich, *Menekrates Zeus und Salmoneus* (Tübinger Beiträge zur Altertumswissenschaft, 18).

10 On the confusion of epilepsy with possession in popular thought at various periods see O. Temkin's comprehensive historical monograph, *The Falling Sickness* (Baltimore, 1945), 15 ff., 84 ff., 138 ff. Many of the highly coloured mediaeval and Renaissance descriptions of "demoniacs" are garnished with symptoms characteristic of epilepsy, e.g., the tongue projecting "like an elephant's trunk," "prodigiously large, long, and hanging down out of her mouth"; the body "tense and rigid all over, with his feet touching his head," "bent backwards like a bow"; and the involuntary discharge of urine at the end of the fit (T. K. Oesterreich, *Possession, Demoniacal and Other*, Eng. trans., 1930, pp. 18, 22, 179, 181, 183). All these were known to rationalist Greek physicians as symptoms of epilepsy: see Aretaeus, *de causis et signis acutorum morborum*, p. 1 ff. Kühn (who also mentions the feeling of being beaten).

11 Cf. Hdt. 4.79.4: ἡμέας ὁ θεὸς λαμβάνει, and the adjs. νυμφόληπτος, θεόληπτος, etc.; Cumont, *L'Égypte des astrologues*, 169, n. 2. But ἐπίληπτος is already used in the *de morbo sacro* without religious implication. Aretaeus, *op. cit.*, 73 K., gives four reasons why epilepsy was called ἱερὰ νόσος: (*a*) δοκέει γὰρ τοῖσι ἐς τὴν σελήνην ἀλιτροῖσι ἀφικνεῖσθαι ἡ νοῦσος (a Hellenistic theory, cf. Temkin, *op. cit.*, 9 f., 90 ff.); (*b*) ἢ μέγεθος τοῦ κακοῦ· ἱερὸν γὰρ τὸ μέγα; (*c*) ἢ ἰήσιος οὐκ ἀνθρωπίνης ἀλλὰ θείης (cf. *morb. sacr.* 1, VI.352.8 Littré); (*d*) ἢ δαίμονος δόξης ἐς τὸν ἄνθρωπον ἐσόδου. The last was probably the original reason; but popular thinking on such matters has always been vague and confused. Plato, who did not believe in the supernatural character of epilepsy, nevertheless defended the term ἱερὰ νόσος, on the ground that it affects the head,

which is the "holy" part of a man (*Tim.* 85AB). It is still called the "heiliges Weh" in Alsace.

12 Morton Prince, *The Dissociation of a Personality*. Cf. also P. Janet, *L'Automatisme psychologique;* A. Binet, *Les Altérations de la personnalité;* Sidis and Goodhart, *Multiple Personality;* F. W. H. Myers, *Human Personality*, chap. ii. The significance of these cases for the understanding of ancient ideas of possession has been emphasised by E. Bevan, *Sibyls and Seers*, 135 f., and was already appreciated by Rohde (*Psyche*, App. viii).

13 Cf. Seligman, *JRAI* 54 (1924) 261: "'among the more primitive folk of whom I have personal knowledge . . . I have observed a more or less widespread tendency to ready dissociation of personality."

14 Sleepwalking is referred to in the *de morbo sacro* (c. 1, VI.354.7 Littré), and is said to be caused, in the opinion of the magical healers, by Hecate and the dead (*ibid.*, 362.3); the ghosts take possession of the living body which its owner leaves unoccupied during sleep. Cf. *trag. adesp.* 375: ἔνυπνον φάντασμα φοβῇ χθονίας θ' Ἑκάτης κῶμον ἐδέξω. For the supernatural origin of fever cf. the fever-daemons Ἠπιάλης, Τῖφυς, Εὐόπας (Didymus *apud* Σ Ar. *Vesp.* 1037); the temple of Febris at Rome, Cic. *N.D.* 3.63, Pliny, *N.H.* 2.15; and *supra*, chap. ii, n. 74.

15 Cf. Oesterreich, *op. cit.*, 124 ff.

16 *Od.* 18.327. In the *Iliad*, on the other hand, such expressions as ἐκ δέ οἱ ἡνίοχος πλήγη φρένας (13.394) imply nothing supernatural: the driver's temporary condition of stupefied terror has a normal human cause. At *Il.* 6.200 ff., Bellerophon is perhaps thought of as mentally afflicted by the gods, but the language used is very vague.

17 *Od.* 20.377. Apoll. Soph. *Lex. Hom.* 73.30 Bekker explains ἐπίμαστος as ἐπίπληκτος, Hesychius as ἐπίληπτος. Cf. W. Havers, *Indogerm. Forschungen*, 25 (1909) 377 f.

18 *Od.* 9.410 ff. Cf. 5.396: στυγερὸς δέ οἱ ἔχραε δαίμων (in a simile); there, however, the illness seems to be physical.

19 See B. Schmidt, *Volksleben der Neugriechen*, 97 f.

20 Hipp. *morb. sacr.* 18 (VI.394.9 ff. Littré). Cf. *aer. aq. loc.* 22 (II.76.16 ff. L.), which is perhaps the work of the same author (Wilamowitz, *Berl. Sitzb.* 1901, i.16); and *flat.* 14 (VI.110 L.). But even medical opinion was not unanimous on this question. The author of the Hippocratic *Prognostikon* seems to believe that certain diseases have "something divine" about them (c. 1, II.112.5 L.). Despite Nestle, *Griech. Studien*, 522 f., this seems to be a

different view from that of *morb. sacr.*: "divine" diseases are a special class which it is important for the physician to recognise (because they are incurable by human means). And the magical treatment of epilepsy never in fact died out: e.g. [Dem.] 25.80 refers to it; and in late antiquity Alexander of Tralles says that amulets and magical prescriptions are used by "some" in treating this malady, not without success (I.557 Puschmann).

²¹ The slave's question, Ar. *Vesp.* 8: ἀλλ' ἦ παραφρονεῖς ἐτεὸν ἢ κορυβαντιᾷς; perhaps implies a distinction between "natural" and "divine" madness. But the difference between παραφρονεῖν and κορυβαντιᾶν may be merely one of degree, milder mental disturbance being attributed to the Corybantes (*infra*, pp. 77 ff.).

²² Ar. *Aves* 524 f. (cf. Plautus, *Poenulus* 527); Theophr. *Char.* 16 (28 J.) 14; Pliny, *N.H.* 28.4.35, "despuimus comitiales morbos, hoc est, contagia regerimus"; and Plautus, *Captivi* 550 ff.

²³ "Mental derangement, which appears to me to be exceedingly common among the Greek peasants, sets the sufferer not merely apart from his fellows but in a sense above them. His utterances are received with a certain awe, and so far as they are intelligible are taken as predictions" (Lawson, *Mod. Greek Folklore and Anc. Greek Religion*, 299). On the prophetic gifts attributed to epileptics see Temkin, *op. cit.*, 149 ff.

²⁴ Soph. *Ajax* 243 f. It is a widespread belief among primitives that persons in abnormal mental states speak a special "divine" language; cf., e.g., Oesterreich, *op. cit.*, 232, 272; N. K. Chadwick, *Poetry and Prophecy*, 18 f., 37 f. Compare also the pseudo-languages spoken by certain automatists and religious enthusiasts, who are often said, like Ajax, to have learned them from "the spirits" (E. Lombard, *De la glossolalie chez les premiers chrétiens et les phénomènes similaires*, 25 ff.).

²⁵ Soph. *O.T.* 1258: λυσσῶντι δ' αὐτῷ δαιμόνων δείκνυσί τις. The Messenger goes on to say that Oedipus was "led" to the right place (1260, ὡς ὑφηγητοῦ τινος); in other words, he is credited with a temporary clairvoyance of supernatural origin.

²⁶ Plato, *Tim.* 71E. Cf. Aristotle, *div. p. somn.* 464ᵃ 24: ἐνίους τῶν ἐκστατικῶν προορᾶν.

²⁷ Heraclitus, fr. 92 D.: Σίβυλλα δὲ μαινομένῳ στόματι ἀγέλαστα καὶ ἀκαλλώπιστα καὶ ἀμύριστα φθεγγομένη χιλίων ἐτῶν ἐξικνεῖται τῇ φωνῇ διὰ τὸν θεόν. The context of the fragment in Plutarch (*Pyth. or.* 6, 397A) makes it practically certain that the words διὰ τὸν θεόν are part of the citation, and that the god in question is Apollo (cf. Delatte, *Conceptions de l'enthousiasme*, 6, n. 1).

[28] *Psyche*, Eng. trans., 260, 289 ff.

[29] Rohde's view is still taken for granted, e.g., by Hopfner in P.-W., s.v. μαντική; E. Fascher, Προφήτης, 66; W. Nestle, *Vom Mythos zum Logos*, 60; Oesterreich, *Possession*, 311. *Contra:* Farnell, *Cults*, IV.190 ff.; Wilamowitz, *Glaube der Hellenen*, II.30; Nilsson, *Geschichte*, I.515 f.; Latte, "The Coming of Pythia," *Harv. Theol. Rev.* 33 (1940) 9 ff. Professor Parke, *Hist. of the Delphic Oracle*, 14, inclines to the opinion that Apollo took over the Pythia from the primitive Earth-oracle at Delphi, on the ground that this accounts for her sex (we should expect Apollo to have a male priest); but this argument is, I think, adequately met by Latte.

[30] Euripides makes Teiresias claim that Dionysus is, among other things, a god of ecstatic prophecy (*Ba.* 298 ff.); and it appears from Hdt. 7.111 that female trance-mediumship was really practised at his Thracian oracle in the country of the Satrae (cf. Eur. *Hec.* 1267, where he is called ὁ Θρῃξὶ μάντις). But in Greece he found a mantic god already in possession, and seems accordingly to have resigned this function, or at any rate allowed it to fall into the background. In the Roman age he had a trance-oracle (with a *male* priest) at Amphikleia in Phocis (Paus. 10.33.11, *IG* IX.1.218); but this is not attested earlier, and the cult shows Orientalising traits (Latte, *loc. cit.*, 11).

[31] Phoenicia: Gressmann, *Altorientalische Texte u. Bilder zum A.T.* I.225 ff. Hittites: A. Götze, *Kleinasiatische Forschungen*, I.219; O. R. Gurney, "Hittite Prayers of Mursili II," *Liverpool Annals*, XXVII. Cf. C. J. Gadd, *Ideas of Divine Rule in the Ancient East* (Schweich Lectures, 1945), 20 ff. We also have a series of Assyrian oracles, dating from the reign of Esarhaddon, in which the goddess Ishtar professedly speaks through the mouth of an (entranced?) priestess whose name is given: see A. Guillaume, *Prophecy and Divination among the Hebrews and Other Semites*, 42 ff. Like the θεομάντεις in Plato, *Apol.* 22c, such prophets are said to "bring forth what they do not know" (A. Haldar, *Associations of Cult Prophets among the Ancient Semites*, 25). Gadd thinks ecstatic prophecy in general older than divination by art ("oracles and prophecy tend to harden into practices of formal divination"); and Halliday is of the same opinion (*Greek Divination*, 55 ff.).

[32] Nilsson, *Greek Popular Religion*, 79, following B. Hrozný, *Arch. Or.* 8 (1936) 171 ff. Unfortunately, the reading "Apulunas," which Hrozný claims to have deciphered in a Hittite hieroglyphic inscription, is disputed by other competent Hittite scholars: see R. D. Barnett, *JHS* 70 (1950) 104.

33 Cf. Wilamowitz, "Apollon," *Hermes*, 38 (1903) 575 ff.; *Glaube*,
I.324 ff.; and (for those who do not read German) his Oxford lecture on Apollo (1908), translated by Murray.

34 Claros, Paus. 7.3.1; Branchidae (Didyma), *ibid*., 7.2.4. Cf. C. Pi-
card, *Ephèse et Claros*, 109 ff.

35 Cf. Farnell's discussion, *Cults*, IV.224. The ancient evidence is
collected *ibid*., 403 ff.

36 Hdt. 1.182. Cf. A. B. Cook, *Zeus*, II.207 ff., and Latte, *loc. cit.*

37 So Curtius, Meillet, Boisacq, Hofmann. Cf. Plato, *Phaedrus* 244c,
and Eur. *Ba*. 299.

38 *Od*. 20.351 ff. I cannot agree with Nilsson, *Gesch*. I.154, that this
scene is "dichterisches Schauen, nicht das sogenannte zweite
Gesicht." The parallel with the symbolism of Celtic vision,
noticed by Monro *ad loc*., seems too close to be accidental. Cf. also
Aesch. *Eum*. 378 ff.: τοῖον ἐπὶ κνέφας ἀνδρὶ μύσους πεπόταται, καὶ
δνοφεράν τιν' ἀχλὺν κατὰ δώματος αὐδᾶται πολύστονος φάτις, and
for the symbolic vision of blood, Hdt. 7.140.3 and the Plutarch
passage quoted in the next note, as well as *Njals Saga*, c. 126.

39 Plut. *Pyrrh*. 31: ἐν τῇ πόλει τῶν Ἀργείων ἡ τοῦ Λυκείου προφῆτις
Ἀπόλλωνος ἐξέδραμε βοῶσα νεκρῶν ὁρᾶν καὶ φόνου κατάπλεω τὴν
πόλιν.

40 It could be made available at set times and seasons only by the
use of some device analogous to the mediaeval "crystal ball." This
was perhaps done at the minor Apolline oracle of Κυανέαι in Lycia,
where Pausanias says it was possible ἔσω ἐνιδόντα τινὰ ἐς τὴν πηγὴν
ὁμοίως πάντα ὁπόσα θέλει θεάσασθαι (7.21.13).

41 ἔνθεος never means that the soul has left the body and is "in
God," as Rohde seems in places to imply, but always that the
body has a god within it, as ἔμψυχος means that it has ψυχή within
it (see Pfister in *Pisciculi F. J. Doelger dargeboten* [Münster, 1939],
183). Nor can I accept the view that the Pythia became ἔνθεος
only in the sense of being "in a state of grace resulting from the accomplishment of rites" and that her "inspired ecstasy" is the invention of Plato, as P. Amandry has recently maintained in a careful and learned study which unfortunately appeared too late for
me to use in preparing this chapter, *La Mantique apollinienne à
Delphes* (Paris, 1950), 234 f. He rightly rejects the "frenzied"
Pythia of Lucan and the vulgar tradition, but his argument is
vitiated by the assumption, still common among people who have
never seen a "medium" in trance, that "possession" is necessarily
a state of hysterical excitement. He also seems to misunderstand
Phaedrus 244B, which surely does not mean that besides her

trance utterances the Pythia also gave oracles (of inferior quality) in her normal state (σωφρονοῦσα), but only that apart from her mediumship she had no particular gifts (cf. n. 53 below).

⁴² Ar. *apud* Sext. Emp. *adv. dogm.* 3.20 f. = fr. 10 Rose (cf. Jaeger, *Aristotle*, Eng. trans., 160 f.); *Probl.* 30, 954ᵃ 34 ff.; R. Walzer, "Un frammento nuovo di Aristotele," *Stud. ital. di Fil. Class.* N.S. 14 (1937) 125 ff.; Cic. *de divin.* 1.18, 64, 70, 113; Plut. *def. orac.* 39 f., 431E ff. Cf. Rohde, *Psyche*, 312 f.

⁴³ Some writers (e.g., Farnell, *Greece and Babylon*, 303) use the terms "shamanism" and "possession" as if they were synonymous. But the characteristic feature of shamanism is not the entry of an alien spirit into the shaman; it is the liberation of the shaman's spirit, which leaves his body and sets off on a mantic journey or "psychic excursion." Supernatural beings may assist him, but his own personality is the decisive element. Cf. Oesterreich, *op. cit.*, 305 ff., and Meuli, *Hermes*, 70 (1935) 144. Greek prophets of the shamanistic type are discussed below, chap. v.

⁴⁴ Cf. Minuc. Felix, *Oct.* 26 f., and the passages collected by Tambornino, *de antiquorum daemonismo* (*RGVV* VII, 3).

⁴⁵ "Deus inclusus corpore humano iam, non Cassandra, loquitur," says Cicero (*de divin.* 1.67) with reference to an old Latin tragedy, probably the *Alexander* of Ennius. Aeschylus presents Cassandra as a clairvoyante rather than a medium; but there is an approach to the idea of possession at *Agam.* 1269 ff., where she suddenly sees her own act in stripping off the symbols of seership (1266 f.) as the act of Apollo himself. For the possession of the Sibyl by Apollo, and of Bakis by the Nymphs, see Rohde, *Psyche*, ix, n. 63. (I doubt if Rohde was right in supposing Bakis to be originally a generic descriptive title, like σίβυλλα, *ibid.*, n. 58. When Aristotle speaks of Σίβυλλαι καὶ Βακίδες καὶ οἱ ἔνθεοι πάντες [*Probl.* 954ᵃ 36], and Plutarch of Σίβυλλαι αὗται καὶ Βακίδες [*Pyth. or.* 10, 399A], they probably mean "people like the Sibyl and Bakis." The term Εὐρυκλεῖς was similarly used [Plut. *def. orac.* 9, 414E; Σ Plato *Soph.* 252C]; but Eurycles was certainly a historical person. And when Philetas, *apud* Σ Ar. *Pax* 1071, distinguishes three different Βακίδες, he is merely using a common expedient of Alexandrian scholars for reconciling inconsistent statements about the same person. Everywhere else Bakis appears as an individual prophet.)

⁴⁶ Plato calls them θεομάντεις and χρησμῳδοί (*Apol.* 22C, *Meno* 99C), or χρησμῳδοί and μάντεις θεῖοι (*Ion* 534C). They fall into ἐνθουσιασμός and utter (in a state of trance?) truths of which they know nothing, and are thus clearly distinguished both from those

μάντεις who "trust birds" (*Phil.* 67B) and those χρησμολόγοι who merely quote or expound old oracles. Plato says nothing to indicate that they have official status. See Fascher, Προφήτης, 66 ff.

47 Plut. *def. orac.* 9, 414E, τοὺς ἐγγαστριμύθους, Εὐρυκλέας πάλαι, νυνὶ Πύθωνας προσαγορευομένους: Hesych., s.v. ἐγγαστρίμυθος· τοῦτόν τινες ἐγγαστρίμαντιν, οἱ δὲ στερνόμαντιν λέγουσι ... τοῦτον ἡμεῖς Πύθωνα νῦν καλοῦμεν. The more dignified term στερνόμαντις comes from the Αἰχμαλωτίδες of Sophocles, fr. 59 P. On private mediumship in late antiquity see App. II, pp. 295 ff.

48 Ar. *Vesp.* 1019, and schol.; Plato, *Soph.* 252C, and schol.

49 ἐντὸς ὑποφθεγγόμενον, Plato, *loc. cit.* L.-S. takes ὑποφθεγγόμενον to mean "speaking in an undertone"; but the other sense, which Cornford adopts, suits the context much better.

50 As Starkie points out *ad loc.*, Ar. *Vesp.* 1019 need not imply ventriloquism in our sense of the word, while some of the other notices definitely exclude it. Cf. Pearson on Soph. fr. 59.

51 Plut. *def. orac.*, *loc. cit.*, where their state of possession is compared to that commonly ascribed to the Pythia, though it is not clear just how far the comparison extends. Schol. Plato, *loc. cit.*, δαίμονα ... τὸν ἐγκελευόμενον αὐτῷ περὶ τῶν μελλόντων λέγειν. Suidas' statement that they called up the souls of the dead is not to be trusted: he took it from I Sam. 28 (witch of Endor), and not, as Halliday asserts, from Philochorus.

52 Hipp. *Epid.* 5.63 (= 7.28), ἀνέπνεεν ὡς ἐκ τοῦ βεβαπτίσθαι ἀναπνέουσι, καὶ ἐκ τοῦ στήθεος ὑπεψόφεεν, ὥσπερ αἱ ἐγγαστρίμυθοι λεγόμεναι. A critical observer's report on the famous "medium" Mrs. Piper states that in full trance "the breathing is slower by one half than normal, and very stertorous," and goes on to suggest that "this profound variation in the breathing, with the lessened oxygenation of the blood ... is probably the agency by means of which the normal consciousness is put out of commission" (Amy Tanner, *Studies in Spiritualism*, 14, 18).

53 Plut. *Pyth. orac.* 22, 405C. Aelius Aristides, *orat.* 45.11 Dind., says that the Pythiae have in their normal condition no particular ἐπιστήμη, and when in trance make no use of such knowledge as they possess. Tacitus asserts that the inspired prophet at Claros was *ignarus plerumque litterarum et carminum* (*Annals* 2.54).

54 Both types occurred in theurgic possession (see App. II, p. 297). Both were known to John Cassian in the fourth century A.D.: "some demoniacs," he observes, "are so excited that they take no account of what they do or say; but others know it and re-

member it afterwards" (*Collationes patrum*, 7.12). And both appear in savage possession and in spirit mediumship.

55 About the priestesses at Dodona the testimony of Aelius Aristides is clear and unambiguous: ὕστερον οὐδὲν ὧν εἶπον ἴσασιν (*orat.* 45.11). What he says about the Pythiae is less explicit: he asks regarding them τίνα ἐπίστανται δή που τέχνην τότε (sc. ἐπειδὰν ἐκστῶσιν ἑαυτῶν), αἴ γε οὐχ οἷαί τέ εἰσι φυλάττειν οὐδὲ μεμνῆσθαι; (45.10). Strictly speaking, this need not imply more than that they cannot remember *why* they said what they did. The language used by other writers about the Pythiae is too vague to admit of any secure inference.

56 Plut. *def. orac.* 51, 438c: οὔτε γὰρ πάντας οὔτε τοὺς αὐτοὺς ἀεὶ διατίθησιν ὡσαύτως ἡ τοῦ πνεύματος δύναμις (the statement is general, but must include the Pythia, as the context shows).

57 *Ibid.*, 438B: ἀλάλου καὶ κακοῦ πνεύματος οὖσα πλήρης. "Dumb" spirits are those which refuse to tell their names (Lagrange on Mark 9: 17; Campbell Bonner, "The Technique of Exorcism," *Harv. Theol. Rev.* 36 [1943] 43 f.). "A dumb exhalation" (Flacelière) is hardly sense.

58 ἀνείλοντο . . . ἔμφρονα. This is the reading of all extant MSS, and makes reasonable sense. In quoting the passage formerly (*Greek Poetry and Life: Essays Presented to Gilbert Murray*, 377) I was careless enough to accept ἔκφρονα from Wyttenbach.

59 I have myself seen an amateur medium break down during trance in a similar way, though without the same fatal results. For cases of possession resulting in death, see Oesterreich, *op. cit.*, 93, 118 f., 222 ff., 238. It is quite unnecessary to assume with Flacelière that the Pythia's death must have been due to inhaling mephitic "vapours" (which would probably kill on the spot if they killed at all, and must in any case have affected the other persons present). Lucan's imaginary picture of the death of an earlier Pythia (*Phars.* 5.161 ff.) was perhaps suggested by the incident Plutarch records, which can be dated to the years 57–62 A.D. (J. Bayet, *Mélanges Grat*, I.53 ff.).

60 It may be said that, strictly, the text proves only that the priests and enquirers were within earshot (R. Flacelière, "Le Fonctionnement de l'Oracle de Delphes au temps de Plutarque," *Annales de l'École des Hautes Études à Gand* [*Études d'archéologie grecque*], 2 [1938] 69 ff.). But it gives no positive support to Flacelière's view that the Pythia was separated from them by a door or curtain. And the phrase δίκην νεὼς ἐπειγομένης rather suggests a visual impression; she shuddered like a ship in a storm. On the procedure

at Delphi in earlier periods I can arrive at no confident judgement:
the literary evidence is either maddeningly vague or impossible to
reconcile with the archaeological findings. At Claros, Tacitus' account suggests (*Ann.* 2.54), and Iamblichus definitely states (*de
myst.* 3.11), that the inspired prophet was not visible. But at Apollo's Ptoan oracle in Boeotia the enquirers themselves hear the inspired πρόμαντις speaking and take down his words (Hdt. 8.135).

61 Plut. *Q. Conv.* 1.5.2, 623B: μάλιστα δὲ ὁ ἐνθουσιασμὸς ἐξίστησι καὶ
παρατρέπει τό τε σῶμα καὶ τὴν φωνὴν τοῦ συνήθους καὶ καθεστηκότος.
The pitch of the voice in which the "possessed" spoke was one of
the symptoms from which the καθαρταί drew inferences about the
possessing spirit (Hipp. *morb. sacr.* 1, VI.360.15 L.). In all parts of
the world the "possessed" are reported as speaking in a changed
voice: see Oesterreich, *op. cit.*, 10, 19–21, 133, 137, 208, 247 f., 252,
254, 277. So too the famous Mrs. Piper, when "possessed" by a male
"control," would speak "in an unmistakably male voice, but
rather husky" (*Proc. Society for Psychical Research*, 8.127).

62 Cf. Parke, *Hist. of the Delphic Oracle*, 24 ff., and Amandry, *op. cit.*,
chaps. xi–xiii, where the ancient evidence on these points is discussed. Contact with a god's sacred tree as a means of procuring
his epiphany may go back to Minoan times (B. Al, *Mnemosyne*,
Ser. III, 12 [1944] 215). On the techniques employed to induce
trance in late antiquity see App. II, pp. 296 f.

63 Oesterreich, *op. cit.*, 319, n. 3.

64 For Claros see Maximus Tyrius, 8.1c, Tac. *Ann.* 2.54, Pliny, *N.H.*
2.232. Pliny's remark that drinking the water shortened the life
of the drinker is probably a mere rationalisation of the widespread
belief that persons in contact with the supernatural die young.
The procedure at Branchidae is uncertain, but the existence of a
spring possessing prophetic properties is now confirmed by an
inscription (Wiegand, *Abh. Berl. Akad.* 1924, Heft 1, p. 22). For
other springs said to cause insanity cf. Halliday, *Greek Divination*,
124 f. For the highly primitive procedure at Argos see Paus.
2.24.1; it has good savage parallels (Oesterreich, *op. cit.*, 137, 143 f.;
Frazer, *Magic Art*, I.383).

65 Wilamowitz, *Hermes*, 38 (1904) 579; A. P. Oppé, "The Chasm at
Delphi," *JHS* 24 (1904) 214 ff.

66 Oppé, *loc. cit.*; Courby, *Fouilles de Delphes*, II.59 ff. But I suspect
that the belief in the existence of some sort of chasm under the
temple is much older than the theory of vapours, and probably
suggested it to rationalists in search of an explanation. At *Cho.*
953, Aeschylus' Chorus address Apollo as μέγαν ἔχων μυχὸν χθονός,

and the corresponding phrase at 807, ὦ μέγα ναίων στόμιον, must also in my judgement refer to Apollo. This seems an unnatural way of speaking if the poet has in mind merely the Pleistos gorge; the temple is not in the gorge, but above it. It looks more like a traditional phraseology going back to the days of the Earth-oracle: for its implications cf. Hes. *Theog.* 119: Τάρταρά τ' ἠερόεντα μυχῷ χθονός: Aesch. *P.V.* 433: "Αιδος . . . μυχὸς γᾶς, Pind. *Pyth.* 4.44: χθόνιον "Αιδα στόμα. The στόμιον which was later interpreted as a channel for vapours (Strabo, 9.3.5, p. 419: ὑπερκεῖσθαι δὲ τοῦ στομίου τρίποδα ὑψηλόν, ἐφ' ὃν τὴν Πυθίαν ἀναβαίνουσαν δεχομένην τὸ πνεῦμα ἀποθεσπίζειν) had originally, I take it, been conceived as an avenue for dreams.

⁶⁷ E.g., Leicester B. Holland, "The Mantic Mechanism of Delphi," *AJA* 1933, 201 ff.; R. Flacelière, *Annales de l'École des Hautes Études à Gand*, 2 (1938) 105 f. See, *contra*, E. Will, *Bull. Corr. Hell.* 66–67 (1942–1943) 161 ff., and now Amandry, *op. cit.*, chap. xix.

⁶⁸ Hdt. 6.66; cf. Paus. 3.4.3. Similarly, it was the Pythia whom Pleistoanax was accused of bribing on a later occasion (Thuc. 5.16.2). Thucydides might be speaking loosely, but Herodotus was not, for he gives the Pythia's name. It is open, however, to the sceptic to say that he is reproducing an "edited" Delphic version of what happened. (Amandry neglects these passages, and is inclined to make the Pythia a mere accessory, *op. cit.*, 120 ff.)

⁶⁹ Parke, *op. cit.*, 37. Fascher, contrasting Greek with Jewish prophecy, doubts if "real prophecy was possible within the framework of an institution" (*op. cit.*, 59); and in regard to responses on matters of public concern the doubt seems justified. Replies to private enquirers—which must have formed the majority at all periods, though very few genuine examples are preserved—may have been less influenced by institutional policy.

⁷⁰ The verse form of response, which had gone out of use in Plutarch's day, was pretty certainly the older; some even maintained that the hexameter was invented at Delphi (Plut. *Pyth. orac.* 17, 402D; Pliny, *N.H.* 7.205, etc.). Strabo asserts that the Pythia herself sometimes spoke ἔμμετρα (9.3.5, p. 419), and Tacitus says the same of the inspired prophet at Claros (*Ann.* 2.54). These statements of Strabo and Tacitus have been doubted (most recently by Amandry, *op. cit.*, 168), but are by no means incredible. Lawson knew a modern Greek prophet, "unquestionably mad," who possessed "an extraordinary power of conducting his part of a conversation in metrical, if not highly poetical, form" (*op. cit.*, 300). And the American missionary Nevius heard a "possessed" woman

in China extemporise verses by the hour together: "Everything she said was in measured verse, and was chanted to an unvarying tune. . . . The rapid, perfectly uniform, and long continued utterances seemed to us such as could not possibly be counterfeited or premeditated" (J. L. Nevius, *Demon Possession and Allied Themes*, 37 f.). Among the ancient Semitic peoples "recitation of verses and doggerel was the mark of one who had converse with the spirits" (A. Guillaume, *Prophecy and Divination among the Hebrews and Other Semites*, 245). In fact, automatic or inspirational speech tends everywhere to fall into metrical patterns (E. Lombard, *De la glossolalie*, 207 ff.). But usually, no doubt, the Pythia's utterances had to be versified by others; Strabo, *loc. cit.*, speaks of poets being retained for this purpose, and Plutarch, *Pyth. orac.* 25, 407B, mentions the suspicion that in old days they sometimes did more than their duty. At Branchidae the existence in the second century B.C. of a χρησμογράφιον (office for drafting, or recording, responses?) is inscriptionally attested (*Rev. de Phil.* 44 [1920] 249, 251); and at Claros the functions of προφήτης (medium?) and θεσπιῳδῶν (versifier?) were distinct, at least in Roman times (Dittenberger, *OGI* II, no. 530). An interesting discussion of the whole problem by Edwyn Bevan will be found in the *Dublin Review*, 1931.

[71] The Greeks were quite alive to the possibility of fraud in particular instances; the god's instruments were fallible. But this did not shake their faith in the existence of a divine inspiration. Even Heraclitus accepted it (fr. 93), contemptuous as he was of superstitious elements in contemporary religion; and Socrates is represented as a deeply sincere believer. On Plato's attitude see below, chap. vii, pp. 217 f., 222 f. Aristotle and his school, while rejecting inductive divination, upheld ἐνθουσιασμός, as did the Stoics; the theory that it was ἔμφυτος, or provoked by vapours, did not invalidate its divine character.

[72] This was so from the first; Delphi was promised its share of the fines to be paid by the collaborators (Hdt. 7.132.2), and also received a tithe of the booty after Plataea (*ibid.*, 9.81.1); the hearths polluted by the presence of the invader were rekindled, at the Oracle's command, from Apollo's own (Plut. *Aristides* 20).

[73] It is worth noting that the nearest approach to an ecclesiastical organisation transcending the individual city-state was the system of ἐξηγηταὶ πυθόχρηστοι who expounded Apolline sacral law at Athens and doubtless elsewhere (cf. Nilsson, *Gesch.* I.603 ff.).

[74] Aesch. *Eum.* 616 ff.: οὐπώποτ' εἶπον μαντικοῖσιν ἐν θρόνοις . . . ὃ μὴ κελεῦσαι Ζεὺς Ὀλυμπίων πατήρ.

75 Cic. *de divin.* 2.117: "quando ista vis autem evanuit? an postquam
homines minus creduli esse coeperunt?" On the social basis of
changes in religious belief see Kardiner, *Psychological Frontiers of
Society,* 426 f. It is significant that the growing social tensions and
increased neurotic anxieties of the late Empire were accompanied
by a revival of interest in oracles: see Eitrem, *Orakel und Mysterien
am Ausgang der Antike.*

76 Ivan M. Linforth, "The Corybantic Rites in Plato," *Univ. of
Calif. Publ. in Class. Philology,* Vol. 13 (1946), No. 5; "Telestic
Madness in Plato, Phaedrus 244DE," *ibid.,* No. 6.

77 "Maenadism in the Bacchae," *Harv. Theol. Rev.* 33 (1940) 155 ff.
See Appendix I in the present book.

78 Cf. Eur. *Ba.* 77, and Varro *apud* Serv. ad Virg. *Georg.* 1.166:
"Liberi patris sacra ad purgationem animae pertinebant." We
should perhaps connect with this the cult of Διόνυσος ἰατρός
which is said to have been recommended to the Athenians by
Delphi (Athen. 22E, cf. 36B).

79 Hesiod, *Erga* 614, *Theog.* 941; Hom. *Il.* 14.325. Cf. also Pindar,
fr. 9.4 Bowra (29 S.): τὰν Διωνύσου πολυγαθέα τιμάν, and the definition of Dionysus' functions at Eur. *Ba.* 379 ff., θιασεύειν τε χοροῖς
μετά τ' αὐλοῦ γελάσαι ἀποπαῦσαί τε μερίμνας, κτλ.

80 Cf. Eur. *Ba.* 421 ff., and my note *ad loc.* Hence the support that
the Dionysiac cult received from Periander and the Peisistratids;
hence also, perhaps, the very slight interest that Homer takes in
it (though he was acquainted with maenads, *Il.* 22.460), and the
contempt with which Heraclitus viewed it (fr. 14 makes his attitude sufficiently clear, whatever may be the sense of fr. 15).

81 See chap. ii, p. 46; and for Λύσιος, App. I, p. 273. The connection of "Dionysiac" mass hysteria with intolerable social conditions is nicely illustrated in E. H. Norman's article, "Mass
Hysteria in Japan," *Far Eastern Survey,* 14 (1945) 65 ff.

82 Cf. *H. Hymn* 7.34 ff. It was, I take it, as Master of Illusions that
Dionysus came to be the patron of a new art, the art of the theatre.
To put on a mask is the easiest way of ceasing to be oneself (cf.
Lévy-Bruhl, *Primitives and the Supernatural,* 123 ff.). The theatri-
cal use of the mask presumably grew out of its magical use: Dionysus became in the sixth century the god of the theatre because he
had long been the god of the masquerade.

83 Herodotus, 4.79.3. For the meaning of μαίνεσθαι cf. Linforth,
"Corybantic Rites," 127 f.

84 Pfister has shown grounds for thinking that ἔκστασις, ἐξίστασθαι,
did not originally involve (as Rohde assumed) the idea of the

soul's departure from the body; they are quite commonly used by classical writers of any abrupt change of mind or mood ("Ekstasis," *Pisciculi F. J. Doelger dargeboten*, 178 ff.). ὁ αὐτός εἰμι καὶ οὐκ ἐξίσταμαι, says Pericles to the Athenians (Thuc. 2.61.2); τὰ μηδὲ προσδοκῶμεν᾽ ἔκστασιν φέρει, says Menander (fr. 149); and in Plutarch's time a person could describe himself as ἐκστατικῶς ἔχων, meaning merely that he felt, as we say, "put out" or "not himself" (Plut. *gen. Socr.* 588A). Cf. also Jeanne Croissant, *Aristote et les mystères*, 41 ff.

85 [Apollod.] *Bibl.* 2.2.2. Cf. Rohde, *Psyche*, 287; Boyancé, *Le Culte des Muses chez les philosophes grecs*, 64 f. It has been the usual opinion of scholars since Rohde that at *Phaedr.* 244DE Plato had the Melampus story in mind; but see, *contra*, Linforth, "Telestic Madness," 169.

86 Boyancé, *op. cit.*, 66 ff., tries to find survivals of the god's original cathartic function (whose importance he rightly stresses) even in his Attic festivals. But his arguments are highly speculative.

87 This appears from Plato, *Laws* 815CD, where he describes, and rejects as "uncivilised" (οὐ πολιτικόν), certain "Bacchic" mimetic dances, imitating Nymphs, Pans, Sileni, and Satyrs, which were performed περὶ καθαρμούς τε καὶ τελετάς τινας. Cf. also Aristides Quintilianus, *de musica* 3.25, p. 93 Jahn: τὰς Βακχικὰς τελετὰς καὶ ὅσαι ταύταις παραπλήσιοι λόγου τινὸς ἔχεσθαί φασιν ὅπως ἂν ἡ τῶν ἀμαθεστέρων ποίησις διὰ βίον ἢ τύχην ὑπὸ τῶν ἐν ταύταις μελῳδιῶν τε καὶ ὀρχήσεων ἅμα παιδιαῖς ἐκκαθαίρηται (quoted by Jeanne Croissant, *Aristote et les mystères*, 121). In other passages which are sometimes cited in this connection, the term βακχεία may be used metaphorically for any excited state: e.g., Plato, *Laws* 790E (cf. Linforth, "Corybantic Rites," 132); Aesch. *Cho.* 698, which I take as referring to the κῶμος of the Ἐρινύες (*Agam.* 1186 ff., cf. *Eum.* 500).

88 Eur. *Hipp.* 141 ff.; Hipp. *morb. sacr.* 1, VI.360.13 ff. L.

89 Pan was believed to cause not only panic (Πανικὸν δεῖμα), but also fainting and collapse (Eur. *Med.* 1172 and Σ). It is a likely enough guess that originally Arcadian shepherds put down the effects of sunstroke to the anger of the shepherd god; and that he was first credited with causing panic by reason of the sudden terror which sometimes infects a herd of beasts (Tambornino, *op. cit.*, 66 f.). Cf. Suidas' definition of panic as occurring ἡνίκα αἰφνίδιον οἵ τε ἵπποι καὶ οἱ ἄνθρωποι ἐκταραχθῶσι, and the observation of Philodemus, π. θεῶν, col. 13 (Scott, *Fragm. Herc.* no. 26), that animals

are subject to worse ταραχαί than men. The association of Apollo
Νόμιος with μανία may have a similar origin.

⁹⁰ Eur. *Hipp.* 143 f. speaks as if the two were distinct, as does Dion.
Hal. *Demosth.* 22. But the Corybantes were originally Cybele's at-
tendants; she, like them, had a healing function (Pind. *Pyth.*
3.137 ff.; Diog. trag. 1.5, p. 776 N.²; Diodorus, 3.58.2); and this
function included the cure of μανία (Dionysus himself is "purged"
of his madness by Rhea-Cybele, [Apollod.] *Bibl.* 3.5.1). And I
think it a reasonable guess that in Pindar's day the rites were
similar, if not identical, since Pindar wrote ἐνθρονισμοί (Suidas,
s.v. Πίνδαρος), which it is natural to connect on the one hand with
the Corybantic rite of θρόνωσις or θρονισμός described by Plato,
Euthyd. 277D, and Dio Chrys. *Or.* 12.33, 387 R., and on the other
with the cult of the Mother which Pindar himself established
(Σ Pind. *Pyth.* 3.137; Paus. 9.25.3). If this is so, we may suppose
the Corybantic rite to be an offshoot from the Cybele-cult, which
took over the goddess's healing function and gradually developed
an independent existence (cf. Linforth, "Corybantic Rites," 157).

⁹¹ The annual τελετή of Hecate at Aegina, though attested for us only
by late writers (testimonies in Farnell, *Cults*, II.597, n. 7), is
doubtless old: it claimed to have been founded by Orpheus (Paus.
2.30.2). Its functions were presumably cathartic and apotropaic
(Dio Chrys. *Or.* 4.90). But the view that they were specifically
directed to the cure of μανία seems to rest only on Lobeck's interpretation of Ar. *Vesp.* 122 διέπλευσεν εἰς Αἴγιναν as referring to
this τελετή (*Aglaophamus*, 242), which is hardly more than a
plausible guess.

⁹² Ar. *Vesp.* 119; Plut. *Amat.* 16, 758F; Longinus, *Subl.* 39.2. Cf.
Croissant, *op. cit.*, 59 ff.; Linforth, "Corybantic Rites," 125 f.;
and below, App. I. The essential similarity of the two rites explains how Plato can use συγκορυβαντιᾶν and συμβακχεύειν as
synonyms (*Symp.* 228B, 234D), and can speak of αἱ τῶν ἐκφρόνων
βακχειῶν ἰάσεις in reference to what he has just described as τὰ
τῶν Κορυβάντων ἰάματα (*Laws* 790DE).

⁹³ Plato, *Symp.* 215E: πολύ μοι μᾶλλον ἢ τῶν κορυβαντιώντων ἥ τε
καρδία πηδᾷ καὶ δάκρυα ἐκχεῖται. I agree with Linforth that the
reference is to the effect of the rites, though similar effects could
occur in spontaneous possession (cf. Menander, *Theophoroumene*
16–28 K.).

⁹⁴ Plato, *Ion* 553E: οἱ κορυβαντιῶντες οὐκ ἔμφρονες ὄντες ὀρχοῦνται,
Pliny, *N.H.* 11.147: "Quin et patentibus dormiunt (oculis) lepores
multique hominum, quos κορυβαντιᾶν Graeci dicunt." The latter

passage can scarcely refer to ordinary sleep, as Linforth assumes ("Corybantic Rites," 128 f.), for (a) the statement would be false, as Pliny must have known, (b) it is hard to see why a habit of sleeping with the eyes open should be taken as evidence of possession. I agree with Rohde (*Psyche*, ix, n. 18) that what Pliny means is "a condition related to hypnosis"; the ecstatic ritual dance might well induce such a state in the susceptible. Lucian, *Jup. Trag.* 30, mentions κίνημα κορυβαντῶδες among symptoms of incipient mantic trance. For the effects of the comparable Dionysiac ritual see Plut. *Mul. Virt.* 13, 249E (App. I, p. 271).

95 Theophrastus, fr. 91 W.; Plato, *Rep.* 398C–401A. Cf. Croissant, *op. cit.*, chap. iii; Boyancé, *op. cit.*, I, chap. vi. The emotional significance of flute-music is illustrated in a bizarre way by two curious pathological cases which have come down to us. In one of them, reported by Galen (VII.60 f. Kühn), an otherwise sane patient was haunted by hallucinatory flute-players, whom he saw and heard by day and night (cf. Aetius, Ἰατρικά 6.8, and Plato, *Crito* 54D). In the other, the patient was seized with panic whenever he heard the flute played at a party (Hipp. *Epid.* 5.81, V.250 L.).

96 *Laws* 790E: δείματα δι' ἕξιν φαύλην τῆς ψυχῆς τινα. Cf. *H. Orph.* 39.1 ff., where the Corybantic daemon is called φόβων ἀποπαύστορα δεινῶν.

97 "Corybantic Rites," 148 ff.

98 See above, n. 87. Elsewhere Aristides tells us that ἐνθουσιασμοί in general are liable, in default of proper treatment, to produce δεισιδαιμονίας τε καὶ ἀλόγους φόβους (*de musica*, p. 42 Jahn). Mlle Croissant has shown reason to think that these statements come from a good Peripatetic source, probably Theophrastus (*op. cit.*, 117 ff.). It may be observed that "anxiety" (φροντίς) is recognised as a special type of pathological state in the Hippocratic treatise *de morbis* (2.72, VII.108 f. L.); and that religious anxieties, especially the fear of δαίμονες, appear in clinical descriptions, e.g., Hipp. *virg.* 1 (VIII.466 L.) and [Galen] XIX.702. Phantasies of exaggerated responsibility were also known, e.g., Galen (VIII. 190) cites melancholics who identified themselves with Atlas, and Alexander of Tralles describes a patient of his own who feared that the world would collapse if she bent her middle finger (I.605 Puschmann). There is an interesting field of study here for a psychologist or psychotherapist with a knowledge of the ancient world and an understanding of the social implications of his subject.

99 *Loc. cit. supra*, n. 88.

¹⁰⁰ As Linforth points out (*op. cit.*, 151), it is nowhere expressly stated that the disorder which the Corybantes cured had been caused by them. But it is a general principle of magical medicine, in Greece and elsewhere, that only he who caused a disease knows how to cure it (ὁ τρώσας καὶ ἰάσεται); hence the importance attached to discovering the identity of the possessing Power. For the cathartic effect, cf. Aretaeus' interesting account of an ἔνθεος μανία (*morb. chron.* 1.6 *fin.*) in which the sufferers gash their own limbs, θεοῖς ἰδίοις ὡς ἀπαιτοῦσι χαριζόμενοι εὐσεβεῖ φαντασίῃ. After this experience they are εὔθυμοι, ἀκηδέες, ὡς τελεσθέντες τῷ θεῷ.

¹⁰¹ Ar. *Vesp.* 118 ff. See above, n. 91.

¹⁰² Plato, *Ion* 536c. Of the two views given in the text, the first corresponds broadly to Linforth's (*op. cit.*, 139 f.), though he might not accept the term "anxiety-state," while the second goes back to Jahn (*NJbb* Supp.-Band X [1844] 231). It is, as Linforth says, "difficult to accept the notion of a divided allegiance in a single religious ceremony." Yet Jahn's theory is supported, not only by the usage of κορυβαντιᾶν elsewhere in Plato, but also, I think, by *Laws* 791A, where in apparent reference to τὰ τῶν Κορυβάντων ἰάματα (790D) Plato speaks of the healed patients as ὀρχουμένους τε καὶ αὐλουμένους μετὰ θεῶν οἷς ἂν καλλιεροῦντες ἕκαστοι θύωσι. Linforth argues that there is a transition here "from the particular to the general, from Corybantic rites at the beginning to the whole class of rites involving madness" (*op. cit.*, 133). But the more natural interpretation of the two passages, taken together, is that the Corybantic rite included (1) a musical diagnosis; (2) a sacrifice by each patient to the god to whose music he had responded, and an observation of omens; (3) a dance of those whose sacrifices were accepted, in which the appeased deities (perhaps impersonated by priests?) were believed to take part. Such an interpretation would also give a more precise sense to the curious phrase used at *Symp.* 215c, where we are told that the tunes attributed to Olympos or Marsyas "are able by themselves [i.e., without an accompanying dance, cf. Linforth, *op. cit.*, 142] to cause possession and to reveal those who need the gods and rites (τοὺς τῶν θεῶν τε καὶ τελετῶν δεομένους, seemingly the same persons who are referred to as τῶν Κορυβαντιώντων at 215E)." On the view suggested, these would be the kind of persons who are called οἱ κορυβαντιῶντες at *Ion* 536c, and the reference in both places would be to the first or diagnostic stage of the Corybantic rite.

¹⁰³ In Hellenistic and Christian times diagnosis (by forcing the intrusive spirit to reveal his identity) was similarly a prerequisite to

successful exorcism: see Bonner, *Harv. Theol. Rev.* 36 (1943) 44 ff. For sacrifices to cure madness cf. Plaut. *Men.* 288 ff., and Varro, *R.R.* 2.4.16.

[104] Plato, *Euthyd.* 277D: καὶ γὰρ ἐκεῖ χορεία τίς ἐστι καὶ παιδιά, εἰ ἄρα καὶ τετέλεσαι (discussed by Linforth, *op. cit.*, 124 f.). It seems to me that the appeal to the experience of the τετελεσμένος is hardly natural save on the lips of one who is τετελεσμένος himself.

[105] See chap. vii, p. 217.

[106] Plato, *Laws* 791A; Arist. *Pol.* 1342ᵃ 7 ff. Cf. Croissant, *op. cit.*, 106 f.; Linforth, *op. cit.*, 162.

[107] Aristoxenus, fr. 26 Wehrli; cf. Boyancé, *op. cit.*, 103 ff.

[108] Theophrastus, fr. 88 Wimmer (= Aristoxenus, fr. 6), seems to describe a musical cure (with the flute) performed by Aristoxenus, though the sense is obscured by textual corruption. Cf. also Aristoxenus, fr. 117, and Martianus Capella, 9, p. 493 Dick: "ad affectiones animi tibias Theophrastus adhibebat ... Xenocrates organicis modulis lymphaticos liberabat."

[109] Theophrastus, *loc. cit.* He also claimed, if he is correctly reported, that music is good for faintness, prolonged loss of reason, sciatica (!), and epilepsy.

[110] Censorinus, *de die natali* 12 (cf. Celsus, III.18); Caelius Aurelianus (i.e., Soranus), *de morbis chronicis* 1.5. Ancient medical theories of insanity and its treatment are usefully summarised in Heiberg's pamphlet, *Geisteskrankheiten im klass. Altertum.*

[111] *Od.* 8.63 f. The Muses also disabled Thamyris, *Il.* 2.594 ff. The danger of an encounter with them is intelligible if scholars are right in connecting μοῦσα with *mons* and regarding them as originally mountain nymphs, since it has always been thought perilous to meet a nymph.

[112] Hesiod, *Theog.* 94 ff.

[113] *Il.* 3.65 f.: οὔ τοι ἀπόβλητ' ἐστὶ θεῶν ἐρικυδέα δῶρα / ὅσσα κεν αὐτοὶ δῶσιν· ἑκὼν δ' οὐκ ἄν τις ἕλοιτο.

[114] Cf. W. Marg, *Der Character in der Sprache der frühgriechischen Dichtung*, 60 ff.

[115] *Il.* 11.218, 16.112, 14.508. The last of these passages has been regarded as a late addition both by Alexandrine and by modern critics; and all of them employ a conventional formula. But even if the appeal itself is conventional, its timing remains a significant clue to the original meaning of "inspiration." Similarly Phemius claimed to have received from the gods not merely his poetic talent, but his stories themselves (*Od.* 22.347 f., cf. chap. i, p. 10).

As Marg rightly says (*op. cit.*, 63), "die Gabe der Gottheit bleibt noch auf das Geleistete, das dinghafte ἔργον ausgerichtet." It corresponds to what Bernard Berenson has called "the planchette element in the pen, which often knows more and better than the person who wields it."

116 *Il.* 2.484 ff. The Muses were the daughters of Memory, and were themselves in some places called Μνεῖαι (Plut. *Q. Conv.* 743D). But I take it that what the poet here prays for is not just an accurate memory—for this, though highly necessary, would be memory only of an inaccurate κλέος—but an actual vision of the past to supplement the κλέος. Such visions, welling up from the unknown depths of the mind, must once have been felt as something immediately "given," and because of its immediacy more trustworthy than oral tradition. So when Odysseus observes that Demodocus can sing about the war of Troy "as if he had been there or heard about it from an eyewitness," he concludes that a Muse, or Apollo, must have "taught" it to him (*Od.* 8.487 ff.). There was a κλέος on this subject too (8.74), but it was evidently not enough to account for Demodocus' accurate mastery of detail. Cf. Latte, "Hesiods Dichterweihe," *Antike u. Abendland*, II (1946), 159; and on the factual inspiration of poets in other cultures, N. K. Chadwick, *Poetry and Prophecy*, 41 ff.

117 Special knowledge, no less than technical skill, is the distinctive mark of a poet in Homer: he is a man who "sings by grace of gods, knowing delightful epic tales" (*Od.* 17.518 f.). Cf. Solon's description of the poet, fr. 13.51 f. B., as ἱμερτῆς σοφίης μέτρον ἐπιστάμενος.

118 Several Indo-European languages have a common term for "poet" and "seer" (Latin *vates*, Irish *fili*, Icelandic *thulr*). "It is clear that throughout the ancient languages of northern Europe the ideas of poetry, eloquence, information (especially antiquarian learning) and prophecy are intimately connected" (H. M. and N. K. Chadwick, *The Growth of Literature*, I.637). Hesiod seems to preserve a trace of this original unity when he ascribes to *the Muses* (*Theog.* 38), and claims for himself (*ibid.*, 32), the same knowledge of "things present, future, and past" which Homer ascribes to Calchas (*Il.* 1.70); the formula is no doubt, as the Chadwicks say (*ibid.*, 625), "a static description of a seer."

119 Hesiod, *Theog.* 22 ff. Cf. chap. iv, p. 117, and the interesting paper by Latte referred to above (n. 116).

120 "The songs made me, not I them," said Goethe. "It is not I who think," said Lamartine; "it is my ideas that think for me." "The mind in creation," said Shelley, "is as a fading coal, which some

invisible influence, like an inconstant wind, awakens to transitory brightness."

121 Pindar, fr. 150 S. (137 B.): μαντεύεο, Μοῖσα, προφατεύσω δ' ἐγώ. Cf. *Paean* 6.6 (fr. 40 B.), where he calls himself ἀοίδιμον Πιερίδων προφάταν, and Fascher, Προφήτης, 12. On Pindar's regard for truth see Norwood, *Pindar*, 166. A similar conception of the Muse as revealing hidden truth is implied in Empedocles' prayer that she will convey to him ὧν θέμις ἐστὶν ἐφημερίοισιν ἀκούειν (fr. 4; cf. Pindar, *Paean* 6.51 ff.). Virgil is true to this tradition when he begs the Muses to reveal to him the secrets of nature, *Geo.* 2.475ff.

122 The same relationship is implied at *Pyth.* 4.279: αὔξεται καὶ Μοῖσα δι' ἀγγελίας ὀρθᾶς: the poet is the Muses' "messenger" (cf. Theognis, 769). We should not confuse this with the Platonic conception of poets ἐνθουσιάζοντες ὥσπερ οἱ θεομάντεις καὶ οἱ χρησμῳδοί (*Apol.* 22c). For Plato, the Muse is actually *inside* the poet: *Crat.* 428c: ἄλλη τις Μοῦσα πάλαι σε ἐνοῦσα ἐλελήθει.

123 *Laws* 719c.

124 The inspirational theory of poetry is directly linked with Dionysus by the traditional view that the best poets have sought and found inspiration in drink. The classical statement of it is in the lines attributed to Cratinus: οἶνός τοι χαρίεντι πέλει ταχὺς ἵππος ἀοιδῷ, ὕδωρ δὲ πίνων οὐδὲν ἂν τέκοι σοφόν (fr. 199 K.). Thence it passed to Horace (*Epist.* 1.19.1 ff.), who has made it a commonplace of literary tradition.

125 Democritus, frs. 17, 18. He appears to have cited Homer as an instance (fr. 21).

126 See the careful study by Delatte, *Les Conceptions de l'enthousiasme*, 28 ff., which makes an ingenious attempt to relate Democritus' views on inspiration to the rest of his psychology; also F. Wehrli, "Der erhabene und der schlichte Stil in der poetisch-rhetorischen Theorie der Antike," *Phyllobolia für Peter von der Mühll*, 9 ff.

127 For the airs which poets gave themselves on the strength of this theory see Horace, *Ars poetica*, 295 ff. The view that personal eccentricity is a more important qualification than technical competence is of course a distortion of Democritus' theory (cf. Wehrli, *op. cit.*, 23); but it is a fatally easy distortion.

IV

Dream-Pattern and Culture-Pattern

S'il était donné à nos yeux de chair de voir dans la conscience d'autrui, on jugerait bien plus sûrement un homme d'après ce qu'il rêve que d'après ce qu'il pense.

VICTOR HUGO

MAN shares with a few others of the higher mammals the curious privilege of citizenship in two worlds. He enjoys in daily alternation two distinct kinds of experience— ὕπαρ and ὄναρ, as the Greeks called them—each of which has its own logic and its own limitations; and he has no obvious reason for thinking one of them more significant than the other. If the waking world has certain advantages of solidity and continuity, its social opportunities are terribly restricted. In it we meet, as a rule, only the neighbours, whereas the dream world offers the chance of intercourse, however fugitive, with our distant friends, our dead, and our gods. For normal men it is the sole experience in which they escape the offensive and incomprehensible bondage of time and space. Hence it is not surprising that man was slow to confine the attribute of reality to one of his two worlds, and dismiss the other as pure illusion. This stage was reached in antiquity only by a small number of intellectuals; and there are still to-day many primitive peoples who attribute to certain types of dream experience a validity equal to that of waking life, though different in kind.[1] Such simplicity drew pitying smiles from nineteenth-century missionaries; but our own age has discovered that the primitives were in principle nearer the truth than the missionaries. Dreams,

[1] For notes to chapter iv see pages 121–134.

as it now appears, are highly significant after all; the ancient art of *oneirocritice* once more provides clever men with a lucrative livelihood, and the most highly educated of our contemporaries hasten to report their dreams to the specialist with as grave an anxiety as the Superstitious Man of Theophrastus.[2]

Against this historical background it seems worth while to look afresh at the attitude of the Greeks towards their dream-experience, and to this subject I propose to devote the present chapter. There are two ways of looking at the recorded dream-experience of a past culture: we may try to see it through the eyes of the dreamers themselves, and thus reconstruct as far as may be what it meant to their waking consciousness; or we may attempt, by applying principles derived from modern dream-analysis, to penetrate from its manifest to its latent content. The latter procedure is plainly hazardous: it rests on an un-proved assumption about the universality of dream-symbols which we cannot control by obtaining the dreamer's associa-tions. That in skilled and cautious hands it might nevertheless yield interesting results, I am willing to believe; but I must not be beguiled into essaying it. My main concern is not with the dream-experience of the Greeks, but with the Greek attitude to dream-experience. In so defining our subject we must, how-ever, bear in mind the possibility that differences between the Greek and the modern attitude to dreams may reflect not only different ways of interpreting the same type of experience, but also variations in the character of the experience itself. For recent enquiries into the dreams of contemporary primitives suggest that, side by side with the familiar anxiety-dreams and wish-fulfilment dreams that are common to humanity, there are others whose manifest content, at any rate, is determined by a local culture-pattern.[3] And I do not mean merely that where, for example, a modern American might dream of travelling by 'plane, a primitive will dream that he is carried to Heaven by an eagle; I mean that in many primitive societies there are types of dream-structure which depend on a socially[4] trans-mitted pattern of belief, and cease to occur when that belief ceases to be entertained. Not only the choice of this or that symbol, but the nature of the dream itself, seems to conform to a rigid traditional pattern. It is evident that such dreams are closely related to myth, of which it has been well said that it is the dream-thinking of the people, as the dream is the myth of the individual.[5]

Keeping this observation in mind, let us consider what sort of dreams are described in Homer, and how the poet presents them. Professor H. J. Rose, in his excellent little book *Primitive Culture in Greece*, distinguishes three prescientific ways of regarding the dream, viz., (1) "to take the dream-vision as objective fact"; (2) "to suppose it . . . something seen by the soul, or one of the souls, while temporarily out of the body, a happening whose scene is in the spirit world, or the like"; (3) "to interpret it by a more or less complicated symbolism."[6] Professor Rose considers these to be three successive "stages of progress," and logically no doubt they are. But in such matters the actual development of our notions seldom follows the logical course. If we look at Homer, we shall see that the first and third of Rose's "stages" coexist in both poems, with no apparent consciousness of incongruity, while Rose's second "stage" is entirely missing (and continues to be missing from extant Greek literature down to the fifth century, when it makes a sensational first appearance in a well-known fragment of Pindar).[7]

In most of their descriptions of dreams, the Homeric poets treat what is seen as if it were "objective fact."[8] The dream usually takes the form of a visit paid to a sleeping man or woman by a single dream-figure (the very word *oneiros* in Homer nearly always means dream-figure, not dream-experience).[9] This dream-figure can be a god, or a ghost, or a preexisting dream-messenger, or an "image" (*eidōlon*) created specially for the occasion;[10] but whichever it is, it exists objectively in space, and is independent of the dreamer. It effects an entry by the keyhole (Homeric bedrooms having neither window nor chimney); it plants itself at the head of the bed to deliver its message; and when that is done, it withdraws by the same route.[11] The dreamer, meanwhile, is almost completely passive: he sees a figure, he hears a voice, and that is practically all. Sometimes, it is true, he will answer in his sleep; once he stretches out his arms to embrace the dream-figure.[12] But these are objective physical acts, such as men are observed to perform in their sleep. The dreamer does not suppose himself to be anywhere else than in his bed, and in fact he knows himself to be asleep, since the dream-figure is at pains to point this out to him: "You are asleep, son of Atreus," says the wicked dream in *Iliad* 2; "You are asleep, Achilles," says the ghost of Patroclus; "You are asleep, Penelope," says the "shadowy image" in the *Odyssey*.[13]

All this bears little resemblance to our own dream-experience, and scholars have been inclined to dismiss it, like so much else in Homer, as "poetic convention" or "epic machinery."[14] It is at any rate highly stylised, as the recurrent formulae show. I shall come back to this point presently. Meanwhile we may notice that the language used by Greeks at all periods in describing dreams of all sorts appears to be suggested by a type of dream in which the dreamer is the passive recipient of an objective vision. The Greeks never spoke as we do of *having* a dream, but always of *seeing* a dream—ὄναρ ἰδεῖν, ἐνύπνιον ἰδεῖν. The phrase is appropriate only to dreams of the passive type, but we find it used even when the dreamer is himself the central figure in the dream action.[15] Again, the dream is said not only to "visit" the dreamer (φοιτᾶν, ἐπισκοπεῖν, προσελθεῖν, etc.)[16] but also to "stand over" him (ἐπιστῆναι). The latter usage is particularly common in Herodotus, where it has been taken for a reminiscence of Homer's στῆ δ' ἄρ' ὑπὲρ κεφαλῆς, "it stood at his head";[17] but its occurrence in the Epidaurian and Lindian Temple Records, and in countless later authors from Isocrates to the Acts of the Apostles,[18] can hardly be explained in this manner. It looks as if the objective, visionary dream had struck deep roots not only in literary tradition but in the popular imagination. And that conclusion is to some extent fortified by the occurrence in myth and pious legend of dreams which *prove* their objectivity by leaving a material token behind them, what our spiritualists like to call an "apport"; the best-known example is Bellerophon's incubation dream in Pindar, in which the apport is a golden bridle.[19]

But let us return to Homer. The stylised, objective dreams I have been describing are not the only dreams with which the epic poets are acquainted. That the common anxiety-dream was as familiar to the author of the *Iliad* as it is to us, we learn from a famous simile: "as in a dream one flees and another cannot pursue him—the one cannot stir to escape, nor the other to pursue him—so Achilles could not overtake Hector in running, nor Hector escape him."[20] The poet does not ascribe such nightmares to his heroes, but he knows well what they are like, and makes brilliant use of the experience to express frustration. Again, in Penelope's dream of the eagle and the geese in *Odyssey* 19 we have a simple wish-fulfilment dream with symbolism and what Freud calls "condensation" and "displacement": Penelope is crying over the murder of her beautiful geese[21] when the eagle suddenly speaks with a human voice and explains that he is Odysseus. This is the only dream in Homer which is interpreted symbolically. Should we say that we have here the work of a late poet who has taken an intellectual leap from the primitiveness of Rose's first stage to the sophistication of his third? I doubt it. On any reasonable theory of the composition of the *Odyssey* it is difficult to suppose that Book 19 is much later than Book 4, in which we meet a dream of the primitive "objective" type. Moreover, the practice of interpreting dreams symbolically was known to the author of *Iliad* 5, which is generally thought one of the oldest parts of the poem: we read there of an *oneiropolos* who failed to interpret his sons' dreams when they went to the Trojan War.[22]

I suggest that the true explanation does not lie in any juxtaposition of "early" and "late" attitudes to dream-experience as such, but rather in a distinction between different types of dream-experience. For the Greeks, as for other ancient peoples,[23] the fundamental distinction was that between significant and nonsignificant dreams; this appears in Homer, in the passage about the gates of ivory and horn, and is maintained throughout antiquity.[24] But within the class of significant dreams several distinct types were recognised. In a classification which is transmitted by Artemidorus, Macrobius, and other late writers, but whose origin may lie much further back, three such types are distinguished.[25] One is the symbolic dream, which "dresses up in metaphors, like a sort of riddles, a meaning which cannot be understood without interpretation." A second is the *horama* or "vision," which is a straightforward preënactment of a future event, like those dreams described in the book of the ingenious J. W. Dunne. The third is called a *chrematismos* or "oracle," and is to be recognised "when in sleep the dreamer's parent, or some other respected or impressive personage, perhaps a priest or even a god, reveals without symbolism what will or will not happen, or should or should not be done."

This last type is not, I think, at all common in our own dream-experience. But there is considerable evidence that dreams of this sort were familiar in antiquity. They figure in other ancient classifications. Chalcidius, who follows a different scheme from the other systematisers,[26] calls such a dream an "admonitio," "when we are directed and admonished by the counsels of angelic goodness," and quotes as examples Socrates' dreams in the *Crito* and the *Phaedo*.[27] Again, the old medical writer Herophilus (early third century B.C.) probably had this type in mind when he distinguished "godsent" dreams from those which owe their origin either to the "natural" clairvoyance of the mind itself or to chance or to wish-fulfilment.[28] Ancient literature is full of these "godsent" dreams in which a single dream-figure presents itself, as in Homer, to the sleeper and gives him prophecy, advice, or warning. Thus an *oneiros* "stood over" Croesus and warned him of coming disasters; Hipparchus saw "a tall and handsome man," who gave him a verse oracle, like the "fair and handsome woman" who revealed to Socrates the day of his death by quoting Homer;

Alexander saw "a very grey man of reverend aspect" who likewise quoted Homer, and in Alexander's opinion *was* in fact
Homer in person.[29]

But we are not dependent on this sort of literary evidence,
whose striking uniformity may naturally be put down to the
conservatism of Greek literary tradition. A common type of
"godsent" dream, in Greece and elsewhere, is the dream which
prescribes a dedication or other religious act;[30] and this has
left concrete evidence of its actual occurrence in the form of
numerous inscriptions stating that their author makes a dedication "in accordance with a dream" or "having seen a
dream."[31] Details are rarely given; but we have one inscription
where a priest is told in a dream by Sarapis to build him a house
of his own, as the deity is tired of living in lodgings; and
another giving detailed rules for the conduct of a house of
prayer which are stated to have been received in sleep from
Zeus.[32] Nearly all the inscriptional evidence is of Hellenistic
or Roman date; but this is probably fortuitous, for Plato
speaks in the *Laws* of dedications which are made on the
strength of dreams or waking visions, "especially by women of
all types, and by men who are sick or in some danger or difficulty, or else have had a special stroke of luck," and we are
told again in the *Epinomis* that "many cults of many gods have
been founded, and will continue to be founded, because of
dream-encounters with supernatural beings, omens, oracles,
and deathbed visions."[33] Plato's testimony to the frequency of
such occurrences is all the more convincing since he himself
has little faith in their supernatural character.

In the light of this evidence we must, I think, recognise that
the stylisation of the "divine dream" or *chrematismos* is not
purely literary; it is a "culture-pattern" dream in the sense I
defined at the beginning of this chapter, and belongs to the religious experience of the people, though poets from Homer
downwards have adapted it to their purposes by using it as a
literary *motif*. Such dreams played an important part in the
life of other ancient peoples, as they do in that of many races

to-day. Most of the dreams recorded in Assyrian, Hittite, and ancient Egyptian literature are "divine dreams" in which a god appears and delivers a plain message to the sleeper, sometimes predicting the future, sometimes demanding cult.[34] As we should expect in monarchical societies, the privileged dreamers are usually kings (an idea which appears also in the *Iliad*);[35] commoners had to be content with the ordinary symbolic dream, which they interpreted with the help of dream-books.[36] A type corresponding to the Greek *chrematismos* also appears among the dreams of contemporary primitives, who usually attach special importance to it. Whether the dream figure is identified as a god or as an ancestor naturally depends on the local culture-pattern. Sometimes he is just a voice, like the Lord speaking to Samuel; sometimes he is an anonymous "tall man," such as we meet in Greek dreams.[37] In some societies he is commonly recognised as the dreamer's dead father;[38] and in other cases the psychologist may be disposed to see in him a father-substitute, discharging the parental functions of admonition and guidance.[39] If that view is right, we may perhaps find a special significance in Macrobius' phrase, "a *parent* or some other respected or impressive personage." And we may further suppose that so long as the old solidarity of the family persisted, such maintenance of contact in dreams with the father-image would have a deeper emotional significance, and a more unquestioned authority, than it possesses in our more individualised society.

However, the "divine" character of a Greek dream seems not to depend entirely on the ostensible identity of the dream-figure. The directness (*enargeia*) of its message was also important. In several Homeric dreams the god or *eidolon* appears to the dreamer in the guise of a living friend,[40] and it is possible that in real life dreams about acquaintances were often interpreted in this manner. When Aelius Aristides was seeking treatment in Asclepius' temple at Pergamum, his valet had a dream about another patient, the consul Salvius, who in the dream talked to the valet about his employer's literary works.

This was good enough for Aristides; he is sure that the dream-figure was the god himself, "disguised as Salvius."[41] It made, of course, some difference that this was a "sought" dream, even though the person to whom it came was not the seeker: any dream experienced in Asclepius' temple was presumed to come from the god.

Techniques for provoking the eagerly desired "divine" dream have been, and still are, employed in many societies. They include isolation, prayer, fasting, self-mutilation, sleeping on the skin of a sacrificed animal, or in contact with some other holy object, and finally incubation (i.e., sleeping in a holy place), or some combination of these. The ancient world relied mainly on incubation, as Greek peasants still do to-day; but traces of some of the other practices are not lacking. Thus fasting was required at certain dream-oracles, such as "Charon's cave" in Asia Minor and the hero-shrine of Amphiaraus in Oropus;[42] at the latter one also slept on the skin of a sacrificed ram.[43] Withdrawal to a sacred cave in quest of visionary wisdom figures in the legends of Epimenides and Pythagoras.[44] Even the Red Indian practice of chopping off a finger joint to procure a dream has an odd partial parallel, which I will mention presently.[45] There were also in later antiquity less painful ways of obtaining an oracle-dream: the dreambooks recommended sleeping with a branch of laurel under your pillow; the magical papyri are full of spells and private rituals for the purpose; and there were Jews at Rome who would sell you any dream you fancied for a few pence.[46]

None of these techniques is mentioned by Homer, nor is incubation itself.[47] But as we have seen, arguments from silence are in his case peculiarly dangerous. Incubation had been practised in Egypt since the fifteenth century B.C. at least, and I doubt if the Minoans were ignorant of it.[48] When we first meet it in Greece, it is usually associated with cults of Earth and of the dead which have all the air of being pre-Hellenic. Tradition said, probably with truth, that the original Earth oracle at Delphi had been a dream-oracle;[49] in historical times, incubation was practised at the shrines of heroes—whether dead men or chthonic daemons—and at certain chasms reputed to be entrances to the world of the dead (*necyomanteia*). The Olympians did not patronise it (which may sufficiently explain Homer's silence); Athena in the Bellerophon story is an exception,[50] but with her it may be a vestige of her pre-Olympian past.

Whether or not incubation had once been more widely practised in Greece, we find it used in historical times mainly for two specialised ends—either to obtain mantic dreams from the dead, or else for medical purposes. The best-known example of the former is Periander's consultation of his dead wife Melissa on a business matter at a *necyomanteion*, when an "image" of the dead woman appeared to Periander's agent, established her identity, prescribed cult, and insisted on satisfaction of this demand before she would answer his question.[51] There is nothing really incredible in this story, and whether true or false, it seems in any case to reflect an old culture-pattern, out of which in some societies a kind of spiritualism has been developed. But in Greece the Homeric Hades-belief, as well as the scepticism of classical times, must have worked to prevent such a development; and in fact mantic dreams from the dead seem to have played only a very minor part in the Classical Age.[52] They may have acquired more importance in some Hellenistic circles, after Pythagoreans and Stoics had brought the dead into more convenient proximity to the living, by transferring the site of Hades to the air. At any rate we read in Alexander Polyhistor that "the whole air is full of souls, who are worshipped as the daemons and heroes, and it is these who send mankind dreams and omens"; and we find a like theory ascribed to Posidonius.[53] But those who held this view had no reason to seek dreams in special places, since the dead were everywhere; there was no future for *necyomanteia* in the ancient world.

Medical incubation, on the other hand, enjoyed a brilliant revival when at the end of the fifth century the cult of Asclepius suddenly rose to Panhellenic importance—a position which it

retained down to the latest pagan times. About the wider implications of this I shall have something to say in a later
chapter.[54] For the moment we are concerned only with the
dreams that the god sent to his patients. Ever since the publication in 1883 of the Epidaurian Temple Record,[55] these have
been much discussed; and the gradual change in our general
attitude towards the nonrational factors in human experience
has been reflected in the opinions of scholars. The earlier
commentators were content to dismiss the Record as a deliberate priestly forgery, or else to suggest unconvincingly that
the patients were drugged, or hypnotised, or somehow mistook
waking for sleeping and a priest in fancy dress for the divine
Healer.[56] Few, perhaps, would now be satisfied with these crude
explanations; and in the three major contributions to the debate
which have been made in the present generation—those of
Weinreich, Herzog, and Edelstein[57]—we can observe a growing
emphasis on the genuinely religious character of the experience.
This seems to me entirely justified. But there are still differences of opinion about the origin of the Record. Herzog thinks
it is based in part on genuine votive tablets dedicated by individual patients—which might, however, be elaborated and
expanded in the process of incorporation—but also in part on a
temple tradition which had attracted to itself miracle stories
from many sources. Edelstein, on the other hand, accepts the
inscriptions as in some sense a faithful reproduction of the
patient's experience.

Certainty in this matter is hardly attainable. But the concept
of the culture-pattern dream or vision may perhaps bring us a
little nearer to understanding the genesis of such documents
as the Epidaurian Record. Experiences of this type reflect a
pattern of belief which is accepted not only by the dreamer but
usually by everyone in his environment; their form is determined by the belief, and in turn confirms it; hence they become
increasingly stylised. As Tylor pointed out long ago, "it is a
vicious circle: what the dreamer believes he therefore sees,
and what he sees he therefore believes."[58] But what if he never-

theless fails to see? That must often have happened at Epidaurus: as Diogenes said of the votive tablets to another deity,
"there would have been far more of them if those who were *not*
rescued had made dedications."[59] But the failures did not
matter, save to the individual; for the will of a god is inscrutable—"therefore hath He mercy on whom He will have
mercy." "I am determined to leave the temple forthwith," says
the sick pimp in Plautus; "for I realise the decision of Asclepius—he does not care for me or want to save me."[60] Many
a sick man must have said that. But the true believer was no
doubt infinitely patient: we know how patiently primitives
wait for the significant vision,[61] and how people return again
and again to Lourdes. Often in practice the sufferer had to be
content with a revelation that was, to say the least, indirect:
we have seen how somebody else's dream about a consul
could be made to serve at a pinch. But Aristides had also experienced, as he believed, the god's personal presence, and described it in terms that are worth quoting.[62] "It was like seeming to touch him," he says, "a kind of awareness that he was
there in person; one was between sleep and waking, one wanted
to open one's eyes, and yet was anxious lest he should withdraw too soon; one listened and heard things, sometimes as in a
dream, sometimes as in waking life; one's hair stood on end;
one cried, and felt happy; one's heart swelled, but not with
vainglory.[63] What human being could put that experience into
words? But anyone who has been through it will share my
knowledge and recognise the state of mind." What is described
here is a condition of self-induced trance, in which the patient
has a strong inward sense of the divine presence, and eventually
hears the divine voice, only half externalised. It is possible
that many of the god's more detailed prescriptions were received by patients in a state of this kind, rather than in actual
dreams.

Aristides' experience is plainly subjective; but occasionally an
objective factor may have come into play. We read in the
Epidaurian Record of a man who fell asleep in the daytime

outside the temple, when one of the god's tame snakes came
and licked his sore toe; he awoke "cured," and said he had
dreamed that a handsome young man put a dressing on his
toe. This recalls the scene in Aristophanes' *Plutus*, where it
is the snakes who administer the curative treatment after the
patients have seen a vision of the god. We also read of cures
performed by the temple dogs who come and lick the affected
part while the patient is wide awake.[64] There is nothing incredible here, if we do not insist on the permanence of the
"cures"; the habits of dogs and the therapeutic virtues of
saliva are well known. Both dogs and snakes were quite real.
A fourth-century Athenian inscription commands an offering
of cakes to the holy dogs, and we have Plutarch's story of the
clever temple-dog who detected a thief stealing the votives and
was rewarded with dinners at the public expense for the rest of
his life.[65] The temple snake figures in Herodas' mime: the visit-
ing ladies remember to pop a little porridge "respectfully" into
his hole.[66]

   In the morning, those who had been favoured with the god's
nocturnal visitation told their experiences. And here we must
make generous allowance for what Freud called "secondary
elaboration," whose effect is, in Freud's words, "that the dream
loses the appearance of absurdity and incoherence, and ap-
proaches the pattern of an intelligible experience."[67] In this
case the secondary elaboration will have operated, without
conscious deception, to bring the dream or vision into closer
conformity with the traditional culture-pattern. For example,
in the dream of the man with the sore toe, the godlike beauty
of the dream-figure is the sort of traditional[68] trait which
would easily be added at this stage. And beyond this I think
we must assume in many cases a tertiary elaboration[69] contributed by the priests, or more often perhaps by fellow-
patients. Every rumour of a cure, bringing as it did fresh hope
to the desperate, will have been seized on and magnified in
that expectant community of suffering, which was bound
together, as Aristides tells us, by a stronger sense of fellow-

ship than a school or a ship's company.[70] Aristophanes gets
the psychology right when he describes the other patients
crowding round Plutus to congratulate him on recovering his
eyesight, and too much excited to go to sleep again.[71] To this
sort of milieu we should probably refer the folktale elements
in the Record, as well as the tall stories of surgical operations
performed by the god on sleeping patients. It is significant
that Aristides knows of no contemporary surgical cures, but
believes that they were frequent "in the time of the present
priest's grandfather."[72] Even at Epidaurus or Pergamum one
had to give a story time to grow.

A word, finally, about the medical aspect of the business. In
the Record the cures are mostly represented as instantaneous,[73]
and possibly some of them were. It is irrelevant to ask how
long the improvement lasted: it is enough that the patient
"departed cured" (ὑγιὴς ἀπῆλθε). Such cures need not have
been numerous: as we see in the case of Lourdes, a healing shrine
can maintain its reputation on a very low percentage of suc-
cesses, provided a few of them are sensational. As for the dream-
prescriptions, their quality naturally varied not only with the
dreamer's medical knowledge, but with his unconscious attitude towards his own illness.[74] In a few instances they are
quite rational, though not exactly original, as when the Divine
Wisdom prescribes gargling for a sore throat and vegetables for
constipation. "Full of gratitude," says the recipient of this
revelation, "I departed cured."[75] More often the god's pharma-
copoeia is purely magical; he makes his patients swallow snake-
poison or ashes from the altar, or smear their eyes with the
blood of a white cock.[76] Edelstein has rightly pointed out that
such remedies still played a biggish part in profane medicine
too;[77] but there remains the important difference that in
the medical schools they were subject, in principle at least, to
rational criticism, whereas in dreams, as Aristotle said, the
element of judgement (τὸ ἐπικρῖνον) is absent.[78]

The influence of the dreamer's unconscious attitude may be
seen in Aristides' dream-prescriptions, many of which he has

recorded. As he says himself, "They are the very opposite of what one would expect, and are indeed just the things which one would naturally most avoid." Their common character-istic is their painfulness: they range from emetics, river-bathing in midwinter, and running barefoot in the frost, to voluntary shipwreck and a demand for the sacrifice of one of his fingers[79]— a symbol whose significance Freud has explained. These dreams look like the expression of a deep-seated desire for self-punish-ment. Aristides always obeyed them (though in the matter of the finger his Unconscious so far relented as to let him dedi-cate a finger-ring as a surrogate). Nevertheless he somehow managed to survive the effects of his own prescriptions; as Pro-fessor Campbell Bonner has said, he must have had the iron constitution of the chronic invalid.[80] Indeed, obedience to such dreams may well have procured a temporary abatement of neurotic symptoms. But plainly on a wider view there is little to be said for a system which placed the patient at the mercy of his own unconscious impulses, disguised as divine monitions. We may well accept the cool judgement of Cicero that "few patients owe their lives to Asclepius rather than Hippocrates";[81] and we should not allow the modern reaction against rationalism to obscure the real debt that mankind owes to those early Greek physicians who laid down the prin-ciples of a rational therapy in the face of age-old superstitions like the one we have been considering.

As I have mentioned self-induced visions in connection with the Asclepius cult, I may add a couple of general remarks on waking visions or hallucinations. It is likely that these were commoner in former times than they are to-day, since they seem to be relatively frequent among primitives; and even with us they are less rare than is often supposed.[82] They have in general the same origin and psychological structure as dreams, and like dreams they tend to reflect traditional culture-patterns. Among the Greeks, by far the commonest type is the appari-tion of a god or the hearing of a divine voice which commands or forbids the performance of certain acts. This type figures, under the name of "spectaculum," in Chalcidius' classification of dreams and visions; his example is the *daemonion* of Socrates.[83] When all allowance has been made for the influence of literary tradition in creating a stereotyped form, we should probably conclude that experiences of this kind had once been fairly frequent, and still occurred occasionally in historical times.[84]

I believe with Professor Latte[85] that when Hesiod tells us how the Muses spoke to him on Helicon[86] this is not allegory or poetic ornament, but an attempt to express a real experience in literary terms. Again, we may reasonably accept as historical Philippides' vision of Pan before Marathon, which resulted in the establishment of a cult of Pan at Athens;[87] and perhaps also Pindar's vision of the Mother of the Gods in the form of a stone statue, which is likewise said to have occasioned the establishment of a cult, though the authority in this case is not contemporary.[88] These three experiences have an interesting point in common: they all occurred in lonely mountainous places, Hesiod's on Helicon, Philippides' on the savage pass of Mount Parthenion, Pindar's during a thunderstorm in the mountains. That is possibly not accidental. Explorers, mountaineers, and airmen sometimes have odd experiences even today: a well-known example is the presence that haunted Shackleton and his companions in the Antarctic.[89] And one of the old Greek doctors in fact describes a pathological state into which a man may fall "if he is travelling on a lonely route and terror seizes him as a result of an apparition."[90] We need to remember in this connection that most of Greece was, and is, a country of small and scattered settlements separated by wide stretches of desolate mountain solitude that dwarf to insignificance the occasional farms, the ἔργα ἀνθρώπων. The psychological influence of that solitude should not be underrated.

It remains to trace briefly the steps by which a handful of Greek intellectuals attained a more rational attitude to dream-experience. So far as our fragmentary knowledge goes, the first man who explicitly put the dream in its proper place was

Heraclitus, with his observation that in sleep each of us retreats to a world of his own.[91] Not only does that rule out the
"objective" dream, but it seems by implication to deny validity
to dream-experience in general, since Heraclitus' rule is "to
follow what we have in common."[92] And it would appear that
Xenophanes too denied its validity, since he is said to have rejected all forms of divination, which must include the veridical
dream.[93] But these early sceptics did not offer to explain, so
far as we know, how or why dreams occurred, and their view
was slow to win acceptance. Two examples will serve to show
how old ways of thinking, or at any rate old ways of speaking,
persisted in the late fifth century. The sceptical Artabanus in
Herodotus points out to Xerxes that most dreams are suggested by our waking preoccupations, yet he still talks of them
in the old "objective" manner as "wandering about among
men."[94] And Democritus' atomist theory of dreams as *eidola*
which continually emanate from persons and objects, and affect
the dreamer's consciousness by penetrating the pores of his
body, is plainly an attempt to provide a mechanistic basis for
the objective dream; it even preserves Homer's word for the
objective dream-image.[95] This theory makes explicit provision
for telepathic dreams by declaring that *eidola* carry representa-
tions (ἐμφάσεις) of the mental activities of the beings from whom
they originate.[96]

We should expect, however, that by the end of the fifth
century the traditional type of "divine dream," no longer
nourished by a living faith in the traditional gods,[97] would
have declined in frequency and importance—the popular
Asclepius cult being for good reasons an exception. And there
are in fact indications that other ways of regarding the dream
were becoming more fashionable about this time. Religious
minds were now inclined to see in the significant dream evidence of the innate powers of the soul itself, which it could
exercise when liberated by sleep from the gross importunities
of the body. That development belongs to a context of ideas, commonly called "Orphic," which I shall consider in the next chap-

ter.[98] At the same time there is evidence of a lively interest in *oneirocritice*, the art of interpreting the private symbolic dream. A slave in Aristophanes talks of hiring a practitioner of this art for a couple of obols; a grandson of Aristides the Just is said to have made his living by it with the help of a πινάκιον or table of correspondences.[99] Out of these πινάκια developed the first Greek dreambooks, the earliest of which may belong to the late fifth century.[100]

The Hippocratic treatise *On Regimen* (περὶ διαίτης), which Jaeger has dated to about the middle of the fourth century,[101] makes an interesting attempt to rationalise *oneirocritice* by relating large classes of dreams to the physiological state of the dreamer and treating them as symptoms important to the physician.[102] This author admits also precognitive "divine" dreams, and he likewise recognises that many dreams are undisguised wish-fulfilments.[103] But the dreams which interest him as a doctor are those which express in symbolic form morbid physiological states. These he attributes to the medical clairvoyance exercised by the soul when in sleep it "becomes its own mistress" and is able to survey its bodily dwelling without distraction[104] (here the influence of the "Orphic" view is evident). From this standpoint he proceeds to justify many of the traditional interpretations by a series of more or less fanciful analogies between the external world and the human body, macrocosm and microcosm. Thus earth stands for the dreamer's flesh, a river for his blood, a tree for his reproductive system; to dream of an earthquake is a symptom of physiological change, while dreams about the dead refer to the food one has eaten, "for from the dead come nourishment and growth and seed."[105] He thus anticipates Freud's principle that the dream is always egocentric,[106] though his application of it is too narrowly physiological. He claims no originality for his interpretations, some of which are known to be older;[107] but he says that earlier interpreters lacked a rational basis for their views, and prescribed no treatment except prayer, which in his opinion is not enough.[108]

Plato in the *Timaeus* offers a curious explanation of mantic dreams: they originate from the insight of the rational soul, but are perceived by the irrational soul as images reflected on the smooth surface of the liver; hence their obscure symbolic character, which makes interpretation necessary.[109] He thus allows dream-experience an indirect relationship to reality, though it does not appear that he rated it very high. A much more important contribution was made by Aristotle in his two short essays *On Dreams* and *On Divination in Sleep*. His approach to the problem is coolly rational without being superficial, and he shows at times a brilliant insight, as in his recognition of a common origin for dreams, the hallucinations of the sick, and the illusions of the sane (e.g., when we mistake a stranger for the person we want to see).[110] He denies that any dreams are godsent (θεόπεμπτα): if the gods wished to communicate knowledge to men, they would do so in the daytime, and they would choose the recipients more carefully.[111] Yet dreams, though not divine, may be called daemonic, "for Nature is daemonic"—a remark which, as Freud said, contains deep meaning if it be correctly interpreted.[112] On the subject of veridical dreams Aristotle in these essays is, like Freud, cautiously noncommittal. He no longer talks of the soul's innate powers of divination, as he had done in his romantic youth;[113] and he rejects Democritus' theory of atomic *eidola*.[114] Two kinds of dreams he accepts as intelligibly precognitive: dreams conveying foreknowledge of the dreamer's state of health, which are reasonably explained by the penetration to consciousness of symptoms ignored in waking hours; and those which bring about their own fulfilment by suggesting a course of action to the dreamer.[115] Where dreams outside these classes prove to be veridical, he thinks it is probably coincidence (σύμπτωμα); alternatively, he suggests a theory of wave-borne stimuli, on the analogy of disturbances propagated in water or air.[116] His whole approach to the problem is scientific, not religious; and one may in fact doubt whether in this matter modern science has advanced very far beyond him.

Certainly later antiquity did not. The religious view of dreams was revived by the Stoics, and eventually accepted even by Peripatetics like Cicero's friend Cratippus.[117] In the considered opinion of Cicero, the philosophers by this "patronage of dreams" had done much to keep alive a superstition whose only effect was to increase the burden of men's fears and anxieties.[118] But his protest went unheeded: the dreambooks continued to multiply; the Emperor Marcus Aurelius thanked the gods for medical advice vouchsafed to him in sleep; Plutarch abstained from eating eggs because of certain dreams; Dio Cassius was inspired by a dream to write history; and even so enlightened a surgeon as Galen was prepared to perform an operation at the bidding of a dream.[119] Whether from an intuitive apprehension that dreams are after all related to man's inmost life, or for the simpler reasons I suggested at the beginning of this chapter, antiquity to the end refused to content itself with the Gate of Ivory, but insisted that there was also, sometimes and somehow, a Gate of Horn.

NOTES TO CHAPTER IV

[1] On the attitude of primitives to dream-experience see L. Lévy-Bruhl, *Primitive Mentality* (Eng. trans., 1923), chap. iii, and *L'Expérience mystique*, chap. iii.

[2] Theophrastus, *Char.* 16 (28 J.).

[3] See Malinowski, *Sex and Repression in Savage Society*, 92 ff., and especially J. S. Lincoln, *The Dream in Primitive Cultures* (London, 1935). Cf. also Georgia Kelchner, *Dreams in Old Norse Literature and Their Affinities in Folklore* (Cambridge, 1935), 75 f.

[4] C. G. Jung would regard such dreams as based on "archetypal images" transmitted through a supposed racial memory. But, as Lincoln points out (*op. cit.*, 24), their disappearance upon the breakdown of a culture indicates that the images are culturally transmitted. Jung himself (*Psychology and Religion*, 20) reports the significant admission of a medicine-man, who "confessed to me that he no longer had any dreams, for they had the District Commissioner now instead. 'Since the English have been in the country

we have no dreams any more,' he said. 'The D. C. knows everything about war and diseases, and about where we have got to live.' "

5 Jane Harrison, *Epilegomena to the Study of Greek Religion*, 32. On the relationship between dream and myth see also W. H. R. Rivers, "Dreams and Primitive Culture," *Bull. of John Rylands Library*, 1918, 26; Lévy-Bruhl, *L'Exp. mystique*, 105 ff.; Clyde Kluckhohn, "Myths and Rituals: A General Theory," *Harv. Theol. Rev.* 35 (1942) 45 ff.

6 *Primitive Culture in Greece*, 151.

7 Pindar, fr. 116 B. (131 S.). Cf. chap. v below, p. 135.

8 The most recent and thorough study of dreams in Homer is Joachim Hundt's *Der Traumglaube bei Homer* (Greifswald, 1935), from which I have learned a good deal. "Objective" dreams are in his terminology "Aussenträume," in contrast with "Innenträume," which are regarded as purely mental experiences, even though they may be provoked by an extraneous cause.

9 ὄνειρος as "dream-experience" seems to occur in Homer only in the phrase ἐν ὀνείρῳ (*Il.* 22.199, *Od.* 19.541, 581 = 21.79).

10 Ghost, *Il.* 23.65 ff·.; god, *Od.* 6.20 ff.; dream-messenger, *Il.* 2.5 ff., where Zeus sends the ὄνειρος on an errand exactly as he elsewhere sends Iris; εἴδωλον created *ad hoc*, *Od.* 4.795 ff. In *Iliad* 2 and the two *Odyssey* dreams, the dream-figure is *disguised* as a living person (cf. *infra*, p. 109); but I see no reason to suppose with Hundt that it is really the "Bildseele" or shadow-soul of the person in question paying a visit to the "Bildseele" of the dreamer (cf. Böhme's criticism, *Gnomon*, 11 [1935]).

11 Entrance and exit by keyhole, *Od.* 4.802, 838; στῆ δ' ἄρ' ὑπὲρ κεφαλῆς, *Il.* 2.20, 23.68, *Od.* 4.803, 6.21; cf. also *Il.* 10.496 (where an actual dream is surely in question).

12 *Il.* 23.99.

13 *Il.* 2.23, 23.69; *Od.* 4.804. Cf. Pindar, *Ol.* 13.67: εὕδεις, Αἰολίδα βασιλεῦ; Aesch. *Eum.* 94: εὕδοιτ' ἄν.

14 Cf. Hundt, *op. cit.*, 42 f., and G. Björck, "ὄναρ ἰδεῖν: De la perception de la rêve chez les anciens," *Eranos*, 44 (1946) 309.

15 Cf. Hdt. 6.107.1, and other examples quoted by Björck, *loc. cit.*, 311.

16 φοιτᾶν, Sappho, *P. Oxy.* 1787; Aesch. *P.V.* 657 (?); Eur. *Alc.* 355; Hdt. 7.16β; Plato, *Phaedo* 60E; Parrhasios *apud* Athen. 543F. ἐπισκοπεῖν, Aesch. *Agam.* 13; πωλεῖσθαι, Aesch. *P.V.* 645; προσελθεῖν, Plato, *Crito* 44A.

17 Hdt. 1.34.1; 2.139.1, 141.3; 5.56; 7.12: cf. Hundt, *op. cit.*, 42 f.

[18] ἰάματα, nos. 4, 7, etc. (see n. 55); *Lindian Chronicle*, ed. Blinkenberg, D 14, 68, 98; Isocrates, 10.65; Acts 23: 11. Many other examples of this usage are collected by L. Deubner, *de incubatione*, pp. 11 and 71.

[19] Pindar, *Ol.* 13.65 ff. Cf. also Paus. 10.38.13, where the dream-figure of Asclepius leaves a letter behind. Old Norse incubation-dreams prove their objectivity in a like manner; cf., e.g., Kelchner, *op. cit.*, 138. The Epidaurian operation-dreams (n. 72 below) are a variation on the same theme. For "apports" in theurgy see App. II, n. 126.

[20] *Il.* 22.199 ff. Aristarchus seems to have rejected the lines; but the grounds given in the scholia—that they are "cheap in style and thought" and "undo the impression of Achilles' swiftness"—are plainly silly, and the objections of some moderns are not much stronger. Leaf, who thinks v. 200 "tautological and awkward," has failed to notice the expressive value of the repeated words in conveying the sense of frustration. Cf. H. Fränkel, *Die homerischen Gleichnisse*, 78, and Hundt, *op. cit.*, 81 ff. Wilamowitz found the simile admirable, but "unerträglich" in its present context (*Die Ilias u. Homer*, 100); his analysis seems to me hypercritical.

[21] *Od.* 19.541 ff. Scholars have thought it a defect in this dream that Penelope is sorry for her geese whereas in waking life she is not sorry for the suitors whom they symbolise. But such "inversion of affect" is common in real dreams (Freud, *The Interpretation of Dreams*, 2nd Eng. ed., 375).

[22] *Il.* 5.148 ff. The ὀνειροπόλος here can only be an interpreter (ἐκρίνατ' ὀνείρους). But in the only other Homeric passage where the word occurs, *Il.* 1.63, it *may* mean a specially favoured *dreamer* (cf. Hundt, *op. cit.*, 102 f.), which would attest the antiquity in Greece of the "sought" dream.

[23] Cf. Sirach 31 (34): 1 ff.; *Laxdaela Saga*, 31.15; etc. As Björck points out (*loc. cit.* 307), without the distinction between significant and nonsignificant dreams the art of ὀνειροκριτική could never have maintained itself. If there was ever a period, before the advent of Freud, when men thought *all* dreams significant, it lies very far back. "Primitives do not accord belief to all dreams indiscriminately. Certain dreams are worthy of credence, others not" (Lévy-Bruhl, *Primitive Mentality*, 101).

[24] *Od.* 19.560 ff.: cf. Hdt. 7.16; Galen, περὶ τῆς ἐξ ἐνυπνίων διαγνώσεως (VI.832 ff. R.); etc. The distinction is implied at Aesch. *Cho.* 534, where I think we should punctuate, with Verrall, οὔτοι μάταιον· ἀνδρὸς ὄψανον πέλει: "it is not a mere nightmare: it is a *symbolic*

vision of a man." Artemidorus and Macrobius recognise the ἐνύπνιον ἀσήμαντον and also another type of nonsignificant dream,
called φάντασμα, which includes, according to Macrobius, (a) the
nightmare (ἐφιάλτης), and (b) the hypnopompic visions which
occur to some persons between waking and sleeping and were first
described by Aristotle (Insomn. 462ᵃ 11).

²⁵ Artemid. 1.2, p. 5 Hercher; Macrobius, in Somn. Scip. 1.3.2;
[Aug.] de spiritu et anima, 25 (P.L. XL.798); Joann. Saresb. Poly-
crat. 2.15 (P.L. CXCIX.429A); Nicephoros Gregoras, in Synesium
de insomn. (P.G. CXLIX.608A.). The passages have been collected, and their relationship discussed, by Deubner, de incubatione, 1 ff. The definitions quoted in the text are from Macrobius.

²⁶ This has been shown by J. H. Waszink, Mnemosyne, 9 (1941)
65 ff. Chalcidius' classification combines Platonist with Jewish
ideas; Waszink conjectures that he may have derived it from
Numenius via Porphyry. Direct converse with a god appears also
in Posidonius' classification, Cic. div. 1.64.

²⁷ Chalcidius, in Tim. 256, quoting Crito 44B and Phaedo 60E.

²⁸ Aetius, Placita 5.2.3: Ἡρόφιλος τῶν ὀνείρων τοὺς μὲν θεοπέμπτους
κατ' ἀνάγκην γίνεσθαι· τοὺς δὲ φυσικοὺς ἀνειδωλοποιουμένης ψυχῆς
τὸ συμφέρον αὐτῇ καὶ τὸ πάντως ἐσόμενον· τοὺς δὲ συγκραματικοὺς
ἐκ τοῦ αὐτομάτου κατ' εἰδώλων πρόσπτωσιν . . . ὅταν ἃ βουλόμεθα
βλέπωμεν, ὡς ἐπὶ τῶν τὰς ἐρωμένας ὁρώντων ἐν ὕπνῳ γίνεται. The last
part of this statement has caused much difficulty (see Diels ad loc.,
Dox Gr. 416). I think the "mixed" dreams (συγκραματικούς) are
dreams of monsters (φαντάσματα) which on Democritus' theory
arise from a fortuitous conjunction of εἴδωλα, ubi equi atque hominis casu convenit imago (Lucr. 5.741). But a dream of one's beloved is not a "mixed" dream in this or any other sense. Galen
has συγκριματικούς, which Wellmann explained as "organic"
(Arch. f. Gesch. d. Med. 16 [1925] 70 ff.). But this does not square
with κατ' εἰδώλων πρόσπτωσιν. I suggest that ὅταν ἃ βουλόμεθα κτλ
illustrates a fourth type, the dream arising from ψυχῆς ἐπιθυμία
(cf. Hippocrates, περὶ διαίτης, 4.93), mention of which has fallen
out.

²⁹ Hdt. 1.34.1, 5.56; Plato, Crito 44A; Plutarch, Alex. 26 (on the authority of Heraclides). The uniformity of the literary tradition has
been noted by Deubner (de incubatione 13); he quotes many other
examples. The type is as common in early Christian as in pagan
literature (Festugière, L'Astrologie et les sciences occultes, 51).

³⁰ E.g., Paus. 3.14.4, the wife of an early Spartan king builds a
temple of Thetis κατὰ ὄψιν ὀνείρατος. Dreams about cult statues,

ibid., 3.16.1, 7.20.4, 8.42.7; Parrhasios *apud* Athen. 543F. Sophocles dedicates a shrine as a result of a dream, *Vit. Soph.* 12, Cic. *div.* 1.54.

31 Dittenberger, *Sylloge*3, offers the following instances: κατ' ὄναρ, 1147, 1148, 1149; κατὰ ὄνειρον, 1150; καθ' ὕπνους, 1152; ὄψιν ἰδοῦσα ἀρετὴν τῆς θεοῦ (Athene), 1151. Probably 1128 καθ' ὅραμα and 1153 κατ' ἐπιταγήν also refer to dreams; 557, an ἐπιφάνεια of Artemis, may be a waking vision. Cf. also Edelstein, *Asclepius*, I, test. 432, 439–442, and for cults originating in waking visions, *infra*, p. 117, and *Chron. Lind.* A 3: τὸ ἱερὸ]ν τᾶς 'Αθάνας τᾶς Λινδίας . . . πολλοῖς κ[αὶ καλοῖς ἀναθέμασι ἐξ ἀρχαιοτ]άτων χρόνων κεκόσμηται διὰ τὰν τᾶς θεοῦ ἐπιφάνειαν.

32 *Syll.*3 663; 985. Cf. also P. Cair. Zenon I.59034, the dreams of Zoilus (who appears to have been a building contractor, and had thus every motive for dreaming that Sarapis required a new temple). Many of Aristides' dreams prescribe sacrifices or other acts of cult.

33 Plato, *Laws* 909E–910A, *Epin.* 985C. The inscriptions tend to confirm Plato's judgement about the kind of person who made a dedication on the strength of a dream; the majority are either dedications to healing deities (Asclepius, Hygieia, Sarapis) or dedications by women.

34 Gadd, *Ideas of Divine Rule*, 24 ff.

35 *Il.* 2.80 ff. seems to imply that the dream-experience of a High King is more trustworthy than that of an ordinary man (cf. Hundt, *op. cit.*, 55 f.). A later Greek view was that the σπουδαῖος was privileged to receive only significant dreams (Artemidorus, 4 *praef.*; cf. Plutarch, *gen. Socr.* 20, 589B), which corresponds to the special status as dreamer accorded by primitives to the medicine-man, and may be based on Pythagorean ideas (cf. Cic. *div.* 2.119).

36 Gadd, *op. cit.*, 73 ff.

37 Voice, e.g., Lincoln, *op. cit.*, 198, cf. I Samuel 3: 4 ff.; tall man, e.g., Lincoln, *op. cit.*, 24, cf. Deubner, *op. cit.*, 12. Some of Jung's patients also reported dreams in which an oracular voice was heard, either disembodied or proceeding "from an authoritative figure"; he calls it "a basic religious phenomenon" (*Psychology and Religion*, 45 f.).

38 Cf. Seligman, *JRAI* 54 (1924) 35 f.; Lincoln, *op. cit.*, 94.

39 Lincoln, *op. cit.*, 96 f.

40 *Il.* 2.20 ff. (Nestor, the ideal father-substitute!); *Od.* 4.796 ff.,

6.22 f. (hardly mother-substitutes, for they are ὁμήλικες with the dreamer).

[41] Aristides, *orat.* 48.9 (II.396.24 Keil); cf. Deubner, *op. cit.*, 9, and Christian examples, *ibid.*, 73, 84. Some primitives are less easily satisfied: see, e.g., Lincoln, *op. cit.*, 255 f., 271 ff.

[42] Strabo, 14.1.44; Philostratus, *vit. Apoll.* 2.37. Other examples in Deubner, *op. cit.*, 14 f.

[43] Paus. 1.34.5. Other examples in Deubner, *op. cit.*, 27 f. Cf. also Halliday, *Greek Divination*, 131 f., who quotes the curious Gaelic incubation rite of "Taghairm," in which the enquirer was wrapped in a bull's hide.

[44] See chap. v, pp. 142, 144.

[45] See n. 79.

[46] Laurel branch, Fulgentius, *Mythologiae*, 1.14 (on the authority of Antiphon and others). Spells, Artemidorus, 4.2, pp. 205 f. H. Sale of dreams, Juv. 6.546 f. On the ὀνειραιτητά in the papyri see Deubner, *op. cit.*, 30 ff.

[47] It has been thought that the Σελλοὶ ἀνιπτόποδες χαμαιεῦναι at Dodona (*Il.* 16.233 ff.) practised incubation; but if they did, did Homer know it?

[48] Cf. Gadd, *op. cit.*, 26 (temple incubation of Amenophis II and Thothmes IV to obtain the god's approval of their occupying the throne). For the Minoans we have no direct evidence; but the terra-cottas found at Petsofa in Crete (*BSA* 9.356 ff.), which represent human limbs and are pierced with holes for suspension, certainly look like votives dedicated at a healing shrine.—For a probable case of incubation in early Mesopotamia see *Ztschr. f. Assyr.* 29 (1915) 158 ff. and 30 (1916) 101 ff.

[49] Eur. *I.T.* 1259 ff. (cf. *Hec.* 70 f.: ὦ πότνια χθών, μελανοπτερύγων μῆτερ ὀνείρων). The authority of this tradition has been doubted; but is any other oracular method so likely? Neither inspired prophecy nor divination by lots is appropriate, so far as our knowledge goes, to an Earth oracle; whereas the author of *Od.* 24.12 already seems to regard dreams as chthonic (cf. Hundt, *op. cit.*, 74 ff.).

[50] Pindar, *Ol.* 13.75 ff. Cf. an inscription from the Athenian Acropolis, *Syll.*[3] 1151: Ἀθηνάᾳ . . . ὄψιν ἰδοῦσα ἀρετὴν τῆς θεοῦ (not necessarily a sought dream, but significant of the goddess' attitude); and the (probably fictitious) epiphany of Athena in a dream, Blinkenberg, *Lindische Tempelchronik*, 34 ff.

[51] Hdt. 5.92η. Melissa was a βιαιοθάνατος, which may have made her εἴδωλον more easily available for consultation. Her complaint

about the cold may be compared with the Norse story of a man who appeared in a dream to say that his feet were cold, the toes of his corpse having been left uncovered (Kelchner, *op. cit.*, 70).

52 Pelias's (unsought) dream in which the soul of Phrixos asks to be brought home (Pindar, *Pyth.* 4.159 ff.) probably reflects the anxiety of the late Archaic Age about translation of relics, and may thus be classed as a "culture-pattern" dream. Other dreams in which the dead appear mostly illustrate the special cases of the Vengeful Dead (e.g., the Erinyes' dream, Aesch. *Eum.* 94 ff., or Pausanias' sought dream, Plutarch, *Cimon* 6, Paus. 3.17.8 f.), or the Grateful Dead (e.g., Simonides' dream, Cic. *div.* 1.56). Dream-apparitions of the recently dead to their surviving relatives are occasionally recorded in their epitaphs as evidence of their continued existence (see Rohde, *Psyche*, 576 f.; Cumont, *After Life in Roman Paganism*, 61 f.). Such dreams are of course natural in all societies; but (apart from Achilles' dream in Homer) the recorded examples of this type are, I think, chiefly postclassical.

53 Alexander Polyhistor *apud* Diog. Laert. 8.32 (= Diels, *Vorsokr.*⁵, 58 B 1a); Posidonius *apud* Cic. *div.* 1.64. Alexander's account was thought by Wellmann (*Hermes*, 54 [1919] 225 ff.) to go back to a fourth-century source which reflected old-Pythagorean views; but see Festugière, *REG.* 58 (1945) 1 ff., who shows reason for dating the source or sources to the third century, and relates the document to the views of the Old Academy and of Diocles of Carystus.

54 See chap. vi, p. 193.

55 ἰάματα τοῦ 'Απόλλωνος καὶ τοῦ 'Ασκλαπιοῦ, *IG* IV², i.121–124. There is a separate edition by R. Herzog, *Die Wunderheilungen von Epidaurus* (*Philol.* Suppl. III.3); and the less mutilated portions are reproduced and translated in Edelstein, *Asclepius*, I, test. 423.

56 The scene in Aristophanes' *Plutus* has been quoted as supporting the last view. But I doubt if the poet intended to hint that the priest of line 676 was identical with "the god" who appears later. Cario's narrative seems to represent, not what Aristophanes thought actually happened, but rather the average patient's imaginative picture of what went on while he slept.

57 O. Weinreich, *Antike Heilungswunder* (*RGVV* VIII.i), 1909; R. Herzog, *op. cit.*, 1931; E. J. and L. Edelstein, *Asclepius: A Collection and Interpretation of the Testimonies* (2 vols., 1945). Mary Hamilton's *Incubation* (1906) provides a very readable general account for the nonspecialist.

58 E. B. Tylor, *Primitive Culture*, II, 49. Cf. G. W. Morgan, "Navaho

Dreams," *American Anthropologist*, 34 (1932) 400: "Myths influence dreams, and these dreams in turn help to maintain the efficacy of the ceremonies."

⁵⁹ Diog. Laert. 6.59.

⁶⁰ Plautus, *Curc.* 216 ff. (= test. 430 Edelstein). Later piety represents failure as a sign of the god's moral disapproval, as in the cases of Alexander Severus (Dio Cass. 78.15.6 f. = test. 395) and the drunken youth in Philostratus (*vit. Apoll.* 1.9 = test. 397). But there were also temple legends to hearten the disappointed (ἰάματα 25). Edelstein thinks these must have been the minority (*op. cit.*, II.163); but the history of Lourdes and other healing shrines suggests that no such assumption is necessary. "If nothing happens," says Lawson, speaking of incubation in Greek churches today, "they return home with hope lessened, but belief unshaken" (*Modern Greek Folklore and Ancient Greek Religion*, 302).

⁶¹ Cf., e.g., Lincoln, *op. cit.*, 271 ff.; and on delays at Epidaurus, Herzog, *op. cit.*, 67. In some narratives of mediaeval incubation the patient waits as much as a year (Deubner, *op. cit.*, 84), and Lawson speaks of peasants today waiting for weeks and months.

⁶² Aristides, *orat.* 48.31 ff. (= test. 417). Maximus of Tyre claims to have had a waking vision of Asclepius (9.7: εἶδον τὸν Ἀσκλη-πιόν, ἀλλ' οὐχὶ ὄναρ). And Iamblichus (*myst.* 3.2, p. 104 P.) regards the state between sleeping and waking as particularly favourable to the reception of divine visions.

⁶³ γνώμης ὄγκος ἀνεπαχθής. ὄγκος was normally a sign of pride, and therefore offensive (ἐπαχθής) to the gods.

⁶⁴ ἰάματα 17; Ar. *Plut.* 733 ff.; ἰάματα 20, 26. On the virtue in the dog's lick see H. Scholz, *Der Hund in der gr.-röm. Magie u. Religion*, 13. A fourth-century relief in the National Museum at Athens, no. 3369, has been interpreted by Herzog (*op. cit.*, 88 ff.) as a parallel to ἰάματα 17. Dedicated by a grateful incubant to the healing hero Amphiaraus, it shows side by side (*a*) the healing of an injured shoulder by Amphiaraus in person (the dream?), (*b*) a snake licking it (the objective event?).

⁶⁵ *IG* II², 4962 (= test. 515); Plutarch, *soll. anim.* 13, 969ᴇ; Aelian, *N.A.* 7.13 (= test. 731a, 731). On the offering "to the dogs and their keepers (κυνηγέταις)" see Farnell, *Hero Cults*, 261 ff.; Scholz, *op. cit.*, 49; Edelstein, *op. cit.*, II.186, n. 9. Plato comicus adapts the phrase to an indecent *double entendre* (fr. 174.16 K.), which possibly indicates that some Athenians found the offering as funny as we do. Are the "keepers" or "dog-leaders" spirits who guide the dog to the appropriate patient? They are anyhow not, I think,

"huntsmen," human or divine: Xen. *Cyneg.* 1.2 is no proof that
Asclepius ever hunted.

⁶⁶ Herodas, 4.90 f. (= test. 482). He is surely a live snake, not a
bronze one. Bronze snakes do not live in holes, and τρώγλη does
not mean "mouth" (as Edelstein, *loc. cit.* and II.188, reproducing
a slip of Knox), nor does it seem likely that a money-box could
be called a τρώγλη (as Herzog, *Arch. f. Rel.* 10 [1907] 205 ff.). The
natural interpretation is confirmed by Paus. 2.11.8 (= test. 700a).

⁶⁷ *The Interpretation of Dreams,* 391.

⁶⁸ Cf. ἰάματα 31, and the many examples in Deubner, *op. cit.,* 12.

⁶⁹ ἰάματα 1 is a clear example, as Herzog has pointed out. Cf. also
G. Vlastos, "Religion and Medicine in the Cult of Asclepius,"
Review of Religion, 1949, 278 ff.

⁷⁰ Aristides, *orat.* 23.16 (= test. 402): οὔτε χοροῦ σύλλογος πρᾶγμα
τοσοῦτον οὔτε πλοῦ κοινωνία οὔτε διδασκάλων τῶν αὐτῶν τυχεῖν, ὅσον
χρῆμα καὶ κέρδος εἰς Ἀσκληπιοῦ τε συμφοιτῆσαι καὶ τελεσθῆναι
τὰ πρῶτα τῶν ἱερῶν.

⁷¹ Ar. *Plut.* 742 ff.

⁷² Aristides, *orat.* 50.64 (= test. 412). Surgical operations on sleeping patients appear also in the fragment of a temple record from
the Asclepieum at Lebena in Crete (*Inscr. Cret.* I.xvii.9 = test.
426), and are attributed to Sts. Cosmas and Damian (Deubner,
op. cit., 74). For an old Norse operation-dream see Kelchner, *op.
cit.,* 110.

⁷³ Instantaneous cures appear also in Christian incubation (Deubner,
op. cit., 72, 82), and are characteristic of savage medicine generally
(Lévy-Bruhl, *Primitive Mentality,* 419 f. [Eng. trans.]).

⁷⁴ Edelstein rightly stresses the first point (*op. cit.,* II.167, "men in
their dreams made the god trust in everything on which they
themselves relied"); he overlooks the second. The older view which
attributed the cures to the medical skill of the priests, and attempted to rationalise the Asclepiea as sanatoriums (cf. Farnell,
Hero Cults, 273 f., Herzog, *op. cit.,* 154 ff.), is rightly abandoned
by Edelstein. As he points out, there is not much real evidence
that at Epidaurus and elsewhere physicians, or priests trained in
medicine, played any part in the temple healings (*op. cit.,* II.158).
The Asclepieum at Cos has been claimed as an exception; but the
medical instruments found there may well be votives dedicated
by physicians. (See, however, Aristides, *orat.* 49.21 f., where Aristides dreams of an ointment and the νεωκόρος provides it; and an
inscription in *JHS* 15 [1895] 121, where the patient thanks his
doctor as well as the god).

75 *IG* IV².i.126 (= test. 432). Cf. Aristides, *orat.* 49.30 (= test. 410): τὰ μὲν (τῶν φαρμάκων) αὐτὸς συντιθείς, τὰ δὲ τῶν ἐν μέσῳ καὶ κοινῶν ἐδίδου (ὁ θεός), and Zingerle's study of the prescriptions given to Granius Rufus, *Comment. Vind.* 3 (1937) 85 ff.

76 Snake poison, Galen, *Subfig. Emp.* 10, p. 78 Deichgräber (= test. 436); ashes, *Inscr. Cret.* I.xvii.17 (= test. 439); cock, *IG* XIV.966 (= test. 438). Cf. Deubner, *op. cit.*, 44 ff.

77 Cf. Edelstein, *op. cit.*, II.171 f.; and, *contra*, Vlastos, *loc. cit.* (n. 69 above), 282 ff. In their admiration for the rational *principles* of Greek medicine, philosophers and historians have been inclined to ignore or slur over the irrational character of many of the remedies employed by ancient physicians (and indeed by all physicians down to fairly recent times). On the difficulty of testing drugs before the development of chemical analysis see Temkin, *The Falling Sickness*, 23 f. Nevertheless, one must still agree with Vlastos that "Hippocratic medicine and Asclepius' cures are polar opposites *in principle.*"

78 Aristotle, *Insomn.* 461ᵇ 6.

79 Aristides, *orat.* 36.124; 47.46–50, 65; 48.18 ff., 27, 74 ff. Aristides' obsessive sense of guilt betrays itself also in two curious passages (*orat.* 48.44 and 51.25) where he interprets the death of a friend as a surrogate for his own; such thoughts are symptomatic not so much of callous egotism as of a deep-seated neurosis. For the dream of sacrificing a finger (*orat.* 48.27 = test. 504) cf. Artemidorus, 1.42. Actual finger-sacrifice is practised by primitives for a variety of purposes (Frazer on Paus. 8.34.2). One object is to procure significant dreams or visions: see Lincoln, *op. cit.*, 147, 256, where the practice is explained as an appeasement of the Father-figure, whose apparition is desired, by an act which symbolises self-castration.

80 Campbell Bonner, "Some Phases of Religious Feeling in Later Paganism," *Harv. Theol. Rev.* 30 (1937) 126.

81 Cic. *N.D.* 3.91 (= test. 416a). Cf. Cic. *div.* 2.123 (= test. 416). For the harm done by reliance on medical dreams cf. Soranus' requirement that a nurse shall not be superstitious, "lest dreams or omens or faith in traditional rituals lead her to neglect proper treatment" (1.2.4.4, *Corp. Med. Graec.* IV.5.28).

82 A "census of hallucinations" conducted by the English Society for Psychical Research (*Proc. S.P.R.* 10 [1894] 25 ff.) seemed to indicate that about one person in ten experiences at some time in his life a hallucination not due to physical or mental illness. A more

recent enquiry by the same society (*Journ. S.P.R.* 34 [1948] 187 ff.) has confirmed this finding.

83 Chalcidius, *in Tim.* 256: spectaculum, ut cum vigilantibus offert se videndam caelestis potestas clare iubens aliquid aut prohibens forma et voce mirabili. The question whether such epiphanies really occurred was the subject of lively controversy in Hellenistic times (Dion. Hal. *Ant. Rom.* 2.68). For a detailed account of an experience in which the same divine figure was simultaneously perceived by one person in a dream and by another in a waking vision, see *P. Oxy.* XI.1381.91 ff.

84 Cf. Wilamowitz, *Glaube*, I.23; Pfister in P.-W., Supp. IV, s.v. "Epiphanie," 3.41. As Pfister says, we cannot doubt that the mass of ancient epiphany-stories corresponds to something in ancient religious experience, even though we can seldom or never be quite sure that any particular story has a historical basis.

85 K. Latte, "Hesiods Dichterweihe," *Antike u. Abendland,* II (1946) 154 ff.

86 Hesiod, *Theog.* 22 ff. (cf. chap. iii, p. 81). Hesiod does not claim to have seen the Muses, but only to have heard their voices; they were presumably κεκαλυμμέναι ἠέρι πολλῇ (*Theog.* 9). Some MSS and citations, reading δρέψασαι in line 31, make the Muses pluck a branch of bay and give it to him, which would put the vision into the class of "apport" stories (n. 19 above). But we should probably prefer the less obvious reading δρέψασθαι, "they granted me to pluck for myself" a branch of the holy tree—the symbolic act expresses his acceptance of his "call."

87 Hdt. 6.105. Here too the experience may have been purely auditory, though φανῆναι is used of it in c. 106.

88 Aristodemus, *apud* Schol. Pind. *Pyth.* 3.79 (137); cf. Paus. 9.25.3, and chap. iii, n. 90.

89 Sir Ernest Shackleton, *South*, 209.

90 Hippocrates, *Int.* 48 (VII.286 L.): αὕτη ἡ νοῦσος προσπίπτει μάλιστα ἐν ἀλλοδημίῃ, καὶ ἤν κου ἐρήμην ὁδὸν βαδίζῃ καὶ ὁ φόβος αὐτὸν λάβῃ ἐκ φάσματος· λαμβάνει δὲ καὶ ἄλλως. The influence of the wild environment on Greek religious ideas has been eloquently stressed by Wilamowitz (*Glaube*, I.155, 177 f., and elsewhere), but this passage seems to have escaped notice.

91 Heraclitus, fr. 89 D.; cf. fr. 73 and Sext. Emp. *adv. dogm.* 1.129 f. (= Heraclitus, A 16). Fr. 26 also seems to refer to dream-experience, but is too corrupt and obscure to build anything on (cf. O. Gigon, *Untersuchungen zu Heraklit*, 95 ff.). Nor can I place much reliance on Chalcidius' statement about the views of "Hera-

clitus and the Stoics" concerning prophecy (*in Tim.* 251 = Heraclitus, A 20).

92 Fr. 2.

93 Cic. *div.* 1.5; Aetius, 5.1.1 (= Xenophanes, A 52).

94 Hdt. 7.16β, ἐνύπνια τὰ ἐς ἀνθρώπους πεπλανημένα. Cf. Lucr. 5.724, "rerum simulacra vagari" (from Democritus?). For dreams reflecting daytime thoughts cf. also Empedocles, fr. 108.

95 This point has been made by Björck, who sees in Democritus' theory an example of the systematising of popular ideas by intellectuals (*Eranos*, 44 [1946] 313). But it is also an attempt to naturalise the "supernatural" dream by giving a mechanistic explanation (Vlastos, *loc. cit.*, 284).

96 Fr. 166, and Plut. ℚ. *Conv.* 8.10.2, 734 F (= Democritus, A 77). Cf. Delatte, *Enthousiasme*, 46 ff., and my paper in *Greek Poetry and Life: Essays Presented to Gilbert Murray*, 369 f.

97 In popular usage terms like θεόπεμπτος came to be largely emptied of their religious content: Artemidorus says that in his day anything unexpected was colloquially called θεόπεμπτον (1.6).

98 See chap. v, p. 135.

99 Ar. *Vesp.* 52 f.; Demetrius of Phaleron *apud* Plut. *Aristides* 27. Cf. also Xen. *Anab.* 7.8.1, where the reading τὰ ἐνύπνια ἐν Λυκείῳ γεγραφότος is probably sound (Wilamowitz, *Hermes*, 54 [1919] 65 f.). ὀνειρομάντεις were referred to by the early comic poet Magnes (fr. 4 K.), and appear to have been satirised in the *Telmessians* of Aristophanes. S. Luria, "Studien zur Geschichte der antiken Traumdeutung," *Bull. Acad. des Sciences de l'U.R.S.S.* 1927, 1041 ff., is perhaps right in distinguishing two schools of dream-interpretation in the Classical Age, one conservative and religious, the other pseudo-scientific, though I cannot follow him in all his detailed conclusions. Faith in the art was not confined to the masses; both Aeschylus and Sophocles recognise the interpretation of dreams as an important branch of μαντική (*P.V.* 485 f.; *El.* 497 ff.).

100 Antiphon ὁ τερατοσκόπος, who is presumably the author of the dreambook quoted by Cicero and Artemidorus (cf. Hermogenes, *de ideis*, 2.11.7 = *Vorsokr.* 87 A 2, ὁ καὶ τερατοσκόπος καὶ ὀνειρο-κρίτης λεγόμενος γενέσθαι) was a contemporary of Socrates (Diog. Laert. 2.46 = Aristotle, fr. 75 R. = *Vorsokr.* 87 A 5). He is often identified, on the authority of Hermogenes, *loc. cit.*, and Suidas, with the sophist Antiphon; but this is not easy to accept. (*a*) It is hard to attribute a deep respect for dreams and portents to the author of the περὶ ἀληθείας, who "disbelieved in providence"

(*Vorsokr.* 87 B 12; cf. Nestle, *Vom Mythos zum Logos*, 389); (*b*) Artemidorus and Suidas call the writer of the dreambook an Athenian (*Vorsokr.* 80 B 78, A 1), while Socrates' use of παρ' ἡμῖν at Xen. *Mem.* 1.6.13 seems to me to imply that the sophist was a foreigner (which would also forbid identification of the sophist with the orator).

101 Jaeger, *Paideia*, III.33 ff. Previous scholars had generally attributed the περὶ διαίτης to the late fifth century.

102 That dreams can be significant symptoms in illness is recognised elsewhere in the Hippocratic corpus (*Epidem.* 1.10, II.670 L.; *Hum.* 4, V.480; *Hebd.* 45, IX.460). In particular, anxiety dreams are seen to be important symptoms of mental trouble, *Morb.* 2.72, VII.110; *Int.* 48, VII.286. Aristotle says the most accomplished physicians believe in taking serious account of dreams, *div. p. somn.* 463ᵃ 4. But the author of περὶ διαίτης carries this essentially sound principle to fantastic lengths.

103 περὶ διαίτης 4.87 (VI.640 L.): ὁκόσα μὲν οὖν τῶν ἐνυπνίων θεῖά ἐστι καὶ προσημαίνει τινὰ συμβησόμενα . . . εἰσὶν οἳ κρίνουσι περὶ τῶν τοιούτων ἀκριβῆ τέχνην ἔχοντες, and *ibid.*, 93: ὁκόσα δὲ δοκέει ὁ ἄνθρωπος θεωρέειν τῶν συνήθων, ψυχῆς ἐπιθυμίην σημαίνει.

104 *Ibid.*, 86: ὁκόταν δὲ τὸ σῶμα ἡσυχάζῃ, ἡ ψυχὴ κινευμένη καὶ ἐπεξέρπουσα τὰ μέρη τοῦ σώματος διοικέει τὸν ἑωυτῆς οἶκον κτλ. Cf. chap.v, p. 135, and Galen's observation that "in sleep the soul seems to sink into the depths of the body, withdrawing from external sense-objects, and so becomes aware of the bodily condition" (περὶ τῆς ἐξ ἐνυπνίων διαγνώσεως, VI.834 Kühn). The influence of "Orphic" ideas on περὶ διαίτης 4.86 has been pointed out by A. Palm, *Studien zur Hippokratischen Schrift π. διαίτης*, 62 ff.

105 *Ibid.*, 90, 92. For the detailed correspondence of macrocosm and microcosm cf. *Hebd.* 6 (IX.436 L.).

106 Freud, *op. cit.*, 299: "every dream treats of one's own person."

107 For the tree as a symbol of reproduction cf. Hdt. 1.108 and Soph. *El.* 419 ff.; a like symbolism is found in some old Norse dreams (Kelchner, *op. cit.*, 56). Similarities of interpretation between the π. διαίτης and ancient Indian dreambooks have led to the suggestion of Oriental influence on the Greek medical writer, or on the Greek dreambook which he used (Palm, *Studien zur Hipp. Schrift π. διαίτης*, 83 ff., followed by Jaeger, *Paideia*, III.39). Others on grounds of the same kind have postulated an early Greek dreambook as a common source of Artemidorus and the π. διαίτης (C. Fredrich, *Hippokratische Untersuchungen*, 213 f.). But such inferences are fragile. The art of ὀνειροκριτική was (and is) an art of

seeing analogies (Arist. *div. p. somn.* 464^b 5), and the more obvious analogies can hardly be missed. Professor Rose has pointed out detailed similarities between Artemidorus' system and that now in vogue in Central Africa (*Man*, 26 [1926] 211 f.). Cf. also Latte, *Gnomon*, 5.159.

[108] *Ibid.*, 87; cf. Palm, *op. cit.*, 75 ff. Theophrastus' Superstitious Man asks the ὀνειροκρίται every time he has a dream τίνι θεῷ ἢ θεᾷ προσεύχεσθαι δεῖ (*Char.* 16).

[109] Plato, *Tim.* 71A–E.

[110] *Insomn.* 458^b 25 ff., 460^b 3 ff.

[111] *Div. p. somn.* 463^b 15 ff., 464^a 20 ff.

[112] *Ibid.*, 463^b 14; cf. Freud, *Interpretation of Dreams*, 2. I cannot agree with Boyancé (*Culte des Muses*, 192) that when Aristotle calls dreams δαιμόνια he is thinking of the Pythagorean (? post-Aristotelian) doctrine that they are caused by δαίμονες in the air (see n. 53). And Boyancé is certainly wrong in claiming Aristotle as an unqualified believer in the mantic dream.

[113] περὶ φιλοσοφίας, fr. 10. Cf. Jaeger, *Aristotle*, 162 f., 333 f. (Eng. ed.).

[114] *Div. p. somn.* 464^a 5.

[115] *Ibid.*, 463^a 4 ff., 27 ff.

[116] *Ibid.*, 464^a 6 ff. Aristotle further suggests that the mind responds best to such minute stimuli when it is empty and passive, as in some types of insanity (464^a 22 ff.); and that there must be a selective factor at work, since veridical dreams usually concern friends, not strangers (464^a 27 ff.)

[117] Cf. Cic. *div.* 1.70 f. Cicero attributes the religious view even to Aristotle's pupil Dicaearchus (*ibid.*, 1.113, 2.100); but this is not easy to reconcile with Dicaearchus' other recorded opinions, and may be due to a misapprehension (F. Wehrli, *Dikaiarchos*, 46).

[118] Cic. *div.* 2.150. The civilised rationalism of *de divinatione*, Book 2, in this closing passage has hardly been sufficiently appreciated.

[119] Cf. the formidable list of authorities on ὀνειροκριτική now lost, in Bouché-Leclercq, *Hist. de la Divination*, I.277. Dreambooks are still much studied in Greece (Lawson, *op. cit.*, 300 f.). Marcus Aurelius' enumeration of his personal debts to Providence includes τὸ δι' ὀνειράτων βοηθήματα δοθῆναι ἄλλα τε καὶ ὡς μὴ πτύειν αἷμα καὶ μὴ ἰλιγγιᾶν (1.17.9); cf. also Fronto, *Epist.* 3.9.1 f. For Plutarch's reliance on dream advice see *Q. Conv.* 2.3.1, 635E; for Galen's, see his commentary on Hipp. περὶ χυμῶν 2.2 (XVI.219 ff. K.). Dio Cassius is instructed by his δαιμόνιον in a dream to write history, 72.23.

V

The Greek Shamans and the Origin of Puritanism

That man should be a thing for immortal souls to sieve through!

HERMAN MELVILLE

IN THE preceding chapter we saw that, side by side with the old belief in objective divine messengers who communicate with man in dreams and visions, there appears in certain writers of the Classical Age a new belief which connects these experiences with an occult power innate in man himself. "Each man's body," says Pindar, "follows the call of overmastering death; yet still there is left alive an image of life (αἰῶνος εἴδωλον), for this alone is from the gods. It sleeps while the limbs are active; but while the man sleeps it often shows in dreams a decision of joy or adversity to come."[1] Xenophon puts this doctrine into plain prose, and provides the logical links which poetry has the right to omit. "It is in sleep," says Xenophon, "that the soul (*psyche*) best shows its divine nature; it is in sleep that it enjoys a certain insight into the future; and this is, apparently, because it is freest in sleep." Then he goes on to argue that in death we may expect the *psyche* to be even freer; for sleep is the nearest approach to death in living experience.[2] Similar statements appear in Plato, and in a fragment of an early work by Aristotle.[3]

Opinions of this kind have long been recognised as elements in a new culture-pattern, expressions of a new outlook on man's nature and destiny which is foreign to the older Greek writers.

[1] For notes to chapter v see pages 156–178.

Discussion of the origin and history of this pattern, and its influence on ancient culture, could easily occupy an entire course of lectures or fill a volume by itself alone. All that I can do here is to consider briefly some aspects of it which crucially affected the Greek interpretation of nonrational factors in human experience. But in attempting even this, I shall have to traverse ground which has been churned to deep and slippery mud by the heavy feet of contending scholars; ground, also, where those in a hurry are liable to trip over the partially decayed remains of dead theories that have not yet been decently interred. We shall be wise, then, to move slowly, and to pick our steps rather carefully among the litter.

Let us begin by asking exactly what it was that was new in the new pattern of beliefs. Certainly not the idea of survival. In Greece, as in most parts of the world,[4] that idea was very old indeed. If we may judge by the furniture of their tombs, the inhabitants of the Aegean region had felt since Neolithic times that man's need for food, drink, and clothing, and his desire for service and entertainment, did not cease with death.[5] I say advisedly "felt," rather than "believed"; for such acts as feeding the dead look like a direct response to emotional drives, not necessarily mediated by any theory. Man, I take it, feeds his dead for the same sort of reason as a little girl feeds her doll; and like the little girl, he abstains from killing his phantasy by applying reality-standards. When the archaic Greek poured liquids down a feeding-tube into the livid jaws of a mouldering corpse, all we can say is that he abstained, for good reasons, from knowing what he was doing; or, to put it more abstractly, that he ignored the distinction between corpse and ghost—he treated them as "consubstantial."[6]

To have formulated that distinction with precision and clarity, to have disentangled the ghost from the corpse, is, of course, the achievement of the Homeric poets. There are passages in both poems which suggest that they were proud of the achievement, and fully conscious of its novelty and importance.[7]

They had indeed a right to be proud; for there is no domain where clear thinking encounters stronger unconscious resistance than when we try to think about death. But we should not assume that once the distinction had been formulated it was universally or even generally accepted. As the archaeological evidence shows, the tendance of the dead, with its implication of identity between corpse and ghost, went quietly on, at any rate in Mainland Greece; it persisted through (some would say despite) the temporary vogue of cremation,[8] and in Attica became so wastefully extravagant that legislation to control it had to be introduced by Solon, and again by Demetrius of Phaleron.[9]

There was no question, then, of "establishing" the idea of survival; that was implicit in age-old custom for the thing in the tomb which is both ghost and corpse, and explicit in Homer for the shadow in Hades which is ghost alone. Nor, secondly, was the idea of rewards and punishments after death a new one. The post-mortem punishment of certain offences against the gods is in my opinion referred to in the *Iliad*,[10] and is undoubtedly described in the *Odyssey;* while Eleusis was already promising its initiates favoured treatment in the afterlife as far back as we can trace its teaching, i.e., probably in the seventh century.[11] No one, I suppose, now believes that the "great sinners" in the *Odyssey* are an "Orphic interpolation,"[12] or that the Eleusinian promises were the result of an "Orphic reform." In Aeschylus, again, the post-mortem punishment of certain offenders is so intimately tied up with the traditional "unwritten laws" and the traditional functions of Erinys and Alastor that I feel great hesitation about pulling the structure to pieces to label one element in it "Orphic."[13] These are special cases, but the idea was there; it looks as if all that the new movement did was to generalise it. And in the new formulation we may sometimes recognise echoes of things that are very old. When Pindar, for example, consoles a bereaved client with a description of the happy afterlife, he assures him that there will be horses and draught-boards in Heaven.[14] That is no new promise: there were horses on Patroclus' funeral pyre, and draught-boards in the tombs of Mycenaean kings. The furniture of Heaven has altered little with the centuries; it remains an idealised replica of the only world we know.

Nor, finally, did the contribution of the new movement consist in equating the *psyche* or "soul" with the personality of the living man. That had already been done, apparently first in Ionia. Homer, indeed, ascribes to the *psyche* no function in the living man, except to leave him; its "esse" appears to be "superesse" and nothing more. But Anacreon can say to his beloved, "You are the master of my *psyche*"; Semonides can talk of "giving his *psyche* a good time"; a sixth-century epitaph from Eretria can complain that the sailor's calling "gives few satisfactions to the *psyche*."[15] Here the *psyche* is the living self, and, more specifically, the appetitive self; it has taken over the functions of Homeric *thumos*, not those of Homeric *noos*. Between *psyche* in this sense and *sōma* (body) there is no fundamental antagonism; *psyche* is just the mental correlate of *soma*. In Attic Greek, both terms can mean "life": the Athenians said indifferently ἀγωνίζεσθαι περὶ τῆς ψυχῆς or περὶ τοῦ σώματος. And in suitable contexts each can mean "person":[16] thus Sophocles can make Oedipus refer to himself in one passage as "my *psyche*," in another as "my *soma*"; in both places he could have said "I."[17] Even the Homeric distinction between corpse and ghost is blurred: not only does an early Attic inscription talk of the *psyche* dying, but Pindar, more surprisingly, can speak of Hades with his wand conducting to "the hollow city" the *somata* of those who die—the corpse and the ghost have reverted here to their old consubstantiality.[18] I think we must admit that the psychological vocabulary of the ordinary man was in the fifth century in a state of great confusion, as indeed it usually is.

But from this confusion one fact emerges which is of importance for our enquiry. It was demonstrated by Burnet in his famous lecture on "The Socratic Doctrine of the Soul,"[19] and for that reason need not detain us long. In fifth-century Attic writers, as in their Ionian predecessors, the "self" which is denoted by the word *psyche* is normally the emotional rather than the rational self. The *psyche* is spoken of as the seat of courage, of passion, of pity, of anxiety, of animal appetite, but before Plato seldom if ever as the seat of reason; its range is broadly that of the Homeric *thumos*. When Sophocles speaks of testing ψυχήν τε καὶ φρόνημα καὶ γνώμην,[20] he is arranging the elements of character on a scale that runs from the emotional (*psyche*) to the intellectual (*gnōmē*) through a middle term, *phrŏnēma*, which by usage involves both. Burnet's further contention that the *psyche* "remains something mysterious and uncanny, quite apart from our normal consciousness," is, as a generalisation, much more open to dispute. We may notice, however, that the *psyche* appears on occasion as the organ of conscience, and is credited with a kind of nonrational intuition.[21] A child can apprehend something in its *psyche* without knowing it intellectually.[22] Helenus has a "divine *psyche*" not because he is cleverer or more virtuous than other men, but because he is a seer.[23] The *psyche* is imagined as dwelling somewhere in the depths of the organism,[24] and out of these depths it can speak to its owner with a voice of its own.[25] In most of these respects it is again a successor to the Homeric *thumos*.

Whether it be true or not that on the lips of an ordinary fifth-century Athenian the word *psyche* had or might have a faint flavour of the uncanny, what it did not have was any flavour of puritanism or any suggestion of metaphysical status.[26] The "soul" was no reluctant prisoner of the body; it was the life or spirit of the body,[27] and perfectly at home there. It was here that the new religious pattern made its fateful contribution: by crediting man with an occult self of divine origin, and thus setting soul and body at odds, it introduced into European culture a new interpretation of human existence, the interpretation we call puritanical. Where did this notion come from? Ever since Rohde called it "a drop of alien blood in the veins of the Greeks,"[28] scholars have been scanning the horizon for the source of the alien drop. Most of them have looked eastward, to Asia Minor or beyond.[29] Personally, I should be inclined to begin my search in a different quarter.

The passages from Pindar and Xenophon with which we started suggest that one source of the puritan antithesis might be the observation that "psychic" and bodily activity vary inversely: the *psyche* is most active when the body is asleep or, as Aristotle added, when it lies at the point of death. This is what I mean by calling it an "occult" self. Now a belief of this kind is an essential element of the shamanistic culture which still exists in Siberia, and has left traces of its past existence over a very wide area, extending in a huge arc from Scandinavia across the Eurasian land-mass as far as Indonesia;[30] the vast extent of its diffusion is evidence of its high antiquity. A shaman may be described as a psychically unstable person who has received a call to the religious life. As a result of his call he undergoes a period of rigorous training, which commonly involves solitude and fasting, and may involve a psychological change of sex. From this religious "retreat" he emerges with the power, real or assumed,[31] of passing at will into a state of mental dissociation. In that condition he is not thought, like the Pythia or like a modern medium, to be possessed by an alien spirit; but his own soul is thought to leave its body and travel to distant parts, most often to the spirit world. A shaman may in fact be seen simultaneously in different places; he has the power of bilocation. From these experiences, narrated by him in extempore song, he derives the skill in divination, religious poetry, and magical medicine which makes him socially important. He becomes the repository of a supernormal wisdom.

Now in Scythia, and probably also in Thrace, the Greeks had come into contact with peoples who, as the Swiss scholar Meuli has shown, were influenced by this shamanistic culture. It will suffice to refer on this point to his important article in *Hermes*, 1935. Meuli has there further suggested that the fruits of this contact are to be seen in the appearance, late in the Archaic Age, of a series of ἰατρομάντεις, seers, magical healers, and religious teachers, some of whom are linked in Greek tradition with the North, and all of whom exhibit shamanistic traits.[32] Out of the North came Abaris, riding, it was said, upon[33] an arrow, as souls, it appears, still do in Siberia.[34] So advanced was he in the art of fasting that he had learned to dispense altogether with human food.[35] He banished pestilences, predicted earthquakes, composed religious poems, and taught the worship of his northern god, whom the Greeks called the Hyperborean Apollo.[36] Into the North, at the bidding of the same Apollo, went Aristeas, a Greek from the Sea of Marmora, and returned to tell his strange experiences in a poem that may have been modelled on the psychic excursions of northern shamans. Whether Aristeas' journey was made in the flesh or in the spirit is not altogether clear; but in any case, as Alföldi has shown, his one-eyed Arimaspians and his treasure-guarding griffons are genuine creatures of Central Asiatic folk-lore.[37] Tradition further credited him with the shamanistic powers of trance and bilocation. His soul, in the form of a bird,[38] could leave his body at will; he died, or fell entranced, at home, yet was seen at Cyzicus; many years later he appeared again at Metapontum in the Far West. The same gift was possessed by another Asiatic Greek, Hermotimus of Clazomenae, whose soul travelled far and wide, observing events in distant places, while his body lay inanimate at home. Such tales of disappearing and reappearing shamans were sufficiently familiar at Athens for Sophocles to refer to them in the *Electra* without any need to mention names.[39]

Of these men virtually nothing is left but a legend, though the pattern of the legend may be significant. The pattern is repeated in some of the tales about Epimenides, the Cretan seer, who purified Athens of the dangerous uncleanness caused by a violation of the right of sanctuary. But since Diels provided him with a fixed date[40] and five pages of fragments, Epimenides has begun to look quite like a person—even though all his fragments were composed, in Diels's opinion, by other people, including the one quoted in the Epistle to Titus. Epimenides came from Cnossos, and to that fact he may perhaps have owed something of his great prestige: a man who had grown up in the shadow of the Palace of Minos might well lay claim to a more ancient wisdom, especially after he had slept for fifty-seven years in the cave of the Cretan mystery-god.[41] Nevertheless, tradition assimilated him to the type of a northern shaman. He too was an expert in psychic excursion; and, like Abaris, he was a great faster, living exclusively on a vegetable preparation whose secret he had learned from the Nymphs and which he was accustomed to store, for reasons best known to himself, in an ox's hoof.[42] Another singular feature of his legend is that after his death his body was observed to be covered with tattoo-marks.[43] Singular, because the Greeks used the tattoo-needle only to brand slaves. It may have been a sign of his dedication as *servus dei;* but in any case to an archaic Greek it would probably suggest Thrace, where all the best people were tattooed, and in particular the shamans.[44] As for the Long Sleep, that is of course a widespread folktale;[45] Rip Van Winkle was no shaman. But its place at the beginning of the Epimenides-saga suggests that the Greeks had heard of the long "retreat" which is the shaman's novitiate and is sometimes largely spent in a condition of sleep or trance.[46]

From all this it seems reasonable to conclude that the opening of the Black Sea to Greek trade and colonisation in the seventh century, which introduced the Greeks for the first time[47] to a culture based on shamanism, at any rate enriched with some remarkable new traits the traditional Greek picture of the Man of God, the θεῖος ἀνήρ. These new elements were, I think, acceptable to the Greek mind because they answered to the needs of the time, as Dionysiac religion had done earlier. Religious experience of the shamanistic type is individual, not collective; but it appealed to the growing individualism of an age for which the collective ecstasies of Dionysus were no longer wholly sufficient. And it is a reasonable further guess that these new traits had some influence on the new and revolutionary conception of the relation between body and soul which appears at the end of the Archaic Age.[48]

One remembers that in Clearchus' dialogue *On Sleep* what convinced Aristotle "that the soul is detachable from the body" was precisely an experiment in psychic excursion.[49] That, however, was a work of fiction, and relatively late at that. Whether any of the Men of God whom I have so far mentioned drew such general theoretical conclusions from his personal experiences, we are entitled to doubt. Aristotle, indeed, thought there were grounds for believing that Hermotimus anticipated his more famous townsman Anaxagoras in his doctrine of *nous*; but this may mean only, as Diels suggested, that for evidence of the separability of *nous* Anaxagoras appealed to the experiences of the old local shaman.[50] Epimenides, again, is said to have claimed that he was a reincarnation of Aeacus and had lived many times on earth[51] (which would explain Aristotle's statement that his divination was concerned not with the future but with the unknown past).[52] Diels thought that this tradition must have an Orphic source; he attributed it to an Orphic poem forged in Epimenides' name by Onomacritus or one of his friends.[53] For a reason which will appear presently, I am less certain about this than Diels was; but whatever view one takes, it would be unwise to build very much on it.

There is, however, another and a greater Greek shaman who undoubtedly drew theoretical consequences and undoubtedly believed in rebirth. I mean Pythagoras. We need not suppose him to have claimed precisely that series of previous incarnations which was attributed to him by Heraclides Ponticus;[54] but there is no good reason to question the statements of our authorities that Pythagoras is the man to whom Empedocles attributed a wisdom gathered in ten or twenty human lives, and that he is also the man whom Xenophanes mocked for believing that a human soul could dwell in a dog.[55] How did Pythagoras come by these opinions? The usual answer is "from Orphic teaching," which, if it is true, only pushes the question one step further back. But it is, I think, possible that he was not directly dependent on any "Orphic" source in this cardinal matter; that both he and Epimenides before him had heard of the northern belief that the "soul" or "guardian spirit" of a former shaman may enter into a living shaman to reinforce his power and knowledge.[56] This need not involve any *general* doctrine of transmigration, and it is noteworthy that Epimenides is credited with no such general doctrine; he merely claimed that he himself had lived before, and was identical with Aeacus, an ancient Man of God.[57] Similarly Pythagoras is represented as claiming identity with the former shaman Hermotimus;[58] but it would appear that Pythagoras extended the doctrine a good deal beyond these original narrow limits. Perhaps that was his personal contribution; in view of his enormous prestige we must surely credit him with some power of creative thinking.

We know at any rate that Pythagoras founded a kind of religious order, a community of men and women[59] whose rule of life was determined by the expectation of lives to come. Possibly there were precedents of a sort even for that: we may remember the Thracian Zalmoxis in Herodotus, who assembled "the best of the citizens" and announced to them, *not* that the human soul is immortal, but that *they and their descendants* were going to live for ever—they were apparently chosen persons, a sort of spiritual *élite*.[60] That there was some analogy between Zalmoxis and Pythagoras must have struck the Greek settlers in Thrace, from whom Herodotus heard the story, for they made Zalmoxis into Pythagoras' slave. That was absurd, as Herodotus saw: the real Zalmoxis was a daemon, possibly a heroised shaman of the distant past.[61] But the analogy was not so absurd: did not Pythagoras promise his followers that they should live again, and become at last daemons or even gods?[62] Later tradition brought Pythagoras into contact with the other northerner, Abaris; credited him with the usual shamanistic powers of prophecy, bilocation, and magical healing; and told of his initiation in Pieria, his visit to the spirit world, and his mysterious identity with the "Hyperborean Apollo."[63] Some of that may be late, but the beginnings of the Pythagoras legend go back to the fifth century at least,[64] and I

am willing to believe that Pythagoras himself did a good deal to
set it going.

I am the more willing to believe it because we can see this
actually happening in the case of Empedocles, whose legend is
largely composed of embroideries upon claims which he himself makes in his poems. Little more than a century after his
death, stories were already in circulation which told how he had
stayed the winds by his magic, how he had restored to life a
woman who no longer breathed, and how he then vanished
bodily from this mortal world and became a god.[65] And by
good fortune we know the ultimate source of these stories: we
have Empedocles' own words, in which he claims that he can
teach his pupils to stay the winds and revive the dead, and that
he is himself, or is thought to be, a god made flesh—ἐγὼ δ' ὑμῖν
θεὸς ἄμβροτος, οὐκέτι θνητός.[66] Empedocles is thus in a sense the
creator of his own legend; and if we can trust his description of
the crowds who came to him in search of occult knowledge or
magical healing, its beginnings date back to his lifetime.[67] In
face of that, it seems to me rash to assume that the legends
of Pythagoras and Epimenides have no roots at all in genuine
tradition, but were deliberately invented from first to last by
the romancers of a later age.

Be that as it may, the fragments of Empedocles are the one
first-hand source from which we can still form some notion of
what a Greek shaman was really like; he is the last belated
example of a species which with his death became extinct in the
Greek world, though it still flourishes elsewhere. Scholars have
been astonished that a man capable of the acute observation
and constructive thought which appear in Empedocles' poem
On Nature should also have written the Purifications and represented himself as a divine magician. Some of them have tried to
explain it by saying that the two poems must belong to different periods of Empedocles' life: either he started as a magician,
lost his nerve, and took to natural science; or else, as others
maintain, he started as a scientist, was converted later to
"Orphism" or Pythagoreanism, and in the lonely exile of his

declining years comforted himself with delusions of grandeur—
he was a god, and would return one day not to Acragas but to
Heaven.[68] The trouble about these explanations is that they
do not really work. The fragment in which Empedocles claims
the power to stay the winds, cause or prevent rain, and revive
the dead, appears to belong, not to the *Purifications*, but to
the poem *On Nature*. So does fragment 23, in which the poet
bids his pupil listen to "the word of a god" (I find it hard to
believe that this refers merely to the conventional inspiration
of the Muse).[69] So does fragment 15, which seems to contrast
"what people call life" with a more real existence before birth
and after death.[70] All this is discouraging for any attempt to
explain Empedocles' inconsistencies on "genetic" lines. Nor is
it easy to accept Jaeger's recent description of him as "a new
synthesising type of philosophical personality,"[71] since any
attempt to synthesise his religious and his scientific opinions is
precisely what we miss in him. If I am right, Empedocles
represents not a new but a very old type of personality, the
shaman who combines the still undifferentiated functions of
magician and naturalist, poet and philosopher, preacher,
healer, and public counsellor.[72] After him these functions fell
apart; philosophers henceforth were to be neither poets nor
magicians; indeed, such a man was already an anachronism in
the fifth century. But men like Epimenides and Pythagoras[73]
may well have exercised all the functions I have named. It
was not a question of "synthesising" these wide domains of
practical and theoretical knowledge; in their quality as Men of
God they practised with confidence in all of them; the "syn-
thesis" was personal, not logical.

What I have thus far suggested is a tentative line of spiritual
descent which starts in Scythia, crosses the Hellespont into
Asiatic Greece, is perhaps combined with some remnants of
Minoan tradition surviving in Crete, emigrates to the Far
West with Pythagoras, and has its last outstanding representative in the Sicilian Empedocles. These men diffused the
belief in a detachable soul or self, which by suitable tech-

niques can be withdrawn from the body even during life, a self which is older than the body and will outlast it. But at this point an inevitable question presents itself: how is this development related to the mythological person named Orpheus and to the theology known as Orphic? And I must attempt a short answer.

About Orpheus himself I can make a guess, at the risk of being called a panshamanist. Orpheus' home is in Thrace, and in Thrace he is the worshipper or companion of a god whom the Greeks identified with Apollo.[74] He combines the professions of poet, magician, religious teacher, and oracle-giver. Like certain legendary shamans in Siberia,[75] he can by his music summon birds and beasts to listen to him. Like shamans everywhere, he pays a visit to the underworld, and his motive is one very common among shamans[76]—to recover a stolen soul. Finally, his magical self lives on as a singing head, which continues to give oracles for many years after his death.[77] That too suggests the North: such mantic heads appear in Norse mythology and in Irish tradition.[78] I conclude that Orpheus is a Thracian figure of much the same kind as Zalmoxis—a mythical shaman or prototype of shamans.

Orpheus, however, is one thing, Orphism quite another. But I must confess that I know very little about early Orphism, and the more I read about it the more my knowledge diminishes. Twenty years ago, I could have said quite a lot about it (we all could at that time). Since then, I have lost a great deal of knowledge; for this loss I am indebted to Wilamowitz, Festugière, Thomas, and not least to a distinguished member of the University of California, Professor Linforth.[79] Let me illustrate my present ignorance by listing a few of the things I once knew.

There was a time when I knew:

That there was an Orphic sect or community in the Classical Age;[80]

That an Orphic "Theogony" was read by Empedocles[81] and Euripides,[82] and parodied by Aristophanes in the *Birds*;[83]

That the poem of which fragments are inscribed on the gold

plates found at Thurii and elsewhere is an Orphic apocalypse;[84]

That Plato took the details of his myths about the Other World from such an Orphic apocalypse;[85]

That the Hippolytus of Euripides is an Orphic figure;[86]

That σῶμα-σῆμα ("Body equals tomb") is an Orphic doctrine.[87]

When I say that I no longer possess these items of information, I do not intend to assert that all of them are false. The last two I feel pretty sure are false: we really must not turn a bloodstained huntsman into an Orphic figure, or call "Orphic" a doctrine that Plato plainly denies to be Orphic. But some of the others may very well happen to be true. All I mean is that I cannot at present convince myself of their truth; and that until I can, the edifice reared by an ingenious scholarship upon these foundations remains for me a house of dreams—I am tempted to call it the unconscious projection upon the screen of antiquity of certain unsatisfied religious longings characteristic of the late nineteenth and early twentieth centuries.[88]

If, then, I decide provisionally to dispense with these cornerstones, and to follow instead the cautious rules of architecture enunciated by Festugière and Linforth,[89] how much of the fabric still stands? Not, I fear, very much, unless I am prepared to patch it with material derived from the fantastic theogonies that Proclus and Damascius read at a time when Pythagoras had been in his grave for nearly a millennium. And that I dare not do, save in the very rare instances where both the antiquity of the material and its Orphic origin are independently guaranteed.[90] I shall quote later what I believe to be such an instance, though the question is a controversial one. But let me first muster such uncontroverted knowledge about Orphism as I still possess, and see what it includes that is germane to the subject of this chapter. I still know that in the fifth and fourth centuries there were in circulation a number of pseudonymous religious poems, which were conventionally ascribed to the mythical Orpheus, but which the critically minded knew or guessed to be of much more recent origin.[91]

Their authorship may have been very diverse, and I have no reason to suppose that they preached any uniform or systematic doctrine; Plato's word for them, βίβλων ὅμαδον, "a hubbub of books,"[92] rather suggests the contrary. Of their contents I know very little. But I do know on good authority that three things were taught in some at least of them, namely, that the body is the prisonhouse of the soul; that vegetarianism is an essential rule of life; and that the unpleasant consequences of sin, both in this world and in the next, can be washed away by ritual means.[93] That they taught the most famous of so-called "Orphic" doctrines, the transmigration of souls, is not, as it happens, directly attested by anyone in the Classical Age; but it may, I think, be inferred without undue rashness from the conception of the body as a prison where the soul is punished for its past sins.[94] Even with this addition, the sum total is not extensive. And it gives me no sure basis for distinguishing an "Orphic" from a "Pythagorean" psychology; for Pythagoreans too are said to have avoided meat, practised catharsis, and viewed the body as a prison,[95] and Pythagoras himself, as we have seen, had experienced transmigration. There cannot in fact have been any very clear-cut distinction between the Orphic teaching, at any rate in some of its forms, and Pythagoreanism; for Ion of Chios, a good fifth-century authority, thought that Pythagoras had composed poems under the name of Orpheus, and Epigenes, who was a specialist on the subject, attributed four "Orphic" poems to individual Pythagoreans.[96] Whether there were any Orphic poems in existence before the time of Pythagoras, and if there were, whether they taught transmigration, remains entirely uncertain. I shall accordingly use the term "Puritan psychology" to cover both early Orphic and early Pythagorean beliefs about the soul.

We have seen—or I hope we have seen—how contact with shamanistic beliefs and practices might suggest to a thoughtful people like the Greeks the rudiments of such a psychology: how the notion of psychic excursion in sleep or trance might sharpen the soul-body antithesis; how the shamanistic "retreat" might provide the model for a deliberate *askēsis*, a conscious training of the psychic powers through abstinence and spiritual exercises; how tales of vanishing and reappearing shamans might encourage the belief in an indestructible magical or daemonic self; and how the migration of the magical power or spirit from dead shamans to living ones might be generalised as a doctrine of reincarnation.[97] But I must emphasise that these are only "mights," logical or psychological possibilities. If they were actualised by certain Greeks, that must be because they were felt, in Rohde's phrase, "to meet Greek spiritual needs."[98] And if we consider the situation at the end of the Archaic Age, as I described it in my second chapter, I think we shall see that they did meet certain needs, logical, moral, and psychological.

Professor Nilsson thinks that the doctrine of rebirth is a product of "pure logic," and that the Greeks invented it because they were "born logicians."[99] And we may agree with him that once people accepted the notion that man has a "soul" distinct from his body, it was natural to ask where this "soul" came from, and natural to answer that it came from the great reservoir of souls in Hades. There are in fact indications of such a line of argument in Heraclitus as well as in the *Phaedo*.[100] I doubt, however, if religious beliefs are often adopted, even by philosophers, on grounds of pure logic—logic is at best *ancilla fidei*. And this particular belief has found favour with many peoples who are by no means born logicians.[101] I am inclined to attach more importance to considerations of a different type.

Morally, reincarnation offered a more satisfactory solution to the Late Archaic problem of divine justice than did inherited guilt or post-mortem punishment in another world. With the growing emancipation of the individual from the old family solidarity, his increasing rights as a judicial "person," the notion of a vicarious payment for another's fault began to be unacceptable. When once human law had recognised that a man is responsible for his own acts only, divine law must sooner or later do likewise. As for post-mortem punishment, that explained well enough why the gods appeared to tolerate the worldly success of the wicked, and the new teaching in fact exploited it to the full, using the device of the "underworld journey" to make the horrors of Hell real and vivid to the imagination.[102] But the post-mortem punishment did not explain why the gods tolerated so much human suffering, and in particular the unmerited suffering of the innocent. Reincarnation did. On that view, no human soul was innocent:[103] all were paying, in various degrees, for crimes of varying atrocity committed in former lives. And all that squalid mass of suffering, whether in this world or in another, was but a part of the soul's long education—an education that would culminate at last in its release from the cycle of birth and return to its divine origin. Only in this way, and on this cosmic time-scale, could justice in its full archaic sense—the justice of the law that "the Doer shall suffer"—be completely realised for every soul.

Plato knows this moral interpretation of rebirth as "a myth or doctrine or what you will" which was taught by "old-time priests."[104] It is certainly an old interpretation, but not, I think, the oldest. To the Siberian shaman, the experience of past lives is not a source of guilt, but an enhancement of power, and that I take to be the original Greek point of view; it was such an enhancement of power that Empedocles perceived in Pythagoras, and that Epimenides, it would seem, had claimed earlier. It was only when rebirth was attributed to *all* human souls that it became a burden instead of a privilege, and was used to explain the inequalities of our earthly portion and to show that, in the words of a Pythagorean poet, man's sufferings are self-incurred ($ai\theta ai\rho \epsilon \tau a$).[105]

Beneath this demand for a solution to what we call "the problem of evil" we may believe that there lay a deeper psychological need—the need to rationalise those unexplained feelings of guilt which, as we saw earlier, were prevalent in the Archaic Age.[106] Men were, I suppose, dimly conscious—and on Freud's view, rightly conscious—that such feelings had their roots in a submerged and long-forgotten past experience. What more natural than to interpret that intuition (which is in fact, according to Freud, a faint awareness of infantile traumata) as a faint awareness of sin committed in a former life? Here we have perhaps stumbled on the psychological source of the peculiar importance attached in the Pythagorean school to "recollection"—not in the Platonic sense of recalling a world of disembodied Forms once seen by the disembodied soul, but in the more primitive sense of training the memory to recall the deeds and sufferings of a previous life on earth.[107]

That, however, is speculation. What is certain is that these beliefs promoted in their adherents a horror of the body and a revulsion against the life of the senses which were quite new in Greece. Any guilt-culture will, I suppose, provide a soil favourable to the growth of puritanism, since it creates an unconscious need for self-punishment which puritanism gratifies. But in Greece it was, apparently, the impact of shamanistic beliefs which set the process going. By Greek minds these beliefs were reinterpreted in a moral sense; and when that was done, the world of bodily experience inevitably appeared as a place of darkness and penance, the flesh became an "alien tunic." "Pleasure," says the old Pythagorean catechism, "is in all circumstances bad; for we came here to be punished and we ought to be punished."[108] In that form of the doctrine which Plato attributes to the Orphic school, the body was pictured as the soul's prison, in which the gods keep it locked up until it has purged its guilt. In the other form mentioned by Plato, puritanism found an even more violent expression: the body was conceived as a tomb wherein the *psyche* lies dead, awaiting its resurrection into true life, which is life without the body. This form seems to be traceable as far back as Heraclitus, who perhaps used it to illustrate his eternal roundabout of opposites, the "Way Up and Down."[109]

To people who equated the *psyche* with the empirical personality, as the fifth century mostly did, such an assertion made no sense at all; it was a fantastic paradox, whose comic possibilities did not escape the eye of Aristophanes.[110] Nor does it make much better sense if we equate "soul" with reason. I should suppose that for people who took it seriously what lay "dead" within the body was neither the reason nor the empirical man, but an "occult" self, Pindar's "image of life," which is indestructible but can function only in the exceptional conditions of sleep or trance. That man has two "souls," one of divine, the other of earthly origin, was already taught (if our late authority can be trusted) by Pherecydes of Syros. And it is significant that Empedocles, on whom our knowledge of early Greek puritanism chiefly depends, avoids applying the term *psyche* to the indestructible self.[111] He appears to have thought of the *psyche* as being the vital warmth which at death is reabsorbed in the fiery element from which it came (that was a fairly common fifth-century view).[112] The occult self which persisted through successive incarnations he called, not *"psyche,"* but "daemon." This daemon has, apparently, nothing to do with perception or thought, which Empedocles held to be mechanically determined; the function of the daemon is to be the carrier of man's potential divinity[113] and actual guilt. It is nearer in some ways to the indwelling spirit which the shaman inherits from other shamans than it is to the rational "soul" in which Socrates believed; but it has been moralised as a guilt-carrier, and the world of the senses has become the Hades in which it suffers torment.[114] That torment Empedocles has described in some of the strangest and most moving religious poetry which has come down to us from antiquity.[115]

The complementary aspect of the doctrine was its teaching on the subject of catharsis—the means whereby the occult self might be advanced on the ladder of being, and its eventual liberation hastened. To judge from its title, this was the central theme of Empedocles' poem, though the parts which dealt with it are mostly lost. The notion of catharsis was no novelty; as we saw earlier,[116] it was a major preoccupation of religious minds throughout the Archaic Age. But in the new pattern of belief it acquired a new content and a new urgency: man must be cleansed not only from specific pollutions, but, so far as might be, from all taint of carnality—that was the condition of his redemption. "From the company of the pure I come, pure Queen of those below"—thus the soul speaks to Persephone in the poem of the gold plates.[117] Purity, rather than justice, has become the cardinal means to salvation. And since it is a magical, not a rational self that has to be cleansed, the techniques of catharsis are not rational but magical. They might consist solely in ritual, as in the Orphic books that Plato denounced for their demoralising effect.[118] Or they might use the incantatory power of music, as in the catharsis attributed to the Pythagoreans, which seems to have developed from primitive charms (ἐπῳδαί).[119] Or they might also involve an "askesis," the practice of a special way of life.

We have seen that the need for some such askesis was implicit from the first in the shamanistic tradition. But the archaic guilt-culture gave it a peculiar direction. The vegetarianism which is the central feature of Orphic and of some Pythagorean askesis is usually treated simply as a corollary to transmigration: the beast you kill for food may be the dwelling-place of a human soul or self. That is how Empedocles explained it. But he is not quite logical: he ought to have felt the same revulsion against eating vegetables, since he believed that his own occult self had once inhabited a bush.[120] Behind his imperfect rationalisation there lies, I suspect, something older—the ancient horror of spilt blood. In scrupulous minds the fear of that pollution may well have extended its domain, as such fears will, until it embraced all shedding of blood, animal as well as human. As Aristophanes tells us, the rule of Orpheus was φόνων ἀπέχεσθαι, "shed no *blood*"; and Pythagoras is said to have avoided contact with butchers and huntsmen—presumably because they were not only wicked, but dangerously unclean, carriers of an infectious pollution.[121] Besides food taboos, the Pythagorean Society seems to have imposed other austerities on its members, such as a rule of silence for novices, and certain sexual restrictions.[122] But it was perhaps only Empedocles who took the final, logical step of the Manichee; I see no reason to dis-

believe the statement that he denounced marriage and all sex
relations,[123] though the verses in which he did so are not
actually preserved. If the tradition is right on this point, puritanism not only originated in Greece, but was carried by a
Greek mind to its extreme theoretical limit.

One question remains. What is the original root of all this
wickedness? How comes it that a divine self sins and suffers
in mortal bodies? As a Pythagorean poet phrased it, "Whence
came mankind, and whence became so evil?"[124] To this un-
escapable question Orphic poetry, at any rate later Orphic
poetry, provided a mythological answer. It all began with the
wicked Titans, who trapped the infant Dionysus, tore him to
bits, boiled him, roasted him, ate him, and were themselves
immediately burned up by a thunderbolt from Zeus; from the
smoke of their remains sprang the human race, who thus in-
herit the horrid tendencies of the Titans, tempered by a tiny
portion of divine soul-stuff, which is the substance of the god
Dionysus still working in them as an occult self. Pausanias says
that this story—or rather, the Titans' part in it—was invented by Onomacritus in the sixth century (he implies that
the rending of Dionysus is older).[125] And everyone believed
Pausanias until Wilamowitz, finding no clear and certain allusion to the Titan myth in any writer earlier than the third
century B.C., inferred it to be a Hellenistic invention.[126] The
inference has been accepted by one or two scholars whose
judgement I respect,[127] and it is with great hesitation that I
differ from them and from Wilamowitz. There are indeed
grounds for discounting Pausanias' statements about Onomacritus;[128] yet several considerations combine to persuade me
that the myth is nevertheless old. The first is its archaic
character: it is founded on the ancient Dionysiac ritual of
Sparagmos and *Omophagia*,[129] and it implies the archaic belief
in inherited guilt, which in the Hellenistic Age had begun to be
a discredited superstition.[130] The second is the Pindar quotation
in Plato's *Meno*, where "the penalty of an ancient grief" is
most naturally explained as referring to human responsibility

for the slaying of Dionysus.[131] Thirdly, in one passage of the *Laws* Plato refers to people who "show off the old Titan nature,"[132] and in another to sacrilegious impulses which are "neither of man nor of god" but arise "from old misdeeds unpurgeable by man."[133] And fourthly, we are told that Plato's pupil Xenocrates somehow connected the notion of the body as a "prison" with Dionysus and the Titans.[134] Individually, these apparent references to the myth can at a pinch be explained away; but taking them together, I find it hard to resist the conclusion that the complete story was known to Plato and his public.[135]

If that is so, ancient like modern puritanism had its doctrine of Original Sin, which explained the universality of guilt-feelings. True, the physical transmission of guilt by bodily inheritance was strictly inconsistent with the view which made the persistent occult self its carrier. But that need not greatly surprise us. The Indian Upanishads similarly managed to combine the old belief in hereditary pollution with the newer doctrine of reincarnation;[136] and Christian theology finds it possible to reconcile the sinful inheritance of Adam with individual moral responsibility. The Titan myth neatly explained to the Greek puritan why he felt himself to be at once a god and a criminal; the "Apolline" sentiment of remoteness from the divine and the "Dionysiac" sentiment of identity with it were both of them accounted for and both of them justified. That was something that went deeper than any logic.

NOTES TO CHAPTER V

[1] Pindar, fr. 116 B. (131 S.). Rohde rightly emphasised the importance of this fragment (*Psyche*, 415), though he was wrong in reading back some of its ideas into Homer (*ibid.*, 7); cf. Jaeger, *Theology of the Early Greek Philosophers*, 75 f.—The view that the experient subject in dreams' is an unchanging "deeper" self is naturally suggested to the mind by the way in which a long dead

and even a forgotten past can be reinstated in sleep. As a modern writer puts it, "In dreams not only are we free of the usual limitations of time and space, not only do we return to our past and probably go forward to our future, but the self that apparently experiences these strange adventures is *a more essential self, of no particular age*" (J. B. Priestley, *Johnson over Jordan*).

² Xen. *Cyrop.* 8.7.21.

³ Plato, *Rep.* 571D ff.: when the λογιστικόν in sleep is αὐτὸ καθ' αὐτὸ μόνον καθαρόν (which is not always the case), it can perceive something it did not know before, whether in the past, the present, or the future, and τῆς ἀληθείας ἐν τῷ τοιούτῳ μάλιστα ἅπτεται. Aristotle, fr. 10 = Sext. Emp. *adv. Phys.* 1.21: ὅταν γὰρ ἐν τῷ ὑπνοῦν καθ' αὑτὴν γίγνεται ἡ ψυχή, τότε τὴν ἴδιον ἀπολαβοῦσα φύσιν προμαντεύεταί τε καὶ προαγορεύει τὰ μέλλοντα. τοιαύτη δέ ἐστι καὶ ἐν τῷ κατὰ τὸν θάνατον χωρίζεσθαι τῶν σωμάτων, cf. Jaeger, *Aristotle*, 162 f. See also Hipp. περὶ διαίτης, 4.86, quoted above, chap. iv, n. 104; and Aesch. *Eum.* 104 f., where the poet has combined the old "objective" dream with the idea that the mind itself is gifted with prescience in sleep, which seems to derive from a different pattern of belief. For the importance attached by the Pythagoreans to dreams cf. Cic. *div.* 1.62; Plut. *gen. Socr.* 585E; Diog. L. 8.24.

⁴ "The question whether one's conscious personality survives after death has been answered by almost all races of men in the affirmative. On this point sceptical or agnostic peoples are nearly, if not wholly, unknown." Frazer, *The Belief in Immortality*, I, 33.

⁵ The archaeological evidence is conveniently assembled and collated in Joseph Wiesner's *Grab und Jenseits* (1938), though doubt may be felt about the validity of some of the inferences he draws from it.

⁶ See Lévy-Bruhl, *The "Soul" of the Primitive*, 202 f., 238 ff., and *L'Exp. mystique*, 151 ff. That the belief in survival was not originally arrived at by any process of logical thought (as Tylor and Frazer had assumed), but rather by a refusal to think, the unconscious turning of a blind eye to unwelcome evidence, is now held by many anthropologists: cf. e.g., Elliot Smith, *The Evolution of the Dragon*, 145 f.; Malinowski, *Magic, Science and Religion*, 32 f.; K. Meuli, "Griech. Opferbräuche," in *Phyllobolia für Peter von der Mühll* (1946); Nilsson in *Harv. Theol. Rev.* 42 (1949) 85 f.

⁷ *Il.* 23.103 f.; *Od.* 11.216–224. The significance of these passages, with their implication of novelty, has been rightly stressed by Zielinski ("La Guerre à l'outretombe," in *Mélanges Bidez*, II. 1021 ff., 1934), though he went a little far in seeing the Homeric

poets as religious reformers comparable in earnestness with the Hebrew prophets.

8 Not only object-offerings but actual feeding-tubes are found even in cremation burials (Nock, *Harv. Theol Rev.* 25 [1932] 332). At Olynthus, where nearly 600 interments of the sixth to the fourth century B.C. have been examined, object-offerings are, in fact, commonest in cremation burials (D. M. Robinson, *Excavations at Olynthus*, XI.176). This must mean one of two things: either that cremation was after all not intended, as Rohde thought, to divorce ghost from corpse by abolishing the latter; or else that the old unreasoning habits of tendance were too deeply rooted to be disturbed by any such measures. Meuli, *loc. cit.*, points out that in Tertullian's time people continued to feed the cremated dead (*carn. resurr.* 1, [vulgus] defunctos atrocissime exurit, quos post modum gulosissime nutrit); and that, despite the initial disapproval of the Church, the use of feeding-tubes has persisted in the Balkans almost down to our own day. Cf. also Lawson, *Mod. Gr. Folklore*, 528 ff., and on the whole question, Cumont, *Lux Perpetua*, 387 ff.

9 Plut. *Solon* 21; Cic. *de legg.* 2.64–66. Cf. also Plato's protest against wasteful funeral expenditure, *Laws* 959C, and the law of the Labyadae, which prohibits *inter alia* the dressing of the corpse in too expensive grave-clothes (Dittenberger, *Syll.*² II.438.134). But the phantasy of the corpse-ghost is of course only one of the feelings which find satisfaction in costly funerals (cf. Nock, *JRS* 38 [1948] 155).

10 *Il.* 3.278 f., 19.259 f. It is extremely unwise to impose eschatological consistency on Homer (or anyone else) at the cost of emendation, excision, or distorting the plain meaning of words. These oath-formulae of the *Iliad* preserve a belief which was older than Homer's neutral Hades (for such formulae archaise, they do not innovate) and had far greater vitality.

11 *H. Dem.* 480 ff. On the probable date of the Hymn (which excludes any likelihood of "Orphic" influence) see Allen and Halliday, *The Homeric Hymns*², 111 ff.

12 This was maintained by Wilamowitz in his rash youth (*Hom. Untersuchungen*, 199 ff.); but he recanted later (*Glaube*, II.200).

13 Aesch. *Eum.* 267 ff., 339 f.; *Suppl.* 414 ff. Cf. Wehrli, Λάθε βιώσας, 90. That in the Classical Age the fear of punishment after death was not confined to "Orphic" or Pythagorean circles, but might haunt any guilty conscience, seems to be implied by Democritus, frs. 199 and 297, and Plato, *Rep.* 330D.

[14] Pindar, fr. 114 B. (130 S.). For the horses cf. *Il.* 23.171 and Wiesner, *op. cit.*, 136³, 152¹¹, 160 etc.; for the πεσσοί, Wiesner, 146.

[15] Anacreon, fr. 4; Semonides of Amorgos, fr. 29.14 D. (= Simonides of Ceos, fr. 85 B.); *IG* XII.9.287 (Friedländer, *Epigrammata*, 79). Hipponax has a similar use of ψυχή, fr. 42 D. (43 B.).

[16] G. R. Hirzel, "Die Person," *Münch. Sitzb.* 1914, Abh. 10.

[17] Soph. *O.T.* 64 f., 643. But although each phrase could be replaced by the personal pronoun, they are not (as Hirzel suggested) interchangeable; σῶμα could not have been used at 64, nor ψυχή at 643.

[18] *IG* I².920 (= Friedländer, *Epigrammata*, 59), ψυχ[ή] ὄλετ' ἐ[ν δαΐ] (*ca.* 500 B.C.); cf. Eur. *Hel.* 52 f., ψυχαὶ δὲ πολλαὶ δι' ἐμέ... ἔθανον, and *Tro.* 1214 f., ψυχὴν σέθεν ἔκτεινε. Pindar, *Ol.* 9.33 ff.: οὐδ' Ἀΐδας ἀκινήταν ἔχε ῥάβδον, βρότεα σώμαθ' ᾇ κατάγει κοίλαν πρὸς ἄγυιαν θνᾳσκόντων (cf. Virg. *Geo.* 4.475 = *Aen.* 6.306).

[19] The Hertz Lecture, 1916, *Proc. Brit. Acad.* VII. L.-S., s.v. ψυχή, has failed to profit by Burnet's investigation. For tragedy, the lexicographical material is collected by Martha Assmann, *Mens et Animus*, I (Amsterdam, 1917).

[20] Soph. *Ant.* 176. Cf. 707 f., where ψυχή is contrasted with φρονεῖν, and Eur. *Alc.* 108.

[21] E.g., Antiphon, 5.93; Soph. *El.* 902 f.

[22] I am inclined to agree with Burnet that this must be the meaning of Eur. *Tro.* 1171 f.; it is hardly natural to construe σῇ ψυχῇ otherwise than with γνούς.

[23] Eur. *Hec.* 87.

[24] Cf. phrases like διὰ μυχῶν βλέπουσα ψυχή, Soph. *Phil.* 1013, and πρὸς ἄκρον μυελὸν ψυχῆς, Eur. *Hipp.* 255.

[25] Soph. *Ant.* 227.

[26] That the word ψυχή carried no puritanical associations is evident from phrases like ψυχῇ τῶν ἀγαθῶν χαριζόμενος (Sem. Amorg. 29.14), ψυχῇ διδόντες ἡδονὴν καθ' ἡμέραν (Aesch. *Pers.* 841), βορᾶς ψυχὴν ἐπλήρουν (Eur. *Ion* 1169). And how remote it was in common speech from religious or metaphysical implications is nicely shown by a passage from the devout Xenophon (if it be his): when he sets out to provide the uninventive with a list of suitable names for dogs, the very first name that occurs to him is Ψυχή (*Cyneg.* 7.5).

[27] Like θυμός in H. *Apoll.* 361 f., ψυχή is sometimes thought of as residing in the blood: Soph. *El.* 785 τοὐμὸν ἐκπίνουσ' ἀεὶ ψυχῆς ἄκρατον αἷμα, and Ar. *Nub.* 712 τὴν ψυχὴν ἐκπίνουσιν (οἱ κόρεις). This is popular usage, not philosophical speculation as in Empedocles, fr. 105. But the medical writers also tend, as we should natu-

rally expect, to stress the close interdependence of mind and body, and the importance of affective elements in the life of both. See W. Muri, "Bemerkungen zur hippokratischen Psychologie," *Festschrift Tièche* (Bern, 1947).

[28] E. Rohde, "Die Religion der Griechen," 27 (*Kl. Schriften*, II.338).

[29] Gruppe's thesis of the origin of Orphism in Asia Minor has lately been reaffirmed by Ziegler, P.-W., s.v. "Orphische Dichtung," 1385. But the weakness of the case is that those divine figures of later Orphism which are certainly of Asiatic origin—Erikepaios, Misa, Hipta, the polymorphic winged Chronos—have no demonstrable existence in early Orphic literature and may easily be importations of a later age. Herodotus' derivation of the rebirth theory from Egypt is impossible, for the good reason that the Egyptians had no such theory (see Mercer, *Religion of Ancient Egypt*, 323, and the authorities cited by Rathmann, *Quaest. Pyth.* 48). A derivation from India is unproved and intrinsically improbable (Keith, *Rel. and Phil. of Veda and Upanishads*, 601 ff.). It seems possible, however, that the Indian and the Greek belief may have the same ultimate source; see below, n. 97.

[30] On the character and diffusion of shamanistic culture see K. Meuli, "Scythica," *Hermes*, 70 (1935) 137 ff., a brilliant paper to which I owe the idea of this chapter; G. Nioradze, *Der Schamanismus bei den Sibirischen Völkern* (Stuttgart, 1925); and the interesting though speculative book of Mrs. Chadwick, *Poetry and Prophecy* (Cambridge, 1942). For detailed descriptions of shamans see W. Radloff, *Aus Sibirien* (1885); V. M. Mikhailovski, *JRAI* 24 (1895) 62 ff., 126 ff.; W. Sieroszewski, *Rev. de l'hist. des rel.* 46 (1902) 204 ff., 299 ff.; M. A. Czaplicka, *Aboriginal Siberia* (1914), who gives a full bibliography; I. M. Kasanovicz, *Smithsonian Inst. Annual Report*, 1924; U. Holmberg, *Finno-Ugric and Siberian Mythology* (1927). The connection of Scythian with Ural-Altaic religious ideas was noticed by the Hungarian scholar Nagy and is accepted by Minns (*Scythians and Greeks*, 85).

[31] It would appear that in some modern forms of shamanism the dissociation is a mere fiction; in others there is evidence that it is quite real (cf. Nioradze, *op. cit.*, 91 f., 100 f.; Chadwick, *op. cit.*, 18 ff.). The latter is presumably the older type, which the former conventionally imitates. A. Ohlmarks, *Arch. f. Rel.* 36 (1939) 171 ff., asserts that genuine shamanistic trance is confined to the arctic region and is due to "arctic hysteria," but see the criticisms of M. Eliade, *Rev. de l'hist. des rel.* 131 (1946) 5 ff. The soul may also leave the body in illness (Nioradze, *op. cit.*, 95; Mikhailovski,

loc. cit., 128), and in ordinary sleep (Nioradze, *op. cit.*, 21 ff.; Czaplicka, *op. cit.*, 287; Holmberg, *op. cit.*, 472 ff.).

32 On these "Greek shamans" see also Rohde, *Psyche*, 299 ff. and 327 ff., where most of the evidence about them is collected and discussed; H. Diels, *Parmenides' Lehrgedicht*, 14 ff.; and Nilsson, *Gesch.* I.582 ff., who accepts Meuli's view of them. It may perhaps be argued that shamanistic behaviour is rooted in man's psycho-physical make-up, and that something of the kind may therefore have appeared among the Greeks independently of foreign influence. But against this there are three things to be said: (1) such behaviour begins to be attested among the Greeks as soon as the Black Sea is opened to Greek colonisation, and not before; (2) of the earliest recorded "shamans," one is a Scythian (Abaris), another a Greek who had visited Scythia (Aristeas); (3) there is sufficient agreement in concrete detail between ancient Greco-Scythian and modern Siberian shamanism to make a hypothesis of simple "convergence" look rather improbable: examples are the shaman's change of sex in Scythia and Siberia (Meuli, *loc. cit.*, 127 ff.), the religious importance of the arrow (n. 34 below), the religious retreat (n. 46), the status of women (n. 59), the power over beasts and birds (n. 75), the underworld journey to recover a soul (n. 76) the two souls (n. 111), and the resemblance in cathartic methods (nn. 118, 119). Some of these things are very likely coincidences; taken separately, none of them is decisive; but their collective weight seems to me considerable.

33 This tradition, though preserved only by later writers, looks older than Herodotus' rationalising version (4.36) in which Abaris *carries* the arrow (his motive for doing so is not explained). Cf. Corssen, *Rh. Mus.* 67 (1912) 40, and Meuli, *loc. cit.*, 159 f.

34 This seems to me to be implicit in the Buryat shaman's use of arrows to summon back the souls of the sick, and also at funerals (Mikhailovski, *loc. cit.*, 128, 135). Shamans also divine from the flight of arrows (*ibid.*, 69, 99); and it is said that the Tatar shaman's "external soul" is sometimes lodged in an arrow (N. K. Chadwick, *JRAI* 66 [1936] 311). Other shamans can ride the air on a "horse-staff" like witches on a broomstick (G. Sandschejew, *Anthropos*, 23 [1928] 980).

35 Hdt. 4.36.

36 For the "Hyperborean Apollo" cf. Alcaeus, fr. 72 Lobel (2 B.); Pindar, *Pyth.* 10.28 ff.; Bacchyl. 3.58 ff.; Soph. fr. 870 N.; A. B. Cook, *Zeus*, II.459 ff. A. H. Krappe, *CPh* 37 (1942) 353 ff., has shown with great probability that the origins of this god are to be

looked for in northern Europe: he is associated with a northern product, amber, and with a northern bird, the whooper swan; and his "ancient garden" lies at the back of the north wind (for the obvious etymology of "Hyperborean" is probably after all the right one). It would seem that the Greeks, hearing of him from missionaries like Abaris, identified him with their own Apollo (possibly from a similarity of name, if Krappe is right in supposing him to be the god of Abalus, "apple island," the mediaeval Avalon), and proved the identity by giving him a place in the temple legend of Delos (Hdt. 4.32 ff.).

[37] Aristeas, frs. 4 and 7 Kinkel; Alföldi, *Gnomon*, 9 (1933) 567 f. I may add that Aeschylus' blind "swan-shaped maidens" who never see the sun (*P.V.* 794 ff., perhaps from Aristeas) have also a good parallel in the "swan-maidens" of Central Asiatic belief, who live in the dark and have eyes of lead (N. K. Chadwick, *JRAI* 66 [1936] 313, 316. As to Aristeas' journey, Herodotus' account (4.13 f.) is ambiguous, and may reflect an attempt to rationalise the story (Meuli, *loc. cit.*, 157 f.). In Maximus of Tyre, 38.3, it is definitely the *soul* of Aristeas which visits the Hyperboreans in the shamanistic manner. The details given in Herodotus 4.16, however, suggest a real journey.

[38] Hdt. 4.15.2; Pliny, *N.H.* 7.174. Compare the soul-birds of the Yakut and Tungus tribes (Holmberg, *op. cit.*, 473, 481); also the bird-costumes worn by Siberian shamans when shamanising (Chadwick, *Poetry and Prophecy*, 58 and pl. 2); and the belief that the first shamans were birds (Nioradze, *op. cit.*, 2). Soul-birds are widely distributed, but it is not certain that early Greece knew them (Nilsson, *Gesch.* I.182 f.).

[39] Soph. *El.* 62 ff. The tone is rationalistic, suggesting the influence of his friend Herodotus; he no doubt has in mind stories like the one Herodotus tells of Zalmoxis (4.95), which rationalises Thracian shamanism. The Lapps used to believe that their shamans "walked" after death (Mikhailovski, *loc. cit.*, 150 f.); and in 1556 the English traveller Richard Johnson saw a Samoyed shaman "die" and then reappear alive (Hakluyt, I.317 f.).

[40] H. Diels, "Ueber Epimenides von Kreta," *Berl. Sitzb.* 1891, I.387 ff. The fragments are now *Vorsokr.* 3 B (formerly 68 B). Cf. also H. Demoulin, *Épiménide de Crète* (Bibl. de la Fac. de Phil. et Lettres Liège, fasc. 12). Wilamowitz' scepticism (*Hippolytos*, 224, 243 f.) appears excessive, though some of E.'s oracles were certainly forged.

[41] The prestige of Cretan καθαρταί in the Archaic Age is attested by

the legend that Apollo was purified after the slaying of Python by Karmanor the Cretan (Paus. 2.30.3, etc.); cf. also the Cretan Thaletas who expelled a plague from Sparta in the seventh century (Pratinas, fr. 8 B.). On the Cretan cave-cult see Nilsson, *Minoan-Myc. Religion*², 458 ff. Epimenides was called νέος Κούρης (Plut. *Sol.* 12, Diog. L. 1.115).

⁴² The tradition of psychic excursion was possibly transferred to Epimenides from Aristeas; Suidas attributes the power to each of them in much the same terms. Similarly Epimenides' post-mortem apparition (Proclus, *in Remp.* II.113 Kr.) may be imitated from that of Aristeas. But the tradition of the fairy food looks older, if only because of the unexplained ox's hoof. It is traceable as far back as Herodorus (fr. 1 J.), whom Jacoby dates *ca.* 400 B.C., and seems to be referred to by Plato, *Laws* 677E. It is tempting to connect it (*a*) with the tradition of Epimenides' miraculously long life, and (*b*) with the Thracian "recipe for escaping death" (n. 60 below).

⁴³ τὸ δέρμα εὑρῆσθαι γράμμασι κατάστικτον, Suid. s.v. (= Epimenides A 2). The source of this may be the Spartan historian Sosibius, *ca.* 300 B.C. (cf. Diog. Laert. 1.115). Suidas adds that τὸ Ἐπιμενίδ-ειον δέρμα was proverbial for anything hidden (ἐπὶ τῶν ἀποθέτων). But I cannot accept the curious theory of Diels (*op. cit.*, 399) and Demoulin (*op. cit.*, 69) that this phrase originally referred to a vellum MS of E.'s works, and was later misunderstood as referring to his tattooed skin. Compare, perhaps, Σ Lucian, p. 124 Rabe, ἐλέγετο γὰρ ὁ Πυθαγόρας ἐντετυπῶσθαι τῷ δεξιῷ αὐτοῦ μηρῷ τὸν Φοῖβον. Is this a rationalisation of the mysterious "golden thigh"? Or was the historical kernel of that tale a sacral tattoo-mark or natural birthmark?

⁴⁴ Hdt. 5.6.2: τὸ μὲν ἐστίχθαι εὐγενὲς κέκριται, τὸ δὲ ἄστικτον ἀγεννές. The Thracian shaman "Zalmoxis" had a tattoo-mark on his forehead which Greek writers, unaware of its religious significance, explained by saying that he had been captured by pirates, who branded him for the slave-market (Dionysophanes *apud* Porph. *vit. Pyth.* 15, where Delatte, *Politique pyth.*, 228, is surely wrong in identifying the fictitious λησταί with local anti-Pythagorean insurgents). That the Thracians practised sacral tattooing was known to Greek vase-painters: Thracian maenads tattooed with a fawn appear on several vases (*JHS* 9 [1888] pl. VI; P. Wolters, *Hermes*, 38 [1903] 268; Furtwängler-Reichhold, III, Tafel 178, where some are also tattooed with a snake). For tattooing as a mark of dedication to a god cf. also Hdt. 2.113 (Egyptian), and the

examples from various sources discussed by Dölger, *Sphragis*, 41 ff. Tattooing was likewise practised by the Sarmatians and Dacians (Pliny, *N.H.* 22.2), the Illyrians (Strabo 7.3.4), the "picti Agathyrsi" in Transylvania whom Virgil represents as worshipping (the Hyperborean) Apollo (*Aen.* 4.146), and other Balkan and Danubian peoples (Cook, *Zeus*, II.123). But the Greeks thought it αἰσχρὸν καὶ ἄτιμον (Sextus Empiricus, *Pyrrh. Hyp.* 3.202; cf. Diels, *Vorsokr.*⁵ 90 [83] 2.13).

⁴⁵ Frazer, *Pausanias*, II, 121 ff.

⁴⁶ Cf. Rohde, *Psyche*, chap. ix, n. 117; Halliday, *Greek Divination*, 91, n. 5; and for the long sleeps of shamans, Czaplicka, *op. cit.*, 179. Holmberg, *op. cit.*, 496, quotes the case of a shaman who had lain "motionless and unconscious" for over two months at the time of his "call." Compare the long underground retreat of Zalmoxis (n. 60 below). Diels thought (*loc. cit.*, 402) that the Long Sleep was invented to reconcile chronological discrepancies in the various tales of Epimenides. But if this were the only motive, Long Sleeps should be very common in early Greek history.

⁴⁷ I leave out of account here Meuli's hazardous speculations about shamanistic elements in the Greek epic (*loc. cit.*, 164 ff.). On the lateness of Greek access to the Black Sea, and the reason for it, see Rhys Carpenter, *AJA* 52 (1948) 1 ff.

⁴⁸ This was already clearly recognised by Rohde, *Psyche*, 301 f.

⁴⁹ Proclus, *in Remp.* II.122.22 ff. Kr. (= Clearchus, fr. 7 Wehrli). The story cannot, unfortunately, be treated as historical (cf. Wilamowitz, *Glaube*, II.256, and H. Lewy, *Harv. Theol. Rev.* 31 [1938] 205 ff.).

⁵⁰ Ar. *Met.* 984ᵇ 19; cf. Diels on Anaxagoras A 58. Zeller-Nestle, I.1269, n. 1, would dismiss Aristotle's statement as entirely baseless. But Iamb. *Protrept.* 48.16 (= Ar. fr. 61) supports the idea that Anaxagoras did appeal to the authority of Hermotimus.

⁵¹ Diog. Laert. 1.114 (*Vorsokr.* 3 A 1): λέγεται δὲ ὡς καὶ πρῶτος (πρῶτον Casaubon, αὐτὸς cj. Diels) αὐτὸν Αἰακὸν λέγοι . . . προσποιηθῆναί τε πολλάκις ἀναβεβιωκέναι. The words αὐτὸν Αἰακὸν λέγοι show that ἀναβεβιωκέναι cannot refer merely to psychic excursion, as Rohde suggested (*Psyche*, 331).

⁵² Ar. *Rhet.* 1418ᵃ 24: ἐκεῖνος γὰρ περὶ τῶν ἐσομένων οὐκ ἐμαντεύετο, ἀλλὰ περὶ τῶν γεγονότων, ἀδήλων δέ. For a different explanation of this statement see Bouché-Leclercq, *Hist. de la divination*, II.100.

⁵³ H. Diels, *loc. cit.* (n. 40 above), 395.

⁵⁴ *Apud* Diog. Laert. 8.4. Cf. Rohde, *Psyche*, App. X, and A. De-

latte, *La Vie de Pythagore de Diogène Laërce*, 154 ff. Others gave him a different series of lives (Dicaearchus, fr. 36 W.).

55 Empedocles, fr. 129 D. (cf. Bidez, *La Biographie d'Empédocle*, 122 f.; Wilamowitz, "Die Καθαρμοί des Empedokles," *Berl. Sitzb.* 1929, 651); Xenophanes, fr. 7 D. I find quite unconvincing Rathmann's attempt to discredit both these traditions in his *Quaestiones Pythagoreae, Orphicae, Empedocleae* (Halle, 1933). Xenophanes seems to have made fun also of the tall stories about Epimenides (fr. 20). Burnet's way of translating the Empedocles fragment, "though he lived ten, yea, twenty generations of men ago" (*EGPh¹*, 236)—which would exclude any reference to Pythagoras—is linguistically quite impossible.

56 Mikhailovski, *loc. cit.* (n. 30 above), 85, 133; Sieroszewski, *loc. cit.*, 314; Czaplicka, *op. cit.*, 213, 280. The last-named attributes a *general* belief in reincarnation to a number of Siberian peoples (130, 136, 287, 290).

57 Aeacus seems to be an old sacral figure, perhaps Minoan: he was in life a magical rainmaker (Isocrates, *Evag.* 14, etc.), and after death was promoted to be Porter of Hellgate (ps.-Apollod. 3.12.6; cf. Eur. *Peirithous* fr. 591, Ar. *Ran.* 464 ff.) or even a Judge of the dead (Plato, *Apol.* 41A, *Gorg.* 524A; cf. Isocr. *Evag.* 15).

58 Diog. Laert. 8.4. Another of Pythagoras' avatars, Aethalides, was said by Pherecydes of Syros to have been given the power of rebirth as a special privilege (Σ Apoll. Rhod. 1.645 = Pherecydes fr. 8). I agree with Wilamowitz (*Platon*, I.251, n. 1) that such stories are not products of philosophical theorising, but that on the contrary the theory is a generalisation suggested (in part, at least) by the stories. On reincarnation as a privilege limited to shamans see P. Radin, *Primitive Religion*, 274 f.

59 The status allowed to women in the Pythagorean community is exceptional for Greek society in the Classical Age. But it is worth noticing that in many Siberian societies today women, as well as men, are eligible for the status of shaman.

60 Hdt. 4.95. Cf. 4.93: Γέτας τοὺς ἀθανατίζοντας, 5.4: Γέται οἱ ἀθανατίζοντες, and Plato, *Charm.* 156D: τῶν Θρᾳκῶν τῶν Ζαλμόξιδος ἰατρῶν, οἳ λέγονται καὶ ἀπαθανατίζειν. These phrases mean, not that the Getae "believe in the immortality of the soul," but that they have a recipe for escaping death (Linforth, *CPh* 13 [1918] 23 ff.). The nature of the escape which "Zalmoxis" promised to his followers is, however, far from clear. It seems possible that Herodotus' informants had fused into one story several distinct ideas, viz., (*a*) the earthly paradise of the "Hyperborean Apollo," to which, as

to the Aegean Elysium, some men are translated bodily without dying (αἰεὶ περιεόντες, cf. Bacchyl. 3.58 ff. and Krappe, *CPh* 37 [1942] 353 ff.): hence the identification of Zalmoxis with Kronos (Mnaseas, *FHG* III, fr. 23); cf. Czaplicka, *op. cit.*, 176: "There exist traditions about shamans who were carried away still living from the earth to the sky"; (*b*) the disappearing shaman who vanishes for long periods into a sacred cave: Hdt.'s κατάγαιον οἴκημα and Strabo's ἀντρῶδές τι χωρίον ἄβατον τοῖς ἄλλοις (7.3.5) look like rationalised versions of the cave where an ἀνθρωποδαίμων dwells undying, *Rhesus*, 970 ff., cf. Rohde, *Psyche*, 279; (*c*) *perhaps* also a belief in transmigration (Rohde, *loc. cit.*); cf. the explicit statement of Mela that some Thracians "redituras putant animas obeuntium" (2.18), and Phot., Suid., *EM*, s.v. Ζάμολξις; but there is nothing about "souls" in Herodotus' account.

⁶¹ Herodotus knows that Zalmoxis is a δαίμων (4.94.1), but leaves open the question whether he may once have been a man (96.2). Strabo's account (7.3.5) strongly suggests that he was either a heroised shaman—all shamans become Üör, heroes, after death (Sieroszewski, *loc. cit.*, 228 f.)—or else a divine prototype of shamans (cf. Nock, *CR* 40 [1926] 185 f., and Meuli, *loc. cit.*, 163). We may compare the status which, according to Aristotle (fr. 192 R. = Iamb. *vit. Pyth.* 31), the Pythagoreans claimed for their founder: τοῦ λογικοῦ ζῴου τὸ μέν ἐστι θεός, τὸ δὲ ἄνθρωπος, τὸ δὲ οἷον Πυθαγόρας. The fact that Zalmoxis gave his name to a particular type of singing and dancing (Hesych. s.v.) seems to confirm his connection with shamanistic performances. The similarities between the Zalmoxis legend and those of Epimenides and Aristeas have been rightly emphasised by Professor Rhys Carpenter (*Folktale, Fiction, and Saga in the Homeric Epics*, Sather Classical Lectures, 1946, 132 f., 161 f.), though I cannot accept his ingenious identification of all three with hibernating bears (was Pythagoras a bear too?). Minar, who tries to elicit a historical kernel from the Zalmoxis stories, ignores their religious background.

⁶² Cf. Delatte, *Études sur la litt. pyth.*, 77 ff.

⁶³ Pythagoras and Abaris, Iamb. *vit. Pyth.* 90–93, 140, 147, who makes Abaris P.'s pupil (Suidas, s.v. Πυθαγόρας, reverses the relation); initiation, *ibid.*, 146. Prophecy, bilocation, and identity with Hyperborean Apollo, Aristotle, fr. 191 R. (= *Vorsokr.*, Pyth. A 7). Healing, Aelian, *V.H.* 4.17, Diog. Laert. 8.12, etc.; visits underworld, Hieronymus of Rhodes *apud* Diog. 8.21, cf. 41. Against the view that the whole Pythagoras-legend can be dismissed as the invention of late romancers see O. Weinreich,

NJbb 1926, 638, and Gigon, *Ursprung d. gr. Philosophie*, 131; and on the irrational character of much early Pythagorean thinking, L. Robin, *La Pensée hellénique*, 31 ff. I do not, of course, suggest that Pythagoreanism can be explained entirely as a development from shamanism; other elements, like number-mysticism and the speculations about cosmic harmony, were also important from an early date.

⁶⁴ As Reinhardt says, the earliest references to Pythagoras—in Xenophanes, Heraclitus, Empedocles, Ion (and one might add Herodotus)—all "presuppose the popular tradition which saw in him an Albertus Magnus" (*Parmenides*, 236). Cf. I. Lévy, *Recherches sur les sources de la légende de Pythagore*, 6 ff. and 19.

⁶⁵ The wind-magic goes back to Timaeus (fr. 94 M. = Diog. L. 8.60); the other stories to Heraclides Ponticus (frs. 72, 75, 76 Voss = Diog. L. 8.60 f., 67 f.). Bidez, *La Biographie d'Empédocle*, 35 ff., argued convincingly that the legend of Empedocles' bodily translation is older than that of his death in the crater of Etna, and was not invented by Heraclides. Similarly, Siberian tradition tells how the great shamans of the past were translated bodily (Czaplicka, *op. cit.*, 176), and how they raised the dead to life (Nioradze, *op. cit.*, 102).

⁶⁶ Frs. 111.3, 9; 112.4.

⁶⁷ Fr. 112.7 ff. Cf. Bidez, *op. cit.*, 135 ff.

⁶⁸ The first of these views was maintained by Bidez, *op. cit.*, 159 ff., and Kranz, *Hermes*, 70 (1935) 115 ff.; the second by Wilamowitz (*Berl. Sitzb.* 1929, 655), after Diels (*Berl. Sitzb.* 1898, i.39 ff.) and others. Against both opinions, see W. Nestle, *Philol.* 65 (1906) 545 ff., A. Diès, *Le Cycle mystique*, 87 ff., Weinreich, *NJbb* 1926, 641, and Cornford, *CAH* IV.568 f. The attempts of Burnet and others to distinguish in a later generation between "scientific" and "religious" Pythagoreans illustrate the same tendency to impose modern dichotomies on a world which had not yet felt the need to define either "science" or "religion."

⁶⁹ This explanation (Karsten's) was accepted by Burnet and Wilamowitz. But see, *contra*, Bidez, *op. cit.*, 166, and Nestle, *loc. cit.*, 549, n. 14.

⁷⁰ In view of these passages, Wilamowitz' description of the poem *On Nature* as "durchaus materialistisch" (*loc. cit.*, 651) is decidedly misleading, though no doubt Empedocles, like other men of his time, thought of mental forces in material terms.

⁷¹ Jaeger, *Theology*, 132.

⁷² Cf. Rohde, *Psyche*, 378. On the wide range of the shaman's func-

tions see Chadwick, *Growth of Literature*, I.637 ff., and *Poetry and Prophecy*, chaps. i and iii. Homeric society is more advanced: there the μάντις, the ἰητρός, the ἀοιδός, are members of distinct professions. The archaic Greek shamans were a throwback to an older type.

73 Later tradition, with its emphasis on the secrecy of Pythagoras' teaching, denied that he put anything in writing; cf., however, Gigon, *Unters. z. Heraklit*, 126. It would seem that there was no such established tradition in the fifth century, since Ion of Chios could attribute Orphic poems to Pythagoras (n. 96 below).

74 Cf. W. K. C. Guthrie, *Orpheus and Greek Religion*, chap. iii.

75 Chadwick, *JRAI* 66 (1936) 300. Modern shamans have lost this power, but they still surround themselves when they shamanise with wooden images of birds and beasts, or with their skins, in order to secure the help of the animal spirits (Meuli, *loc. cit.*, 147); they also imitate the cries of these helpers (Mikhailovski, *loc. cit.*, 74, 94). The same tradition appears in the legend of Pythagoras, who "is believed to have tamed an eagle, by certain cries checking it in its flight overhead and calling it down" (Plut. *Numa* 8); this may be compared with the Yenissean belief that "the eagles are the shaman's helpers" (Nioradze, *op. cit.*, 70). He also tames another animal very important to northern shamans, the bear (Iamb. *vit. Pyth.* 60).

76 Chadwick, *ibid.*, 305 (underworld journey of Kan Märgän to look for his sister), and *Poetry and Prophecy*, 93; Mikhailovski, *loc. cit.*, 63, 69 f.; Czaplicka, *op. cit.*, 260, 269; Meuli, *loc. cit.*, 149.

77 Cf. Guthrie, *op. cit.*, 35 ff.

78 E.g., the mantic head of Mímir, *Ynglinga saga*, chaps. iv and vii. In Ireland, "heads that speak have been a well-attested phenomenon for more than a thousand years" (G. L. Kittredge, *A Study of Gawain and the Green Knight*, 177, where numerous examples are quoted). Cf. also W. Déonna, *REG* 38 (1925) 44 ff.

79 Wilamowitz, *Glaube*, II.193 ff. (1932); Festugière, *Revue Biblique*, 44 (1935) 372 ff.; *REG* 49 (1936) 306 ff.; H. W. Thomas, Ἐπέκεινα (1938); Ivan M. Linforth, *The Arts of Orpheus* (1941). A spirited counter-attack on this "reactionary" scepticism was delivered in 1942 by Ziegler, representing the Old Guard of pan-Orphists, in the guise of an article in a work of reference (P.-W., s.v. "Orphische Dichtung"). But while he has no difficulty in scoring some direct hits on his immediate adversary Thomas, I cannot feel that Ziegler has stilled my doubts about the foundations on which the traditional account of "Orphism" rests, even in the modified form in

which it is presented by such careful writers as Nilsson ("Early Orphism," *Harv. Theol. Rev.* 28 [1935]) and Guthrie (*op. cit.*).

80 See, *contra*, Wilamowitz, II.199. To his generalisation that no writer of the Classical Age speaks of Ὀρφικοί, Herodotus 2.81 can be claimed as a possible exception only if we adopt the "short text" (the reading of ABC) in that disputed passage. But an accidental omission in an ancestor of ABC, caused by homoioteleuton and leading to a subsequent change in the number of the verb, appears to me much likelier than an interpolation in DRSV; and I cannot resist the conviction that the choice of the word ὀργίων in the next sentence was determined by the word Βακχικοῖσι in the "long text" of this one (cf. Nock, *Studies Presented to F. Ll. Griffith*, 248, and Boyancé, *Culte des Muses*, 94, n. 1).

81 See, *contra*, Bidez, *op. cit.*, 141 ff. There is in my judgement a stronger case for attaching Empedocles to the Pythagorean tradition (Bidez, 122 ff.; Wilamowitz, *Berl. Sitzb.* 1929, 655; Thomas, 115 ff.) than for connecting him with anything that is demonstrably and distinctively early-Orphic (Kern, Kranz, etc.). But it is probably a mistake to regard him as a member of any "school": he was an independent shaman who had his own way of putting things.

82 In *Hypsipyle* fr. 31 Hunt (= Kern, *O.F.* 2) the quite common adjective πρωτόγονος has no proved association with the older Orphic literature, while Ἔρως and Νύξ have been imported by conjecture. Nor has *Cretans*, fr. 472, any demonstrable connection with "Orphism" (Festugière, *REG* 49.309).

83 See, *contra*, Thomas, 43 f.

84 See, *contra*, Wilamowitz, II.202 f.; Festugière, *Rev. Bibl.* 44.381 f.; Thomas, 134 ff.

85 That this hypothesis is both superfluous and intrinsically improbable is the central thesis of Thomas's book.

86 See, *contra*, Linforth, 56 ff.; D. W. Lucas, "Hippolytus," *CQ* 40 (1946) 65 ff. It may be added that the Pythagorean tradition explicitly coupled hunters with butchers as unclean persons (Eudoxus, fr. 36 Gisinger = Porph. *vit. Pyth.* 7). The Orphic view of them can hardly have been very different.

87 This hoary error has in recent years been exposed again and again: see R. Harder, *Ueber Ciceros Somnium Scipionis*, 121, n. 4; Wilamowitz, II.199; Thomas, 51 f.; Linforth, 147 f. Since, however, it is still repeated by highly respected scholars, it seems worth while to say once more (*a*) that what is attributed by Plato, *Crat.* 400c, to οἱ ἀμφ' Ὀρφέα is a derivation of σῶμα (τοῦτο τὸ

ὄνομα) from σῴζειν, ἵνα σῴζηται (ἡ ψυχή): this is placed beyond doubt by the words καὶ οὐδὲν δεῖν παράγειν οὐδ' ἕν γράμμα, which contrast σῶμα-σῴζω with σῶμα-σῆμα and σῶμα-σημαίνω; (b) that σῶμα-σῆμα is attributed in the same passage to τινές, without further specification; (c) that when an author says, "Some persons connect σῶμα with σῆμα, but I think it was probably the Orphic poets who coined the word, deriving it from σῴζω," we cannot suppose "the Orphic poets" to be either identical with, or included among, "some persons" (I am inclined to think this remains true even if μάλιστα is understood as qualifying ὡς δίκην διδούσης κτλ).

88 As Mr. D. W. Lucas has put it (CQ 40.67), "the modern reader, baffled and dismayed by the apparent crudity of much of conventional Greek religion, is inclined to look everywhere for signs of Orphism, because he feels it gives more of what he has come to expect from religion, and he is loath to believe that the Greeks did not demand it too." Cf. also Jaeger, Theology, 61. I cannot help suspecting that "the historic Orphic Church," as it appears, e.g., in Toynbee's Study of History, V.84 ff., will one day be quoted as a classic instance of the kind of historical mirage which arises when men unknowingly project their own preoccupations into the distant past.

89 Festugière, REG 49.307; Linforth, xiii f.

90 Parallels between Plato or Empedocles and these late compilations do not in my opinion constitute such a guarantee, unless in any particular case we can exclude the possibility that the compiler lifted the phrase or the idea from those accepted masters of mystical thought.

91 The sceptics appear to have included Herodotus, Ion of Chios, and Epigenes (n. 96 below), as well as Aristotle: see Linforth's admirable discussion, 155 ff.

92 Rep. 364E. The etymology and usage of the word ὅμαδος suggest that what Plato had in mind was not so much the confused noise of gabbling recitation as the confused noise of a lot of books each propounding its own nostrum; it takes more than one to make a ὅμαδος. Euripides' phrase, πολλῶν γραμμάτων καπνούς (Hipp. 954), also stresses the multiplicity of Orphic authorities, as well as their futility. It is anachronistic, as Jaeger points out (Theology, 62), to postulate a uniform Orphic "dogma" in the Classical Age.

93 Plato, Crat. 400C; Eur. Hipp. 952 f. (cf. Ar. Ran. 1032, Plato, Laws 782C); Plato, Rep. 364E–365A.

94 Ziegler, loc. cit., 1380, seems to me to be right on this point, against

the ultra-sceptical Thomas. Aristotle's words at *de anima* 410ᵇ 19
(= *O.F.* 27), far from excluding transmigration from the range of
Orphic beliefs, go some way to confirm its inclusion by showing
that some writers of 'Ορφικά believed at any rate in a preëxistent
detachable soul.

⁹⁵ Pythagoreans are portrayed in Middle Comedy as pretending to
be strict vegetarians (Antiphanes, fr. 135 K., Aristophon, fr. 9,
etc.) and even as living on bread and water (Alexis, fr. 221). But
the Pythagorean rule had various forms; the oldest may have
prohibited the eating only of certain "sacred" animals or parts of
animals (Nilsson, "Early Orphism," 206 f.; Delatte, *Études sur
la litt. pyth.*, 289 ff.). The σῶμα-φρουρά idea was put by Clearchus
(fr. 38 W.) into the mouth of a real or imaginary Pythagorean
called Euxitheos. (Plato, *Phaedo* 62B, does not in my opinion support the view that it was taught by Philolaus; and I have little
faith in "Philolaus," fr. 15.) On Pythagorean κάθαρσις see below, n. 119, and on the close general similarity of old-Pythagorean
and old-Orphic ideas, E. Frank, *Platon u. d. sogenannten Pythagoreer*, 67 ff., 356 ff., and Guthrie, *op. cit.*, 216 ff. The most clearly
recognisable differences are not doctrinal, but are concerned with
cult (Apollo is central for Pythagoreanism, Dionysus apparently
for the 'Ορφικά); with social status (Pythagoreanism is aristocratic, the 'Ορφικά probably were not); and, above all, with the
fact that Orphic thought remained on the mythological level,
while the Pythagoreans at an early date, if not from the first, attempted to translate this way of thinking into more or less rational
terms.

⁹⁶ Diog. Laert. 8.8 (= Kern, *Test.* 248); Clem. Alex. *Strom.* 1.21, 131
(= *Test.* 222). I find it difficult to accept Linforth's identification
of this Epigenes with an obscure member of the Socratic circle
(*op. cit.*, 115 ff.); the sort of linguistic interests attributed to him
by Clement (*ibid.*, 5.8, 49 = *O.F.* 33) and Athenaeus (468c)
strongly suggest Alexandrian scholarship. But he was in any case
a man who had made a special study of Orphic poetry, and in view
of the poverty of our own information it seems unwise to dismiss
his statements in the cavalier manner of Delatte (*Études sur la
litt. pyth.*, 4 f.). We do not know on what his particular ascriptions
were based; but for the general view that early Pythagoreans had
had a hand in the manufacture of 'Ορφικά he could appeal to good
fifth-century authority, not only to Ion of Chios but also, I think,
to Herodotus, if I am right in understanding the famous sentence
in 2.81 to mean "These Egyptian practices agree (ὁμολογέει

RSV) with the practices called Orphic and Dionysiac, which really originated in Egypt and (some of which) were brought thence by Pythagoras" (on the text see n. 80 above). Since Hdt. elsewhere (2.49) attributes the importation of the βακχικά to Melampus, the practices imported by Pythagoras are presumably limited to the 'Ορφικά. Cf. 2.123, where he says he knows but will not name the plagiarists who imported the doctrine of transmigration from Egypt and claimed it as their own.

97 Something of the same sort may have happened in India, where the belief in reincarnation also emerges relatively late and appears to be neither indigenous nor part of the creed of the I.-E. incomers. W. Ruben, *Acta Orientalia*, 17 (1939) 164 ff., finds its starting-point in contacts with the shamanistic culture of Central Asia. One interesting fact is that in India, as in Greece, the reincarnation theory and the interpretation of the dream as a psychic excursion make their first appearance together (*Br. Upanishad* 3.3 and 4.3; cf. Ruben, *loc. cit.*, 200). It looks as if they were elements of the same belief-pattern. If so, and if shamanism is the source of the latter element, it is probably the source of both.

98 Rohde, "Orpheus," *Kl. Schriften*, II.306.

99 *Eranos*, 39 (1941) 12. See, *contra*, Gigon, *Ursprung*, 133 f.

100 Heraclitus, fr. 88 D., cf. Sext. Emp. *Pyrrh. Hyp.* 3.230 (quoted below, n. 109); Plato, *Phaedo* 70C-72D (the "argument from ἀνταπόδοσις").

101 "This doctrine of the transmigration or reincarnation of the soul is found among many tribes of savages," Frazer, *The Belief in Immortality*, I.29. "The belief in some form of reincarnation is universally present in all the simple food-gathering and fishing-hunting civilisations," P. Radin, *Primitive Religion*, 270.

102 Cf. Plato, *Phaedo* 69C, *Rep.* 363D, etc., and for the Pythagorean belief in Tartarus, Arist. *Anal. Post.* 94^b 33 (= *Vorsokr.* 58 C 1). An *Underworld Journey* is among the poems ascribed by Epigenes to the Pythagorean Cercops (n. 96). The specific fancy of a hell of mud is usually called "Orphic" on the not very impressive authority of Olympiodorus (*in Phaed.* 48.20 N.). Aristides, *orat.* 22.10 K. (p. 421 Dind.), attributes it to Eleusis (cf. Diog. L. 6.39). Plato, *Rep.* 363D and *Phaedo* 69C, is quite vague. I suspect it to be an old popular notion derived from the consubstantiality of ghost and corpse and the consequent confusion of Hades with the grave: the stages of its growth may be traced in Homer's 'Αΐδεω δόμον εὐρώεντα (*Od.* 10.512, cf. Soph. *Aj.* 1166, τάφον εὐρώεντα); Aeschylus' λάμπα or λάπα (*Eum.* 387, cf. Blass *ad loc.*); and

Aristophanes' βόρβορον πολὺν καὶ σκῶρ ἀείνων (Ran. 145). At some point in its development it was interpreted as the appropriate punishment of the uninitiated or "unclean" (τῶν ἀκαθάρτων); this might be the contribution of Eleusis or of the 'Ορφικά or of both.

103 To the question, τί ἀληθέστατον λέγεται; the old Pythagorean catechism replied, ὅτι πονηροὶ οἱ ἄνθρωποι (Iamb. vit. Pyth. 82 = Vorsokr. 45 C 4).

104 Laws 872DE. Cf. the Pythagorean view of justice, Arist. E.N. 1132ᵇ 21 ff.

105 γνώσει δ' ἀνθρώπους αὐθαίρετα πήματ' ἔχοντας, quoted as Pythagorean by Chrysippus apud Aul. Gell. 7.2.12. Cf. Delatte, Études, 25.

106 See above, chap. ii.

107 Against Burnet's ascription of Platonic ἀνάμνησις to the Pythagoreans (Thales to Plato, 43) see L. Robin, "Sur la doctrine de la réminiscence," REG 32 (1919) 451 ff. (= La Pensée hellénique, 337 ff.), and Thomas, 78 f. On Pythagorean memory-training, Diod. 10.5 and Iamb. vit. Pyth. 164 ff. These authors do not connect it with the attempt to recover memory of past lives, but it seems a reasonable guess that this was originally its ultimate purpose. 'Ανάμνησις in this sense is an exceptional feat, attainable only by special gifts or special training; it is a highly esteemed spiritual accomplishment in India today. The belief in it is probably assisted by the curious psychological illusion, to which some persons are subject, known as "déjà vu."

108 Iamb. vit. Pyth. 85 (= Vorsokr. 58 C 4). Cf. Crantor apud [Plut.] cons. ad Apoll. 27, 115B, who attributes to "many wise men" the view that human life is a τιμωρία, and Arist. fr. 60, where the same view is ascribed to οἱ τὰς τελετὰς λέγοντες (Orphic poets?).

109 Heraclitus, frs. 62, 88; cf. Sext. Emp. Pyrrh. Hyp. 3.230: ὁ δὲ 'Ηράκλειτός φησιν ὅτι καὶ τὸ ζῆν καὶ τὸ ἀποθανεῖν καὶ ἐν τῷ ζῆν ἡμᾶς ἐστι καὶ ἐν τῷ τεθνάναι· ὅτε μὲν γὰρ ἡμεῖς ζῶμεν, τὰς ψυχὰς ἡμῶν τεθνάναι καὶ ἐν ἡμῖν τεθάφθαι, ὅτε δὲ ἡμεῖς ἀποθνήσκομεν, τὰς ψυχὰς ἀναβιοῦν καὶ ζῆν, and Philo, Leg. alleg. 1.108. Sextus' quotation is doubtless not verbatim; but it seems unsafe to discount it completely, as some do, because of its "Pythagorean" language. For the similar view held by Empedocles, see below, n. 114; and for later developments of this line of thought, Cumont, Rev. de Phil. 44 (1920) 230 ff.

110 Ar. Ran. 420, ἐν τοῖς ἄνω νεκροῖσι, and the parody of Euripides, ibid., 1477 f. (Cf. 1082, καὶ φασκούσας οὐ ζῆν τὸ ζῆν, where the doctrine is presented as a climax of perversity.)

111 Pherecydes, A 5 Diels. On the two souls in Empedocles see Gom-

perz, *Greek Thinkers*, I.248 ff. (Eng. trans.); Rostagni, *Il Verbo di Pitagora*, chap. vi; Wilamowitz, *Berl. Sitzb.* 1929, 658 ff.; Delatte, *Enthousiasme*, 27. Failure to distinguish the ψυχή from the δαίμων has led various scholars to discover an imaginary contradiction between the *Purifications* and the poem *On Nature* in regard to immortality. Apparent contradictions on the same subject in the fragments of Alcmaeon are perhaps to be explained in a like manner (Rostagni, *loc. cit.*). Another view of the persistent "occult" self, attributed by Aristotle to "some Pythagoreans" (*de anima* 404ᵃ 17), represented it as a tiny material particle (ξύσμα), a notion which has plenty of primitive parallels. This again is quite distinct from the breath-soul which is the principle of life on the ordinary empirical level. The notion of a plurality of "souls" may have been taken over from shamanistic tradition: most of the Siberian peoples today believe in two or more souls (Czaplicka, *op. cit.*, chap. xiii). But, as Nilsson has lately said, "pluralistic teaching about the soul is founded in the nature of things, and only our habits of thought make it surprising that man should have several 'souls' " (*Harv. Theol. Rev.* 42 [1949] 89).

¹¹² Empedocles, A 85 (Aetius, 5.25.4), cf. frs. 9–12. Return of ψυχή or πνεῦμα to the fiery aether: Eur. *Supp.* 533, fr. 971, and the Potidaea epitaph (Kaibel, *Epigr. gr.* 21). It seems to be based on the simple idea that ψυχή is breath or warm air (Anaximenes, fr. 2), which will tend to float upwards when released at death into the atmosphere (Empedocles, fr. 2.4, καπνοῖο δίκην ἀρθέντες).

¹¹³ A similar paradox is attributed by Clement to Heraclitus, *Paedag.* 3.2.1. But what is missing in the fragments of Heraclitus is the Empedoclean preoccupation with guilt. Like Homer, he is apparently more concerned about τιμή (fr. 24).

¹¹⁴ Rohde's view, that the "unfamiliar place" (fr. 118) and the "Meadow of Ate" (fr. 121) are simply the world of men, has the support of ancient authority, and seems to me almost certainly right. It was challenged by Maass and Wilamowitz, but is accepted by Bignone (*Empedocle*, 492), Kranz (*Hermes*, 70 [1935] 114, n. 1), and Jaeger (*Theology*, 148 f., 238).

¹¹⁵ The imaginative qualities of the *Purifications* have been well brought out by Jaeger, *Theology*, chap. viii, especially 147 f. Empedocles was a true poet, not a philosopher who happened to write in verse.

¹¹⁶ See above, pp. 35 ff. Certain cathartic functions are exercised by the primitive Siberian shaman (Radloff, *op. cit.*, II.52 ff.); so that the role of καθαρτής would come natural to his Greek imitators.

117 *O.F.*, 32 (c) and (d).

118 *Rep.* 364E: διὰ θυσιῶν καὶ παιδιᾶς ἡδονῶν. Empedocles, fr. 143, prescribes washing in water drawn in a bronze vessel from five springs—which recalls the "futile prescription" offered by a speaker in Menander (fr. 530.22 K.), ἀπὸ κρουνῶν τριῶν ὕδατι περιρράναι, and the catharsis practised by Buryat shamans with water drawn from three springs (Mikhailovski, *loc. cit.*, 87).

119 Aristoxenus, fr. 26, and Wehrli's note; Iamb. *vit. Pyth.* 64 f., 110–114, 163 f.; Porph. *vit. Pyth.* 33; Boyancé, *Le Culte des Muses*, 100 ff., 115 ff. Music is much used by modern shamans to summon or banish spirits—it is "the language of spirits" (Chadwick, *JRAI* 66 [1936] 297). And it seems likely that the Pythagorean use of it derives in part at least from shamanistic tradition: cf. the ἐπῳδαί by which the Thracian followers of Zalmoxis are said to "heal the soul" (Plato, *Charm.* 156D–157A).

120 Empedocles, fr. 117.

121 Ar. *Ran.* 1032 (cf. Linforth, 70); Eudoxus *apud* Porph. *vit. Pyth.* 7. Vegetarianism is associated with Cretan mystery cults by Euripides (fr. 472) and by Theophrastus (*apud* Porph. *de abst.* 2.21), and it may well be that the Cretan vegetarian Epimenides played a part in its diffusion. But the other form of the Pythagorean rule, which forbade only the eating of certain "sacred" creatures, such as the white cock (n. 95 above), may possibly derive from shamanism, since to-day "animals, and especially birds, which play some part in shamanistic beliefs may not be killed or even molested" (Holmberg, *op. cit.*, 500), though a general prohibition of flesh-eating is reported only of certain clans among the Buryats (*ibid.*, 499).

122 The "Pythagorean silence" is proverbial from Isocrates (11.29) onwards. Iamblichus speaks of five years' complete silence for novices (*vit. Pyth.* 68, 72), but this may be a later exaggeration. Sexual restraint, Aristoxenus, fr. 39 W., Iamb. *vit. Pyth.* 132, 209 ff.; sex relations harmful, Diog. Laert. 8.9, Diod. 10.9.3 ff., Plut. *Q. Conv.* 3.6.3, 654B. Celibacy is not required of the modern Siberian shaman. But it is worth noticing that, according to Posidonius, celibacy was practised by certain holy men (shamans?) among the Thracian Getae (Strabo, 7.3.3 f.).

123 Hippolytus (*Ref. haer.* 7.30 = Empedocles B 110) accuses Marcion of emulating the καθαρμοί of Empedocles in trying to get rid of marriage: διαιρεῖ γὰρ ὁ γάμος κατὰ Ἐμπεδοκλέα τὸ ἓν καὶ ποιεῖ πολλά. This is explained by another statement which he attributes to E. (*ibid.*, 7.29 = Emp. B 115), that sexual intercourse helps

the disruptive work of strife. It is not clear, however, whether E. went to the length of preaching race-suicide.

[124] Hippodamas *apud* Iamb. *vit. Pyth.* 82.

[125] Paus. 8.37.5 (= Kern, *Test.* 194).

[126] Wilamowitz, *Glaube*, II.193, 378 f.

[127] Notably by Festugière, *Rev. Bibl.* 44 (1935) 372 ff. and *REG* 49 (1936) 308 f. On the other hand the antiquity of the myth is maintained—not always on what seem to me the strongest grounds—by Guthrie (107 ff.), Nilsson ("Early Orphism," 202), and Boyancé ("Remarques sur le salut selon l'Orphisme," *REA* 43 [1941] 166). The fullest and most careful survey of the evidence is Linforth's, *op. cit.*, chap. v. He inclines on the whole to the earlier dating, though his conclusions are in some other respects negative.

[128] For the probable meaning of the attribution to Onomacritus see Wilamowitz, *Glaube*, II.379, n. 1; Boyancé, *Culte des Muses*, 19 f.; Linforth, 350 ff. I should also be hesitant about building much on the finds in the Theban Kabeirion (Guthrie, 123 ff.), which would be more impressive as evidence if there were anything to connect them directly with Titans or with σπαραγμός. Nor are we helped by S. Reinach's ingenious discovery (*Rev. Arch.* 1919, i.162 ff.) of an allusion to the myth in one of the "additional" Aristotelian προβλήματα (Didot Aristotle, IV.331.15), so long as the date of this πρόβλημα remains uncertain; the evidence of Athen. 656AB is not sufficient to show that the πρόβλημα was known to Philochorus.

[129] See App. I, pp. 276 ff.; and on the connection between the rite and the myth, Nilsson, "Early Orphism," 203 f. Those who deny, like Wilamowitz, that the older Ὀρφικά had *any* connection with Dionysus have to explain away the evidence of Hdt. 2.81 (or eliminate it by adopting the transcriptionally less probable reading).

[130] See above, pp. 33 f.

[131] Pindar, fr. 127 B. (133 S.) = Plato, *Meno* 81BC. This interpretation was offered by Tannery, *Rev. de Phil.* 23, 126 f. The case for it has been persuasively argued by Rose in *Greek Poetry and Life: Essays Presented to Gilbert Murray*, 79 ff. (cf. also his note in *Harv. Theol. Rev.* 36 [1943] 247 ff.).

[132] Plato, *Laws* 701C. The thought is unfortunately as elliptical as the syntax is crabbed; but all explanations which assume that τὴν λεγομένην παλαιὰν Τιτανικὴν φύσιν refers merely to the war of the Titans and the gods seem to me to suffer shipwreck on the phrase ἐπὶ τὰ αὐτὰ πάλιν ἐκεῖνα ἀφικομένους (or ἀφικομένοις,

Schanz), which makes no known sense as applied to Titans, and not much sense (in view of πάλιν) as applied to men unless the human race sprang from Titans. To Linforth's objection (*op. cit.*, 344) that Plato is talking only of degenerates, whereas the myth made the Τιτανικὴ φύσις a permanent part of *all* human nature, the answer surely is that while all men have the Titan nature in their breasts, only degenerates "show it off and emulate it." (ἐπιδεικνῦσι implies that they are proud to have it in them, while μιμουμένοις means that they follow the example of their mythical ancestors.)

133 *Ibid.*, 854B: to a person tormented by impulses to sacrilege we must say: ὦ θαυμάσιε, οὐκ ἀνθρώπινόν σε κακὸν οὐδὲ θεῖον κινεῖ τὸ νῦν ἐπὶ τὴν ἱεροσυλίαν προτρέπον ἰέναι, οἶστρος δέ σέ τις ἐμφυόμενος ἐκ παλαιῶν καὶ ἀκαθάρτων τοῖς ἀνθρώποις ἀδικημάτων, περιφερόμενος ἀλιτηριώδης. The ἀδικήματα are usually thought to be crimes committed by the person's immediate ancestors (so England, etc.), or by the person himself in a previous incarnation (Wilamowitz, *Platon*, I.697). But (*a*) if the temptation arises in some way from past human acts, why is it called οὐκ ἀνθρώπινον κακόν? (*b*) Why is it specifically a temptation to *sacrilege?* (*c*) Why are the original acts ἀκάθαρτα τοῖς ἀνθρώποις (words which are naturally taken together, and must in fact be so taken, since they evidently lead up to the advice in the next sentence to seek purgation *from the gods*)? I cannot resist the conclusion (which I find has been reached on other grounds by Rathmann, *Quaestt. Pyth.*, 67) that Plato is thinking of the Titans, whose incessant irrational promptings (οἶστρος) haunt the unhappy man wherever he goes (περιφερό-μενος), tempting him to emulate their sacrilege. Cf. Plut. *de esu carn.* I, 996C: τὸ γὰρ ἐν ἡμῖν ἄλογον καὶ ἄτακτον καὶ βίαιον, οὐ θεῖον <ὂν> ἀλλὰ δαιμονικόν, οἱ παλαιοὶ Τιτᾶνας ὠνόμασαν (which seems to come from Xenocrates); and for οἶστρος resulting from man's evil inheritance, Olymp. *in Phaed.* 87.13 ff. N. (= *O.F.* 232).

134 Olymp. *in Phaed.* 84.22 ff.: ἡ φρουρά . . . ὡς Ξενοκράτης, Τιτανική ἐστιν καὶ εἰς Διόνυσον ἀποκορυφοῦται (= Xenocrates, fr. 20). Cf. Heinze *ad loc.*; E. Frank, *Platon u. d. sog. Pythagoreer*, 246; and the more cautious views of Linforth, 337 ff.

135 It must be conceded to Linforth that none of the older writers explicitly equates the divine in man with the Dionysiac. But it can, I think, be shown that this equation is not (as Linforth maintains, p. 330) the invention of Olympiodorus (*in Phaed.* 3.2 ff.), or (as might be suggested) of his source Porphyry (cf. Olymp. *ibid.*, 85.3). (*a*) It appears in Olympiodorus, not merely "as a desperate

device to explain a puzzling passage in Plato" (Linforth, p. 359), but as an explanation in mythical terms of moral conflict and the redemption of man, *in Phaed.* 87.1 ff.: τὸν ἐν ἡμῖν Διόνυσον διασπῶμεν . . . οὕτω δ' ἔχοντες Τιτᾶνές ἐσμεν· ὅταν δὲ εἰς ἐκεῖνο συμβῶμεν, Διόνυσοι γινόμεθα τετελειωμένοι ἀτεχνῶς. When Linforth says (p. 360) that the connection of these ideas with the Titan myth "is not suggested by Olympiodorus and is merely the gratuitous assertion of modern scholars," he seems to have overlooked this passage. (*b*) Iamblichus says of the old Pythagoreans, *vit. Pyth.* 240, παρήγγελλον γὰρ θαμὰ ἀλλήλοις μὴ διασπᾶν τὸν ἐν ἑαυτοῖς θεόν. It has apparently escaped notice that he is alluding to the same doctrine as Olympiodorus (the use of the verb διασπᾶν makes this fairly certain). We do not know what his source was; but even Iamblichus would hardly represent as an old-Pythagorean σύμβολον something which had just been invented by Porphyry. Its real age cannot be exactly determined; but it is a reasonable guess that, like the Titan myth itself, Porphyry found it in Xenocrates. If so, Plato will hardly have been ignorant of it. But Plato had a good reason for not using this element of the myth: he could identify the irrational impulses with the Titans, but to equate the divine in man with the Dionysiac was repugnant to a rationalist philosophy.

[136] Keith, *Rel. and Phil. of Veda and Upanishads*, 579.

VI

Rationalism and Reaction in the Classical Age

The major advances in civilisation are processes which all but wreck the societies in which they occur.

A. N. Whitehead

In the previous chapters of this book I have tried to illustrate within a particular field of belief the slow, age-long building up, out of the deposit left by successive religious movements, of what Gilbert Murray in a recently published lecture has called "the Inherited Conglomerate."[1] The geological metaphor is apt, for religious growth is geological: its principle is, on the whole and with exceptions, *agglomeration*, not substitution. A new belief-pattern very seldom effaces completely the pattern that was there before: either the old lives on as an element in the new—sometimes an unconfessed and half-unconscious element—or else the two persist side by side, logically incompatible, but contemporaneously accepted by different individuals or even by the same individual. As an example of the first situation, we have seen how Homeric notions like *ate* were taken up into, and transformed by, the archaic guilt-culture. As an example of the second, we have seen how the Classical Age inherited a whole series of inconsistent pictures of the "soul" or "self"—the living corpse in the grave, the shadowy image in Hades, the perishable breath that is spilt in the air or absorbed in the aether, the daemon that is reborn in other bodies. Though of varying age and derived from different culture-patterns, all

[1] For notes to chapter vi see pages 195–206.

these pictures persisted in the background of fifth-century thinking; you could take some one of them seriously, or more than one, or even all, since there was no Established Church to assure you that this was true and the other false. On questions like that there was no "Greek view," but only a muddle of conflicting answers.

Such, then, was the Inherited Conglomerate at the end of the Archaic Age, historically intelligible as the reflex of changing human needs over many successive generations, but intellectually a mass of confusion. We saw in passing how Aeschylus attempted to master this confusion and to elicit from it something which made moral sense.[2] But in the period between Aeschylus and Plato the attempt was not renewed. In that period the gap between the beliefs of the people and the beliefs of the intellectuals, which is already implicit in Homer,[3] widens to a complete breach, and prepares the way for the gradual dissolution of the Conglomerate. With certain consequences of this process, and of the attempts that were made to check it, I shall be concerned in the remaining chapters.

The process itself does not, in its general aspect, form part of my subject. It belongs to the history of Greek rationalism, which has been written often enough.[4] But certain things are perhaps worth saying about it. One is that the "Aufklärung" or Enlightenment was not initiated by the Sophists. It seems desirable to say this, because there are still people who talk as if "Enlightenment" and Sophistic Movement were the same thing, and proceed to envelope both in the same blanket of condemnation or (less often) approval. The Enlightenment is of course much older; its roots are in sixth-century Ionia; it is at work in Hecataeus, Xenophanes, and Heraclitus, and in a later generation is carried further by speculative scientists like Anaxagoras and Democritus. Hecataeus is the first Greek who admitted that he found Greek mythology "funny,"[5] and set to work to make it less funny by inventing rationalist explanations, while his contemporary Xenophanes attacked the Homeric and Hesiodic myths from the moral angle.[6] More

important for our purposes is the statement that Xenophanes
denied the validity of divination (μαντική):[7] if this is true, it
means that, almost alone among classical Greek thinkers, he
swept aside not only the pseudo-science of reading omens
but the whole deep-seated complex of ideas about inspiration
which occupied us in an earlier chapter. But his decisive contribution was his discovery of the relativity of religious ideas.
"If the ox could paint a picture, his god would look like an
ox":[8] once that had been said, it could only be a matter of
time before the entire fabric of traditional belief began to
loosen. Xenophanes was himself a deeply religious man; he had
his private faith in a god "who is not like men in appearance or
in mind."[9] But he was conscious that it was faith, not knowledge. No man, he says, has ever had, or ever will have, sure
knowledge about gods; even if he should chance to hit on the
exact truth, he cannot *know* that he has done so, though we
can all have our opinions.[10] That honest distinction between
what is knowable and what is not appears again and again in
fifth-century thought,[11] and is surely one of its chief glories;
it is the foundation of scientific humility.

Again, if we turn to the fragments of Heraclitus, we find
a whole series of direct assaults on the Conglomerate, some of
which concern the types of belief we have considered in previous chapters. His denial of validity to dream-experience we
have already noticed.[12] He made fun of ritual catharsis, comparing those who purge blood with blood to a man who should
try to wash off dirt by bathing in mud.[13] That was a direct blow
at the consolations of religion. So was his complaint that "the
customary mysteries" were conducted in an unholy manner,
though unluckily we do not know on what the criticism was
based or exactly what mysteries he had in mind.[14] Again, the
saying νεκύες κοπρίων ἐκβλητότεροι, "dead is nastier than dung,"
might have been approved by Socrates, but it was a studied
insult to ordinary Greek sentiment: it dismisses in three words
all the pother about burial rites which figures so largely both in
Attic tragedy and in Greek military history, and indeed the

whole tangle of feelings which centred round the ghost-corpse.[15] Another three-word maxim, ἦθος ἀνθρώπῳ δαίμων, "character is destiny," similarly dismisses by implication the whole set of archaic beliefs about inborn luck and divine temptation.[16] And finally, Heraclitus had the temerity to attack what to this day is still a leading feature of Greek popular religion, the cult of images, which he declared was like talking to a man's house instead of talking to its owner.[17] Had Heraclitus been an Athenian, he would pretty certainly have been had up for blasphemy, as Wilamowitz says.[18]

However, we must not exaggerate the influence of these early pioneers. Xenophanes, and still more Heraclitus, give the impression of being isolated figures even in Ionia,[19] and it was a long time before their ideas found any echo on the Mainland. Euripides is the first Athenian of whom we can say with confidence that he had read Xenophanes,[20] and he is also represented as introducing the teaching of Heraclitus for the first time to the Athenian public.[21] But by Euripides' day the Enlightenment had been carried much further. It was probably Anaxagoras who taught him to call the divine sun "a golden clod,"[22] and it may have been the same philosopher who inspired his mockery of the professional seers;[23] while it was certainly the Sophists who set him and his whole generation discussing fundamental moral questions in terms of *Nŏmŏs* versus *Physis*, "Law" or "Custom" or "Convention" versus "Nature."

I do not propose to say much about this celebrated antithesis, whose origin and ramifications have been carefully examined in a recent book by a young Swiss scholar, Felix Heinimann.[24] But it may not be superfluous to point out that thinking in these terms could lead to widely different conclusions according to the meaning you assigned to the terms themselves. *Nomos* could stand for the Conglomerate, conceived as the inherited burden of irrational custom; or it could stand for an arbitrary rule consciously imposed by certain classes in their own interest; or it could stand for a rational system of State law, the achievement which distinguished Greeks from barbarians. Similarly *Physis* could represent an unwritten, unconditionally valid "natural law," against the particularism of local custom; or it could represent the "natural rights" of the individual, against the arbitrary requirements of the State; and this in turn could pass—as always happens when rights are asserted without a corresponding recognition of duties—into a pure anarchic immoralism, the "natural right of the stronger" as expounded by the Athenians in the Melian Dialogue and by Callicles in the *Gorgias*. It is not surprising that an antithesis whose terms were so ambiguous led to a vast amount of argument at cross-purposes. But through the fog of confused and for us fragmentary controversy we can dimly perceive two great issues being fought out. One is the ethical question concerning the source and the validity of moral and political obligation. The other is the psychological question concerning the springs of human conduct—why do men behave as they do, and how can they be induced to behave better? It is only the second of these issues which concerns us here.

On that issue the first generation of Sophists, in particular Protagoras, seem to have held a view whose optimism is pathetic in retrospect, but historically intelligible. "Virtue or Efficiency (*arete*) could be taught": by criticising his traditions, by modernising the *Nomos* which his ancestors had created and eliminating from it the last vestiges of "barbarian silliness,"[25] man could acquire a new Art of Living, and human life could be raised to new levels hitherto undreamed of. Such a hope is understandable in men who had witnessed the swift growth of material prosperity after the Persian Wars, and the unexampled flowering of the spirit that accompanied it, culminating in the unique achievements of Periclean Athens. For that generation, the Golden Age was no lost paradise of the dim past, as Hesiod had believed; for them it lay not behind but ahead, and not so very far ahead either. In a civilised community, declared Protagoras robustly, the very worst citizen was already a better man than the supposedly noble savage.[26] Better, in fact, fifty years of Europe than a cycle of Cathay. But history has, alas, a short way with optimists. Had Tennyson experienced the latest fifty years of Europe he might, I fancy, have reconsidered his preference; and Protagoras before he died had ample ground for revising his. Faith in the inevitability of progress had an even shorter run in Athens than in England.[27]

In what I take to be a quite early dialogue, Plato set this Protagorean view of human nature over against the Socratic. Superficially, the two have much in common. Both use the traditional[28] utilitarian language: "good" means "good for the individual," and is not distinguished from the "profitable" or the "useful." And both have the traditional[29] intellectualist approach: they agree, against the common opinion of their time, that if a man really knew what was good for him he would act on his knowledge.[30] Each, however, qualifies his intellectualism with a different sort of reservation. For Protagoras, *arete* can be taught, but not by an intellectual discipline: one "picks it up," as a child picks up his native language;[31] it is transmitted not by formal teaching, but by what the anthropologists call "social control." For Socrates, on the other hand, *arete* is or should be *epistēmē*, a branch of scientific knowledge: in this dialogue he is even made to talk as if its appropriate method were the nice calculation of future pains and pleasures, and I am willing to believe that he did at times so talk.[32] Yet he is also made to doubt whether *arete* can be taught at all, and this too I am willing to accept as historical.[33] For to Socrates *arete* was something which proceeded from within outward; it was not a set of behaviour-patterns to be acquired through habituation, but a consistent attitude of mind springing from a steady insight into the nature and meaning of human life. In its self-consistency it resembled a science;[34] but I think we should be wrong to interpret the insight as purely logical—it involved the whole man.[35] Socrates no doubt believed in "following the argument wherever it led"; but he found that too often it led only to fresh questions, and where it failed him he was prepared to follow other guides. We should not forget that he took both dreams and oracles very seriously,[36] and that he habitually heard and obeyed an inner voice which knew more than he did (if we can believe Xenophon,[37] he called it, quite simply, "the voice of God").

Thus neither Protagoras nor Socrates quite fits the popular modern conception of a "Greek rationalist." But what seems to us odd is that both of them dismiss so easily the part played by emotion in determining ordinary human behavior. And we know from Plato that this seemed odd to their contemporaries also; on this matter there was a sharp cleavage between the intellectuals and the common man. "Most people," says Socrates, "do not think of knowledge as a force (ἰσχυρόν), much less a dominant or ruling force: they think a man may often have knowledge while he is ruled by something else, at one time anger, at another pleasure or pain, sometimes love, very often fear; they really picture knowledge as a slave which is kicked about by all these other things."[38] Protagoras agrees that this is the common view, but considers it not worth discussing—"the common man will say anything."[39] Socrates, who does discuss it, explains it away by translating it into intellectual terms: the nearness of an immediate pleasure or pain leads to false judgements analogous to errors of visual perspective; a scientific moral arithmetic would correct these.[40]

It is unlikely that such reasoning impressed the common man. The Greek had always felt the experience of passion as something mysterious and frightening, the experience of a force that was in him, possessing him, rather than possessed by him. The very word páthos testifies to that: like its Latin equivalent passio, it means something that "happens to" a man, something of which he is the passive victim. Aristotle compares the man in a state of passion to men asleep, insane, or drunk: his reason, like theirs, is in suspense.[41] We saw in earlier chapters[42] how Homer's heroes and the men of the Archaic Age interpreted such experience in religious terms, as ate, as a communication of menos, or as the direct working of a daemon who uses the human mind and body as his instrument.

That is the usual view of simple people: "the primitive under the influence of strong passion considers himself as possessed, or ill, which for him is the same thing."[43] That way of thinking was not dead even in the late fifth century. Jason at the end of the *Medea* can explain his wife's conduct only as the act of an *alastor*, the daemon created by unatoned bloodguilt; the Chorus of the *Hippolytus* think that Phaedra may be possessed, and she herself speaks at first of her condition as the *ate* of a daemon.[44]

But for the poet, and for the educated part of his audience, this language has now only the force of a traditional symbolism. The daemonic world has withdrawn, leaving man alone with his passions. And this is what gives Euripides' studies of crime their peculiar poignancy: he shows us men and women nakedly confronting the mystery of evil, no longer as an alien thing assailing their reason from without, but as a part of their own being—ἦθος ἀνθρώπῳ δαίμων. Yet, for ceasing to be supernatural, it is not the less mysterious and terrifying. Medea knows that she is at grips, not with an *alastor*, but with her own irrational self, her *thumos*. She entreats that self for mercy, as a slave begs mercy of a brutal master.[45] But in vain: the springs of action are hidden in the *thumos* where neither reason nor pity can reach them. "I know what wickedness I am about to do; but the *thumos* is stronger than my purposes, *thumos*, the root of man's worst acts."[46] On these words, she leaves the stage; when she returns, she has condemned her children to death and herself to a lifetime of foreseen unhappiness. For Medea has no Socratic "illusions of perspective"; she makes no mistake in her moral arithmetic, any more than she mistakes her passion for an evil spirit. Therein lies her supreme tragic quality.

Whether the poet had Socrates in mind when he wrote the *Medea*, I do not know. But a conscious rejection of the Socratic theory has been seen,[47] I think rightly, in the famous words that he put into the mouth of Phaedra three years later. Misconduct, she says, does not depend on a failure of insight, "for plenty of people have a good understanding." No, we know and

recognise our good, but fail to act on the knowledge: either
a kind of inertia obstructs us, or we are distracted from
our purpose by "some pleasure."[48] This does look as if it
had a controversial point, for it goes beyond what the dramatic situation requires or even suggests.[49] Nor do these passages stand alone; the moral impotence of the reason is asserted
more than once in fragments from lost plays.[50] But to judge
from extant pieces, what chiefly preoccupied Euripides in his
later work was not so much the impotence of reason in man as
the wider doubt whether any rational purpose could be seen
in the ordering of human life and the governance of the world.[51]
That trend culminates in the *Bacchae*, whose religious content
is, as a recent critic has said,[52] the recognition of a "Beyond"
which is outside our moral categories and inaccessible to our
reason. I do not maintain that a consistent philosophy of life
can be extracted from the plays (nor should we demand this of
a dramatist writing in an age of doubt). But if we must attach
a label, I still think that the word "irrationalist," which I
once suggested,[53] fits Euripides better than any other.

This does not imply that Euripides followed the extreme
Physis school, who provided human weakness with a fashionable
excuse by declaring that the passions were "natural" and therefore right, morality a convention and therefore a shackle to be
cast off. "Be natural," says the Unjust Cause in the *Clouds;*
"kick up your heels, laugh at the world, take no shame for
anything."[54] Certain characters in Euripides follow this counsel, if in a less lighthearted manner. "Nature willed it," says
an erring daughter, "and nature pays no heed to rules: we
women were made for this."[55] "I don't need your advice," says
a homosexual; "I can see for myself, but nature constrains
me."[56] Even the most deeply rooted of man's taboos, the prohibition of incest, is dismissed with the remark, "There's
nothing shameful but thinking makes it so."[57] There must
have been young people in Euripides' circle who talked like
that (we are familiar with their modern counterparts). But I
doubt if the poet shared their opinions. For his Choruses re-

peatedly go out of their way to denounce, without much dramatic relevance, certain persons who "slight the law, to gratify lawless impulse," whose aim is εὖ κακουργεῖν, "to do wrong and get away with it," whose theory and practice is "above the laws," for whom *aidos* and *arete* are mere words.[58] These unnamed persons are surely the *Physis* men, or the pupils of the *Physis* men, the "realist" politicians whom we meet in Thucydides.

Euripides, then, if I am right about him, reflects not only the Enlightenment, but also the reaction against the Enlightenment—at any rate he reacted against the rationalist psychology of some of its exponents and the slick immoralism of others. To the violence of the *public* reaction there is, of course, other testimony. The audience that saw the *Clouds* was expected to enjoy the burning down of the Thinking Shop, and to care little if Socrates were burnt with it. But satirists are bad witnesses, and with sufficient good will it is possible to believe that the *Clouds* is just Aristophanes' friendly fun.[59] More secure deductions can perhaps be drawn from a less familiar bit of evidence. A fragment of Lysias[60] makes us acquainted with a certain dining-club. This club had a curious and shocking name: its members called themselves Κακοδαιμονισταί, a profane parody of the name Ἀγαθοδαιμονισταί which respectable social clubs sometimes adopted. Liddell and Scott translate it "devil-worshippers," and that would be the literal meaning; but Lysias is no doubt right in saying that they chose the title "to make fun of the gods and of Athenian custom." He further tells us that they made a point of dining on unlucky days (ἡμέραι ἀποφράδες), which suggests that the club's purpose was to exhibit its scorn of superstition by deliberately tempting the gods, deliberately doing as many unlucky things as possible, including the adoption of an unlucky name. One might think this pretty harmless. But according to Lysias the gods were not amused: most of the members of the club died young, and the sole survivor, the poet Kinesias,[61] was afflicted with a chronic disease so painful as to be worse than death. This un-

important story seems to me to illustrate two things rather well.
It illustrates the sense of liberation—liberation from meaningless rules and irrational guilt-feelings—which the Sophists
brought with them, and which made their teaching so attractive to the high-spirited and intelligent young. And it also
shows how strong was the reaction against such rationalism in
the breast of the average citizen: for Lysias evidently relies on
the awful scandal of the dining-club to discredit Kinesias' testimony in a lawsuit.

But the most striking evidence of the reaction against the
Enlightenment is to be seen in the successful prosecutions of
intellectuals on religious grounds which took place at Athens in
the last third of the fifth century. About 432 B.C.[62] or a year or
two later, disbelief in the supernatural[63] and the teaching of
astronomy[64] were made indictable offences. The next thirty-
odd years witnessed a series of heresy trials which is unique in
Athenian history. The victims included most of the leaders of
progressive thought at Athens—Anaxagoras,[65] Diagoras, Socrates, almost certainly Protagoras also,[66] and possibly Euripides.[67]
In all these cases save the last the prosecution was successful:
Anaxagoras may have been fined and banished; Diagoras
escaped by flight; so, probably, did Protagoras; Socrates, who
could have done the same, or could have asked for a sentence of
banishment, chose to stay and drink the hemlock. All these
were famous people. How many obscurer persons may have
suffered for their opinions we do not know.[68] But the evidence
we have is more than enough to prove that the Great Age of
Greek Enlightenment was also, like our own time, an Age of
Persecution—banishment of scholars, blinkering of thought,
and even (if we can believe the tradition about Protagoras)[69]
burning of books.

This distressed and puzzled nineteenth-century professors,
who had not our advantage of familiarity with this kind of
behaviour. It puzzled them the more because it happened at
Athens, the "school of Hellas," the "headquarters of philosophy," and, so far as our information goes, nowhere else.[70]

Hence a tendency to cast doubt on the evidence wherever possible; and where this was not possible, to explain that the real motive behind the prosecutions was political. Up to a point, this was doubtless true, at least in some of the cases: the accusers of Anaxagoras were presumably, as Plutarch says, striking at his patron Pericles; and Socrates might well have escaped condemnation had he not been associated with men like Critias and Alcibiades. But granting all this, we have still to explain why at this period a charge of irreligion was so often selected as the surest means of suppressing an unwelcome voice or damaging a political opponent. We seem driven to assume the existence among the masses of an exasperated religious bigotry on which politicians could play for their own purposes. And the exasperation must have had a cause.

Nilsson has suggested[71] that it was whipped up by the professional diviners, who saw in the advance of rationalism a threat to their prestige, and even to their livelihood. That seems quite likely. The proposer of the decree which set off the series of prosecutions was the professional diviner Diopeithes; Anaxagoras had exposed the true nature of so-called "portents";[72] while Socrates had a private "oracle"[73] of his own which may well have aroused jealousy.[74] The influence of diviners, however, had its limits. To judge by the constant jokes at their expense in Aristophanes, they were not greatly loved or (save at moments of crisis)[75] wholly trusted: like the politicians, they might exploit popular sentiment, but they were hardly in a position to create it.

More important, perhaps, was the influence of wartime hysteria. If we allow for the fact that wars cast their shadows before them and leave emotional disturbances behind them, the Age of Persecution coincides pretty closely with the longest and most disastrous war in Greek history. The coincidence is hardly accidental. It has been observed that "in times of danger to the community the whole tendency to conformity is greatly strengthened: the herd huddles together and becomes more intolerant than ever of 'cranky' opinion."[76] We have seen this observation confirmed in two recent wars, and we may assume that it was not otherwise in antiquity. Antiquity had indeed a conscious reason for insisting on religious conformity in wartime, where we have only unconscious ones. To offend the gods by doubting their existence, or by calling the sun a stone, was risky enough in peacetime; but in war it was practically treason—it amounted to helping the enemy. For religion was a collective responsibility. The gods were not content to strike down the individual offender: did not Hesiod say that whole cities often suffered for one bad man?[77] That these ideas were still very much alive in the minds of the Athenian populace is evident from the enormous hysterical fuss created by the mutilation of the Hermae.[78]

That, I think, is part of the explanation—superstitious terror based on the solidarity of the city-state. I should like to believe that it was the whole explanation. But it would be dishonest not to recognise that the new rationalism carried with it real as well as imaginary dangers for the social order. In discarding the Inherited Conglomerate, many people discarded with it the religious restraints that had held human egotism on the leash. To men of strong moral principle—a Protagoras or a Democritus—that did not matter: their conscience was adult enough to stand up without props. It was otherwise with most of their pupils. To them, the liberation of the individual meant an unlimited freedom of self-assertion; it meant rights without duties, unless self-assertion is a duty; "what their fathers had called self-control they called an excuse for cowardice."[79] Thucydides put that down to war mentality, and no doubt this was the immediate cause; Wilamowitz rightly remarked that the authors of the Corcyraean massacres did not have to learn about the transvaluation of values from a course of lectures by Hippias. The new rationalism did not *enable* men to behave like beasts—men have always been able to do that. But it enabled them to justify their brutality to themselves, and that at a time when the external temptations to brutal conduct were particularly strong. As someone has said in reference to our own enlightened age, seldom have so many babies been poured out with so little bath-water.[80] Therein lay the immediate danger, a danger which has always shown itself when an Inherited Conglomerate was in process of breaking down. In Professor Murray's words, "Anthropology seems to show that these Inherited Conglomerates have practically no chance of being true or even sensible; and, on the other hand, that no society can exist without them or even submit to any drastic correction of them without social danger."[81] Of the latter truth there was, I take it, some confused inkling in the minds of the men who charged Socrates with corrupting the young. Their fears were not groundless; but as people do when they are frightened, they struck with the wrong weapon and they struck the wrong man.

The Enlightenment also affected the social fabric in another and more permanent way. What Jacob Burckhardt said of nineteenth-century religion, that it was "rationalism for the few and magic for the many," might on the whole be said of Greek religion from the late fifth century onwards. Thanks to the Enlightenment, and the absence of universal education, the divorce between the beliefs of the few and the beliefs of the many was made absolute, to the injury of both. Plato is almost the last Greek intellectual who seems to have real social roots; his successors, with very few exceptions, make the impression of existing beside society rather than in it. They are "sapientes" first, citizens afterwards or not at all, and their touch upon contemporary social realities is correspondingly uncertain. This fact is familiar. What is less often noticed is the regressiveness of popular religion in the Age of Enlightenment. The first signs of this regression appeared during the Peloponnesian War, and were doubtless in part due to the war. Under the stresses that it generated, people began to slip back from the too difficult achievement of the Periclean Age; cracks appeared in the fabric, and disagreeably primitive things poked up here and there through the cracks. When that happened, there was no longer any effective check on their growth. As the intellectuals withdrew further into a world of their own, the popular mind was left increasingly defenceless, though it must be said that for several generations the comic poets continued to do their best. The loosening of the ties of civic religion began to set men free to choose their own gods, instead of simply worshipping as their fathers had done; and, left without guidance, a growing number relapsed with a sigh of relief into the pleasures and comforts of the primitive.

I shall conclude this chapter by giving some examples of what I call regression. One instance we have already had occasion to notice[82]—the increased demand for magical healing which within a generation or two transformed Asclepius from a minor hero into a major god, and made his temple at Epidaurus a place of pilgrimage as famous as Lourdes is to-day. It is a reasonable guess that his fame at Athens (and perhaps elsewhere too) dated from the Great Plague of 430.[83] That visitation, according to Thucydides, convinced some people that religion was useless,[84] since piety proved no protection against bacilli; but it must have set others looking for a new and better magic. Nothing could be done at the time; but in 420, during the interval of peace, Asclepius was solemnly inducted into Athens, accompanied, or more probably represented, by his Holy Snake.[85] Until a house could be built for him, he enjoyed the hospitality of no less a person than the poet Sophocles—a fact which has its bearing on the understanding of Sophocles' poetry. As Wilamowitz observed,[86] one cannot think that either Aeschylus or Euripides would have cared to entertain a Holy Snake. But nothing illustrates better the polarisation of the Greek mind at this period than the fact that the generation which paid such honour to this medical reptile saw also the publication of some of the most austerely scientific of the Hippocratic treatises.[87]

A second example of regression may be seen in the fashion for foreign cults, mostly of a highly emotional, "orgiastic" kind, which developed with surprising suddenness during the Peloponnesian War.[88] Before it was over, there had appeared at

Athens the worship of the Phrygian "Mountain Mother," Cybele, and that of her Thracian counterpart, Bendis; the mysteries of the Thraco-Phrygian Sabazius, a sort of savage un-Hellenised Dionysus; and the rites of the Asiatic "dying gods," Attis and Adonis. I have discussed this significant development elsewhere,[89] so shall not say more about it here.

A generation or so later, we find the regression taking an even cruder form. That in the fourth century there was at Athens plenty of "magic for the many," and in the most literal sense of the term, we know from the first-hand evidence of the "defixiones." The practice of *defixio* or κατάδεσις was a kind of magical attack. It was believed that you could bind a person's will, or cause his death, by invoking upon him the curse of the underworld Powers; you inscribed the curse on something durable, a leaden tablet or a potsherd, and you placed it for choice in a dead man's grave. Hundreds of such "defixiones" have been found by excavators in many parts of the Mediterranean world,[90] and indeed similar practices are observed occasionally to-day, both in Greece[91] and in other parts of Europe.[92] But it seems significant that the oldest examples so far discovered come from Greece, most of them from Attica; and that while exceedingly few examples can be referred with certainty to the fifth century, in the fourth they are suddenly quite numerous.[93] The persons cursed in them include well-known public figures like Phocion and Demosthenes,[94] which suggests that the practice was not confined to slaves or aliens. Indeed, it was sufficiently common in Plato's day for him to think it worth while to legislate against it,[95] as also against the kindred method of magical attack by maltreating a wax image of one's enemy.[96] Plato makes it clear that people were really afraid of this magical aggression, and he would prescribe severe legal penalties for it (in the case of professional magicians the death penalty), not because he himself believes in black magic—as to that he professes to have an open mind[97]—but because black magic expresses an evil will and has evil psychological effects. Nor was this merely the private fussiness of an

elderly moralist. From a passage in the speech *Against Aristogei-
ton*[98] we may infer that in the fourth century attempts were
actually made to repress magic by drastic legal action. Taking
all this evidence together, in contrast with the almost complete
silence of our fifth-century sources,[99] I am inclined to conclude that one effect of the Enlightenment was to provoke in
the second generation[100] a revival of magic. That is not so
paradoxical as it sounds: has not the breakdown of another
Inherited Conglomerate been followed by similar manifestations in our own age?

All the symptoms I have mentioned—the revival of incubation, the taste for orgiastic religion, the prevalence of magical
attack—can be viewed as regressive; they were in a sense a
return of the past. But they were also, in another aspect,
portents of things to come. As we shall see in the final chapter,
they point forward to characteristic features of the Greco-
Roman world. But before we come to that, we must consider
Plato's attempt to stabilise the situation.

NOTES TO CHAPTER VI

[1] Gilbert Murray, *Greek Studies*, 66 f.

[2] Chap. ii, pp. 39 f.

[3] This point is made most forcibly, if with some exaggeration, by
Pfister, *Religion d. Griechen u. Römer*, Bursian's Jahresbericht, 229
(1930) 219. Cf. chap. ii, pp. 43 f.

[4] See, in particular, the recent book of Wilhelm Nestle, *Vom
Mythos zum Logos*, the purpose of which is to exhibit "the progressive replacement of mythological by rational thinking among
the Greeks."

[5] Hecataeus, fr. 1 Jacoby; cf. Nestle, *op. cit.*, 134 ff. Hecataeus rationalised mythological bogies like Cerberus (fr. 27), and possibly
all the other horrors of τὰ ἐν Ἀΐδου. That he was personally
ἀδεισιδαίμων appears from his advice to his countrymen to appropriate to secular uses the treasures of Apollo's oracle at Branchidae (Hdt. 5.36.3). Cf. Momigliano, *Atene e Roma*, 12 (1931) 139,

and the way in which Diodorus and Plutarch present the similar action of Sulla (Diod. 38/9, fr. 7; Plut. *Sulla* 12).

[6] Xenophanes, frs. 11 and 12 Diels.

[7] Cic. *div.* 1.5; Aetius, 5.1.1 (= Xenophanes, A 52). Cf. his naturalistic explanations of the rainbow (fr. 32) and of St. Elmo's fire (A 39), both of which are traditional portents.

[8] Xenophanes, fr. 15 (cf. 14 and 16).

[9] Fr. 23. Cf. Jaeger, *Theology*, 42 ff. As Murray says (*op. cit.*, 69), "That 'or in mind' gives food for thought. It reminds one of the mediaeval Arab mystic who said that to call God 'just' was as foolishly anthropomorphic as to say that he had a beard." Cf. the God of Heraclitus, for whom human distinctions of "just" and "unjust" are meaningless, since he perceives everything as just (fr. 102 Diels).

[10] Fr. 34.

[11] Cf. Heraclitus, fr. 28; Alcmaeon, fr. 1; Hipp. *vet. med.* 1, with Festugière *ad loc.*; Gorgias, *Hel.* 13; Eur. fr. 795.

[12] See chap. iv, p. 118.

[13] Heraclitus, fr. 5. If fr. 69 is to be trusted, he did not dispense altogether with the concept of κάθαρσις; but he may have transposed it, like Plato, to the moral and intellectual plane.

[14] Fr. 14. The antecedent reference to βάκχοι and λῆναι suggests that he had Dionysiac (not "Orphic") mysteries especially in mind; but in the form in which it is transmitted, his condemnation appears not to be limited to these. Whether he intended to condemn mysteries as such, or only their methods, cannot, I think, be determined with certainty, though it is plain from the company in which he puts them that he had little sympathy with μύσται. Fr. 15 throws no light on the question, even if we could be sure of its meaning: the φαλλικά were not a μυστήριον. As to the much-discussed equation of Dionysus with Hades in that fragment, I take this to be a Heraclitean paradox, not an "Orphic mystery-doctrine," and am inclined to agree with those who see in it a condemnation of the φαλλικά, not an excuse for them (the life of the senses is the death of the soul, cf. frs. 77, 117, and Diels, *Herakleitos*, 20).

[15] Fr. 96. Cf. Plato, *Phaedo* 115c; and for the sentiments attacked, chap. v, pp. 136 f.

[16] Fr. 119; cf. chap. ii, p. 42. Fr. 106 similarly attacks the superstition about "lucky" and "unlucky" days.

[17] Fr. 5. On the modern cult of holy icons (statues being forbidden) see B. Schmidt, *Volksleben*, 49 ff.

[18] *Glaube*, II.209. Heraclitus' significance as an *Aufklärer* is rightly emphasised by Gigon, *Untersuchungen zu Heraklit*, 131 ff., and (despite what seems to me a questionable interpretation of fr. 15) by Nestle, *op. cit.*, 98 ff. His doctrine has, of course, other and no less important aspects, but they do not concern the subject of this book.

[19] Cf. Xenophanes, fr. 8; Heraclitus, frs. 1, 57, 104, etc.

[20] The similarity between Eur. fr. 282 and Xenophanes, fr. 2 was noticed by Athenaeus, and seems too close to be accidental; cf. also Eur. *Her.* 1341–1346 with Xenophanes A 32 and B 11 and 12. On the other hand, the resemblance of Aesch. *Supp.* 100–104 to Xenophanes B 25–26, though interesting, is hardly specific enough to establish that Aeschylus had read or heard the Ionian.

[21] Diog. Laert. 2.22. Heraclitus' critique of irrational ritual has in fact echoes in Euripides (Nestle, *Euripides*, 50, 118); though these need not be direct borrowings (Gigon, *op. cit.*, 141). Euripides is described as a noted collector of books (Athen. 3A; cf. Eur. fr. 369 on the pleasures of reading, and Ar. *Ran.* 943).

[22] Eur. fr. 783.

[23] Cf. P. Decharme, *Euripide et l'esprit de son théâtre*, 96 ff.; L. Radermacher, *Rh. Mus.* 53 (1898) 501 ff.

[24] F. Heinimann, *Nomos und Physis* (Basel, 1945). For a bibliography of earlier studies see W. C. Greene, *Moira*, App. 31.

[25] Cf. Hdt. 1.60.3: ἀπεκρίθη ἐκ παλαιτέρου τοῦ βαρβάρου ἔθνεος τὸ Ἑλληνικόν, ἐὸν καὶ δεξιώτερον καὶ εὐηθίης ἠλιθίου ἀπηλλαγμένον μᾶλλον.

[26] Plato, *Prot.* 327CD.

[27] A measure of the swift decline in confidence is the changed tone of the Sophist known as "Anonymus Iamblichi" (*Vorsokr.*[5], 89), who shared Protagoras' belief in νόμος and was perhaps his pupil. Writing, we may guess, in the later years of the Peloponnesian War, he speaks in the despondent voice of one who has seen the whole social and moral order crumble about his head.

[28] On the traditional character of the identification of the "good" with the useful, see Snell, *Die Entdeckung des Geistes*, 131 ff. For Socratic utilitarianism cf. Xen. *Mem.* 3.9.4, etc.

[29] Cf. chap. i, p. 17. So long as ἀρετή was conceived in the positive way as efficiency, "being good at doing things," it was naturally thought of as dependent on knowing how to do them. But by the fifth century the masses (to judge from *Prot.* 352B and *Gorg.* 491D) were more impressed by the negative aspect of ἀρετή as control of passion, in which the intellectual factor is less obvious.

30 Plato, *Prot.* 352A–E.

31 *Ibid.*, 327E. The comparison is a fifth-century one, and was probably used by the historical Protagoras, since it appears in the same context in Euripides, *Suppl.* 913 ff. In general, I incline to think with Taylor, Wilamowitz, and Nestle that Protagoras' discourse (320C–328D) can be taken as a broadly faithful reproduction of views which Protagoras actually held, though certainly not as an excerpt or précis from one of his works.

32 Cf. R. Hackforth, "Hedonism in Plato's Protagoras," *CQ* 22 (1928) 39 ff., whose arguments seem very hard to answer.

33 *Prot.* 319A–320C. This is often said to be "merely ironical," in order to eliminate the difference between the sceptical Socrates of this dialogue and the Socrates of the *Gorgias* who has discovered what true statesmanship is. But to take it so is to destroy the point of the paradox with which the dialogue ends (361A). Plato must have felt that there was in his master's teaching on this matter a real inconsistency, or at any rate obscurity, which needed clearing up. In the *Gorgias* he cleared it up, but in doing so stepped beyond the position of the historical Socrates.

34 The reciprocal implication of the virtues is among the few positive doctrines which we can attribute with confidence to the historical Socrates (cf. *Prot.* 329D ff., *Laches*, *Charmides*, Xen. *Mem.* 3.9.4 f., etc.).

35 Cf. Festugière, *Contemplation et vie contemplative chez Platon*, 68 f.; Jaeger, *Paideia*, II.65 ff.

36 Plato, *Apol.* 33C: ἐμοὶ δὲ τοῦτο, ὡς ἐγώ φημι, προστέτακται ὑπὸ τοῦ θεοῦ πράττειν καὶ ἐκ μαντείων καὶ ἐξ ἐνυπνίων. For dreams cf. also *Crito* 44A, *Phaedo* 60E; for oracles, *Apol.* 21B, Xen. *Mem.* 1.4.15 (where Socrates believes in τέρατα too), *Anab.* 3.1.5. But Socrates also warned his hearers against treating μαντική as a substitute for "counting and measuring and weighing" (Xen. *Mem.* 1.1.9); it was a supplement and (as in the case of Chaerephon's oracle) a stimulus to rational thought, not a surrogate for it.

37 Xen. *Apol.* 12, θεοῦ μοι φωνὴ φαίνεται. Cf. *Mem.* 4.8.6; Plato (?), *Alc.* I, 124C.

38 Plato, *Prot.* 352BC.

39 *Ibid.*, 353A.

40 *Ibid.*, 356C–357E.

41 Aristotle, *E.N.* 1147ᵃ 11 ff.

42 Chap. i, pp. 5 ff.; chap. ii, pp. 38 ff.

43 Combarieu, *La Musique et la magie* (Études de philologie musicale, III [Paris, 1909]), 66 f., quoted by Boyancé, *Culte des Muses*,

108). Plato speaks of animals in the grip of sexual desire as νοσοῦντα (*Symp.* 207A); and of hunger, thirst, and sexual passion as τρία νοσήματα (*Laws* 782E–783A).

44 Eur. *Med.* 1333; *Hipp.* 141 ff., 240. M. André Rivier, in his interesting and original *Essai sur le tragique d'Euripide* (Lausanne, 1944), thinks that we are meant to take these opinions seriously: Medea is *literally* possessed by a devil (p. 59), and a supernatural hand is pouring a poison into Phaedra's soul. But I find this hard to accept, anyhow as regards Medea. She, who sees deeper into things than the conventional-minded Jason, uses none of this religious language (contrast Aeschylus' Clytemnestra, *Agam.* 1433, 1475 ff., 1497 ff.). And Phaedra too, when once she has brought herself to face her situation, analyses it in purely human terms (on the significance of Aphrodite see "Euripides the Irrationalist," *CR* 43 [1929] 102). Decisive for the poet's attitude is the *Troades*, where Helen blames her misconduct on a divine agency (940 f., 948 ff.) only to be crushed by Hecuba's retort, μὴ ἀμαθεῖς ποίει θεοὺς τὸ σὸν κακὸν κοσμοῦσα, μὴ οὐ πείσῃς σοφούς (981 f.).

45 *Med.* 1056 ff. Cf. Heraclitus, fr. 85: θυμῷ μάχεσθαι χαλεπόν· ὃ γὰρ ἂν θέλῃ, ψυχῆς ὠνεῖται.

46 *Ibid.*, 1078–1080. Wilamowitz deleted 1080, which from the standpoint of a modern producer injures the effectiveness of the "curtain." But it is in keeping with Euripides' habit of mind that he should make Medea generalise her self-analysis, as Phaedra does hers. My case, she implies, is not unique: there is civil war in every human heart. And in fact these lines became a standard textbook example of inner conflict (see below, chap. viii, n. 16).

47 Wilamowitz, *Einleitung i. d. gr. Tragoedie*, 25, n. 44; Decharme, *Euripide et l'esprit de son théâtre*, 46 f.; and especially Snell, *Philologus*, 97 (1948) 125 ff. I feel much more doubt about the assumption of Wilamowitz (*loc. cit.*) and others that *Prot.* 352B ff. is Plato's (or Socrates') "reply" to Phaedra. Why should Plato think it necessary to reply to the incidental remarks of a character in a play written more than thirty years earlier? And if he did, or if he knew that Socrates had done so, why should he not cite Euripides by name as he does elsewhere (Phaedra cannot quote Socrates by name, but Socrates can quote Phaedra)? I see no difficulty in supposing that "the many" at *Prot.* 352B are just the many: the common man has never ignored the power of passion, in Greece or elsewhere, and in this place he is credited with no subtleties.

48 *Hipp.* 375 ff.

49 For an attempt to relate the passage as a whole to the dramatic

situation and Phaedra's psychology, see *CR* 39 (1925) 102 ff. But cf. Snell, *Philologus, loc. cit.*, 127 ff., with whom I am now inclined to agree.

50 Cf. frs. 572, 840, 841, and Pasiphaë's speech in her own defence (*Berl. Kl. Texte*, II.73 = Page, *Gk. Lit. Papyri*, I.74). In the two last the traditional religious language is used.

51 Cf. W. Schadewaldt, *Monolog u. Selbstgespräch*, 250 ff.: the "tragedy of endurance" replaces the "tragedy of πάθος." I should suppose, however, that the *Chrysippus*, though a late play (produced along with the *Phoenissae*), was a tragedy of πάθος: it became, like the *Medea*, a stock example of the conflict between reason and passion (see Nauck on fr. 841), and it clearly reëmphasised the point about human irrationality.

52 Rivier, *op. cit.*, 96 f. Cf. my edition of the play, pp. xl ff.

53 *CR* 43 (1929) 97 ff.

54 Ar. *Nub.* 1078.

55 Quoted by Menander, *Epitrep.* 765 f. Koerte, from the *Auge* (part of it was previously known, fr. 920 Nauck).

56 *Chrysippus*, fr. 840.

57 *Aeolus*, fr. 19, τί δ' αἰσχρὸν ἦν μὴ τοῖσι χρωμένοις δοκῇ; The Sophist Hippias argued that the incest prohibition was conventional, not "divinely implanted" or instinctive, since it was not universally observed (Xen. *Mem.* 4.4.20). But Euripides' line understandably created a scandal: it showed where unlimited ethical relativism landed you. Cf. Aristophanes' parody (*Ran.* 1475); the courtesan's use of it against its author (Machon *apud* Athen. 582CD); and the later stories which make Antisthenes or Plato reply to it (Plut. *aud. poet.* 12, 33C, Serenus *apud* Stob. 3.5.36 H.).

58 *Her.* 778, *Or.* 823, *Ba.* 890 ff., *I.A.* 1089 ff. Cf. Murray, *Euripides and His Age*, 194, and Stier, "Nomos Basileus," *Philol.* 83 (1928) 251.

59 So Murray, *Aristophanes*, 94 ff., and more recently Wolfgang Schmid, *Philol.* 97 (1948) 224 ff. I feel less sure about it than they do.

60 Lysias, fr. 73 Th. (53 Scheibe), *apud* Athen. 551E.

61 Best known as a favourite butt of Aristophanes (*Aves* 1372–1409 and elsewhere). He was accused of insulting a shrine of Hecate (Σ Ar. *Ran.* 366), which would be exactly in keeping with the spirit of the club, the Ἑκάταια being foci of popular superstition (cf. Nilsson, *Gesch.* I.685 f.). Plato cites him as a typical example of the kind of poet who plays to the gallery instead of trying to make his audience better men (*Gorg.* 501E).

[62] This is the date indicated for the decree of Diopeithes by Diod. 12.38 f. and Plut. *Per.* 32. Adcock, *CAH* V.478, is inclined to put it in 430 and connect it with "the emotions evoked by the plague, the visible sign of the anger of heaven"; that may well be right.

[63] τὰ θεῖα μὴ νομίζειν (Plut. *Per.* 32). On the meaning of this expression see R. Hackforth, *Composition of Plato's Apology*, 60 ff., and J. Tate, *CR* 50 (1936) 3 ff., 51 (1937) 3 ff. ἀσέβεια in the sense of sacrilege had no doubt always been an offence; what was new was the prohibition of neglect of cult or antireligious teaching. Nilsson, who clings to the old pretence that "freedom of thought and expression was absolute in Athens" (*Greek Piety*, 79), tries to restrict the scope of the prosecutions to offences against cult. But the tradition unanimously represents the prosecutions of Anaxagoras and Protagoras as based on their theoretical views, not their actions. And a society which forbade the one to describe the sun as a material object and the other to express uncertainty about the existence of gods surely did *not* allow "absolute freedom of thought."

[64] λόγους περὶ τῶν μεταρσίων διδάσκειν (Plut. *ibid.*). This was doubtless aimed especially at Anaxagoras, but the disapproval of μετεωρολογία was widespread. It was thought to be not only foolish and presumptuous (Gorg. *Hel.* 13, Hipp. *vet. med.* 1, Plato, *Rep.* 488E, etc.), but also dangerous to religion (Eur. fr. 913, Plato, *Apol.* 19B, Plut. *Nicias* 23), and was in the popular mind associated especially with Sophists (Eupolis, fr. 146, Ar. *Nub.* 360, Plato, *Pol.* 299B). Cf. W. Capelle, *Philol.* 71 (1912) 414 ff.

[65] Taylor's dating of the trial of Anaxagoras to 450 (*CQ* 11 [1917] 81 ff.) would make the Enlightenment at Athens and the reaction against it start much earlier than the rest of the evidence suggests. His arguments seem to me to have been disposed of by E. Derenne, *Les Procès d'impiété*, 30 ff., and J. S. Morrison, *CR* 35 (1941) 5, n. 2.

[66] Burnet (*Thales to Plato*, 112), and others after him, dismiss the widely attested tradition of Protagoras' trial as unhistorical because of Plato, *Meno* 91E. But Plato is speaking there of Protagoras' international reputation *as a teacher*, which would not be diminished by an Athenian heresy-hunt; he was not accused of corrupting the young, but of atheism. The trial cannot have taken place so late as 411, but the tradition does not say that it did (cf. Derenne, *op. cit.*, 51 ff.).

[67] Satyros, *vit. Eur.* fr. 39, col. x (Arnim, *Suppl. Eur.* 6). Cf. Bury, *CAH* V.383 f.

[68] It is rash to assume that there were no prosecutions but those we

happen to have heard of. Scholars have hardly paid enough attention to what Plato makes Protagoras say (*Prot.* 316c–317b) about the risks attendant on the Sophists' trade, which exposes them to "great jealousy, and other forms of ill-will and conspiracy, so that most of them find it necessary to work under cover." He himself has his private safeguards (the friendship of Pericles?) which have so far kept him from harm.

[69] Diog. Laert. 9.52, Cic. *nat. deor.* 1.63, etc. For the dangers of the reading habit cf. Aristophanes, fr. 490: τοῦτον τὸν ἄνδρ' ἢ βυβλίον διέφθορεν ἢ Πρόδικος ἢ τῶν ἀδολεσχῶν εἷς γέ τις.

[70] This may well be an accident of our defective information. If it is not, it seems to contradict the claim which Plato puts into Socrates' mouth (*Gorg.* 461E), that Athens allows greater freedom of speech than any other place in Greece (the dramatic date of this is *after* the decree of Diopeithes). It is worth noticing, however, that Lampsacus honoured Anaxagoras with a public funeral after Athens had cast him out (Alcidamas *apud* Ar. *Rhet.* 1398[b] 15).

[71] Nilsson, *Greek Popular Religion*, 133 ff.

[72] Plut. *Pericles* 6.

[73] Plato, *Apol.* 40A: ἡ εἰωθυῖά μου μαντικὴ ἡ τοῦ δαιμονίου.

[74] Xen. *Apol.* 14: οἱ δικασταὶ ἐθορύβουν, οἱ μὲν ἀπιστοῦντες τοῖς λεγομένοις, οἱ δὲ καὶ φθονοῦντες, εἰ καὶ παρὰ θεῶν μειζόνων ἢ αὐτοὶ τυγχάνοι. Despite Taylor's ingenious arguments to the contrary (*Varia Socratica*, 10 ff.), I think it impossible to separate the charge of introducing καινὰ δαιμόνια from the δαιμόνιον with which both Plato and Xenophon connect it. Cf. A. S. Ferguson, *CQ* 7 (1913) 157 ff.; H. Gomperz, *NJbb* 1924, 141 ff.; R. Hackforth, *Composition of Plato's Apology*, 68 ff.

[75] Cf. Thuc. 5.103.2, when things are going badly the masses ἐπὶ τὰς ἀφανεῖς (ἐλπίδας) καθίστανται, μαντικήν τε καὶ χρησμούς. Contrast Plato, *Euthyphro* 3c: ὅταν τι λέγω ἐν τῇ ἐκκλησίᾳ περὶ τῶν θείων, προλέγων αὐτοῖς τὰ μέλλοντα, καταγελῶσιν ὡς μαινομένου.

[76] R. Crawshay-Williams, *The Comforts of Unreason*, 28.

[77] Hesiod, *Erga* 240; cf. Plato, *Laws* 910B, and chap. ii, n. 43. Lysias' attitude is illuminating. "Our ancestors," he says, "by performing the prescribed sacrifices left us a city the greatest and most prosperous in Greece: surely we ought to offer the same sacrifices as they did, if only for the sake of the fortune which has resulted from those rites" (30.18). This pragmatist view of religion must have been pretty common.

[78] Thuc. 6.27 f., 60. Thucydides naturally stresses the political aspects of the affair, and indeed it is impossible to read 6.60 without

being reminded of the political "purges" and "witch-hunts" of our own time. But the root cause of the popular excitement was δεισιδαιμονία: the act was an οἰωνὸς τοῦ ἔκπλου (6.27.3).

[79] Thuc. 3.82.4.

[80] Nigel Balchin, *Lord, I was afraid*, 295.

[81] Gilbert Murray, *Greek Studies*, 67. Cf. Frazer's judgement that "society has been built and cemented to a great extent on a foundation of religion, and it is impossible to loosen the cement and shake the foundation without endangering the superstructure" (*The Belief in Immortality*, I.4). That there is a real causal connection between the breakdown of a religious tradition and the unrestricted growth of power politics seems to be confirmed by the experience of other ancient cultures, notably the Chinese, where the secularist positivism of the Fa Hia school had its practical counterpart in the ruthless militarism of the Ts'in Empire.

[82] Chap. iv, pp. 111 ff.

[83] So Kern, *Rel. der Griechen*, II.312, and W. S. Ferguson, "The Attic Orgeones," *Harv. Theol. Rev.* 37 (1944) 89, n. 26. It was for a like reason that the Asclepius cult was brought to Rome in 293 B.C. It was in fact, in Nock's words, "a religion of emergencies" (*CPh* 45 [1950] 48). The first extant reference to incubation in an Asclepius temple occurs in the *Wasps*, written within a few years of the cessation of the plague.

[84] Thuc. 2.53.4: κρίνοντες ἐν ὁμοίῳ καὶ σέβειν καὶ μή, ἐκ τοῦ πάντας ὁρᾶν ἐν ἴσῳ ἀπολλυμένους.

[85] *IG* II.2, 4960. On the details see Ferguson, *loc. cit.*, 88 ff.

[86] *Glaube*, II.233. The most probable interpretation of the evidence seems to be that Asclepius appeared in a dream or vision (Plutarch, *non posse suaviter* 22, 1103B) and said, "Fetch me from Epidaurus," whereupon they fetched him δράκοντι εἰκασμένον, just as the Sicyonians did on the occasion described by Pausanias (2.10.3; cf. 3.23.7).

[87] E.g., *de vetere medicina*, which Festugière dates *ca.* 440–420; *de aeribus, aquis, locis* (thought by Wilamowitz and others to be earlier than 430); *de morbo sacro* (probably somewhat later, cf. Heinimann, *Nomos u. Physis*, 170 ff.). Similarly, the appearance of the first known "dreambooks" (chap. iv, p. 119) is contemporary with the first attempts to explain dreams on naturalistic lines: here too there is polarisation.

[88] The Second Punic War was to produce very similar effects at Rome (cf. Livy, 25.1, and J. J. Tierney, *Proc. R.I.A.* 51 [1947] 94).

[89] *Harv. Theol. Rev.* 33 (1940) 171 ff. Since then, see Nilsson, *Gesch.*

I.782 ff., and the important article of Ferguson (above, n. 83), which throws much light on the naturalisation of Thracian and Phrygian cults at Athens and their diffusion among Athenian citizens. The establishment of the public cult of Bendis can now be dated, as Ferguson has elsewhere shown (*Hesperia*, Suppl. 8 [1949] 131 ff.), to the plague year, 430–429.

⁹⁰ Over 300 examples were collected and studied by A. Audollent, *Defixionum tabellae* (1904), and others have been found since. A supplementary list from central and northern Europe is given by Preisendanz, *Arch. f. Rel.* 11 (1933).

⁹¹ Lawson, *Mod. Greek Folklore*, 16 ff.

⁹² See *Globus*, 79 (1901) 109 ff. Audollent, *op. cit.*, cxxv f., also quotes a number of instances, including the case of "a wealthy and cultivated gentleman" in Normandy who, when his offer of marriage was rejected, ran a needle through the forehead of a photograph of the lady and added the inscription, "God curse you!" This anecdote indicates the simple psychological roots of this kind of magic. Guthrie has cited an interesting example from nineteenth-century Wales (*The Greeks and Their Gods*, 273).

⁹³ The Attic examples known before 1897 (over 200 in number) were separately edited by R. Wünsch, *IG* III.3, Appendix. Additional Attic *defixiones* have since been published by Ziebarth, *Gött. Nachr.* 1899, 105 ff., and *Berl. Sitzb.* 1934, 1022 ff., and others have been found in the Kerameikos (W. Peek, *Kerameikos*, III.89 ff.) and the Agora. Among all these there seem to be only two examples (Kerameikos 3 and 6) which can be assigned with confidence to the fifth century or earlier; on the other hand, a good many are shown by persons named to belong to the fourth, and there are many in which the spelling and style of the lettering suggest that period (R. Wilhelm, *Öst. Jahreshefte*, 7 [1904] 105 ff.).

⁹⁴ Wünsch, no. 24; Ziebarth, *Gött. Nachr.* 1899, no. 2, *Berl. Sitzb.* 1934, no. 1 B.

⁹⁵ Plato, *Laws* 933A–E. He refers to κατάδεσμοι also at *Rep.* 364C as performed for their clients by ἀγύρται καὶ μάντεις, and at *Laws* 909B to necromancy as practised by similar people. The witch Theoris (n. 98 below) claimed some kind of religious status: Harpocration s.v. calls her a μάντις, Plutarch, *Dem.* 14, a ἱέρεια. There was thus no sharp line separating superstition from "religion." And in fact the gods invoked in the older Attic καταδέσεις are the chthonic deities of ordinary Greek belief, most often Hermes and Persephone. It is noteworthy, however, that the meaningless formulae ('Εφέσια γράμματα) characteristic of later magic were al-

Rationalism and Reaction 205

ready coming into use, as appears from Anaxilas, fr. 18 Kock, and with more certainty from Menander, fr. 371.

⁹⁶ *Laws* 933B: κηρινὰ μιμήματα πεπλασμένα, εἴτ᾽ ἐπὶ θύραις εἴτ᾽ ἐπὶ τριόδοις εἴτ᾽ ἐπὶ μνήμασι γονέων. So far as I know, the earliest extant reference to this technique is in an inscription of the early fourth century from Cyrene, where κηρινά are said to have been publicly used as part of the sanction of an oath taken at the time of Cyrene's foundation (Nock, *Arch. f. Rel.* 24 [1926] 172). The wax images have naturally perished; but figurines in more durable materials with the hands bound behind the back (a literal κατά-δεσις), or with other marks of magical attack, have been found fairly often, at least two of them in Attica: see Ch. Dugas's list, *Bull. Corr. Hell.* 39 (1915) 413.

⁹⁷ *Laws* 933A: ταῦτ᾽ οὖν καὶ περὶ τοιαῦτα σύμπαντα οὔτε ῥᾴδιον ὅπως ποτὲ πέφυκεν γιγνώσκειν οὔτ᾽ εἴ τις γνοίη, πείθειν εὐπετὲς ἑτέρους. The second part of this sentence perhaps hints at a greater degree of scepticism than he chooses to express, since the tone of *Rep.* 364C (as well as *Laws* 909B) is definitely sceptical.

⁹⁸ [Dem.] 25.79 f., the case of a φαρμακίς from Lemnos named Theoris, who was put to death at Athens "with her entire family" on the information of her maidservant. That this φαρμακίς was not merely a poisoner appears from the reference in the same sentence to her φάρμακα καὶ ἐπῳδάς (and cf. Ar. *Nub.* 749 ff.). According to Philochorus, *apud* Harpocration, s.v. Θεωρίς, the formal charge was one of ἀσέβεια, and this is probably right: the savage destruction of the whole family implies a pollution of the community. Plutarch (who gives a different account of the charge) says, *Dem.* 14, that the accuser was Demosthenes—who was himself, as we have seen, more than once the object of magical attack.

⁹⁹ Mythology apart, there are surprisingly few direct references in Attic fifth-century literature to *aggressive* magic, other than love-philtres (Eur. *Hipp.* 509 ff., Antiphon, 1.9, etc.) and the ἐπῳδὴ Ὀρφέως, Eur. *Cycl.* 646. The author of *morb. sacr.* speaks of persons allegedly πεφαρμακευμένους, "placed under a spell" (VI.362 L.), and the same thing may be meant at Ar. *Thesm.* 534. Otherwise the nearest approach is perhaps to be seen in the word ἀναλύτης, an "undoer" of spells, said to have been used by the early comic poet Magnes (fr. 4). Protective or "white" magic was no doubt common: e.g., people wore magic rings as amulets (Eupolis, fr. 87, Ar. *Plut.* 883 f. and Σ). But if you wanted a really potent witch you had to buy one from Thessaly (Ar. *Nub.* 749 ff.).

¹⁰⁰ There was a comparable gap in the nineteenth century between the

breakdown of the belief in Christianity among intellectuals and the rise of spiritualism and similar movements in the semi-educated classes (from which some of them have spread to a section of the educated). But in the case of Athens one cannot exclude the possibility that the revival of aggressive magic dated from the despairing last years of the Peloponnesian War. For other possible reasons which may have contributed to its popularity in the fourth century see Nilsson, *Gesch.* I.759 f. I cannot think that the multiplication of "defixiones" at this time reflects merely an increase in literacy, as has been suggested; for they could be written, and probably often were written (Audollent, *op. cit.*, xlv), by professional magicians employed for the purpose (Plato speaks as if this were so, *Rep.* 364c).

VII

Plato, the Irrational Soul, and the Inherited Conglomerate

> *There is no hope in returning to a traditional faith after it has once been abandoned, since the essential condition in the holder of a traditional faith is that he should not know he is a traditionalist.*
>
> AL GHAZALI

THE LAST chapter described the decay of the inherited fabric of beliefs which set in during the fifth century, and some of its earlier results. I propose here to consider Plato's reaction to the situation thus created. The subject is important, not only because of Plato's position in the history of European thought, but because Plato perceived more clearly than anyone else the dangers inherent in the decay of an Inherited Conglomerate, and because in his final testament to the world he put forward proposals of great interest for stabilising the position by means of a counter-reformation. I am well aware that to discuss this matter fully would involve an examination of Plato's entire philosophy of life; but in order to keep the discussion within manageable limits I propose to concentrate on seeking answers to two questions:

First, what importance did Plato himself attach to non-rational factors in human behaviour, and how did he interpret them?

Secondly, what concessions was he prepared to make to the irrationalism of popular belief for the sake of stabilising the Conglomerate?

It is desirable to keep these two questions distinct as far as possible, though, as we shall see, it is not always easy to decide where Plato is expressing a personal faith and where he is merely using a traditional language. In trying to answer the first question, I shall have to repeat one or two things which I have already said in print,[1] but I shall have something to add on matters which I did not previously consider.

One assumption I shall make. I shall assume that Plato's philosophy did not spring forth fully mature, either from his own head or from the head of Socrates; I shall treat it as an organic thing which grew and changed, partly in obedience to its inner law of growth, but partly also in response to external stimuli. And here it is relevant to remind you that Plato's life, like his thought, all but bridges the wide gulf between the death of Pericles and the acceptance of Macedonian hegemony.[2] Though it is probable that all his writings belong to the fourth century, his personality and outlook were moulded in the fifth, and his earlier dialogues are still bathed in the remembered light of a vanished social world. The best example is to my mind the *Protagoras*, whose action is set in the golden years before the Great War; in its optimism, its genial worldliness, its frank utilitarianism, and its Socrates who is still no more than life-size, it seems to be an essentially faithful reproduction of the past.[3]

Plato's starting-point was thus historically conditioned. As the nephew of Charmides and kinsman of Critias, no less than as one of Socrates' young men, he was the child of the Enlightenment. He grew up in a social circle which not only took pride in settling all questions before the bar of reason, but had the habit of interpreting all human behaviour in terms of rational self-interest, and the belief that "virtue," *arete*, consisted essentially in a technique of rational living. That pride, that habit, and that belief remained with Plato to the end; the framework of his thought never ceased to be rationalist. But the contents of the framework came in time to be strangely transformed. There were good reasons for that. The transition from the fifth century to the fourth was marked (as our

[1] For notes to chapter vii see pages 224–235.

own time has been marked) by events which might well induce any rationalist to reconsider his faith. To what moral
and material ruin the principle of rational self-interest might
lead a society, appeared in the fate of imperial Athens; to
what it might lead the individual, in the fate of Critias and
Charmides and their fellow-tyrants. And on the other hand,
the trial of Socrates afforded the strange spectacle of the wisest
man in Greece at the supreme crisis of his life deliberately and
gratuitously flouting that principle, at any rate as the world
understood it.

It was these events, I think, which compelled Plato, not to
abandon rationalism, but to transform its meaning by giving
it a metaphysical extension. It took him a long time, perhaps a
decade, to digest the new problems. In those years he no doubt
turned over in his mind certain significant sayings of Socrates,
for example, that "the human *psyche* has something divine
about it" and that "one's first interest is to look after its
health."[4] But I agree with the opinion of the majority of scholars that what put Plato in the way of expanding these hints
into a new transcendental psychology was his personal contact
with the Pythagoreans of West Greece when he visited them
about 390. If I am right in my tentative guess about the historical antecedents of the Pythagorean movement, Plato in
effect cross-fertilised the tradition of Greek rationalism with
magico-religious ideas whose remoter origins belong to the
northern shamanistic culture. But in the form in which we
meet them in Plato these ideas have been subjected to a double
process of interpretation and transposition. A well-known passage of the *Gorgias* shows us in a concrete instance how certain
philosophers—such men, perhaps, as Plato's friend Archytas—
took over old mythical fancies about the fate of the soul and
read into them new allegorical meanings which gave them moral
and psychological significance.[5] Such men prepared the way for
Plato; but I should guess that it was Plato himself who by a
truly creative act transposed these ideas definitively from the
plane of revelation to the plane of rational argument.

The crucial step lay in the identification of the detachable "occult" self which is the carrier of guilt-feelings and potentially divine with the rational Socratic *psyche* whose virtue is a kind of knowledge. That step involved a complete reinterpretation of the old shamanistic culture-pattern. Nevertheless the pattern kept its vitality, and its main features are still recognisable in Plato. Reincarnation survives unchanged. The shaman's trance, his deliberate detachment of the occult self from the body, has become that practice of mental withdrawal and concentration which purifies the rational soul—a practice for which Plato in fact claims the authority of a traditional *lŏgos*.[6] The occult knowledge which the shaman acquires in trance has become a vision of metaphysical truth; his "recollection" of past earthly lives[7] has become a "recollection" of bodiless Forms which is made the basis of a new epistemology; while on the mythical level his "long sleep" and "underworld journey" provides a direct model for the experiences of Er the son of Armenius.[8] Finally, we shall perhaps understand better Plato's much-criticised "Guardians" if we think of them as a new kind of rationalised shamans who, like their primitive predecessors, are prepared for their high office by a special kind of discipline designed to modify the whole psychic structure; like them, must submit to a dedication that largely cuts them off from the normal satisfactions of humanity; like them, must renew their contact with the deep sources of wisdom by periodic "retreats"; and like them, will be rewarded after death by receiving a peculiar status in the spirit world.[9] It is likely that an approximation to this highly specialised human type already existed in the Pythagorean societies; but Plato dreamed of carrying the experiment much further, putting it on a serious scientific basis, and using it as the instrument of his counter-reformation.

This visionary picture of a new sort of ruling class has often been cited as evidence that Plato's estimate of human nature was grossly unrealistic. But shamanistic institutions are not built on ordinary human nature; their whole concern is to exploit the possibilities of an exceptional type of personality. And the *Republic* is dominated by a similar concern. Plato admitted frankly that only a tiny fraction of the population (φύσει ὀλίγιστον γένος) possessed the natural endowment which would make it possible to transform them into Guardians.[10] For the rest—that is to say, the overwhelming majority of mankind—he seems to have recognised at all stages of his thought that, so long as they are not exposed to the temptations of power, an intelligent hedonism provides the best practicable guide to a satisfactory life.[11] But in the dialogues of his middle period, preoccupied as he then was with exceptional natures and their exceptional possibilities, he shows scant interest in the psychology of the ordinary man.

In his later work, however, after he had dismissed the philosopher-kings as an impossible dream, and had fallen back on the rule of Law as a second-best,[12] he paid more attention to the motives which govern ordinary human conduct, and even the philosopher is seen not to be exempt from their influence. To the question whether any one of us would be content with a life in which he possessed wisdom, understanding, knowledge, and a complete memory of the whole of history, but experienced no pleasure or pain, great or small, the answer given in the *Philebus*[13] is an emphatic "No": we are anchored in the life of feeling which is part of our humanity, and cannot surrender it even to become "spectators of all time and all existence"[14] like the philosopher-kings. In the *Laws* we are told that the only practicable basis for public morals is the belief that honesty pays: "for no one," says Plato, "would consent, if he could help it, to a course of action which did not bring him more joy than sorrow."[15] With that we seem to be back in the world of the *Protagoras* and of Jeremy Bentham. The legislator's position, however, is not identical with that of the common man. The common man wants to be happy; but Plato, who is legislating for him, wants him to be good. Plato therefore labours to persuade him that goodness and happiness go together. That this is true, Plato happens to believe; but did he not believe it, he would still pretend it true, as being "the most salutary lie that was ever told."[16] It is not Plato's own position that has changed: if anything has changed, it is his assessment of human capacity. In the *Laws*, at any rate, the virtue of the common man is evidently not based on knowledge, or even on true opinion as such, but on a process of conditioning or habituation[17] by which he is induced to accept and act on certain "salutary" beliefs. After all, says Plato, this is not too difficult: people who can believe in Cadmus and the dragon's teeth will believe anything.[18] Far from supposing, as his master had done, that "the unexamined life is no life for a human being,"[19] Plato now appears to hold that the majority of human beings can be kept in tolerable moral health only by a carefully chosen diet of "incantations" (ἐπῳδαί),[20]—that is to say, edifying myths and bracing ethical slogans. We may say that in principle he accepts Burckhardt's dichotomy—rationalism for the few, magic for the many. We have seen, however, that his rationalism is quickened with ideas that once were magical; and on the other hand we shall see later how his "incantations" were to be made to serve rational ends.

In other ways too, Plato's growing recognition of the importance of affective elements carried him beyond the limits of fifth-century rationalism. This appears very clearly in the development of his theory of Evil. It is true that to the end of his life[21] he went on repeating the Socratic dictum that "No one commits an error if he can help it"; but he had long ceased to be content with the simple Socratic opinion which saw moral error as a kind of mistake in perspective.[22] When Plato took over the magico-religious view of the *psyche*, he at first took over with it the puritan dualism which attributed all the sins and sufferings of the *psyche* to the pollution arising from contact with a mortal body. In the *Phaedo* he transposed that doctrine into philosophical terms and gave it the formulation that was to become classical: only when by death or by self-discipline the rational self is purged of "the folly of the body"[23] can it resume its true nature which is divine and sinless; the good life is the practice of that purgation, μελέτη θανάτου. Both in antiquity and to-day, the general reader has been inclined to regard this as Plato's last word on the matter. But Plato was too penetrating and, at bottom, too realistic a thinker to be satisfied for long with the theory of the *Phaedo*. As soon as he turned from the occult self to the empirical man, he found himself driven to recognise an irrational factor within the mind itself, and thus to think of moral evil in terms of psychological conflict (στάσις).[24]

That is already so in the *Republic:* the same passage of Homer which in the *Phaedo* had illustrated the soul's dialogue with "the passions of the body" becomes in the *Republic* an internal dialogue between two "parts" of the soul;[25] the passions are no longer seen as an infection of extraneous origin, but as a necessary part of the life of the mind as we know it, and even as a source of energy, like Freud's *libido*, which can be "canalised" either towards sensuous or towards intellectual activity.[26] The theory of inner conflict, vividly illustrated in the *Republic* by the tale of Leontius,[27] was precisely formulated in the *Sophist*,[28] where it is defined as a psychological maladjustment resulting "from some sort of injury,"[29] a kind of disease of the soul, and is said to be the cause of cowardice, intemperance, injustice, and (it would seem) moral evil in general, as distinct from ignorance or intellectual failure. This is something quite different both from the rationalism of the earliest dialogues and from the puritanism of the *Phaedo*, and goes a good deal deeper than either; I take it to be Plato's personal contribution.[30]

Yet Plato had not abandoned the transcendent rational self, whose perfect unity is the guarantee of its immortality. In the *Timaeus*, where he is trying to reformulate his earlier vision of man's destiny in terms compatible with his later psychology and cosmology, we meet again the unitary soul of the *Phaedo;* and it is significant that Plato here applies to it the old religious term that Empedocles had used for the occult self—he calls it the daemon.[31] In the *Timaeus*, however, it has another sort of soul or self "built on to it," "the mortal kind wherein are terrible and indispensable passions."[32] Does not this mean that for Plato the human personality has virtually broken in two? Certainly it is not clear what bond unites or could unite an indestructible daemon resident in the human head with a set of irrational impulses housed in the chest or "tethered like a beast untamed" in the belly. We are reminded of the naïve opinion of that Persian in Xenophon to whom it was quite obvious that he must have two souls: for, said he, the same soul could not be at once good and bad—it could not desire simultaneously noble actions and base ones, will and not will to perform a particular act at a particular moment.[33]

But Plato's fission of the empirical man into daemon and beast is perhaps not quite so inconsequent as it may appear to the modern reader. It reflects a similar fission in Plato's view of human nature: the gulf between the immortal and the mortal soul corresponds to the gulf between Plato's vision of man as he might be and his estimate of man as he is. What Plato had come to think of human life as it is actually lived, appears most clearly in the *Laws*. There he twice informs us that man is a puppet. Whether the gods made it simply as a plaything or for some serious purpose one cannot tell; all we know is that the creature is on a string, and its hopes and fears, pleasures and pains, jerk it about and make it dance.[34] In a later passage the Athenian observes that it is a pity we have to take human affairs seriously, and remarks that man is God's plaything, "and that is really the best that can be said of him": men and women should accordingly make this play as charming as possible, sacrificing to the gods with music and dancing; "thus they will live out their lives in accordance with their nature, being puppets chiefly, and having in them only a small portion of reality." "You are making out our human race very mean," says the Spartan. And the Athenian apologises: "I thought of God, and I was moved to speak as I did just now. Well, if you will have it so, let us say that our race

is not mean—that it is worth taking a little bit seriously
(σπουδῆς τινος ἄξιον)."[35]

Plato suggests here a religious origin for this way of thinking;
and we often meet it in later religious thinkers, from Marcus
Aurelius to Mr. T. S. Eliot—who has said in almost the same
words, "Human nature is able to endure only a very little
reality." It agrees with the drift of much else in the *Laws*—
with the view that men are as unfit to rule themselves as a
flock of sheep,[36] that God, not man, is the measure of things,[37]
that man is the gods' property (κτῆμα),[38] and that if he wishes
to be happy, he should be ταπεινός, "abject," before God—a
word which nearly all pagan writers, and Plato himself elsewhere, employ as a term of contempt.[39] Ought we to discount
all this as a senile aberration, the sour pessimism of a tired and
irritable old man? It might seem so: for it contrasts oddly with
the radiant picture of the soul's divine nature and destiny
which Plato painted in his middle dialogues and certainly never
abjured. But we may recall the philosopher of the *Republic*,
to whom, as to Aristotle's megalopsych, human life cannot
appear important (μέγα τι);[40] we may remember that in the
Meno the mass of men are likened to the shadows that flit in
Homer's Hades, and that the conception of human beings as the
chattels of a god appears already in the *Phaedo*.[41] We may think
also of another passage in the *Phaedo*, where Plato predicts
with undisguised relish the future of his fellow-men: in their
next incarnation some of them will be donkeys, others wolves,
while the μέτριοι, the respectable bourgeoisie, may look forward to becoming bees or ants.[42] No doubt this is partly Plato's
fun; but it is the sort of fun which would have appealed to
Jonathan Swift. It carries the implication that everybody except the philosopher is on the verge of becoming subhuman,
which is (as ancient Platonists saw)[43] hard to reconcile with the
view that every human soul is essentially rational.

In the light of these and other passages I think we have to
recognise two strains or tendencies in Plato's thinking about
the status of man. There is the faith and pride in human reason

which he inherited from the fifth century, and for which he found religious sanction by equating the reason with the occult self of shamanistic tradition. And there is the bitter recognition of human worthlessness which was forced upon him by his experience of contemporary Athens and Syracuse. This too could be expressed in the language of religion, as a denial of all value to the activities and interests of this world in comparison with "the things Yonder." A psychologist might say that the relation between the two tendencies was not one of simple opposition, but that the first became a compensation—or overcompensation—for the second: the less Plato cared for actual humanity, the more nobly he thought of the soul. The tension between the two was resolved for a time in the dream of a new Rule of the Saints, an *élite* of purified men who should unite the incompatible virtues of (to use Mr. Koestler's terms) the Yogi and the Commissar, and thereby save not only themselves but society. But when that illusion faded, Plato's underlying despair came more and more to the surface, translating itself into religious terms, until it found its logical expression in his final proposals for a completely "closed" society,[44] to be ruled not by the illuminated reason, but (under God) by custom and religious law. The "Yogi," with his faith in the possibility and necessity of intellectual conversion, did not wholly vanish even now, but he certainly retreated before the "Commissar," whose problem is the conditioning of human cattle. On this interpretation the pessimism of the *Laws* is not a senile aberration: it is the fruit of Plato's personal experience of life, which in turn carried in it the seed of much later thought.[45]

It is in the light of this estimate of human nature that we must consider Plato's final proposals for stabilising the Conglomerate. But before turning to that, I must say a word about his opinions on another aspect of the irrational soul which has concerned us in this book, namely, the importance traditionally ascribed to it as the source or channel of an intuitive insight. In this matter, it seems to me, Plato remained throughout his life faithful to the principles of his master. Knowledge, as dis-

tinct from true opinion, remained for him the affair of the intellect, which can justify its beliefs by rational argument. To
the intuitions both of the seer and of the poet he consistently
refused the title of knowledge, not because he thought them
necessarily groundless, but because their grounds could not be
produced.[46] Hence Greek custom was right, he thought, in
giving the last word in military matters to the commander-in-
chief, as a trained expert, and not to the seers who accompanied
him on campaign; in general, it was the task of σωφροσύνη,
rational judgement, to distinguish between the true seer and
the charlatan.[47] In much the same way, the products of poetic
intuition must be subject to the rational and moral censorship
of the trained legislator. All that was in keeping with Socratic
rationalism.[48] Nevertheless, as we have noticed,[49] Socrates
had taken irrational intuition quite seriously, whether it expressed itself in dreams, in the inner voice of the "daemonion,"
or in the utterance of the Pythia. And Plato makes a great show
of taking it seriously too. Of the pseudo-sciences of augury and
hepatoscopy he permits himself to speak with thinly veiled
contempt;[50] but "the madness that comes by divine gift," the
madness that inspires the prophet or the poet, or purges men
in the Corybantic rite—this, as we saw in an earlier chapter,
is treated as if it were a real intrusion of the supernatural into
human life.

How far did Plato intend this way of talking to be taken *au
pied de la lettre?* In recent years the question has been often
raised, and variously answered;[51] but unanimity has not been
reached, nor is it likely to be. I should be inclined myself to
say three things about it:

a) That Plato perceived what he took to be a real and significant analogy between mediumship, poetic creation, and certain pathological manifestations of the religious consciousness,
all three of which have the appearance of being "given"[52]
ab extra;

b) That the traditional religious explanations of these phenomena were, like much else in the Conglomerate, accepted

by him provisionally, not because he thought them finally adequate, but because no other language was available to express that mysterious "givenness";[53]

c) That while he thus accepted (with whatever ironical reservations) the poet, the prophet, and the "Corybantic" as being in some sense channels[54] of divine or daemonic[55] grace, he nevertheless rated their activities far below those of the rational self,[56] and held that they must be subject to the control and criticism of reason, since reason was for him no passive plaything of hidden forces, but an active manifestation of deity in man, a daemon in its own right. I suspect that, had Plato lived to-day, he would have been profoundly interested in the new depth-psychology, but appalled by the tendency to reduce the human reason to an instrument for rationalising unconscious impulses.

Much of what I have said applies also to Plato's fourth type of "divine madness," the madness of Eros. Here too was a "given," something which happens to a man without his choosing it or knowing why—the work, therefore, of a formidable daemon.[57] Here too—here, indeed, above all[58]—Plato recognised the operation of divine grace, and used the old religious language[59] to express that recognition. But Eros has a special importance in Plato's thought as being the one mode of experience which brings together the two natures of man, the divine self and the tethered beast.[60] For Eros is frankly rooted in what man shares with the animals,[61] the physiological impulse of sex (a fact which is unfortunately obscured by the persistent modern misuse of the term "Platonic love"); yet Eros also supplies the dynamic impulse which drives the soul forward in its quest of a satisfaction transcending earthly experience. It thus spans the whole compass of human personality, and makes the one empirical bridge between man as he is and man as he might be. Plato in fact comes very close here to the Freudian concept of *libido* and sublimation. But he never, as it seems to me, fully integrated this line of thought with the rest of his philosophy; had he done so, the notion of the intellect as a self-

sufficient entity independent of the body might have been im-
perilled, and Plato was not going to risk that.[62]

I turn now to Plato's proposals for reforming and stabilising
the Inherited Conglomerate.[63] They are set forth in his last
work, the *Laws*, and may be briefly summarised as follows.

1. He would provide religious faith with a logical foundation
by *proving* certain basic propositions.

2. He would give it a legal foundation by incorporating these
propositions in an unalterable legal code, and imposing legal
penalties on any person propagating disbelief in them.

3. He would give it an educational foundation by making
the basic propositions a compulsory subject of instruction for
all children.

4. He would give it a social foundation by promoting an
intimate union of religious and civic life at all levels—as we
should phrase it, a union of Church and State.

It may be said that most of these proposals were designed
merely to strengthen and generalise existing Athenian practice.
But when we take them together we see that they represent the
first attempt to deal systematically with the problem of controlling religious belief. The problem itself was new: in an
age of faith no one thinks of proving that gods exist or inventing
techniques to induce belief in them. And some of the methods
proposed were apparently new: in particular, no one before
Plato seems to have realised the importance of early religious
training as a means of conditioning the future adult. Moreover,
when we look more closely at the proposals themselves, it becomes evident that Plato was trying not only to stabilise but
also to reform, not only to buttress the traditional structure
but also to discard so much of it as was plainly rotten and
replace it by something more durable.

Plato's basic propositions are:

a) That gods exist;

b) That they are concerned with the fate of mankind;

c) That they cannot be bribed.

The arguments by which he attempted to prove these statements do not concern us here; they belong to the history of theology. But it is worth noticing some of the points on which he felt obliged to break with tradition, and some on which he compromised.

Who, in the first place, are the gods whose existence Plato sought to prove and whose worship he sought to enforce? The answer is not free from ambiguity. As regards worship, a passage in *Laws* iv provides a completely traditional list—gods of Olympus, gods of the city, gods of the underworld, local daemons and heroes.[64] These are the conventional figures of public cult, the gods who, as he puts it elsewhere in the *Laws*, "exist according to customary usage."[65] But are they the gods whose existence Plato thought he could prove? We have ground for doubting it. In the *Cratylus* he makes Socrates say that we know nothing about these gods, not even their true names, and in the *Phaedrus*, that we *imagine* a god (πλάττομεν) without having seen one or formed any adequate idea of what he is like.[66] The reference in both passages is to mythological gods. And the implication seems to be that the cult of such gods has no rational basis, either empirical or metaphysical. Its level of validity is, at best, of the same order as that which Plato allows to the intuitions of the poet or the seer.

The supreme god of Plato's personal faith was, I take it, a very different sort of being, one whom (in the words of the *Timaeus*) "it is hard to find and impossible to describe to the masses."[67] Presumably Plato felt that such a god could not be introduced into the Conglomerate without destroying it; at any rate he abstained from the attempt. But there was one kind of god whom everyone could see, whose divinity could be recognised by the masses,[68] and about whom the philosopher could make, in Plato's opinion, logically valid statements. These "visible gods" were the heavenly bodies—or, more exactly, the divine minds by which those bodies were animated or controlled.[69] The great novelty in Plato's project for religious reform was the emphasis he laid, not merely on the divinity of sun, moon, and stars (for that was nothing new), but on their cult. In the *Laws*, not only are the stars described as "the gods in heaven," the sun and moon as "great gods," but Plato insists that prayer and sacrifice shall be made to them by all;[70] and the focal point of his new State Church is to be a joint cult of Apollo and the sun-god Helios, to which the High Priest will be attached and the highest political officers will be solemnly dedicated.[71] This joint cult—in place of the expected cult of Zeus—expresses the union of old and new, Apollo standing for the traditionalism of the masses, and Helios for the new "natural religion" of the philosophers;[72] it is Plato's last desperate attempt to build a bridge between the intellectuals and the people, and thereby save the unity of Greek belief and of Greek culture.

A similar mixture of necessary reform with necessary compromise may be observed in Plato's handling of his other basic propositions. In dealing with the traditional problem of divine justice, he firmly ignores not only the old belief in "jealous" gods,[73] but (with certain exceptions in religious law)[74] the old idea that the wicked man is punished in his descendants. That the doer shall suffer in person is for Plato a demonstrable law of the cosmos, which must be taught as an article of faith. The detailed working of the law is not, however, demonstrable: it belongs to the domain of "myth" or "incantation."[75] His own final belief in this matter is set forth in an impressive passage of *Laws* x:[76] the law of cosmic justice is a law of spiritual gravitation; in this life and in the whole series of lives every soul gravitates naturally to the company of its own kind, and therein lies its punishment or its reward; Hades, it is hinted, is not a place but a state of mind.[77] And to this Plato adds another warning, a warning which marks the transition from the classical to the Hellenistic outlook: if any man demands personal happiness from life, let him remember that the cosmos does not exist for his sake, but he for the sake of the cosmos.[78] All this, however, was above the head of the common man, as Plato well knew; he does not, if I understand him rightly, propose to make it part of the compulsory official creed.

On the other hand, Plato's third proposition—that the gods cannot be bribed—implied a more drastic interference with traditional belief and practice It involved rejecting the ordinary interpretation of sacrifice as an expression of gratitude for favours to come, "do ut des " a view which he had long ago stigmatised in the *Euthyphro* as the application to religion of a commercial technique (ἐμπορικὴ τις τέχνη).[79] But it seems plain that the great emphasis he lays on this point both in the *Republic* and in the *Laws* is due not merely to theoretical considerations; he is attacking certain widespread practices which in his eyes constitute a threat to public morality. The "travelling priests and diviners" and purveyors of cathartic ritual who are denounced in a much-discussed passage of *Republic* ii, and again in the *Laws*,[80] are not, I think, merely those minor charlatans who in all societies prey upon the ignorant and superstitious. For they are said in both places to mislead whole cities,[81] an eminence that minor charlatans seldom achieve. The scope of Plato's criticism is in my view wider than some scholars have been willing to admit: he is attacking, I believe, the entire tradition of ritual purification, so far as it was in the hands of private, "unlicensed" persons.[82]

This does not mean that he proposed to abolish ritual purification altogether. For Plato himself, the only truly effective catharsis was no doubt the practice of mental withdrawal and concentration which is described in the *Phaedo:*[83] the trained philosopher could cleanse his own soul without the help of ritual. But the common man could not, and the faith in ritual catharsis was far too deeply rooted in the popular mind for Plato to propose its complete elimination. He felt, however, the need for something like a Church, and a canon of authorised rituals, if religion was to be prevented from running off the rails and becoming a danger to public morality. In the field of religion, as in that of morals, the great enemy which had to be fought was antinomian individualism; and he looked to Delphi to organise the defence. We need not assume that Plato believed the Pythia to be verbally inspired. My own guess would be that his attitude to Delphi was more like that of a modern "political Catholic" towards the Vatican: he saw in Delphi a great conservative force which could be harnessed to the task of stabilising the Greek religious tradition and checking both the spread of materialism and the growth of aberrant tendencies within the tradition itself. Hence his insistence, both in the *Republic* and in the *Laws*, that the authority of Delphi is to be absolute in all religious matters.[84] Hence also the choice of Apollo to share with Helios the supreme position in the hierarchy of State cults: while Helios provides the few with a relatively rational form of worship, Apollo will dispense to the many, in regulated and harmless doses, the archaic ritual magic which they demand.[85]

Of such legalised magic the *Laws* provides many examples, some of them startlingly primitive. For instance, an animal, or even an inanimate object, which has caused the death of a man, is to be tried, condemned, and banished beyond the frontiers of the State, because it carries a "miasma" or pollution.[86] In this and many other matters Plato follows Athenian practice and Delphic authority. We need not suppose that he himself attached any value to proceedings of this kind; they were the price to be paid for harnessing Delphi and keeping superstition within bounds.

It remains to say a few words about the sanctions by which Plato proposes to enforce acceptance of his reformed version of the traditional beliefs. Those who offend against it by speech or act are to be denounced to the courts, and, if found guilty, are to be given not less than five years' solitary confinement in a reformatory, where they will be subjected to intensive religious propaganda, but denied all other human intercourse; if this fails to cure them, they will be put to death.[87] Plato in fact wishes to revive the fifth-century heresy trials (he makes it plain that he would condemn Anaxagoras unless he mended his opinions);[88] all that is new is the proposed psychological treatment of the guilty. That the fate of Socrates did not warn Plato of the danger inherent in such measures may seem strange, indeed.[89] But he apparently felt that freedom of thought in religious matters involved so grave a *threat to society* that the measures had to be taken. "Heresy" is perhaps a misleading word to use in this connection. Plato's proposed theocratic State does in certain respects foreshadow the mediaeval theocracy. But the mediaeval Inquisition was chiefly concerned lest people should suffer in the next world for having held false opinions in this one; overtly, at any rate, it was trying to save souls at the expense of bodies. Plato's concern was quite different. He was trying to save society from contamination by dangerous thoughts, which in his view were visibly destroying the springs of social conduct.[90] Any teaching which weakens the conviction that honesty is the best policy he feels obliged to prohibit as antisocial. The motives behind his legislation are thus practical and secular; in this respect the nearest historical analogue is not the Inquisition, but those trials of "intellectual deviationists" with which our own generation has become so familiar.

Such, then, in brief, were Plato's proposals for reforming the Conglomerate. They were not carried out, and the Conglomerate was not reformed. But I hope that the next and final chapter will show why I have thought it worth while to spend time in describing them.

NOTES TO CHAPTER VII

[1] "Plato and the Irrational," *JHS* 65 (1945) 16 ff. This paper was written before the present book was planned; it leaves untouched some of the problems with which I am here concerned, and on the other hand deals with some aspects of Plato's rationalism and irrationalism which fall outside the scope of the present volume.

[2] Plato was born in the year of Pericles' death or the year following, and died in 347, a year before the Peace of Philocrates and nine years before the battle of Chaeronea.

[3] Cf. chap. vi, nn. 31–33.

[4] Xen. *Mem.* 4.3.14; Plato, *Apol.* 30AB, *Laches* 185E.

⁵ *Gorgias* 493A–C. Frank's view of what is implied in this passage (*Platon u. die sog. Pythagoreer*, 291 ff.) seems to me right in the main, though I should question certain details. Plato distinguishes, as 493B 7 shows, (*a*) τις μυθολογῶν κομψὸς ἀνήρ, ἴσως Σικελός τις ἢ Ἰταλικός, whom I take to be the anonymous author of an old Underworld Journey (not necessarily "Orphic") which was current in West Greece and may have been somewhat after the style of the poem quoted on the gold plates; (*b*) Socrates' informant, τις τῶν σοφῶν, who read into the old poem an allegorical meaning (much as Theagenes of Rhegium had allegorised Homer). This σοφός I suppose to be a Pythagorean, since such formulae are regularly used by Plato when he has to put Pythagorean ideas into Socrates' mouth: 507E, φασὶ δ᾽ οἱ σοφοί that there is a moral world-order (cf. Thompson *ad loc.*); *Meno* 81A, ἀκήκοα ἀνδρῶν τε καὶ γυναικῶν σοφῶν about transmigration; *Rep.* 583B, δοκῶ μοι τῶν σοφῶν τινος ἀκηκοέναι that physical pleasures are illusory (cf. Adam *ad loc.*). Moreover, the view that underworld myths are an allegory of this life appears in Empedocles (cf. chap. v, n. 114), and in later Pythagoreanism (Macrob. *in Somn. Scip.* I.10.7–17). I cannot agree with Linforth ("Soul and Sieve in Plato's *Gorgias*," *Univ. Calif. Publ. Class. Philol.* 12 [1944] 17 ff.) that "the whole of what Socrates professes to have heard from someone else . . . was original with Plato himself": if it were, he would hardly make Socrates describe it as ἐπιεικῶς ὑπό τι ἄτοπα (493C) or call it the product of a certain school (γυμνασίου, 493D).

⁶ *Phaedo* 67C, cf. 80E; 83A–C. For the meaning of λόγος ("religious doctrine") cf. 63C, 70C, *Epist.* vii. 335A, etc. In thus reinterpreting the old tradition about the importance of dissociated states, Plato was no doubt influenced by Socrates' practice of prolonged mental withdrawal, as described in the *Symposium*, 174D–175C and 220CD, and (it would seem) parodied in the *Clouds:* cf. Festugière, *Contemplation et vie contemplative chez Platon*, 69 ff.

⁷ See chap. v, n. 107.

⁸ Proclus, *in Remp.* II.113.22, quotes as precedents Aristeas, Hermotimus (so Rohde for Hermodorus), and Epimenides.

⁹ As the Siberian shaman becomes an Üör after death (Sieroszewski, *Rev. de l'hist. des rel.* 46 [1902] 228 f.), so the men of Plato's "golden breed" will receive post-mortem cult not merely as heroes —which would have been within the range of contemporary usage —but (subject to Delphic approval) as δαίμονες (*Rep.* 468E–469B). Indeed, such men may already be called δαίμονες in their lifetime (*Crat.* 398C). In both passages Plato appeals to the precedent of

Hesiod's "golden race" (*Erga* 122 f.). But he is almost certainly influenced also by something less remotely mythical, the Pythagorean tradition which accorded a special status to the θεῖος or δαιμόνιος ἀνήρ (see above, chap. v, n. 61). The Pythagoreans—like Siberian shamans today—had a special funeral ritual of their own, which secured for them a μακαριστὸν καὶ οἰκεῖον τέλος (Plut. *gen. Socr.* 16, 585E, cf. Boyancé, *Culte des Muses*, 133 ff.; Nioradze, *Schamanismus*, 103 f.), and may well have provided the model for the elaborate and unusual regulations laid down in the *Laws* for the funerals of εὔθυνοι (947B–E, cf. O. Reverdin, *La Religion de la cité platonicienne*, 125 ff.). On the disputed question whether Plato himself received divine (or daemonic) honours after death, see Wilamowitz, *Aristoteles u. Athen*, II.413 ff.; Boyancé, *op. cit.*, 250 ff.; Reverdin, *op. cit.*, 139 ff.; and *contra*, Jaeger, *Aristotle*, 108 f.; Festugière, *Le Dieu cosmique*, 219 f.

¹⁰ *Rep.* 428E–429A, cf. *Phaedo* 69C.

¹¹ *Phaedo* 82AB, *Rep.* 500D, and the passages quoted below from *Philebus* and *Laws*.

¹² *Politicus* 297DE, 301DE; cf. *Laws* 739DE.

¹³ *Philebus* 21DE.

¹⁴ *Rep.* 486A.

¹⁵ *Laws* 663B; cf. 733A.

¹⁶ *Ibid.*, 663D.

¹⁷ *Ibid.*, 653B: ὀρθῶς εἰθίσθαι ὑπὸ τῶν προσηκόντων ἐθῶν.

¹⁸ *Ibid.*, 664A.

¹⁹ *Apol.* 38A. Professor Hackforth, *CR* 59 (1945) 1 ff., has sought to convince us that Plato remained loyal to this maxim throughout his life. But though he certainly paid lip service to it as late as the *Sophist* (230C–E), I see no escape from the conclusion that the educational policy of the *Republic*, and still more clearly that of the *Laws*, is in reality based on very different assumptions. Plato could never confess to himself that he had abandoned any Socratic principle; but that did not prevent him from doing it. Socrates' θεραπεία ψυχῆς surely implies respect for the human mind as such; the techniques of suggestion and other controls recommended in the *Laws* seem to me to imply just the opposite.

²⁰ In the *Laws*, ἐπῳδή and its cognates are continually used in this metaphorical sense (659E, 664B, 665C, 666C, 670E, 773D, 812C, 903B, 944B). Cf. Callicles' contemptuous use of the word, *Gorg.* 484A. Its application in the *Charmides* (157A–C) is significantly different: there the "incantation" turns out to be a Socratic cross-examination. But in the *Phaedo*, where the myth is an ἐπῳδή

(114D, cf. 77E–78A), we already have a suggestion of the part which ἐπῳδαί were to play in the *Laws*. Cf. Boyancé's interesting discussion, *Culte des Muses*, 155 ff.

21 *Tim.* 86DE, *Laws* 731C, 860D.

22 See above, chap. vi, p. 185.

23 *Phaedo* 67A: καθαροὶ ἀπαλλαττόμενοι τῆς τοῦ σώματος ἀφροσύνης. Cf. 66C: τὸ σῶμα καὶ αἱ τούτου ἐπιθυμίαι, 94E: ἄγεσθαι ὑπὸ τῶν τοῦ σώματος παθημάτων, *Crat.* 414A: καθαρὰ πάντων τῶν περὶ τὸ σῶμα κακῶν καὶ ἐπιθυμιῶν. In the *Phaedo*, as Festugière has lately put it, "le corps, c'est le mal, et c'est tout le mal" (*Rev. de Phil.* 22 [1948] 101). Plato's teaching here is the main historical link between the Greek "shamanistic" tradition and Gnosticism.

24 For a fuller account of the unitary and the tripartite soul in Plato see G. M. A. Grube, *Plato's Thought*, 129–149, where the importance of the concept of στάσις, "one of the most startlingly modern things in Platonic philosophy," is rightly stressed. Apart from the reason given in the text, the extension of the notion of ψυχή to embrace the whole of human activity is doubtless connected with Plato's later view that ψυχή is the source of all motion, bad as well as good (cf. *Tim.* 89E: τρία τριχῇ ψυχῆς ἐν ἡμῖν εἴδη κατῴκισται, τυγχάνει δὲ ἕκαστον κινήσεις ἔχον, *Laws* 896D: τῶν τε ἀγαθῶν αἰτίαν εἶναι ψυχὴν καὶ τῶν κακῶν). On the ascription in the *Laws* (896E) of an irrational, and potentially evil, secondary soul to the κόσμος see Wilamowitz, *Platon*, II.315 ff., and the very full and fair discussion of this passage by Simone Pétrement, *Le Dualisme chez Platon, les Gnostiques et les Manichéens* (1947), 64 ff. I have stated my own view briefly in *JHS* 65 (1945) 21.

25 *Phaedo* 94DE; *Rep.* 441BC.

26 *Rep.* 485D: ὥσπερ ῥεῦμα ἐκεῖσε ἀπωχετευμένον. Grube, *loc. cit.*, has called attention to the significance of this passage, and others in the *Republic*, as implying that "the aim is not repression but sublimation." But Plato's presuppositions are, of course, very different from Freud's, as Cornford has pointed out in his fine essay on the Platonic Eros (*The Unwritten Philosophy*, 78 f.).

27 *Rep.* 439E. Cf. 351E–352A, 554D, 486E, 603D.

28 *Soph.* 227D–228E. Cf. also *Phdr.* 237D–238B and *Laws* 863A–864B.

29 ἔκ τινος διαφθορᾶς διαφοράν (so Burnet, from the indirect tradition in Galen).

30 The first hints of an approach to this view may be detected in the *Gorgias* (482BC, 493A). But I cannot believe that Socrates, or Plato, took it over from the Pythagoreans ready-made, as Burnet and Taylor supposed. The unitary soul of the *Phaedo* comes (with

a changed significance) from Pythagorean tradition; the evidence that the tripartite one does is late and weak. Cf. Jaeger, *Nemesios von Emesa*, 63 ff.; Field, *Plato and His Contemporaries*, 183 f.; Grube, *op. cit.*, 133. Plato's recognition of an irrational element in the soul was seen in the Peripatetic School to mark an important advance beyond the intellectualism of Socrates (*Magna Moralia* 1.1, 1182ᵃ 15 ff.); and his views on the training of the irrational soul, which will respond only to an irrational ἐθισμός, were later invoked by Posidonius in his polemic against the intellectualist Chrysippus (Galen, *de placitis Hippocratis et Platonis*, pp. 466 f. Kühn, cf. 424 f.). See below, chap. viii, p. 239.

31 *Tim.* 90A. Cf. *Crat.* 398C. Plato does not explain the implications of the term; on its probable meaning for him see L. Robin, *La Théorie platonicienne de l'amour*, 145 ff., and V. Goldschmidt, *La Religion de Platon*, 107 ff. The irrational soul, being mortal, is not a δαίμων; but the *Laws* seem to hint that the "heavenly" δαίμων has an evil daemonic counterpart in the "Titan nature" which is a hereditary root of wickedness in man (701C, 854B: cf. chap. v, nn. 132, 133).

32 *Tim.* 69C. In the *Politicus*, 309C, Plato had already referred to the two elements in man as τὸ ἀειγενὲς ὄν τῆς ψυχῆς μέρος and τὸ ζῳογενές, which implies that the latter is mortal. But there they are still "parts" of the same soul. In the *Timaeus* they are usually spoken of as distinct "kinds" of soul; they have a different origin; and the lower "kinds" are shut away from the divine element lest they pollute it "beyond the unavoidable minimum" (69D). If we are meant to take this language literally, the unity of the personality is virtually abandoned. Cf., however, *Laws* 863B, where the question whether θυμός is a πάθος or a μέρος of the soul is left open, and *Tim.* 91E, where the term μέρη is used.

33 Xen. *Cyrop.* 6.1.41. Xenophon's imaginary Persian is no doubt a Mazdean dualist. But it is unnecessary to suppose that the psychology of the *Timaeus* (in which the irrational soul is conceived as educable, and therefore *not* incurably depraved) is borrowed from Mazdean sources. It has Greek antecedents in the archaic doctrine of the indwelling δαίμων (chap. ii, p. 42), and in Empedocles' distinction between δαίμων and ψυχή (chap. v, p. 153); and Plato's adoption of it can be explained in terms of the development of his own thought. On the general question of Oriental influence on Plato's later thought I have said something in *JHS* 65 (1945). Since then, the problem has been fully discussed by Jula Kerschensteiner, *Plato u. d. Orient* (Diss. München, 1945);

by Simone Pétrement, *Le Dualisme chez Platon;* and by Festugière in an important paper, "Platon et l'Orient," *Rev. de Phil.* 21 (1947) 5 ff. So far as concerns the suggestion of a Mazdean origin for Plato's dualism, the conclusions of all three writers are negative.

[34] *Laws* 644DE. The germ of this idea may be seen already in the *Ion*, where we are told that God, operating on the passions through the "inspired" poets, ἕλκει τὴν ψυχὴν ὅποι ἂν βούληται τῶν ἀνθρώπων (536A), though the image there is that of the magnet. Cf. also *Laws* 903D, where God is "the gamester" (πεττευτής) and men are his pawns.

[35] *Laws*, 803B–804B.

[36] *Ibid.*, 713CD.

[37] *Ibid.*, 716C.

[38] *Ibid.*, 902B, 906A; cf. *Critias*, 109B.

[39] *Ibid.*, 716A. For the implications of ταπεινός, cf., e.g., 774C, δουλεία ταπεινὴ καὶ ἀνελεύθερος. To be ταπεινός towards the gods was for Plutarch a mark of superstition (*non posse suaviter*, 1101E), as it was also for Maximus of Tyre (14.7 Hob.) and probably for most Greeks.

[40] *Ibid.*, 486A; cf. *Theaet.* 173C–E, Arist. *E.N.* 1123[b] 32.

[41] *Meno* 100A, *Phaedo* 62B.

[42] *Phaedo* 81E–82B.

[43] Plot. *Enn.* 6.7.6: μεταλαβούσης δὲ θηρεῖον σῶμα θαυμάζεται πῶς, λόγος οὖσα ἀνθρώπου. Cf. *ibid.*, 1.1.11; Alex. Aphrod. *de anima* p. 27 Br. (Suppl. Arist. II.i); Porphyry *apud* Aug. *Civ. Dei*, 10.30; Iamblichus *apud* Nemes. *nat. hom.* 2 (*PG* 40, 584A); Proclus, *in Tim.* III.294, 22 ff. The notion of reincarnation in animals was in fact transferred from the occult self of Pythagoreanism to the rational ψυχή which it did not fit: cf. Rostagni, *Il Verbo di Pitagora*, 118.

[44] *Laws* 942AB: "The principal thing is that none, man or woman, should ever be without an officer set over him, and that none should get the mental habit of taking any step, whether in earnest or in jest, on his individual responsibility: in peace as in war he must live always with his eye on his superior officer, following his lead and guided by him in his smallest actions . . . in a word, we must train the mind not even to consider acting as an individual or know how to do it."

[45] On later developments of the theme of the unimportance of τὰ ἀνθρώπινα see Festugière in *Eranos*, 44 (1946) 376 ff. For man as a puppet cf. M. Ant. 7.3 and Plot. *Enn.* 3.2.15 (I.244.26 Volk.).

[46] *Apol.* 22c, poets and inspired seers λέγουσι μὲν πολλὰ καὶ καλά, ἴσασιν δ᾽ οὐδὲν ὧν λέγουσι. The same thing is said of *politicians* and seers, *Meno* 99cd; of poets, *Ion* 533e–534d, *Laws* 719c; of seers, *Tim.* 72a.

[47] *Laches* 198e; *Charm.* 173c.

[48] The attack on poetry in the *Republic* is usually taken to be Platonic rather than Socratic: but the view of poetry as irrational, on which the attack depends, appears already in the *Apology* (n. 46 above).

[49] Chap. vi, p. 185.

[50] *Phaedrus* 244cd; *Tim.* 72b.

[51] Cf. R. G. Collingwood, "Plato's Philosophy of Art," *Mind* N.S. 34 (1925) 154 ff.; E. Fascher, Προφήτης, 66 ff.; Jeanne Croissant, *Aristote et les mystères*, 14 ff.; A. Delatte, *Les Conceptions de de l'enthousiasme*, 57 ff.; P. Boyancé, *Le Culte des Muses*, 177 ff.; W. J. Verdenius, "L'*Ion* de Platon," *Mnem.* 1943, 233 ff., and "Platon et la poésie," *ibid.*, 1944, 118 ff.; I. M. Linforth, "The Corybantic Rites in Plato," *Univ. Calif. Publ. Class. Philol.* 13 (1946) 160 ff. Some of these critics would divorce Plato's religious language from any sort of religious feeling: it is "no more than a pretty dress in which he clothes his thought" (Croissant); "to call art a divine force or an inspiration is simply to call it a *je ne sais quoi*" (Collingwood). This seems to me to miss part of Plato's meaning. On the other hand, those who, like Boyancé, take his language quite literally seem to overlook the ironical undertone which is evident in passages like *Meno* 99cd and may be suspected elsewhere.

[52] *Phdr.* 244a: μανίας θείᾳ δόσει διδομένης.

[53] Cf. chap. iii, p. 80.

[54] *Laws* 719c, the poet οἷον κρήνη τις τὸ ἐπιὸν ῥεῖν ἑτοίμως ἐᾷ.

[55] *Symp.* 202e: διὰ τούτου (sc. τοῦ δαιμονίου) καὶ ἡ μαντικὴ πᾶσα χωρεῖ καὶ ἡ τῶν ἱερέων τέχνη τῶν τε περὶ τὰς θυσίας καὶ τελετὰς καὶ τὰς ἐπῳδὰς καὶ τὴν μαντείαν πᾶσαν καὶ γοητείαν.

[56] In the "rating of lives," *Phdr.* 248d, the μάντις or τελεστής and the poet are placed in the fifth and sixth classes respectively, below even the business man and the athlete. For Plato's opinion of μάντεις cf. also *Politicus* 290cd; *Laws* 908d. Nevertheless both μάντεις and poets are assigned a function, though a subordinate one, in his final project for a reformed society (*Laws* 660a, 828b); and we hear of a μάντις who had studied under him in the Academy (Plut. *Dion.* 22).

[57] Chap. ii, p. 41; chap. vi, pp. 185 f. Cf. Taylor, *Plato*, 65: "In the

Greek literature of the great period, Eros is a god to be dreaded
for the havoc he makes of human life, not to be coveted for the
blessings he bestows; a tiger, not a kitten to sport with."

58 *Phdr.* 249E, the erotic madness is πασῶν τῶν ἐνθουσιάσεων ἀρίστη.

59 This religious language does not, however, exclude for Plato an
explanation of erotic attraction in mechanistic terms—suggested,
perhaps, by Empedocles or Democritus—by postulating physical
"emanations" from the eye of the beloved which are eventually
reflected back upon their author (*Phdr.* 251B, 255CD). Cf. the
mechanistic explanation of the catharsis produced by Corybantic
rites, *Laws* 791A (which is called Democritean by Delatte and
Croissant, Pythagorean by Boyancé, but may quite possibly be
Plato's own).

60 Eros as a δαίμων has the general function of linking the human
with the divine, ὥστε τὸ πᾶν αὐτὸ αὐτῷ συνδεδέσθαι (*Symp.*
202E). In conformity with that function, Plato sees the sexual and
the nonsexual manifestations of Eros as expressions of the same
basic impulse towards τόκος ἐν καλῷ—a phrase which is for him the
statement of a deep-seated organic law. Cf. I. Bruns, "Attische
Liebestheorien," *NJbb* 1900, 17 ff., and Grube, *op. cit.*, 115.

61 *Symp.* 207AB.

62 It is significant that the theme of immortality, in its usual Platonic sense, is completely missing from the *Symposium;* and that in
the *Phaedrus*, where a sort of integration is attempted, this can
be achieved only at the level of myth, and only at the cost of treating the irrational soul as persisting after death and retaining its
carnal appetites in the discarnate state.

63 In the following pages I am especially indebted to the excellent
monograph of O. Reverdin, *La Religion de la cité platonicienne*
(Travaux de l'École Française d'Athènes, fasc. VI, 1945), which
I have not found the less valuable because the writer's religious
standpoint is very different from my own.

64 *Laws* 717AB. Cf. 738D: every village is to have its local god, δαίμων,
or hero, as every village in Attica probably in fact had (Ferguson,
Harv. Theol. Rev. 37 [1944] 128 ff.).

65 *Ibid.*, 904A, οἱ κατὰ νόμον ὄντες θεοί (cf. 885B and, if the text
is sound, 891E).

66 *Crat.* 400D, *Phdr.* 246c. Cf. also *Critias* 107AB; *Epin.* 984D (which
sounds definitely contemptuous). Those who, like Reverdin
(*op. cit.*, 53), credit Plato with a wholehearted personal belief in
the traditional gods, because he prescribes their cult and nowhere
explicitly denies their existence, seem to me to make insufficient

allowance for the compromises necessary to any practical scheme of religious reform. To detach the masses completely from their inherited beliefs, had it been possible, would in Plato's view have been disastrous; and no reformer can openly reject for himself what he would prescribe for others. See further my remarks in *JHS* 65 (1945) 22 f.

67 *Tim.* 28c. On the much-debated question of Plato's God see especially Diès, *Autour de Platon*, 523 ff.; Festugière, *L'Idéal religieux des Grecs et l'Évangile*, 172 ff.; Hackforth, "Plato's Theism," *CQ* 30 (1936) 4 ff.; F. Solmsen, *Plato's Theology* (Cornell, 1942). I have stated my own tentative view, *JHS, loc. cit.*, 23.

68 The heavenly bodies are everywhere the natural representatives or symbols of what Christopher Dawson calls "the transcendent element in external reality" (*Religion and Culture*, 29). Cf. *Apol.* 26D, where we are told that "everybody," including Socrates himself, believes the sun and the moon to be gods; and *Crat.* 397CD, where the heavenly bodies are represented as the primitive gods of Greece. But in the fourth century, as we learn from the *Epinomis*, 982D, this belief was beginning to fade before the popularising of mechanistic explanations (cf. *Laws* 967A; *Epin.* 983C). Its revival in the Hellenistic Age was in no small degree due to Plato himself.

69 On the question of animation *versus* external control see *Laws* 898E–899A, *Epin.* 983C. Animation was no doubt the popular theory, and was to prevail in the coming age; but Plato refuses to decide (the stars are either θεοί or θεῶν εἰκόνες ὡς ἀγάλματα, θεῶν αὐτῶν ἐργασαμένων, *Epin.* 983E; for the latter view cf. *Tim.* 37C).

70 *Laws* 821B–D. In itself, prayer to the sun was not foreign to Greek tradition: Socrates prays to him at sunrise (*Symp.* 220D), and a speaker in a lost play of Sophocles prays: ἥλιος, οἰκτείρειέ με, | ὃν οἱ σοφοὶ λέγουσι γεννητὴν θεῶν | καὶ πατέρα πάντων (fr. 752 P.). Elsewhere in the *Laws* (887D) Plato speaks of προκυλίσεις ἅμα καὶ προσκυνήσεις Ἑλλήνων τε καὶ βαρβάρων at the rising and setting of the sun and moon. Festugière has accused him of misrepresenting the facts here: "ni l'objet de culte ni le geste d'adoration ne sont grecs: ils sont barbares. Il s'agit de l'astrologie chaldéenne et de la προσκύνησις en usage à Babylone et chez les Perses" (*Rev. de Phil.* 21 [1947] 23). But while we may allow that the προκυλίσεις, and perhaps the moon-cult, are barbarian rather than Greek, Plato's statement seems sufficiently justified by Hesiod's rule of prayer and offerings at sunrise and sundown

(*Erga* 338 f.) and by Ar. *Plut.* 771: καὶ προσκυνῶ γε πρῶτα μὲν τὸν ἥλιον, κτλ. Nevertheless, the proposals of the *Laws* do seem to give the heavenly bodies a religious importance which they lacked in ordinary Greek cult, though there may have been partial precedents in Pythagorean thought and usage (cf. chap. viii, n. 68). And in the *Epinomis*—which I am now inclined to regard either as Plato's own work or as put together from his "Nachlass"—we meet with something that is certainly Oriental, and is frankly presented as such, the proposal for *public* worship of the *planets*.

71 *Laws* 946BC, 947A. The dedication is not merely formal: the εὔθυνοι are to be actually housed in the τέμενος of the joint temple (946CD). It should be added that the proposal to institute a High Priest (ἀρχιερεύς) appears to be an innovation; at any rate the title is nowhere attested before Hellenistic times (Reverdin, *op. cit.*, 61 f.). Presumably it reflects Plato's sense of the need for a tighter organisation of the religious life of Greek communities. The High Priest will be, however, like other priests, a layman, and will hold office only for a year; Plato did not conceive the idea of a professional clergy, and would certainly, I think, have disapproved it, as tending to impair the unity of "Church" and State, religious and political life.

72 See Festugière, *Le Dieu cosmique* (= *La Révélation d'Hermès*, II, Paris, 1949); and my chap. viii, p. 240.

73 Divine φθόνος is explicitly rejected, *Phdr.* 247A, *Tim.* 29E (and Arist. *Met.* 983ᵃ 2).

74 See chap. ii, n. 32.

75 *Laws* 903B, ἐπῳδῶν μύθων: cf. 872E, where the doctrine of requital in future earthly lives is called μῦθος ἢ λόγος ἢ ὅ τι χρὴ προσαγορεύειν αὐτό, and L. Edelstein, "The Function of the Myth in Plato's Philosophy," *Journal of the History of Ideas*, 10 (1949) 463 ff.

76 *Ibid.*, 904C–905D; cf. also 728BC, and Plotinus' development of this idea, *Enn.* 4.3.24.

77 904D: Ἀίδην τε καὶ τὰ τούτων ἐχόμενα τῶν ὀνομάτων ἐπονομάζοντες σφόδρα φοβοῦνται καὶ ὀνειροπολοῦσιν ζῶντες διαλυθέντες τε τῶν σωμάτων. Plato's language here (ὀνομάτων, ὀνειροπολοῦσιν) suggests that popular beliefs about the Underworld have no more than symbolic value. But the last words of the sentence are puzzling: they can hardly mean "when in sleep or trance" (England), since they are antithetic to ζῶντες, but seem to assert that the fear of Hades continues *after death*. Does Plato intend to hint that to experience this fear—the fruit of a guilty conscience—is

already to *be* in Hades? That would accord with the general doctrine which he preached from the *Gorgias* onward, that wrongdoing is its own punishment.

[78] 903CD, 905B. On the significance of this point of view see Festugière, *La Sainteté*, 60 ff., and V. Goldschmidt, *La Religion de Platon*, 101 f. It became one of the commonplaces of Stoicism, e.g., Chrysippus *apud* Plut. *Sto. rep.* 44, 1054F, M. Ant. 6.45, and reappears in Plotinus, e.g., *Enn.* 3.2.14. Men live in the cosmos like mice in a great house, enjoying splendours not designed for them (Cic. *nat. deor.* 2.17).

[79] *Euthyphro*, 14E. Cf. *Laws* 716E–717A.

[80] *Rep.* 364B–365A; *Laws* 909B (cf. 908D). The verbal similarities of the two passages are, I think, sufficient to show that Plato has in view the same class of persons (Thomas, Ἐπέκεινα, 30, Reverdin, *op. cit.*, 226).

[81] *Rep.* 364E: πείθοντες οὐ μόνον ἰδιώτας ἀλλὰ καὶ πόλεις (cf. 366AB, αἱ μέγισται πόλεις), *Laws* 909B: ἰδιώτας τε καὶ ὅλας οἰκίας καὶ πόλεις χρημάτων χάριν ἐπιχειρῶσιν κατ' ἄκρας ἐξαιρεῖν. Plato may have in mind famous historical instances like the purification of Athens by Epimenides (mentioned at *Laws* 642D, where the respectful tone is in character for the Cretan speaker) or of Sparta by Thaletas: cf. Festugière, *REG* 51 (1938) 197. Boyancé, *REG* 55 (1942) 232, has objected that Epimenides was unconcerned with the Hereafter. But this is true only on Diels' assumption that the writings attributed to him were "Orphic" forgeries—an assumption which, whether it be correct or not, Plato is unlikely to have made.

[82] I find it hard to believe—as many still do, on the strength of "Musaeus and his son" (*Rep.* 363C)—that Plato intended to condemn the official Mysteries of Eleusis: cf. Nilsson, *Harv. Theol. Rev.* 28 (1935) 208 f., and Festugière, *loc. cit.* Certainly he cannot have meant to suggest in the *Laws* that the Eleusinian priesthood should be brought to trial for an offence which he regards as worse than atheism (907B). On the other hand, the *Republic* passage does not justify restricting Plato's condemnation to "Orphic" books and practices, though these are certainly included. The parallel passage in the *Laws* does not mention Orpheus at all.

[83] See above, n. 6.

[84] *Rep.* 427BC; *Laws* 738BC, 759C.

[85] I do not intend to imply that for Plato Apolline religion is simply a pious lie, a fiction maintained for its social usefulness. Rather it reflects or symbolises religious truth at the level of εἰκασία at

which it can be assimilated by the people. Plato's universe was a graded one: as he believed in degrees of truth and reality, so he believed in degrees of religious insight. Cf. Reverdin, *op. cit.*, 243 ff.

[86] *Laws* 873E. Pollution is incurred in all cases of homicide, even involuntary (865CD), or of suicide (873D), and requires a κάθαρσις which will be prescribed by the Delphic ἐξηγηταί. The infectiousness of μίασμα is recognised within certain limits (881DE, cf. 916c, and chap. ii, n. 43).

[87] *Laws* 907D–909D. Those whose irreligious teaching is aggravated by antisocial conduct are to suffer solitary confinement for life (909BC) in hideous surroundings (908A)—a fate which Plato rightly regards as worse than death (908E). Grave *ritual* offences, such as sacrificing to a god when in a state of impurity, are to be punishable by death (910CE), as they were at Athens: this is defended on the old ground that such acts bring the anger of the gods on the entire city (910B).

[88] *Ibid.*, 967BC, "certain persons" who formerly got themselves into trouble through falsely asserting that the heavenly bodies were "a pack of stones and earth" had only themselves to blame for it. But the view that astronomy is a dangerous science is, thanks to modern discoveries, now out of date (967A); some smattering of it is indeed a necessary part of religious education (967D-968A).

[89] Cornford has drawn a striking parallel between Plato's position and that of the Grand Inquisitor in the story told in *The Brothers Karamazov* (*The Unwritten Philosophy*, 66 f.).

[90] Cf. *Laws*, 885D: οὐκ ἐπὶ τὸ μὴ δρᾶν τὰ ἄδικα τρεπόμεθα οἱ πλεῖστοι, δράσαντες δ' ἐξακεῖσθαι πειρώμεθα, and 888B: μέγιστον δέ . . . τὸ περὶ τοὺς θεοὺς ὀρθῶς διανοηθέντα ζῆν καλῶς ἢ μή. For the wide diffusion of materialism see 891B.

VIII
The Fear of Freedom

A man's worst difficulties begin when he is able to do as he likes.

T. H. HUXLEY

I MUST begin this final chapter by making a confession. When the general idea of the lectures on which this book is based first formed itself in my mind, my notion was to illustrate the Greek attitude to certain problems over the whole stretch of time that lies between Homer and the last pagan Neoplatonists, a stretch about as long as that which separates antiquity from ourselves. But as material accumulated and the lectures got themselves written, it became evident that this could not be done, save at the price of a hopeless superficiality. Thus far I have in fact covered about one-third of the period in question, and even there I have left many gaps. The greater part of the story remains untold. All that I can now do is to look down a perspective of some eight centuries and ask myself in very general terms what changes took place in certain human attitudes, and for what reasons. I cannot hope in so brief a survey to arrive at exact or confident answers. But it will be something if we can get a picture of what the problems are, and can formulate them in the right terms.

Our survey starts from an age when Greek rationalism appeared to be on the verge of final triumph, the great age of intellectual discovery that begins with the foundation of the Lyceum about 335 B.C. and continues down to the end of the third century. This period witnessed the transformation of Greek science from an untidy jumble of isolated observations mixed with *a priori* guesses into a system of methodical disciplines. In the more

236

abstract sciences, mathematics and astronomy, it reached a
level that was not to be attained again before the sixteenth century; and it made the first organised attempt at research in
many other fields, botany, zoology, geography, and the history
of language, of literature, and of human institutions. Nor was
it only in science that the time was adventurous and creative.
It is as if the sudden widening of the spatial horizon that resulted from Alexander's conquests had widened at the same
time all the horizons of the mind. Despite its lack of political
freedom, the society of the third century B.C. was in many
ways the nearest approach to an "open"[1] society that the world
had yet seen, and nearer than any that would be seen again
until very modern times. The traditions and institutions
of the old "closed" society were of course still there and
still influential: the incorporation of a city-state in one or
other of the Hellenistic kingdoms did not cause it to lose
its moral importance overnight. But though the city was
there, its walls, as someone has put it, were down: its institutions stood exposed to rational criticism; its traditional ways of
life were increasingly penetrated and modified by a cosmopoli-
tan culture. For the first time in Greek history, it mattered little
where a man had been born or what his ancestry was: of the
men who dominated Athenian intellectual life in this age,
Aristotle and Theophrastus, Zeno, Cleanthes, and Chrysippus
were all of them foreigners; only Epicurus was of Athenian
stock, though by birth a colonial.

And along with this levelling out of local determinants, this
freedom of movement in space, there went an analogous
levelling out of temporal determinants, a new freedom for the
mind to travel backwards in time and choose at will from the
past experience of men those elements which it could best
assimilate and exploit. The individual began consciously to *use*
the tradition, instead of being used by it. This is most obvious
in the Hellenistic poets, whose position in this respect was like
that of poets and artists to-day. "If we talk of tradition to-

day," says Mr. Auden, "we no longer mean what the eighteenth century meant, a way of working handed down from one generation to the next; we mean a consciousness of the whole of the past in the present. Originality no longer means a slight personal modification of one's immediate predecessors; it means the capacity to find in any other work of any date or locality clues for the treatment of one's own subject-matter."[2] That this is true of most, if not all, Hellenistic poetry hardly needs proving: it explains both the strength and the weakness of works like the *Argonautica* of Apollonius or the *Aetia* of Callimachus. But we can apply it also to Hellenistic philosophy: Epicurus' use of Democritus and the Stoic use of Heraclitus are cases in point. As we shall find presently,[3] it has likewise some bearing on the field of religious beliefs.

Certainly it is in this age that the Greek pride in human reason attains its most confident expression. We should reject, says Aristotle, the old rule of life that counselled humility, bidding man think in mortal terms (θνητὰ φρονεῖν τὸν θνητόν); for man has within him a divine thing, the intellect, and so far as he can live on that level of experience, he can live as though he were not mortal.[4] The founder of Stoicism went further still: for Zeno, man's intellect was not merely akin to God, it *was* God, a portion of the divine substance in its pure or active state.[5] And although Epicurus made no such claim, he yet held that by constant meditation on the truths of philosophy one could live "like a god among men."[6]

But ordinary human living, of course, is not like that. Aristotle knew that no man can sustain the life of pure reason for more than very brief periods;[7] and he and his pupils appreciated, better perhaps than any other Greeks, the necessity of studying the irrational factors in behaviour if we are to reach a realistic understanding of human nature. I have briefly illustrated the sanity and subtlety of their approach to this kind of problem in dealing with the cathartic influence of music, and with the theory of dreams.[8] Did circumstances permit, I should have liked to devote an entire chapter to Aristotle's treatment of the

Irrational; but the omission may perhaps be excused, since there exists an excellent short book, Mlle Croissant's *Aristote et les Mystères*, which deals in an interesting and thorough manner, not indeed with the whole subject, but with some of its most important aspects.[9]

Aristotle's approach to an empirical psychology, and in particular to a psychology of the Irrational, was unhappily carried no further after the first generation of his pupils. When the natural sciences detached themselves from the study of philosophy proper, as they began to do early in the third century, psychology was left in the hands of the philosophers (where it remained—I think to its detriment—down to very recent times). And the dogmatic rationalists of the Hellenistic Age seem to have cared little for the objective study of man as he is; their attention was concentrated on the glorious picture of man as he might be, the ideal *sapiens* or sage. In order to make the picture seem possible, Zeno and Chrysippus deliberately went back, behind Aristotle and behind Plato, to the naïve intellectualism of the fifth century. The attainment of moral perfection, they said, was independent both of natural endowment and of habituation; it depended solely on the exercise of reason.[10] And there was no "irrational soul" for reason to contend with: the so-called passions were merely errors of judgement, or morbid disturbances resulting from errors of judgement.[11] Correct the error, and the disturbance will automatically cease, leaving a mind untouched by joy or sorrow, untroubled by hope or fear, "passionless, pitiless, and perfect."[12]

This fantastic psychology was adopted and maintained for two centuries, not on its merits, but because it was thought necessary to a moral system which aimed at combining altruistic action with complete inward detachment.[13] Posidonius, we know, rebelled against it and demanded a return to Plato,[14] pointing out that Chrysippus' theory conflicted both with observation, which showed the elements of character to be innate,[15] and with moral experience, which revealed irrationality and evil as ineradicably rooted in human nature and control-

lable only by some kind of "catharsis."[16] But his protest did
not avail to kill the theory; orthodox Stoics continued to talk
in intellectualist terms, though perhaps with diminishing conviction. Nor was the attitude of Epicureans or of Sceptics very
different in this matter. Both schools would have liked to
banish the passions from human life; the ideal of both was
ataraxia, freedom from disturbing emotions; and this was to
be achieved in the one case by holding the right opinions about
man and God, in the other by holding no opinions at all.[17] The
Epicureans made the same arrogant claim as the Stoics, that
without philosophy there can be no goodness[18]—a claim which
neither Aristotle nor Plato ever made.

This rationalist psychology and ethic was matched by a
rationalised religion. For the philosopher, the essential part of
religion lay no longer in acts of cult, but in a silent contemplation of the divine and in a realisation of man's kinship with it.
The Stoic contemplated the starry heavens, and read there the
expression of the same rational and moral purpose which he
discovered in his own breast; the Epicurean, in some ways the
more spiritual of the two, contemplated the unseen gods who
dwell remote in the *intermundia* and thereby found strength to
approximate his life to theirs.[19] For both schools, deity has
ceased to be synonymous with arbitrary Power, and has become
instead the embodiment of a rational ideal; the transformation
was the work of the classical Greek thinkers, especially Plato.
As Festugière has rightly insisted,[20] the Stoic religion is a
direct inheritance from the *Timaeus* and the *Laws*, and even
Epicurus is at times closer in spirit to Plato than he would have
cared to acknowledge.

At the same time, all the Hellenistic schools—even perhaps
the Sceptics[21]—were as anxious as Plato had been to avoid a
clean break with traditional forms of cult. Zeno indeed declared that temples were superfluous—God's true temple was
the human intellect.[22] Nor did Chrysippus conceal his opinion
that to represent gods in human shape was childish.[23] Nevertheless, Stoicism found room for the anthropomorphic gods by

treating them as allegorical figures or symbols;[24] and when in the Hymn of Cleanthes we find the Stoic God decked out with the epithets and attributes of Homer's Zeus, this is more, I think, than a stylistic formality—it is a serious attempt to fill the old forms with a new meaning.[25] Epicurus too sought to keep the forms and purify their content. He was scrupulous, we are told, in observing all the usages of cult,[26] but insisted that they must be divorced from all fear of divine anger or hope of material benefit; to him, as to Plato, the "do ut des" view of religion is the worst blasphemy.[27]

It would be unwise to assume that such attempts to purge the tradition had much effect on popular belief. As Epicurus said, "the things which I know, the multitude disapproves, and of what the multitude approves, I know nothing."[28] Nor is it easy for us to know what the multitude approved in Epicurus' time. Then as now, the ordinary man became articulate about such things only, as a rule, upon his tombstone—and not always even there. Extant tombstones of the Hellenistic Age are less reticent than those of an earlier time, and suggest, for what they are worth, that the traditional belief in Hades is slowly fading, and begins to be replaced either by explicit denial of any Afterlife or else by vague hopes that the deceased has gone to some better world—"to the Isles of the Blessed," "to the gods," or even "to the eternal Kosmos."[29] I should not care to build very much on the latter type of epitaph: we know that the sorrowing relatives are apt to order "a suitable inscription" which does not always correspond to any actively held belief.[30] Still, taken as a whole, the tombstones do suggest that disintegration of the Conglomerate has gone a stage further.

As for public or civic religion, we should expect it to suffer from the loss of civic autonomy: in the city-state, religion and public life were too intimately interlocked for either to decline without injury to the other. And that public religion had in fact declined pretty steeply at Athens in the half-century after Chaeronea we know from Hermocles' hymn to Demetrius

Poliorcetes:[31] at no earlier period could a hymn sung on a great public occasion have declared that the gods of the city were either indifferent or nonexistent, and that these useless stocks and stones were now replaced by a "real" god, Demetrius himself.[32] The flattery may be insincere; the scepticism plainly is not, and it must have been generally shared, since we are told that the hymn was highly popular.[33] That Hellenistic ruler-worship was *always* insincere—that it was a political stunt *and nothing more*—no one, I think, will believe who has observed in our own day the steadily growing mass adulation of dictators, kings, and, in default of either, athletes.[34] When the old gods withdraw, the empty thrones cry out for a successor, and with good management, or even without management,[35] almost any perishable bag of bones may be hoisted into the vacant seat. So far as they have religious meaning for the individual, ruler-cult and its analogues,[36] ancient and modern, are primarily, I take it, expressions of helpless dependence; he who treats another human being as divine thereby assigns to himself the relative status of a child or an animal. It was, I think, a related sentiment that gave rise to another characteristic feature of the Early Hellenistic Age, the wide diffusion of the cult of Tyche, "Luck" or "Fortune." Such a cult is, as Nilsson has said, "the last stage in the secularising of religion";[37] in default of any positive object, the sentiment of dependence attaches itself to the purely negative idea of the unexplained and unpredictable, which is Tyche.

I do not want to give a false impression of a complex situation by oversimplifying it. Public worship of the city gods of course continued; it was an accepted part of public life, an accepted expression of civic patriotism. But it would, I think, be broadly true to say of it what has been said of Christianity in our own time, that it had become "more or less a social routine, without influence on goals of living."[38] On the other hand, the progressive decay of tradition set the religious man free to choose his own gods,[39] very much as it set the poet free to choose his own style; and the anonymity and loneliness of life in the great new cities, where the individual felt himself a cipher, may have enforced on many the sense of need for some divine friend and helper. The celebrated remark of Whitehead, that "religion is what the individual does with his own solitariness,"[40] whatever one may think of it as a general definition, describes fairly accurately the religious situation from Alexander's time onwards. And one thing that the individual did with his solitariness in this age was to form small private clubs devoted to the worship of individual gods, old or new. Inscriptions tell us something of the activities of such "Apolloniasts" or "Hermaists" or "Iobacchi" or "Sarapiasts," but we cannot see far into their minds. All we can really say is that these associations served both social and religious purposes, in unknown and probably varying proportions: some may have been little more than dining-clubs; others may have given their members a real sense of community with a divine patron or protector of their own choice, to replace the inherited local community of the old closed society.[41]

Such, in the broadest outline, were the relations between religion and rationalism in the third century.[42] Looking at the picture as a whole, an intelligent observer in or about the year 200 B.C. might well have predicted that within a few generations the disintegration of the inherited structure would be complete, and that the perfect Age of Reason would follow. He would, however, have been quite wrong on both points—as similar predictions made by nineteenth-century rationalists look like proving wrong. It would have surprised our imaginary Greek rationalist to learn that half a millennium after his death Athena would still be receiving the periodic gift of a new dress from her grateful people;[43] that bulls would still be sacrificed in Megara to heroes killed in the Persian Wars eight hundred years earlier;[44] that ancient taboos concerned with ritual purity would still be rigidly maintained in many places.[45] For the *vis inertiae* that keeps this sort of thing going—what Matthew Arnold once called "the extreme slowness of things"[46]—no rationalist ever makes sufficient allowance. Gods withdraw, but their rituals live on, and no one except a few intellectuals notices that they have ceased to mean anything. In a material sense the Inherited Conglomerate did not in the end perish by disintegration; large portions of it were left standing through the centuries, a familiar, shabby, rather lovable façade, until one day the Christians pushed the façade over and discovered that there was virtually nothing behind it—only a faded local patriotism and an antiquarian sentiment.[47] So, at least, it happened in the cities; it appears that to the country folk, the *pagani*, certain of the old rites still did mean something, as indeed a few of them, in a dim half-comprehended manner, still do.

A prevision of this history would have surprised an observer in the third century B.C. But it would have surprised him far more painfully to learn that Greek civilisation was entering, not on the Age of Reason, but on a period of slow intellectual decline which was to last, with some deceptive rallies and some brilliant individual rear-guard actions, down to the capture of Byzantium by the Turks; that in all the sixteen centuries of existence still awaiting it the Hellenic world would produce no poet as good as Theocritus, no scientist as good as Eratosthenes, no mathematician as good as Archimedes, and that the one great name in philosophy would represent a point of view believed to be extinct—transcendental Platonism.

To understand the reasons for this long-drawn-out decline is one of the major problems of world history. We are concerned here with only one aspect of it, what may be called for convenience the Return of the Irrational. But even that is so big a subject that I can only illustrate what I have in mind by pointing briefly to a few typical developments.

We saw in an earlier chapter how the gap between the beliefs of the intellectuals and the beliefs of the people, already discernible in the oldest Greek literature, widened in the late fifth century to something approaching a complete divorce, and how the growing rationalism of the intellectuals was matched by regressive symptoms in popular belief. In the relatively "open" Hellenistic society, although the divorce was on the whole maintained, rapid changes in social stratification, and the opening of education to wider classes, created more opportunities of interaction between the two groups. We have noticed evidence that in third-century Athens a scepticism once confined to intellectuals had begun to infect the general population; and the same thing was to happen later at Rome.[48] But after the third century a different kind of interaction shows itself, with the appearance of a pseudo-scientific literature, mostly pseudonymous and often claiming to be based on divine revelation, which took up the ancient superstitions of the East or the more recent phantasies of the Hellenistic masses, dressed them in trappings borrowed from Greek science or Greek philosophy, and won for them the acceptance of a large part of the educated class. Assimilation henceforth works both ways: while rationalism, of a limited and negative kind, continues to spread from above downwards, antirationalism spreads from below upwards, and eventually wins the day.

Astrology is the most familiar example.[49] It has been said that it "fell upon the Hellenistic mind as a new disease falls upon some remote island people."[50] But the comparison does not quite fit the facts, so far as they are known. Invented in Babylonia, it spread to Egypt, where Herodotus appears to have met with it.[51] In the fourth century, Eudoxus reported its existence in Babylonia, along with the achievements of Babylonian astronomy; but he viewed it with scepticism,[52] and there is no evidence that it was taken up, although in the *Phaedrus* myth Plato amused himself by playing his own variation on an astrological theme.[53] About 280 B.C. more detailed information was made available to Greek readers in the writings of the Babylonian priest Berossus, without (it would seem) causing any great excitement. The real vogue of astrology seems to start in the second century B.C., when a number of popular manuals—especially one composed in the name of an imaginary Pharaoh, the *Revelations of Nechepso and Petosiris*[54]—began to circulate widely, and practising

astrologers appeared as far afield as Rome.[55] Why did it occur
then and not sooner? The idea was by then no novelty, and the
intellectual ground for its reception had long been prepared in
the astral theology which was taught alike by Platonists, Aris-
totelians, and Stoics, though Epicurus warned the world of its
dangers.[56] One may guess that its spread was favoured by political conditions: in the troubled half-century that preceded the
Roman conquest of Greece it was particularly important to
know what was going to happen. One may guess also that the
Babylonian Greek who at this time occupied the Chair of
Zeno[57] encouraged a sort of "trahison des clercs" (the Stoa had
already used its influence to kill the heliocentric hypothesis of
Aristarchus which, if accepted, would have upset the foundations both of astrology and of Stoic religion).[58] But behind such
immediate causes we may perhaps suspect something deeper
and less conscious: for a century or more the individual had
been face to face with his own intellectual freedom, and now
he turned tail and bolted from the horrid prospect—better
the rigid determinism of the astrological Fate than that terrifying burden of daily responsibility. Rational men like Panaetius
and Cicero tried to check the retreat by argument, as Plotinus
was to do later,[59] but without perceptible effect; certain motives
are beyond the reach of argument.

Besides astrology, the second century B.C. saw the development of another irrational doctrine which deeply influenced the
thought of later antiquity and the whole Middle Age—the
theory of occult properties or forces immanent in certain
animals, plants, and precious stones. Though its beginnings
are probably much older, this was first systematically set forth
by one Bolus of Mendes, called "the Democritean," who appears
to have written about 200 B.C.[60] His system was closely linked
with magical medicine and with alchemy; it was also soon combined with astrology, to which it formed a convenient supplement. The awkward thing about the stars had always been
their inaccessibility, alike to prayer and to magic.[61] But if
each planet had its representative in the animal, vegetable,

and mineral kingdoms, linked to it by an occult "sympathy," as was now asserted, one could get at them magically by manipulating these earthly counterparts.[62] Resting as they did on the primitive conception of the world as a magical unity, Bolus' ideas were fatally attractive to the Stoics, who already conceived the cosmos as an organism whose parts had community of experience ($\sigma\upsilon\mu\pi\acute{\alpha}\theta\epsilon\iota\alpha$).[63] From the first century B.C. onwards Bolus begins to be quoted as a scientific authority comparable in status with Aristotle and Theophrastus,[64] and his doctrines become incorporated in the generally accepted world picture.

Many students of the subject have seen in the first century B.C. the decisive period of *Weltwende*, the period when the tide of rationalism, which for the past hundred years had flowed ever more sluggishly, has finally expended its force and begins to retreat. There is no doubt that all the philosophical schools save the Epicurean took a new direction at this time. The old religious dualism of mind and matter, God and Nature, the soul and the appetites, which rationalist thought had striven to overcome, reasserts itself in fresh forms and with a fresh vigour. In the new unorthodox Stoicism of Posidonius this dualism appears as a tension of opposites within the unified cosmos and unified human nature of the old Stoa.[65] About the same time an internal revolution in the Academy puts an end to the purely critical phase in the development of Platonism, makes it once more a speculative philosophy, and sets it on the road that will lead eventually to Plotinus.[66] Equally significant is the revival, after two centuries of apparent abeyance, of Pythagoreanism, not as a formal teaching school, but as a cult and as a way of life.[67] It relied frankly on authority, not on logic: Pythagoras was presented as an inspired Sage, the Greek counterpart of Zoroaster or Ostanes, and numerous apocrypha were fathered on him or on his immediate disciples. What was taught in his name was the old belief in a detachable magic self, in the world as a place of darkness and penance, and in the necessity of catharsis; but this was now combined with ideas derived from astral religion (which had in fact certain links with old Pythagoreanism),[68] from Plato (who was represented as a Pythagorean), from the occultism of Bolus,[69] and from other forms of magical tradition.[70]

All these developments are perhaps symptoms, rather than causes, of a general change in the intellectual climate of the Mediterranean world—something whose nearest historical analogue may be the romantic reaction against rationalist "natural theology" which set in at the beginning of the nineteenth century and is still a powerful influence to-day.[71] The adoration of the visible cosmos, and the sense of unity with it which had found expression in early Stoicism, began to be replaced in many minds[72] by a feeling that the physical world— at any rate the part of it below the moon—is under the sway of evil powers, and that what the soul needs is not unity with it but escape from it. The thoughts of men were increasingly preoccupied with techniques of individual salvation, some relying on holy books allegedly discovered in Eastern temples or dictated by the voice of God to some inspired prophet,[73] others seeking a personal revelation by oracle, dream, or waking vision;[74] others again looking for security in ritual, whether by initiation in one or more of the now numerous "mysteria" or by employing the services of a private magician.[75] There was a growing demand for occultism, which is essentially an attempt to capture the Kingdom of Heaven by material means —it has been well described as "the vulgar form of transcendentalism."[76] And philosophy followed a parallel path on a higher level. Most of the schools had long since ceased to value the truth for its own sake,[77] but in the Imperial Age they abandon, with certain exceptions,[78] any pretence of disinterested curiosity and present themselves frankly as dealers in salvation. It is not only that the philosopher conceives his lecture-room as a dispensary for sick souls;[79] in principle, that was nothing new. But the philosopher is not merely a psychotherapist; he is also, as Marcus Aurelius put it, "a kind of priest and minister of the gods,"[80] and his teachings claim to have religious rather than scientific worth. "The aim of Platonism," says a Christian observer in the second century A.D., "is to see God face to face."[81] And profane knowledge was valued only so far as it contributed to such aims. Seneca, for example, quotes with approval the view that we should not trouble to investigate things that it is neither possible nor useful to know, such as the cause of the tides or the principle of perspective.[82] In such sayings we already feel the intellectual climate of the Middle Ages. It is the climate in which Christianity grew up; it made the triumph of the new religion possible, and it left its mark on Christian teaching;[83] but it was not created by Christians.

What, then, did create it? One difficulty in the way of attempting any answer at the present time is the lack of a comprehensive and balanced survey of all the relevant facts which might help us to grasp the relationship between the trees and the wood. We have brilliant studies of many individual trees, though not of all; but of the wood we have only impressionistic sketches. When the second volume of Nilsson's *Geschichte* appears,[84] when Nock has published his long-awaited Gifford Lectures on Hellenistic Religion, and when Festugière has completed the important series of studies in the history of religious thought misleadingly entitled *La Révélation d'Hermès Trismégiste*,[85] the ordinary nonspecialist like myself may be in a better position to make up his mind; meanwhile he had better abstain from snap judgements. I should like, however, to conclude by saying a word about some suggested explanations of the failure of Greek rationalism.

Certain of these merely restate the problem which they claim to solve. It is not helpful to be told that the Greeks had become decadent, or that the Greek mind had succumbed to Oriental influences, unless we are also told why this happened. Both statements may be true in some sense, though I think the best scholars to-day would hesitate to accord to either the unqualified acceptance which was usual in the last century.[86] But even if true, such sweeping assertions will not advance matters until the nature and causes of the alleged degeneration are made clear. Nor shall I be content to accept the fact of racial interbreeding as a sufficient explanation until it is established either that cultural attitudes are transmitted in the germ-plasm or that cross-bred strains are necessarily inferior to "pure" ones.[87]

If we are to attempt more precise answers, we must try to be sure that they really square with the facts and are not dictated solely by our own prejudices. This is not always done. When a well-known British scholar assures me that "there can be little doubt that the over-specialisation of science and the development of popular education in the Hellenistic Age led to the decline of mental activity,"[88] I fear he is merely projecting into the past his personal diagnosis of certain contemporary ills. The sort of specialisation we have to-day was quite unknown to Greek science at any period, and some of the greatest names at all periods are those of nonspecialists, as may be seen if you look at a list of the works of Theophrastus or Eratosthenes, Posidonius, Galen, or Ptolemy. And universal education was equally unknown: there is a better case for the view that Hellenistic thought suffered from too little popular education rather than too much.

Again, some favourite sociological explanations have the drawback of not quite fitting the historical facts.[89] Thus the loss of political freedom may have helped to discourage intellectual enterprise, but it was hardly the determining factor; for the great age of rationalism, from the late fourth to the late third century, was certainly not an age of political freedom. Nor is it quite easy to put the whole blame on war and economic impoverishment. There is indeed some evidence that such conditions do favour an increased resort to magic and divination[90] (very recent examples are the vogue of spiritualism during and after the First World War, of astrology during and after the Second);[91] and I am willing to believe that the disturbed conditions of the first century B.C. helped to start the direct retreat from reason, while those of the third century A.D. helped to make it final. But if this were the only force at work, we should expect the two intervening centuries—an exceptionally long period of domestic peace, personal security, and, on the whole, decent government—to show a reversal of this tendency instead of its gradual accentuation.

Other scholars have emphasised the *internal* breakdown of Greek rationalism. It "wasted away," says Nilsson, "as a fire burns itself out for lack of fuel. While science ended in fruitless logomachies and soulless compilations, the religious will to believe got fresh vitality."[92] As Festugière puts it, "on avait trop discuté, on était las des mots. Il ne restait que la technique."[93] To a modern ear the description has a familiar and disquieting ring, but there is much ancient evidence to support it. If we go on to ask why fresh fuel was lacking, the answer of both authors is the old one, that Greek science had failed to develop the experimental method.[94] And if we ask further why it failed to do so, we are usually told that the Greek habit of mind was deductive—which I do not find very illuminating. Here Marxist analysis has hit on a cleverer answer: experiment failed to develop because there was no serious technology; there was no serious technology because human labour was cheap; human labour was cheap because slaves were abundant.[95] Thus by a neat chain of inference the rise of the mediaeval world-view is shown to depend on the institution of slavery. Some of its links, I suspect, may need testing; but this is a task for which I am not qualified. I will, however, venture to make two rather obvious comments. One is that the economic argument explains better the stagnation of mechanics after Archimedes than it does the stagnation of medicine after Galen or of astronomy after Ptolemy. The other is that the paralysis of scientific thought in general may very well account for the boredom and restlessness of the intellectuals, but what it does not so well account for is the new attitude of the masses. The vast majority of those who turned to astrology or magic, the vast majority of the devotees of Mithraism or Christianity, were evidently not the sort of people to whom the stagnation of science was a *direct* and conscious concern; and I find it hard to be certain that their religious outlook would have been fundamentally different even if some scientist had changed their economic lives by inventing the steam engine.

If future historians are to reach a more complete explanation of what happened, I think that, without ignoring either the intellectual or the economic factor, they will have to take account of another sort of motive, less conscious and less tidily rational. I have already suggested that behind the acceptance of astral determinism there lay, among other things, the fear of freedom —the unconscious flight from the heavy burden of individual choice which an open society lays upon its members. If such a motive is accepted as a *vera causa* (and there is pretty strong evidence that it is a *vera causa* to-day),[96] we may suspect its operation in a good many places. We may suspect it in the hardening of philosophical speculation into quasi-religious dogma which provided the individual with an unchanging rule of life; in the dread of inconvenient research expressed even by a Cleanthes or an Epicurus; later, and on a more popular level, in the demand for a prophet or a scripture; and more generally, in the pathetic reverence for the written word characteristic of late Roman and mediaeval times—a readiness, as Nock puts it, "to accept statements because they were in books, or even because they were said to be in books."[97]

When a people has travelled as far towards the open society as the Greeks had by the third century B.C., such a retreat does not happen quickly or uniformly. Nor is it painless for the individual. For the refusal of responsibility in any sphere there is always a price to be paid, usually in the form of neurosis. And we may find collateral evidence that the fear of freedom is not a mere phrase in the increase of irrational anxieties and the striking manifestations of neurotic guilt-feeling observable in the later[98] stages of the retreat. These things were not new in the religious experience of the Greeks: we encountered them in studying the Archaic Age. But the centuries of rationalism had weakened their social influence and thus, indirectly, their power over the individual. Now they show themselves in new forms and with a new intensity. I cannot here go into the evidence; but we can get some measure of the change by comparing the "Superstitious Man" of Theophrastus, who is hardly more than an old-fashioned observer of traditional taboos, with Plutarch's idea of a superstitious man as one who "sits in a public place clad in sackcloth or filthy rags, or wallows naked in the mire, proclaiming what he calls his sins."[99] Plutarch's picture of religious neurosis can be amplified from a good many other sources: striking individual documents are Lucian's portrait of Peregrinus, who turned from his sins first to Christianity, then to pagan philosophy, and after a spectacular suicide became a miracle-working pagan saint;[100] and the self-portrait of another interesting neurotic, Aelius Aristides.[101] Again, the presence of a diffused anxiety among the masses shows itself clearly, not only in the reviving dread of post-mortem punishments[102] but in the more immediate terrors revealed by extant prayers and amulets.[103] Pagan and Christian alike prayed in the later Imperial Age for protection against invisible perils—against the evil eye and daemonic possession, against "the deceiving demon" or "the headless dog."[104] One amulet promises protection "against every malice of a frightening dream or of beings in the air"; a second, "against enemies, accusers, robbers, terrors, and apparitions in dreams"; a third—a Christian one—against "unclean spirits" hiding under your bed or in the rafters or even in the rubbish-pit.[105] The Return of the Irrational was, as may be seen from these few examples, pretty complete.

There I must leave the problem. But I will not end this book without making a further confession. I have purposely been sparing in the use of modern parallels, for I know that such parallels mislead quite as often as they illuminate.[106] But as a man cannot escape from his own shadow, so no generation can pass judgement on the problems of history without reference, conscious or unconscious, to its own problems. And I will not pretend to hide from the reader that in writing these chapters, and especially this last one, I have had our own situation constantly in mind. We too have witnessed the slow disintegration of an inherited conglomerate, starting among the educated class but now affecting the masses almost everywhere, yet still very far from complete. We too have experienced a great age of rationalism, marked by scientific advances beyond anything that earlier times had thought possible, and confronting mankind with the prospect of a society more open than any it has ever known. And in the last forty years we have also experienced something else—the unmistakable symptoms of a recoil from that prospect. It would appear that, in the words used recently by André Malraux, "Western civilisation has begun to doubt its own credentials."[107]

What is the meaning of this recoil, this doubt? Is it the hesitation before the jump, or the beginning of a panic flight? I do not know. On such a matter a simple professor of Greek is in no position to offer an opinion. But he can do one thing. He can remind his readers that once before a civilised people rode to this jump—rode to it and refused it. And he can beg them to examine all the circumstances of that refusal.

Was it the horse that refused, or the rider? That is really the crucial question. Personally, I believe it was the horse—in other words, those irrational elements in human nature which govern without our knowledge so much of our behaviour and so much of what we think is our thinking. And if I am right about this, I can see in it grounds for hope. As these chapters have, I trust, shown, the men who created the first European rationalism were never—until the Hellenistic Age—"mere" rationalists: that is to say, they were deeply and imaginatively aware of the power, the wonder, and the peril of the Irrational. But they could describe what went on below the threshold of consciousness only in mythological or symbolic language; they had no instrument for understanding it, still less for controlling it; and in the Hellenistic Age too many of them made the fatal mistake of thinking they could ignore it. Modern man, on the other hand, is beginning to acquire such an instrument. It is still very far from perfect, nor is it always skilfully handled; in many fields, including that of history,[108] its possibilities and its limitations have still to be tested. Yet it seems to offer the hope that if we use it wisely we shall eventually understand our horse better; that, understanding him better, we shall be able by better training to overcome his fears; and that through the overcoming of fear horse and rider will one day take that decisive jump, and take it successfully.

NOTES TO CHAPTER VIII

[1] A completely "open" society would be, as I understand the term, a society whose modes of behaviour were entirely determined by a rational choice between possible alternatives and whose adaptations were all of them conscious and deliberate (in contrast with the completely "closed" society in which all adaptation would be unconscious and no one would ever be aware of making a choice). Such a society has never existed and will never exist; but one can usefully speak of relatively closed and relatively open societies, and can think in broad terms of the history of civilisation as the history of a movement away from the former type and in the general direction of the latter. Cf. K. R. Popper, *The Open Society and Its Enemies* (London, 1945), and the paper by Auden quoted below. On the novelty of the third-century situation see Bevan, *Stoics and Sceptics*, 23 ff.

[2] W. H. Auden, "Criticism in a Mass Society," *The Mint*, 2 (1948) 4. Cf. also Walter Lippmann, *A Preface to Morals*, 106 ff., on "the burden of originality."

[3] See pp. 242 f.

[4] Aristotle, *E.N.* 1177ᵇ 24–1178ᵃ 2. Cf. fr. 61: man is quasi mortalis deus.

[5] *Stoicorum Veterum Fragmenta*, ed. Arnim (cited henceforth as *SVF*), I.146: Ζήνων ὁ Κιτιεὺς ὁ Στωικὸς ἔφη . . . δεῖν . . . ἔχειν τὸ θεῖον ἐν μόνῳ τῷ νῷ, μᾶλλον δὲ θεὸν ἡγεῖσθαι τὸν νοῦν. God himself (or itself) is "the right reason which penetrates all things" (Diog. Laert. 7.88, cf. *SVF* I.160–162). For such a view there were precedents in earlier speculation (cf., e.g., Diogenes of Apollonia fr. 5); but it appeared now for the first time as the foundation of a systematic theory of human life.

[6] Epicurus, *Epist.* 3.135: ζήσεις δὲ ὡς θεὸς ἐν ἀνθρώποις. Cf. also

Sent. Vat. 33; Aelian, *V.H.* 4.13 (= fr. 602 Usener); and Lucr. 3.322.

7 Aristotle, *Met.* 1072ᵇ 14: διαγωγὴ δ᾽ ἐστὶν οἵα ἡ ἀρίστη μικρὸν χρόνον ἡμῖν.

8 Chap. iii, pp. 79 f.; iv, p. 120.

9 Cf. also Jaeger, *Aristotle*, 159 ff., 240 f., 396 f.; Boyancé, *Culte des Muses*, 185 ff.

10 Cic. *Acad. post.* 1.38 = *SVF* I.199.

11 Unity of the ψυχή, *SVF* II.823, etc. Zeno defined πάθος as "an irrational and *unnatural* disturbance of the mind" (*SVF* I.205). Chrysippus went further, actually identifying the πάθη with erroneous judgements: *SVF* III.456, 461, Χρύσιππος μέν ... ἀποδεικνύναι πειρᾶται, κρίσεις τινὰς εἶναι τοῦ λογιστικοῦ τὰ πάθη, Ζήνων δ᾽ οὐ τὰς κρίσεις αὐτάς, ἀλλὰ τὰς ἐπιγιγνομένας αὐταῖς συστολὰς καὶ χύσεις, ἐπάρσεις τε καὶ πτώσεις τῆς ψυχῆς ἐνόμιζεν εἶναι τὰ πάθη.

12 *SVF* III.444: Stoici affectus omnes, quorum impulsu animus commovetur, ex homine tollunt, cupiditatem, laetitiam, metum, maestitiam. .... Haec quattuor morbos vocant, non tam natura insitos quam prava opinione susceptos: et idcirco eos censent exstirpari posse radicitus, si bonorum malorumque opinio falsa tollatur. The characterisation of the Sage is Tarn's (*Hellenistic Civilisation*, 273).

13 Cf. Bevan's interesting discussion, *op. cit.*, 66 ff.

14 In his περὶ παθῶν, on which Galen drew in his treatise *de placitis Hippocratis et Platonis*. Cf. Pohlenz, *NJbb* Supp. 24 (1898) 537 ff., and *Die Stoa*, I.89 ff.; Reinhardt, *Poseidonios*, 263 ff.; Edelstein, *AJP* 47 (1936) 305 ff. It would seem that the false unity of the Zenonian psychology had already been modified by Panaetius (Cicero, *Off.* 1.101), but Posidonius carried the revision much further.

15 A newly recovered treatise by Galen, in which most of the material seems to be taken from Posidonius, develops this argument at some length, citing the differences of character observable in infants and animals: see R. Walzer, "New Light on Galen's Moral Philosophy," *CQ* 43 (1949) 82 ff.

16 Galen, ὅτι ταῖς τοῦ σώματος κράσεσιν κτλ, p. 78.8 ff. Müller: οὐ τοίνυν οὐδὲ Ποσειδωνίῳ δοκεῖ τὴν κακίαν ἔξωθεν ἐπεισιέναι τοῖς ἀνθρώποις οὐδεμίαν ἔχουσαν ῥίζαν ἐν ταῖς ψυχαῖς ἡμῶν, ὅθεν ὁρμωμένη βλαστάνει τε καὶ αὐξάνεται, ἀλλ᾽ αὐτὸ τοὐναντίον. καὶ γὰρ οὖν καὶ τῆς κακίας ἐν ἡμῖν αὐτοῖς σπέρμα, καὶ δεόμεθα πάντες οὐχ οὕτω τοῦ φεύγειν τοὺς πονηροὺς ὡς τοῦ διώκειν τοὺς

καθαρίσοντάς τε καὶ κωλύσοντας ἡμῶν τὴν αὔξησιν τῆς κακίας. Cf.
plac. Hipp. et Plat., pp. 436.7 ff. Müller: in his treatment (θεραπεία) of the passions Posidonius followed Plato, not Chrysippus.
It is interesting that the inner conflict of Euripides' Medea, in
which the fifth-century poet had expressed his protest against
the crudities of rationalist psychology (chap. vi, p. 186), also
played a part in this controversy, being quoted, oddly enough,
by both sides (Galen, *plac. Hipp. et Plat.*, p. 342 Müller; *ibid.*,
p. 382 = *SVF* III.473 *ad fin.*).

17 Cf. Epicurus, *Epist.* 1.81 f.; Sextus Emp. *Pyrrh. Hyp.* 1.29.

18 Seneca, *Epist.* 89.8: nec philosophia sine virtute est nec sine
philosophia virtus. Cf. the Epicurean *Pap. Herc.* 1251, col. xiii.6:
φιλοσοφίας δι' ἧς μόνης ἔστιν ὀρθοπραγεῖν.

19 Cf. Philodemus, *de dis* III, fr. 84 Diels = Usener, *Epicurea* fr. 386:
the wise man πειρᾶται συνεγγίζειν αὐτῇ (sc. the divine character)
καὶ καθαπερεὶ γλίχεται θιγεῖν καὶ συνεῖναι.

20 Festugière, *Le Dieu cosmique*, xii f.; *Épicure et ses dieux*, 95 ff.
Against the view that early Stoicism represents an intrusion of
"Oriental mysticism" into Greek thought see *Le Dieu cosmique*,
266, n. 1, and Bevan, *op. cit.*, 20 ff. The general relation of philosophy to religion in this age is well stated by Wendland, *Die
hellenistisch-römische Kultur²*, 106 ff.

21 Pyrrho is said to have held a high-priesthood (Diog. Laert. 9.64).

22 *SVF* I.146, 264–267.

23 *SVF* II.1076.

24 Chrysippus, *ibid.* A like allegorisation is attributed to the Platonist Xenocrates (Aetius, 1.7.30 = Xen. fr. 15 Heinze).

25 Cf. W. Schubart, "Die religiöse Haltung des frühen Hellenismus,"
Der Alte Orient, 35 (1937) 22 ff.; M. Pohlenz, "Kleanthes' Zeus-
hymnus," *Hermes*, 75 (1940) esp. 122 f. Festugière has now given
us an illuminating commentary on Cleanthes' Hymn (*Le Dieu
cosmique*, 310 ff.).

26 Philodemus, *de pietate*, pp. 126–128 Gomperz = Usener, *Epicurea*,
frs. 12, 13, 169, 387. Cf. Festugière, *Épicure et ses dieux*, 86 ff.

27 ἀνυ]πέρβλητον ἀ[σέβει]αν, Philod., *ibid.*, p. 112. For Plato, cf.
chap. vii, p. 222. Epicurus accepted the first and third of the
basic propositions of *Laws* x, but rejected the second, belief in
which seemed to him a main source of human unhappiness.

28 Epicurus *apud* Sen. *Epist.* 29.10, who adds: idem hoc omnes tibi
conclamabunt, Peripatetici, Academici, Stoici, Cynici.

29 Down to the end of the fifth century, Greek epitaphs rarely include any pronouncement on the fate of the dead; when they do,

they nearly always speak in terms of the Homeric Hades (on the most striking exception, the Potidaea epitaph, see chap. v, n. 112). Hopes of personal immortality begin to appear in the fourth century—when they are sometimes couched in language suggestive of Eleusinian influence—and become somewhat less rare in the Hellenistic Age, but show little trace of being based on specific religious doctrines. Reincarnation is never referred to (Cumont, *Lux Perpetua*, 206). Explicitly sceptical epitaphs seem to begin with Alexandrian intellectuals. But a man like Callimachus could exploit by turns the conventional view (*Epigr.* 4 Mein.), the optimistic (*Epigr.* 10), or the sceptical (*Epigr.* 13). On the whole, there is nothing in the evidence to contradict Aristotle's statement that most people consider the mortality or immortality of the soul an open question (*Soph. Elench.* 176^b 16). On the whole subject see Festugière, *L'Idéal rel. des grecs*, Pt. II, chap. v, and R. Lattimore, "Themes in Greek and Latin Epitaphs," *Illinois Studies*, 28 (1942).

30 Cf. Schubart's cautious verdict (*loc. cit.*, 11): "wo in solchen Äusserungen wirklicher Glaube spricht und wo nur eine schöne Wendung klingt, das entzieht sich jedem sicheren Urteil."

31 Athenaeus, 253D = Powell, *Collectanea Alexandrina*, p. 173. The date is not quite certain, probably 290 B.C.

32 ἄλλοι μὲν ἢ μακρὰν γὰρ ἀπέχουσιν θεοί,
   ἢ οὐκ ἔχουσιν ὦτα,
   ἢ οὐκ εἰσίν, ἢ οὐ προσέχουσιν ἡμῖν οὐδὲ ἕν,
   σὲ δὲ παρόνθ᾽ ὁρῶμεν,
   οὐ ξύλινον οὐδὲ λίθινον, ἀλλ᾽ ἀληθινόν.

I do not understand how Rostovtzoff can say in his Ingersoll Lecture ("The Mentality of the Hellenistic World and the After-Life," Harvard Divinity School *Bulletin*, 1938–1939) that there is "no blasphemy and no ἀσέβεια" here, if he is using these terms in the traditional Greek sense. And how does he know that the hymn is "an outburst of sincere religious feeling"? That was not the view of the contemporary historian Demochares (*apud* Athen. 253A), and I can find nothing in the words to suggest it. The piece was presumably written to order (on Demetrius' attitude see Tarn, *Antigonos Gonatas*, 90 f.), and could well have been composed in the spirit of Demosthenes advising the Assembly "to recognise Alexander as the son of Zeus—or Poseidon if he fancies it." Demetrius is the son of Poseidon and Aphrodite? Certainly— why not?—provided he will prove it by bringing peace and dealing with those Aetolians.

33 Athen. 253F (from Duris or Demochares?): ταῦτ' ᾖδον οἱ Μαραθω-
νομάχαι οὐ δημοσίᾳ μόνον, ἀλλὰ καὶ κατ' οἰκίαν.

34 We are not unique in this. The fifth century, with Delphic approval,
"heroised" its great athletes, and occasionally its great men, presumably in response to popular demand: not, however, until
they were dead. A tendency to this sort of thing has perhaps
existed at all times and places, but a serious supernaturalism
keeps it within bounds. The honours paid to a Brasidas pale
before those of almost any Hellenistic king, and Hitler got nearer
to being a god than any conqueror of the Christian period.

35 It would seem that once the habit had been established, divine
honours were often offered spontaneously, even by Greeks; and
in some cases to the genuine embarrassment of the recipients, e.g.
Antigonos Gonatas, who on hearing himself described as a god
retorted drily, "The man who empties my chamberpot has not
noticed it" (Plut. *Is. et Os.* 24, 360CD).

36 Not kings only, but private benefactors were worshipped, sometimes even in their lifetime (Tarn, *Hellenistic Age*, 48 f.). And the
Epicurean practice of referring to their founder as a god (Lucr.
5.8, deus ille fuit, Cic. *Tusc.* 1.48, eumque venerantur ut deum)
was rooted in the same habit of mind—was not Epicurus a greater
εὐεργέτης than any king? Plato again, if he did not actually receive divine honours after death (chap. vii, n. 9), was already
believed in his nephew's day to have been a son of Apollo (Diog.
Laert. 3.2). These facts seem to me to tell against W. S. Ferguson's
view (*Amer. Hist. Rev.* 18 [1912–1913] 29 ff.) that Hellenistic
ruler-worship was essentially a political device and nothing more,
the religious element being merely formal. In the case of rulers,
reverence for the εὐεργέτης or σωτήρ was doubtless reinforced,
consciously or unconsciously, by the ancient sense of a "royal
mana" (cf. Weinreich, *NJbb* 1926, 648 f.), which in turn may be
thought to rest upon unconscious identification of king with father.

37 Nilsson, *Greek Piety* (Eng. trans., 1948), 86. For the deep impression left on men's minds in the late fourth century by the
occurrence of unpredictable revolutionary events see the striking
words of Demetrius of Phaleron *apud* Polyb. 29.21, and Epicurus'
remark that οἱ πολλοί believe τύχη to be a goddess (*Epist.* 3.134).
An early example of actual cult is Timoleon's dedication of an
altar to Αὐτοματία (Plut. *Timol.* 36, *qua quis rat.* 11, 542E). This
sort of impersonal morally neutral Power—with which New
Comedy made so much play, cf. Stob. *Ecl.* 1.6—is something
different from the "luck" of an individual or a city, which has

older roots (cf. chap. ii, nn. 79, 80). The best study of the whole subject will be found in Wilamowitz, *Glaube*, II.298–309.

[38] A. Kardiner, *The Psychological Frontiers of Society*, 443. Cf. Wilamowitz, *Glaube*, II.271, "Das Wort des Euripides, νόμῳ καὶ θεοὺς ἡγούμεθα, ist volle Wahrheit geworden."

[39] On the earlier phases of this development see Nilsson, *Gesch.* I.760 ff.; on its importance for the Hellenistic period, Festugière, *Épicure et ses dieux*, 19.

[40] A. N. Whitehead, *Religion in the Making*, 6.

[41] The standard book on the Hellenistic clubs is F. Poland's *Geschichte des griechischen Vereinswesens*. For a short account in English see M. N. Tod, *Sidelights on Greek History*, lecture iii. The psychological function of such associations in a society where traditional bonds have broken down is well brought out by de Grazia, *The Political Community*, 144 ff.

[42] In this brief sketch I have taken no account of the position in the newly Hellenised East, where the incoming Greeks found firmly established local cults of non-Greek gods, to whom they duly paid their respects, sometimes under Greek names. On the lands of old Greek culture, Oriental influence was still relatively slight; further east, Greek and Oriental forms of worship lived side by side, without hostility, but apparently as yet without much attempt at syncretism (cf. Schubart, *loc. cit.*, 5 f.).

[43] Dittenberger, *Syll.*³ 894 (A.D., 262/3).

[44] *IG* VII.53 (fourth century A.D.).

[45] Cf. Festugière et Fabre, *Monde gréco-romain*, II.86.

[46] Matthew Arnold to Grant Duff, August 22, 1879: "But I more and more learn the extreme slowness of things; and that, though we are all disposed to think that everything will change in our lifetime, it will not."

[47] This is not to deny that there was an organised and bitter opposition to the Christianisation of the Empire. But it came from a small class of Hellenising intellectuals, supported by an active group of conservative-minded senators, rather than from the masses. On the whole subject see J. Geffcken, *Der Ausgang des griechisch-römischen Heidentums* (Heidelberg, 1920).

[48] For the prevalence of scepticism among the Roman populace cf., e.g., Cic. *Tusc.* 1.48: quae est anus tam delira quae timeat ista?; Juv. 2.149 ff.: esse aliquid Manes, et subterranea regna . . . nec pueri credunt, nisi qui nondum aere lavantur; Sen. *Epist.* 24.18: nemo tam puer est ut Cerberum timeat, etc. Such rhetorical statements should not, however, be taken too literally (cf. W. Kroll,

"Die Religiosität in der Zeit Ciceros," *NJbb* 1928, 514 ff.). We have on the other side the express testimony of Lucian, *de luctu*.

49 In the following paragraphs I am especially indebted to Festugière's *L'Astrologie et les sciences occultes* (= *La Révélation d'Hermès Trismégiste*, I [Paris, 1944]), which is much the best introduction to ancient occultism as a whole. For astrology see also Cumont's *Astrology and Religion among the Greeks and Romans*, and the excellent short account in H. Gressmann's *Die Hellenistische Gestirnreligion*.

50 Murray, *Five Stages of Greek Religion*, chap. iv.

51 Hdt. 2.82.1. It is not quite certain that the reference is to astrology.

52 Cic. *Div.* 2.87: Eudoxus, . . . sic opinatur, id quod scriptum reliquit, Chaldaeis in praedictione et in notatione cuiusque vitae ex natali die minime esse credendum. Plato also rejects it, at least by implication, at *Tim.* 40CD; the passage was understood in later antiquity as referring specifically to astrology (see Taylor on 40D 1), but it is quite possible that Plato had in mind only the traditional Greek view of eclipses as portents. Of other fourth-century writers, it is probable that Ctesias knew something of astrology, and there is a slight indication that Democritus may have done so (W. Capelle, *Hermes*, 60 [1925] 373 ff.).

53 The souls of the unborn take on the characters of the gods whom they "follow" (252CD), and these twelve θεοὶ ἄρχοντες seem to be located in the twelve signs of the zodiac (247A) with which Eudoxus had associated them, though Plato does not say this in so many words. But Plato, unlike the astrologers, is careful to safeguard free will. Cf. Bidez, *Eos*, 60 ff., and Festugière, *Rev. de Phil.* 21 (1947) 24 ff. I agree with the latter that the "astrology" of this passage is no more than a piece of imaginative decoration. It is significant that Theophrastus (*apud* Proclus, *in Tim.* III. 151.1 ff.) still spoke of astrology as if it were a purely foreign art (whether he felt for it all the admiration that Proclus attributes him may reasonably be doubted).

54 Festugière, *L'Astrologie*, 76 ff. Some of the fragments of "Nechepso's" work, which has been called "the astrologer's Bible," were collected by Riess, *Philologus*, Supp.-Band 6 (1892) 327 ff.

55 Cato includes "Chaldaei" among the riff-raff whom the farm steward should be warned not to consult (*de agri cultura* 5.4). A little later, in 139 B.C., they were expelled from Rome for the first but by no means the last time (Val. Max. 1.3.3). In the follow-

ing century they were back again, and by then senators as well as farm stewards were numbered among their clients.

⁵⁶ Epicurus, *Epist.* 1.76 ff., 2.85 ff. (cf. Festugière, *Épicure et ses dieux*, 102 ff.). A sentence in 1.79 sounds like a specific warning against the astrologers (Bailey *ad loc.*).

⁵⁷ Diogenes of Seleucia, called "the Babylonian," who died *ca.* 152 B.C. According to Cicero (*div.* 2.90), he admitted some but not all of the claims made for astrology. Earlier Stoics had perhaps not thought it necessary to express any view, since Cicero says definitely that Panaetius (Diogenes' immediate successor) was the only Stoic who *rejected* astrology (*ibid.*, 2.88), while Diogenes is the only one he quotes in its favour. See, however, *SVF* II.954, which seems to imply that Chrysippus believed in horoscopes.

⁵⁸ Cleanthes thought that Aristarchus ought to be had up (like Anaxagoras before him and Galileo after him) for ἀσέβεια (Plut. *de facie* 6, 923A = *SVF* I.500). In the third century that was no longer possible; but it seems likely that theological prejudice played some part in securing the defeat of heliocentrism. Cf. the horror of it expressed by the Platonist Dercylîdes, *apud* Theon Smyrn., p. 200.7 Hiller.

⁵⁹ Cicero, *div.* 2.87–99; Plot. *Enn.* 2.3 and 2.9.13. The astrologers were delighted by Plotinus' painful end, which they explained as the merited punishment of his blasphemous lack of respect for the stars.

⁶⁰ See M. Wellmann, "Die Φυσικά des Bolos," *Abh. Berl. Akad.*, phil.-hist. Kl., 1928; W. Kroll, "Bolos und Demokritos," *Hermes*, 69 (1934) 228 ff.; and Festugière, *L'Astrologie*, 196 ff., 222 ff.

⁶¹ Hence Epicurus thought it better even to follow popular religion than to be a slave to astral εἱμαρμένη, since the latter ἀπαραίτητον ἔχει τὴν ἀνάγκην (*Epist.* 3.134). The futility of prayer was emphasised by orthodox astrologers: cf. Vettius Valens, 5.9; 6 procem.; 6.1 Kroll.

⁶² Cf. App. II, pp. 292 f., also *PGM* i.214, xiii.612, and A. D. Nock, *Conversion*, 102, 288 f.

⁶³ *SVF* II.473 *init.*, Chrysippus held that by virtue of the all-penetrating πνεῦμα, συμπαθές ἐστιν αὐτῷ τὸ πᾶν. Cf. also II.912. This is of course something different from the doctrine of specific occult "sympathies"; but it probably made it easier for educated men to accept the latter.

⁶⁴ Festugière, *op. cit.*, 199. Hence Nilsson's remark that "antiquity could not differentiate between natural and occult potencies" (*Greek Piety*, 105). But the aims and methods of Aristotle and his

pupils are as distinct from those of the occultists as science is from superstition (cf. Festugière, 189 ff.).

65 A generation ago there was a fashion, started by Schmekel in his *Philosophie der mittleren Stoa*, for attributing to Posidonius almost every "mystical" or "otherworldly" or "Orientalising" tendency which appeared in later Greco-Roman thought. These exaggerations were exposed by R. M. Jones in a valuable series of articles in *CP* (1918, 1923, 1926, 1932). For a more cautious account of Posidonius' system see L. Edelstein, *AJP* 57 (1936) 286 ff. Edelstein finds no evidence in the *attested* fragments that he was either an Orientaliser or a man of deep religious feeling. But it remains true that his dualism suited the religious tendencies of the new age.

66 On the significance of this revolution in the Academy see O. Gigon, "Zur Geschichte der sog. Neuen Akademie," *Museum Helveticum*, 1 (1944) 47 ff.

67 "Its sectaries formed a church rather than a school, a religious order, not an academy of sciences," Cumont, *After Life in Roman Paganism*, 23. A good general picture of Neopythagoreanism is to be found in Festugière's article, *REG* 50 (1937) 470 ff. (cf. also his *L'Idéal religieux des Grecs*, Pt. I, chap. v). Cumont's *Recherches sur le symbolisme funéraire des Romains* attributes to Neopythagoreanism a wide influence on popular eschatological ideas; but cf. the doubts expressed in Nock's review, *AJA* 50 (1946) 140 ff., particularly 152 ff.

68 Cf. Diog. Laert. 8.27, and the first question in the Pythagorean catechism, τί ἐστιν αἱ μακάρων νῆσοι; ἥλιος καὶ σελήνη (Iamb. *vit. Pyth.* 82 = Diels, *Vorsokr.* 58 C 4), with Delatte's commentary, *Études sur la litt. pyth.*, 274 ff.; also Boyancé, *REG* 54 (1941) 146 ff., and Gigon, *Ursprung*, 146, 149 f. I am not satisfied that these old Pythagorean beliefs are necessarily due to Iranian influence. Such fancies seem to have originated independently in many parts of the world.

69 This was especially stressed by Wellmann (*op. cit. supra*, n. 60). Wellmann regarded Bolus himself as a Neopythagorean (after Suidas), which seems to be wrong (cf. Kroll, *loc. cit.*, 231); but such men as Nigidius Figulus were evidently influenced by him.

70 Nigidius Figulus, a leading figure in the Pythagorean revival, not not only wrote on dreams (fr. 82) and quoted the wisdom of the Magi (fr. 67), but was reputed to be a practising occultist who had discovered a hidden treasure by the use of boy mediums (Apul.

Apol. 42). Vatinius, who "called himself a Pythagorean," and Appius Claudius Pulcher, who probably belonged to the same group, are said by Cicero to have engaged in necromancy (*in Vat.* 14; *Tusc.* 1.37; *div.* 1.132). And Varro seems to have credited Pythagoras himself with necromancy or hydromancy, doubtless on the strength of Neopythagorean apocrypha (Aug. *Civ. Dei* 7.35). Professor Nock is inclined to attribute to Neopythagoreans a substantial share in the systematising of magical theory, as well as in its practice (*J. Eg. Arch.* 15 [1929] 227 f.).

71 The romantic reaction against natural theology has been well characterised by Christopher Dawson, *Religion and Culture*, 10 ff. Its typical features are (*a*) the insistence on transcendence, against a theology which, in Blake's words, "calls the Prince of this World 'God' "; (*b*) the insistence on the reality of evil and "the tragic sense of life," against the insensitive optimism of the eighteenth century; (*c*) the insistence that religion is rooted in feeling and imagination, not in reason, which opened the way to a deeper understanding of religious experience, but also to a revival of occultism and a superstitious respect for "the Wisdom of the East." The new trend of religious thought which began in the first century B.C. can be described in exactly the same terms.

72 In the early centuries of the Empire, monism and dualism, "cosmic optimism" and "cosmic pessimism," persisted side by side—both are found, for example, in the *Hermetica*—and it was only gradually that the latter gained the upper hand. Plotinus, while sharply criticising both the extreme monism of the Stoics and the extreme dualism of Numenius and the Gnostics, endeavours to construct a system which shall do justice to both tendencies. The starry heavens are still for the Emperor Julian an object of deeply felt adoration: cf. *orat.* 5, 130CD, where he tells how the experience of walking in starlight caused him in boyhood to fall into a state of entranced abstraction.

73 Cf. Festugière, *L'Astrologie*, chap. ix.

74 Cf. Nock, "A Vision of Mandulis Aion," *Harv. Theol. Rev.* 27 (1934) 53 ff.; and Festugière, *op. cit.*, 45 ff., where a number of interesting texts are translated and discussed.

75 Theurgy was primarily a technique for attaining salvation by magical means; see App. II, p. 291. And the same may be said of some of the rituals preserved in the magical papyri, such as the famous "recipe for immortality" (*PGM* iv. 475 ff.). Cf. Nock, "Greek Magical Papyri," *J. Eg. Arch.* 15 (1929) 230 ff.; Festugière, *L'Idéal religieux*, 281 ff.; Nilsson, "Die Religion in den gr.

Zauberpapyri,"*Bull. Soc. Roy. des Lettres de Lund*, 1947–1948, ii.59 ff.

76 Nilsson, *Greek Piety*, 150. Occultism, I should add, is to be distinguished from the primitive magic described by anthropologists, which is prescientific, prephilosophical, and perhaps prereligious, whereas occultism is a pseudo-science or system of pseudo-sciences, often supported by an irrationalist philosophy, and always exploiting the disintegrated débris of preexisting religions. Occultism is also, of course, to be distinguished from the modern discipline of psychical research, which attempts to eliminate occultism by subjecting supposedly "occult" phenomena to rational scrutiny and thus either establishing their subjective character or integrating them with the general body of scientific knowledge.

77 Epicurus was particularly frank in expressing his contempt for culture (fr. 163 Us., παιδείαν πᾶσαν φεῦγε, cf. Cic. *fin.* 1.71 ff. = fr. 227), and also for science, so far as it does not promote ἀταραξία (*Epist.* 1.79, 2.85; Κύριαι Δόξαι, 11). Professor Farrington seems to me altogether mistaken in making him a representative of the scientific spirit, in contrast with the "reactionary" Stoics. But Stoicism too was generally indifferent to research save in so far as it confirmed Stoic dogmas, and was prepared to suppress it where it conflicted with them (n. 58).

78 Plotinus is the outstanding exception. He organised his teaching on the basis of a sort of seminar system, with free discussion (Porph. *vit. Plot.* 13); he recognised the value of music and mathematics as a preparation for philosophy (*Enn.* 1.3.1, 1.3.3), and is said to have been himself well versed in these subjects, as well as in mechanics and optics, though he did not lecture on them (*vit. Plot.* 14); above all, as Geffcken has put it (*Ausgang*, 42), "he does not stand on top of a system and preach: he investigates."

79 Epictetus, *Diss.* 3.23.30: ἰατρεῖόν ἐστιν, ἄνδρες, τὸ τοῦ φιλοσόφου σχολεῖον; Sen. *Epist.* 48.4: ad miseros advocatus es . . . perditae vitae perituraeque auxilium aliquod implorant. This language is common to all the schools. The Epicureans held that their concern was περὶ τὴν ἡμῶν ἰατρείαν (*Sent. Vat.* 64, cf. Epicurus, *Epist.* 3.122, πρὸς τὸ κατὰ ψυχὴν ὑγιαῖνον). Philo of Larissa ἐοικέναι φησὶ τὸν φιλόσοφον ἰατρῷ (Stob. *Ecl.* 2.7.2, pp. 39 f. W.), and Plato himself is described in the anonymous *vita*, 9.36 ff., as a physician of souls. The ultimate source of all this is, no doubt, the Socratic θεραπεία ψυχῆς, but the frequency of the medical metaphor is nevertheless significant. On the social function of philosophy in the Hellenistic Age and later see especially Nock, *Conversion*, chap. xi.

[80] M. Ant. 3.4.3: ἱερεύς τίς ἐστι καὶ ὑπουργὸς θεῶν.

[81] Justin Martyr, *Dial.* 2.6. Cf. Porphyry, *ad Marcellam* 16: ψυχὴ δὲ σοφοῦ ἁρμόζεται πρὸς θεόν, ἀεὶ θεὸν ὁρᾷ, σύνεστιν ἀεὶ θεῷ.

[82] Demetrius Cynicus (saec. I A.D.) *apud* Seneca, *de beneficiis* 7.1.5. f.

[83] As Wendland points out (*Die hellenistisch-römische Kultur²*, 226 ff.), the attitude of pagans like Demetrius is matched by that of Christian writers like Arnobius who held all secular learning to be unnecessary. And there is not a vast difference between the view of the Shorter Catechism that "the whole duty of man is to glorify God and enjoy him for ever" and the view of the pagan Hermetist who wrote that "philosophy consists exclusively in seeking to know God by habitual contemplation and holy piety" (*Asclepius* 12).

[84] Meanwhile, see his *Greek Piety* (Eng. trans., 1948), and his articles on "The New Conception of the Universe in Late Greek Paganism" (*Eranos*, 44 [1946] 20 ff.) and "The Psychological Background of Late Greek Paganism" (*Review of Religion*, 1947, 115 ff.).

[85] Vol. I, *L'Astrologie et les sciences occultes* (Paris, 1944), containing also a brilliantly written introduction to the series; Vol. II, *Le Dieu cosmique* (Paris, 1949). Two further volumes, *Les Doctrines de l'âme* and *Le Dieu inconnu et la Gnose*, are promised. Cumont's posthumous book, *Lux Perpetua*, which does for the Greco-Roman world something of what Rohde's *Psyche* did for the Hellenic, appeared too late for me to use it.

[86] Bury thought that no misuse of "that vague and facile word 'decadent'" could be more flagrant than its application to the Greeks of the third and second centuries (*The Hellenistic Age*, 2); and Tarn "ventures to entertain considerable doubts whether the true Greek really degenerated" (*Hellenistic Civilisation*, 5). As to Oriental influence on later Greek thought, the present tendency is to diminish the importance assigned to it in comparison with that of earlier Greek thinkers, especially Plato (cf. Nilsson, *Greek Piety*, 136 ff.; Festugière, *Le Dieu cosmique*, xii ff.). Such men as Zeno of Citium, Posidonius, Plotinus, and even the authors of the philosophic *Hermetica*, are no longer considered as "Orientalisers" in any fundamental sense. There is also now a reaction against exaggerated estimates of the influence of Eastern mystery cults: cf. Nock, *CAH* XII.436, 448 f.; Nilsson, *op. cit.*, 161.

[87] Cf. the remarks of N. H. Baynes, *JRS* 33 (1943) 33. It is worth remembering that the creators of Greek civilisation were themselves to all appearance the products of a cross between Indo-European and non-Indo-European stocks.

[88] W. R. Halliday, *The Pagan Background of Early Christianity*, 205. Others, with more reason, have blamed the thinness of the civilised upper crust and the total failure of higher education to reach or influence the masses (so, e.g., Eitrem, *Orakel und Mysterien am Ausgang der Antike*, 14 f.).

[89] Cf. Festugière, *L'Astrologie*, 5 ff.

[90] See chap. ii, n. 92.

[91] A book published in 1946 states that there are at present some 25,000 practising astrologers in the United States, and that about 100 American newspapers now provide their readers with daily divinations (Bergen Evans, *The Natural History of Nonsense*, 257). I regret that I have no comparable figures for Britain or Germany.

[92] Nilsson, *Greek Piety*, 140.

[93] Festugière, *L'Astrologie*, 9.

[94] There are important exceptions to this, particularly in the work of Strato in physics (cf. B. Farrington, *Greek Science*, II.27 ff.), and in the fields of anatomy and physiology. In optics Ptolemy devised a number of experiments, as A. Lejeune has shown in his *Euclide et Ptolemée*.

[95] Cf. Farrington, *op. cit.*, II.163 ff., and Walbank, *Decline of the Roman Empire in the West*, 67 ff. I have simplified the argument, but I hope without doing it serious injustice.

[96] Cf. Erich Fromm, *Escape from Freedom*.

[97] Nock, *Conversion*, 241. Cf. Fromm's conception of dependence on a "magic helper" and the resulting blockage of spontaneity, *op. cit.*, 174 ff.

[98] That we have so little evidence from the Hellenistic Age may well be due to the almost total loss of the prose literature of that period. But its history does provide one very striking instance of a mass upsurge of irrationalist religion, the Dionysiac movement in Italy which was suppressed in 186 B.C. and the following years. It claimed to have a vast following, "almost a second people." Cf. Nock, *op. cit.*, 71 ff.; E. Fraenkel, *Hermes*, 67 (1932) 369 ff.; and most recently J. J. Tierney, *Proc. R.I.A.* 51 (1947) 89 ff.

[99] Theophrastus, *Char.* 16 (28 J.); Plut. *de superstitione* 7, 168D. Cf. "The Portrait of a Greek Gentleman," *Greece and Rome*, 2 (1933) 101 f.

[100] If we can trust Lucian, Peregrinus too used to smear his face with mud (*Peregr.* 17), though perhaps from other motives. Lucian explained everything in Peregrinus' strange career as due to a craving for notoriety. And there may be an element of truth in his diagnosis: P.'s exhibitionism *à la* Diogenes (*ibid.*), if it is not simply

a trait conventionally ascribed to extreme Cynics, seems to confirm it better than Lucian could know. Yet it is difficult to read
Lucian's angry narrative without feeling that the man was a good
deal more than a vulgar charlatan. Neurotic he certainly was,
possibly to a point not far removed at times from actual insanity;
yet many, both Christian and pagan, had seen in him a θεῖος ἀνήρ,
even a second Socrates (*ibid.*, 4 f., 11 f.), and he enjoyed a post-
mortem cult (Athenagoras, *Leg. pro Christ.* 26). A psychologist
might be disposed to find the leitmotiv of his life in an inner
need to defy authority (cf. K. v. Fritz in P.-W., s.v.). And he
might go on to conjecture that this need was rooted in a family
situation, remembering the sinister rumour that Peregrinus was a
parricide, and remembering also those unexpected last words
before he leapt upon the pyre—δαίμονες μητρῷοι καὶ πατρῷοι,
δέξασθέ με εὐμενεῖς (*Peregr.* 36).

¹⁰¹ Cf. Wilamowitz, "Der Rhetor Aristides," *Berl. Sitzb.* 1925, 333 ff.;
Campbell Bonner, "Some Phases of Religious Feeling in Later
Paganism," *Harv. Theol. Rev.* 30 (1937) 124 ff.; and above, chap.
iv, p. 116.

¹⁰² Cf. Cumont, *After Life*, lecture vii. Plutarch's δεισιδαίμων pictures "the deep gates of Hell opening," rivers of fire, the shrieks
of the damned, etc. (*de superst.* 4, 167A)—quite in the style of
the *Apocalypse of Peter*, which may have been written in Plutarch's lifetime.

¹⁰³ On amulets, see the important paper by Campbell Bonner in
Harv. Theol. Rev. 39 (1946) 25 ff. He points out that from the
first century A.D. onwards there was apparently a great increase
in the magical use of engraved gems (with which his paper is
primarily concerned). The compilation known as *Kyranides*,
whose older parts may go back to that century, abounds in recipes
for amulets against demons, phantasms, night fears, etc. How
far the fear of demons had gone in late antiquity, even in the educated class, may be seen from Porphyry's opinion that every house
and every animal body was full of them (*de philosophia ex oraculis
haurienda*, pp. 147 f. Wolff), and from the assertion of Tertullian
nullum paene hominem carere daemonio (*de anima* 57). It is true
that as late as the third and fourth centuries A.D. there were
rational men who protested against these beliefs (cf. Plot. *Enn.*
2.9.14; Philostorgius, *Hist. Eccl.* 8. 10; and other examples quoted
by Edelstein, "Greek Medicine in Its Relation to Religion and
Magic," *Bull. Hist. Med.* 5 [1937] 216 ff.). But they were a diminishing band. For Christians, the view that the pagan gods were

truly existent evil spirits greatly added to the burden of fear. Nock goes so far as to say that "for the Apologists as a group and for Tertullian in his apologetic work the redemptive operation of Christ lay in deliverance from demons rather than in deliverance from sin" (*Conversion*, 222).

104 *PGM* viii.33 ff. (cf. P. Christ. 3); ἀντίθεος πλανοδαίμων, vii.635; κύων ἀκέφαλος, P. Christ. 15B.

105 *PGM* vii.311 ff.; x.26 ff.; P. Christ. 10. The fear of terrifying dreams is also prominent in Plutarch's picture of the δεισιδαίμων (*de superst.* 3, 165E ff.).

106 I believe that there are elements in our situation to-day which make it essentially different from any earlier human situation, and thus invalidate such cyclic hypotheses as Spengler's. The point has been well put by Lippmann, *A Preface to Morals*, 232 ff.

107 A. Malraux, *Psychologie de l'art* (Paris, 1949). Cf. Auden's observation that "the failure of the human race to acquire the habits that an open society demands if it is to function properly, is leading an increasing number of people to the conclusion that an open society is impossible, and that, therefore, the only escape from economic and spiritual disaster is to return as quickly as possible to a closed type of society" (*loc. cit. supra*, n. 2). Yet it is less than thirty years since Edwyn Bevan could write that "the idea of some cause going forward is so bred in the bone of modern men that we can hardly imagine a world in which the hope of improvement and advance is absent" (*The Hellenistic Age*, 101).

108 The late R. G. Collingwood held that "irrational elements . . . the blind forces and activities in us, which are part of human life . . . are not parts of the historical process." This agrees with the practice of nearly all historians, past and present. My own conviction, which these chapters attempt to illustrate, is that our chance of understanding the historical process depends very largely on removing this quite arbitrary restriction upon our notion of it. The same point was repeatedly stressed by Cornford in relation to the history of thought: see especially *The Unwritten Philosophy*, 32 ff. As to the general position, I should accept L. C. Knights' conclusion in his *Explorations:* "what we need is not to abandon reason, but simply to recognise that reason in the last three centuries has worked within a field which is not the whole of experience, that it has mistaken the part for the whole, and imposed arbitrary limits on its own working" (p. 111).

Appendix I
Maenadism

"IN ART, as well as in poetry, the representation of these wild states of enthusiasm was apparently due to the imagination alone, for in prose literature we have very little evidence, in historic times, of women actually holding revels[1] in the open air. Such a practice would have been alien to the spirit of seclusion which pervaded the life of womankind in Greece. . . . The festivals of the Thyiads were mainly confined to Parnassus." Thus Sandys in the introduction to his justly admired edition of the *Bacchae*. Diodorus, on the other hand, tells us (4.3) that "in many Greek states congregations (βακχεῖα) of women assemble every second year, and the unmarried girls are allowed to carry the thyrsus and share the transports of the elders (συνενθουσιάζειν)." And since Sandys's day inscriptional evidence from various parts of the Greek world has confirmed Diodorus' statement. We know now that such biennial festivals (τριετηρίδες) existed at Thebes, Opus, Melos, Pergamum, Priene, Rhodes; and they are attested for Alea in Arcadia by Pausanias, for Mitylene by Aelian, for Crete by Firmicus Maternus.[2] Their character may have varied a good deal from place to place, but we can hardly doubt that they normally included women's ὄργια of the ecstatic or quasi-ecstatic type described by Diodorus, and that these often, if not always, involved nocturnal ὀρειβασία or mountain dancing. This strange rite, described in the *Bacchae* and practised by women's societies at the Delphic τριετηρίς down to Plutarch's time, was certainly practised elsewhere also: at Miletus the priestess of Dionysus still "led the women to the mountain" in late Hellenistic times;[3] at Erythrae the title Μιμαντοβάτης points to an ὀρειβασία on Mount Mimas.[4] Dionysus himself is ὄρειος (Festus, p. 182), ὀρειμά-

These pages originally formed part of an article published in the *Harvard Theological Review*, Vol. 33 (1940). They are reprinted here with a few corrections and additions. I am indebted to Professor A. D. Nock, Dr. Rudolf Pfeiffer, and others for valuable criticisms.

[1] For numbered notes to Appendix I see pages 278–280 below.

νης (Tryph. 370), ὀρέσκιος, οὐρεσιφοίτης (*Anth. Pal.* 9.524); and Strabo in discussing Dionysiac and other related mystery-cults speaks quite generally of τὰς ὀρειβασίας τῶν περὶ τὸ θεῖον σπουδαζόντων (10.3.23). The oldest literary allusion is in the Homeric *Hymn to Demeter*, 386: ἤιξ᾽ ἤυτε μαινὰς ὄρος κατὰ δάσκιον ὕλης.

The ὀρειβασία took place at night in midwinter, and must have involved great discomfort and some risk: Pausanias[5] says that at Delphi the women went to the very summit of Parnassus (which is over 8,000 feet high), and Plutarch[6] describes an occasion, apparently in his own lifetime, when they were cut off by a snowstorm and a rescue party had to be sent out—when they returned, their clothes were frozen as stiff as boards. What was the object of this practice? Many people dance to make their crops grow, by sympathetic magic. But such dances elsewhere are annual like the crops, not biennial like the ὀρειβασία; their season is spring, not midwinter; and their scene is the cornland, not the barren mountaintops. Late Greek writers thought of the dances at Delphi as commemorative: they dance, says Diodorus (4.3), "in imitation of the maenads who are said to have been associated with the god in the old days." Probably he is right, as regards his own time; but ritual is usually older than the myth by which people explain it, and has deeper psychological roots. There must have been a time when the maenads or thyiads or βάκχαι really became for a few hours or days what their name implies—wild women whose human personality has been temporarily replaced by another. Whether this might still be so in Euripides' day we have no sure means of knowing; a Delphic tradition recorded by Plutarch[7] suggests that the rite sometimes produced a true disturbance of personality as late as the fourth century, but the evidence is very slender, nor is the nature of the change at all clear. There are, however, parallel phenomena in other cultures which may help us to understand the πάροδος of the *Bacchae* and the punishment of Agave.

In many societies, perhaps in all societies, there are people for whom, as Mr. Aldous Huxley puts it, "ritual dances provide a religious experience that seems more satisfying and convincing than any other. . . . It is with their muscles that they most easily obtain knowledge of the divine."[8] Mr. Huxley thinks that Christianity made a mistake when it allowed the dance to become completely secularised,[9] since, in the words of a Mohammedan sage, "he that knows the Power of the Dance dwells in God." But the Power of the Dance is a dangerous power. Like other forms of self-surrender, it is easier to begin than to stop. In the extraordinary dancing madness which periodically invaded Europe from the fourteenth to the seventeenth century, people danced until they dropped—like the dancer at *Bacchae* 136 or the dancer on a Berlin vase, no. 2471[10]—and lay unconscious, trodden underfoot by their fellows.[11] Also the thing is highly infectious. As Pentheus observes at *Bacchae* 778, it spreads like wildfire. The will to dance takes possession of people without the consent of the conscious mind: e.g., at Liège in 1374, after certain possessed folk had come dancing half-naked into the town with garlands on their heads, dancing in the name of St. John, we are told that "many persons seemingly sound in mind and body were suddenly possessed by the devils and joined the dancers"; these persons left house and home, like the Theban women in the play; even young girls cut themselves off from their family and friends and wandered away with the dancers.[12] Against a similar mania in seventeenth-century Italy "neither youth nor age," it is said, "afforded any protection; so that even old men of ninety threw aside their crutches at the sound of the tarantella, and as if some magic potion, restorative of youth and vigour, flowed through their veins, they joined the most extravagant dancers."[13] The Cadmus-Teiresias scene of the *Bacchae* was thus, it would appear, frequently reenacted, justifying the poet's remark (206 ff.) that Dionysus imposes no age limit. Even sceptics were sometimes, like Agave, infected with the mania against their will, and contrary to their professed belief.[14] In Alsace it was held in the fifteenth and sixteenth centuries that the dancing madness could be imposed on a victim by cursing him with it.[15] In some cases the compulsive obsession reappeared at regular intervals, growing in intensity until St. John's or St. Vitus' day, when an outbreak occurred and was followed by a return to normality;[16] while in Italy the periodic "cure" of afflicted patients by music and ecstatic dancing seems to have developed into an annual festival.[17]

This last fact suggests the way in which in Greece the ritual *oreibasia* at a fixed date may originally have developed out of spontaneous attacks of mass hysteria. By canalising such hysteria in an organised rite once in two years, the Dionysiac cult kept it within bounds and gave it a relatively harmless outlet. What the πάροδος of the *Bacchae* depicts is hysteria subdued to the service of religion; what happened on Mount Cithaeron was hysteria in the raw, the

dangerous Bacchism[18] which descends as a punishment on the too respectable and sweeps them away against their will. Dionysus is present in both: like St. John or St. Vitus, he is the cause of madness and
the liberator from madness, Βάκχος and Λύσιος.[19] We must keep this
ambivalence in mind if we are rightly to understand the play. To resist Dionysus is to repress the elemental in one's own nature; the
punishment is the sudden complete collapse of the inward dykes
when the elemental breaks through perforce and civilisation vanishes.

There are, further, certain resemblances in points of detail between
the orgiastic religion of the *Bacchae* and orgiastic religion elsewhere,
which are worth noticing because they tend to establish that the
"maenad" is a real, not a conventional figure, and one that has
existed under different names at widely different times and places.
The first concerns the flutes and tympana or kettledrums which ac-
company the maenad dance in the *Bacchae* and on Greek vases.[20]
To the Greeks these were the "orgiastic" instruments *par excellence:*[21]
they were used in all the great dancing cults, those of the Asiatic
Cybele and the Cretan Rhea as well as that of Dionysus. They could
cause madness, and in homoeopathic doses they could also cure it.[22]
And 2,000 years later, in the year 1518, when the crazy dancers of St.
Vitus were dancing through Alsace, a similar music—the music of
drum and pipe—was used again for the same ambiguous purpose, to
provoke the madness and to cure it: we still have the minute of the
Strassburg Town Council on the subject.[23] That is certainly not tradition, probably not coincidence: it looks like the rediscovery of a real
causal connection, of which to-day only the War Office and the
Salvation Army retain some faint awareness.

A second point is the carriage of the head in Dionysiac ecstasy.
This is repeatedly stressed in the *Bacchae:* 150, "flinging his long hair
to the sky"; 241, "I will stop you tossing back your hair"; 930,
"tossing my head forwards and backwards like a bacchanal"; similarly elsewhere the possessed Cassandra "flings her golden locks when
there blows from God the compelling wind of second-sight" (*I.A.*
758). The same trait appears in Aristophanes, *Lysist.* 1312, ταὶ δὲ
κόμαι σείονθ' ἅπερ βακχᾶν, and is constant, though less vividly described, in later writers: the maenads still "toss their heads" in
Catullus, in Ovid, in Tacitus.[24] And we see this back-flung head and
upturned throat in ancient works of art, e.g., the gems figured by
Sandys, pages 58 and 73, or the maenad on the bas-relief in the

British Museum (Marbles II, pl. xiii, Sandys, p. 85).[25] But the gesture is not simply a convention of Greek poetry and art; at all times and everywhere it characterizes this particular type of religious hysteria. I take three independent modern descriptions: "the continual jerking their heads back, causing their long black hair to twist about, added much to their savage appearance";[26] "their long hair was tossed about by the rapid to-and-fro movements of the head";[27] "the head was tossed from side to side or thrown far back above a swollen and bulging throat."[28] The first phrase is from a missionary's account of a cannibal dance in British Columbia which led up to the tearing asunder and eating of a human body; the second describes a sacral dance of goat-eaters in Morocco; the third is from a clinical description of possessive hysteria by a French doctor.

Nor is this the only analogy which links these scattered types. The ecstatic dancers in Euripides "carried fire on their heads and it did not burn them" (757).[29] So does the ecstatic dancer elsewhere. In British Columbia he dances with glowing coals held in his hands, plays with them recklessly, and even puts them in his mouth;[30] so he does in South Africa;[31] and so also in Sumatra.[32] In Siam[33] and in Siberia[34] he claims to be invulnerable so long as the god remains within him—just as the dancers on Cithaeron were invulnerable (*Ba.* 761). And our European doctors have found an explanation or half-explanation in their hospitals; during his attacks the hysterical patient is often in fact analgesic—all sensitiveness to pain is repressed.[35]

An interesting account of the use, both spontaneous and curative, of ecstatic dancing and ecstatic music (trumpet, drum, and fife) in Abyssinia at the beginning of the nineteenth century is to be found in *The Life and Adventures of Nathaniel Pearce, written by himself during a Residence in Abyssinia from the years 1810 to 1819*, I.290 ff. It has several points in common with Euripides' description. At the culminating moment of the dance the patient "made a start with such swiftness that the fastest runner could not come up with her [cf. *Bacch.* 748, 1090], and when at a distance of about 200 yards she dropped on a sudden as if shot" (cf. *Bacch.* 136 and n. 11 below). Pearce's native wife, who caught the mania, danced and jumped "more like a deer than a human being" (cf. *Bacch.* 866 ff., 166 ff.). Again, "I have seen them in these fits dance with a bruly, or bottle of maize, upon their heads without spilling the liquor, or letting the bottle fall, although they have put themselves into the most extravagant postures" (cf. *Bacch.* 775 f., Nonnus, 45.294 ff.).

The whole description of the maenads' raid on the Theban villages (*Bacch.* 748–764) corresponds to the known behaviour of comparable groups elsewhere. Among many peoples persons in abnormal states, whether natural or induced, are privileged to plunder the community: to interfere with their acts would be dangerous, since they are for the time being in contact with the supernatural. Thus in Liberia the novices who are undergoing initiation in the forest are licensed to raid and plunder neighbouring villages, carrying off everything they want; so also the members of secret societies in Senegal, the Bismarck Archipelago, etc., during the period when their rites have set them apart from the community.[36] This state of affairs belongs no doubt to a stage of social organisation which fifth-century Greece had long outgrown; but legend or ritual may have preserved the memory of it, and Euripides may have encountered the actuality in Macedonia. An attenuated ritual survival is perhaps to be seen even to-day in the behaviour of the Viza mummers: "in general," says Dawkins, "anything lying about may be seized as a pledge to be redeemed, and the Koritzia [girls] especially carry off babies with this object."[37] Are these girls the direct descendants of the baby-stealing maenads of *Bacch.* 754 (who appear also in Nonnus and on vases)?[38]

Another obviously primitive element is the snake-handling (*Bacch.* 101 ff., 698, 768). Euripides has not understood it, although he knows that Dionysus can appear as a snake (1017 f.). It is shown on vases, and after Euripides it becomes part of the conventional literary portrait of the maenad;[39] but it would seem that only in the more primitive cult of Sabazius,[40] and perhaps in Macedonian Bacchism,[41] was the living snake, as vehicle of the god, actually handled in ritual in classical times.[42] That such handling, even without any underlying belief in the snake's divinity, may be a powerful factor in producing religious excitement is shown by a curious recent account,[43] with photographs, of the rattlesnake ritual practised in the Holiness Church in remote mining villages in Leslie and Perry counties, Kentucky. According to this report the snake-handling (which is ostensibly based on Mark 16:18, "They shall take up serpents") forms part of a religious service, and is preceded and accompanied by ecstatic dancing and followed by exhaustion. The snakes are taken from boxes and passed from hand to hand (apparently by both sexes); photographs show them held high

above the worshipper's head (cf. Demos. *de cor.* 259 ὑπὲρ τῆς κεφαλῆς
αἰωρῶν) or close to the face. "One man thrust one inside his shirt and
caught it as it wriggled out before it could fall to the floor"—an
oddly exact parallel to the ritual act of the Sabaziasts described by
Clement and Arnobius,[44] and one which may lead us to hesitate
before agreeing with Dieterich[45] that the act in question "can signify
absolutely nothing else than the sexual union of the god with the
initiate"!

It remains to say something of the culminating act of the Dionysiac
winter dance, which was also the culminating act of the Columbian
and Moroccan dances mentioned above—the tearing to pieces, and
swallowing raw, of an animal body, σπαραγμός and ὠμοφαγία. The
gloating descriptions of this act in certain Christian Fathers may well
be discounted, and it is hard to know how much weight to attach to
the anonymous evidence of scholiasts and lexicographers on the subject;[46] but that it still had some place in the Greek orgiastic ritual in
classical times is attested not only by the respectable authority of
Plutarch,[47] but by the regulations of the Dionysiac cult at Miletus in
276 b.c.,[48] where we read μὴ ἐξεῖναι ὠμοφάγιον ἐμβαλεῖν μηθενὶ πρότε-
ρον ἢ ἡ ἱέρεια ὑπὲρ τῆς πόλεως ἐμβάλῃ. The phrase ὠμοφάγιον ἐμβαλεῖν
has puzzled scholars. I do not think that it means "to throw a sacrificial
animal into a pit" (Wiegand, *ad loc.*) or "to throw a joint of beef into
a sacred place" (Haussoulier, *R.E.G.* 32.266). A bloodier but more
convincing picture is suggested by Ernest Thesiger's account of an
annual rite which he witnessed in Tangier in 1907:[49] "A hill-tribe
descends upon the town in a state of semi-starvation and drugged
delirium. After the usual beating of tom-toms, screaming of the pipes
and monotonous dancing, a sheep is thrown into the middle of the
square, upon which all the devotees come to life and tear the animal
limb from limb and eat it raw." The writer adds a story that "one
year a Tangier Moor, who was watching the proceedings, got infected with the general frenzy of the crowd and threw his baby into
the middle of them." Whether the last is true or not, the passage
gives a clue to the meaning of ἐμβαλεῖν, and also illustrates the possible
dangers of unregulated ὠμοφαγία. The administration at Miletus
was engaged in the ever-recurrent task of putting Dionysus in a strait
waistcoat.

In the *Bacchae*, σπαραγμός is practised first on the Theban cattle
and then on Pentheus; in both cases it is described with a gusto which

the modern reader has difficulty in sharing. A detailed description of the ὠμοφαγία would perhaps have been too much for the stomachs even of an Athenian audience; Euripides speaks of it twice, *Bacchae* 139 and *Cretans* fragm. 472, but in each place he passes over it swiftly and discreetly. It is hard to guess at the psychological state that he describes in the two words ὠμοφάγον χάριν; but it is noteworthy that the days appointed for ὠμοφαγία were "unlucky and black days,"[50] and in fact those who practise such a rite in our time seem to experience in it a mixture of supreme exaltation and supreme repulsion: it is at once holy and horrible, fulfilment and uncleanness, a sacrament and a pollution—the same violent conflict of emotional attitudes that runs all through the *Bacchae* and lies at the root of all religion of the Dionysiac type.[51]

Late Greek writers explained the ὠμοφαγία as they did the dancing, and as some would explain the Christian communion: it was merely a commemorative rite, in memory of the day when the infant Dionysus was himself torn to pieces and devoured.[52] But the practice seems to rest in fact on a very simple piece of savage logic. The homoeopathic effects of a flesh diet are known all over the world. If you want to be lion-hearted, you must eat lion; if you want to be subtle, you must eat snake; those who eat chickens and hares will be cowards, those who eat pork will get little piggy eyes.[53] By parity of reasoning, if you want to be like god you must eat god (or at any rate something which is θεῖον). And you must eat him quick and raw, before the blood has oozed from him: only so can you add his life to yours, for "the blood is the life." God is not always there to be eaten, nor indeed would it be safe to eat him at common times and without due preparation for the reception of the sacrament. But once in two years he is present among his mountain dancers: "the Boeotians," says Diodorus (4.3), "and the other Greeks and Thracians believe that at this time he has his epiphany among men"—just as he has in the *Bacchae*. He may appear in many forms, vegetable, bestial, human; and he is eaten in many forms. In Plutarch's day it was the ivy that was torn to pieces and chewed:[54] that may be primitive, or it may be a surrogate for something bloodier. In Euripides bulls are torn,[55] the goat torn and eaten;[56] we hear elsewhere of ὠμοφαγία of fawns[57] and rending of vipers.[58] Since in all these we may with greater or less probability recognise embodiments of the god, I incline to accept Gruppe's view[59] that the ὠμοφαγία was a sacrament in which God was present in his beast-vehicle and was torn and eaten in that shape by his people. And I have argued elsewhere[60] that there once existed a more potent, because more dreadful, form of this sacrament, viz., the rending, and perhaps the eating, of God in the shape of man; and that the story of Pentheus is in part a reflection of that act—in opposition to the fashionable euhemerism which sees in it *only* the reflection of a historical conflict between Dionysiac missionaries and their opponents.

To sum up: I have tried to show that Euripides' description of maenadism is not to be accounted for in terms of "the imagination alone"; that inscriptional evidence (incomplete as it is) reveals a closer relationship with actual cult than Victorian scholars realised; and that the maenad, however mythical certain of her acts, is not in essence a mythological character[61] but an observed and still observable human type. Dionysus has still his votaries or victims,.though we call them by other names; and Pentheus was confronted by a problem which other civil authorities have had to face in real life.

NOTES TO APPENDIX I

[1] This traditional rendering of βακχεύειν has unfortunate associations. βακχεύειν is not to have a good time, but to share in a particular religious rite and (or) have a particular religious experience—the experience of communion with a god which transformed a human being into a βάκχος or a βάκχη.

[2] *Fouilles de Delphes*, III.i.195; *IG* IX.282, XII.iii.1089; Fraenkel, *In. Perg.* 248 (cf. Suidas, s.v. τριετηρίς); Hiller v. Gärtringen, *In. Priene* 113, l. 79; *IG* XII.i.155, 730; Paus. 8.23.1; Ael. *Var. Hist.* 13.2; Firm. Mat. *Err. prof. rel.* 6.5. Also τριετηρίδες among the half-Hellenised Budini in Thrace, Hdt. 4.108.

[3] Wiegand, *Milet*, IV.547 εἰς ὄρος ἦγε: cf. *Bacch.* 116, 165, 977, which suggest that εἰς ὄρος may have been a ritual cry.

[4] Waddington, *Explic. des Inscr. d'Asie Mineur*, p. 27, no. 57. That the title is Dionysiac is not certain. But there is literary evidence of Dionysiac ὀρειβασία on Tmolus, the eastern part of the same mountain range: Nonnus 40.273: εἰς σκοπιὰς Τμώλοιο θεόσσυτος ἤιε βάκχη, *H. Orph.* 49.6: Τμῶλος . . . καλὸν Λυδοῖσι θόασμα (hence ἱερὸν Τμῶλον, Eur. *Bacch.* 65).

[5] 10.32.5. The statement has naturally been doubted.

[6] *de primo frigido* 18, 953D.

7 *mul. virt.* 13, 249E.

8 *Ends and Means*, 232, 235.

9 Dancing as a form of worship long survived in certain of the American sects. Ray Strachey, *Group Movements of the Past*, 93, quotes the exhortation of the Shaker elder a hundred years ago: "Go forth, old men, young men and maidens, and worship God with all your might in the dance." And it appears that the sacral dance is still practised by members of the Holiness Church in Kentucky (*Picture Post*, December 31, 1938), as it is by the Jewish Hasidim (L. H. Feldman, *Harv. Theol. Rev.* 42 [1949] 65 ff.).

10 Beazley, *ARV* 724.1; Pfuhl, *Malerei u. Zeichnung*, fig. 560; Lawler, *Memoirs of the American Academy at Rome*, 6 (1927) pl. 21, no. 1.

11 *Chronicle of Limburg* (1374), quoted by A. Martin, "Gesch. der Tanzkrankheit in Deutschland," *Zeitschrift d. Vereins f. Volkskunde*, 24 (1914). Similarly the Ghost Dance, for which North American Indians developed a passion in the 1890's, went on "till the dancers, one after another, fell rigid, prostrate on the ground" (Benedict, *Patterns of Culture*, 92).

12 Quoted by Martin, *loc. cit.*, from various contemporary documents. His account supplements, and in some points corrects, the classic work of J. F. K. Hecker, *Die Tanzwuth* (1832: I quote from the Eng. trans. by Babington, Cassell's Library, 1888).

13 Hecker, *op. cit.*, 152 f. So Brunel says of certain Arab dances that "the contagious madness infects everybody" (*Essai sur la confrérie religieuse des Aissâoûa au Maroc*, 119). The dancing madness in Thuringia in 1921 was similarly infectious (see my edition of the *Bacchae*, p. xiii, n. 1).

14 Hecker, 156.

15 Martin, 120 f.

16 Hecker, 128 ff.; Martin, 125 ff.

17 Hecker, 143 f., 150. Martin, 129 ff., finds a formal and regulated survival of the Rhenish compulsive-curative dances in the annual dancing procession of Esternach, which is still believed to be a cure for epilepsy and similar psychopathic complaints.

18 Perhaps expressed in Laconia by the term Δύσμαιναι (the title of a tragedy by Pratinas, Nauck, *TGF²*, p. 726). Failure to distinguish the "black" maenadism described by the Messengers from the "white" maenadism described by the Chorus has been responsible for much misunderstanding of the *Bacchae*.

19 Cf. Rohde, *Psyche*, ix, n. 21; Farnell, *Cults*, V.120. Others explain Λύσιος and Λυαῖος as the liberator from convention (Wilamowitz)

or the liberator of the imprisoned (Weinreich, *Tübinger Beiträge*, V [1930] 285 f., comparing *Bacch.* 498).

20 In vase paintings of maenads Lawler, *loc. cit.*, 107 f., finds 38 occurrences of the flute and 26 of the tympanum, also 38 of crotala or castanets (cf. Eur. *Cycl.* 204 f.). She notes that "tranquil scenes never show the use of the tympanum."

21 For the flute cf. Ar. *Pol.* 1341ᵃ 21: οὐκ ἔστιν ὁ αὐλὸς ἠθικὸν ἀλλὰ μᾶλλον ὀργιαστικόν, Eur. *Her.* 871, 879, and chap. iii, n. 95, above. For the τύμπανον in orgiastic cults at Athens, Aristoph. *Lys.* 1–3, 388.

22 See chap. iii, pp. 78–80.

23 Martin, 121 f. So too the Turkish drum and shepherd's pipe were used in Italy (Hecker, 151).

24 Cat. *Attis* 23; Ovid, *Metam.* 3.726; Tac. *Ann.* 11.31.

25 Further examples may be seen in Furtwängler, *Die antike Gemmen*, pl. 10, no. 49; pl. 36, nos. 35–37; pl. 41, no. 29; pl. 66, no. 7. Lawler, *loc. cit.*, 101, finds a "strong backward bend" of the head in 28 figures of maenads on vases.

26 Quoted in Frazer, *Golden Bough*, V.i.19. Similarly in voodoo dances "their heads are thrown weirdly back as if their necks were broken" (W. B. Seabrook, *The Magic Island*, 47).

27 Frazer, *ibid.*, V.i.21.

28 P. Richer, *Études cliniques sur la grande hystérie*, 441. Cf. S. Bazdechi, "Das Psychopathische Substrät der *Bacchae*," *Arch. Gesch. Med.* 25 (1932) 288.

29 For other ancient evidence on this point see Rohde, *Psyche*, viii, n. 43.

30 Benedict, *Patterns of Culture*, 176.

31 O. Dapper, *Beschreibung von Afrika*, quoted in T. K. Oesterreich, *Possession*, 264 (Eng. trans.). Lane watched the Mohammedan dervishes do the same thing (*Manners and Customs of the Modern Egyptians*, 467 f., Everyman's Library edition). See also Brunel, *op. cit.*, 109, 158.

32 J. Warneck, *Religion der Batak*, quoted by Oesterreich, *ibid.*, 270.

33 A. Bastian, *Völker des Oestlichen Asiens*, III.282 f.: "When the Chao (demon lord) is obliged by the conjurations to descend into the body of the Khon Song (a person dressed as the demon lord), the latter remains invulnerable so long as he is there, and cannot be touched by any kind of weapon" (quoted *ibid.*, 353).

34 Czaplicka, *Aboriginal Siberia*, 176.

35 Binswanger, *Die Hysterie*, 756.

36 A. van Gennep, *Les Rites de passage*, 161 f.

37 *JHS* 26 (1906) 197; cf. Wace, *BSA* 16 (1909–1910) 237.

38 Nonnus, 45.294 ff. Cf. the maenad on a British Museum pyxis by the Meidias Painter (Beazley, *ARV* 833.14; Curtius, *Pentheus*, fig. 15) which is closely contemporary with the *Bacchae*. The child she carries is hardly her own, since it is brutally slung by the leg over her shoulder.

39 Cf. Beazley, *ARV* 247.14; Horace, *Odes* 2.19.19.

40 Demos. *de cor.* 259.

41 Plut. *Alex.* 2; Lucian, *Alex.* 7.

42 Cf. Rapp, *Rh. Mus.* 27 (1872) 13. Even Sabazius, if we may believe Arnobius, eventually spared his worshippers' nerves by allowing them to use a metal snake (see n. 44). The snakes in the Dionysiac procession of Ptolemy Philadelphus at Alexandria (Athen. 5.28) were doubtless sham ones (like the imitation ivy and grapes described in the same passage) since the ladies were ἐστεφανωμέναι ὄφεσιν: a wreath of live snakes, however tame, would come undone and spoil the effect.

43 *Picture Post*, December 31, 1938. I am indebted to Professor R. P. Winnington-Ingram for calling my attention to this article. I am informed that the ritual has resulted in deaths from snakebite, and has therefore now been prohibited by law. Snake-handling is also practised at Cocullo in the Abruzzi as the central feature of a religious festival; see Marian C. Harrison, *Folklore*, 18 (1907) 187 ff., and T. Ashby, *Some Italian Scenes and Festivals*, 115 ff.

44 *Protrept.* 2.16: δράκων δέ ἐστιν οὗτος (sc. Σαβάζιος) διελκόμενος τοῦ κόλπου τῶν τελουμένων, Arnob. 5.21: aureus coluber in sinum demittitur consecratis et eximitur rursus ab inferioribus partibus atque imis. Cf. also Firmicus Maternus, *Err. prof. rel.* 10.

45 *Mithrasliturgie*², 124. The unconscious motive may of course be sexual in both cases.

46 Collected in Farnell, *Cults*, V. 302 f., nn. 80–84.

47 *Def. orac.* 14, 417C: ἡμέρας ἀποφράδας καὶ σκυθρωπάς, ἐν αἷς ὠμοφαγίαι καὶ διασπασμοί.

48 *Milet*, VI.22.

49 Kindly communicated to me by Miss N. C. Jolliffe. The Arab rite is also described by Brunel, *op. cit.* (n. 13 above), 110 ff., 177 ff. He adds the significant points that the animal is thrown from a roof or platform, where it is kept until the proper moment, *lest the crowd should tear it to pieces too soon;* and that the fragments of the creatures (bull, calf, sheep, goat, or hen) are preserved for use as amulets.

50 See n. 47.

[51] Cf. Benedict, *Patterns of Culture*, 179: "The very repugnance which the Kwakiutl (Indians of Vancouver Island) felt towards the act of eating human flesh made it for them a fitting expression of the Dionysian virtue that lies in the terrible and the forbidden."

[52] Schol. Clem. Alex. 92 P. (Vol. I, p. 318, Stählin); Photius, s.v. νεβρίζειν; Firm. Mat. *Err. prof. rel.* 6.5.

[53] Frazer, *Golden Bough*, V.ii, chap. 12.

[54] Plut. *Q. Rom.* 112, 291A.

[55] *Bacch.* 743 ff., cf. Schol. Aristoph. *Ranae* 360.

[56] *Bacch.* 138, cf. Arnob. *adv. Nat.* 5.19.

[57] Photius, s.v. νεβρίζειν. Cf. the art type of the maenad νεβροφόνος most recently discussed by H. Philippart, *Iconographie des "Bacchantes,"* 41 ff.

[58] Galen, *de antidot.* 1.6.14 (in a *spring* festival, probably of Sabazius).

[59] *Griech. Myth. u. Rel.* 732.

[60] See my introduction to the *Bacchae*, xvi f., xxiii ff.

[61] As argued by Rapp, *Rh. Mus.* 27.1 ff., 562 ff., and accepted, e.g., by Marbach in P.-W., s.v., and Voigt in Roscher, s.v. "Dionysos."

Appendix II
Theurgy

THE LAST half-century has seen a remarkable advance in our knowledge of the magical beliefs and practices of later antiquity. But in comparison with this general progress the special branch of magic known as theurgy has been relatively neglected and is still imperfectly understood. The first step towards understanding it was taken more than fifty years ago by Wilhelm Kroll, when he collected and discussed the fragments of the *Chaldaean Oracles*.[1] Since then the late Professor Joseph Bidez has disinterred and explained[2] a number of interesting Byzantine texts, mainly from Psellus, which appear to derive from Proclus' lost commentary on the *Chaldaean Oracles*, perhaps through the work of Proclus' Christian opponent, Procopius of Gaza; and Hopfner[3] and Eitrem[4] have made valuable contributions, especially in calling attention to the many common features linking theurgy with the Greco-Egyptian magic of the papyri.[5] But much is still obscure, and is likely to remain so until the scattered texts bearing on theurgy have been collected and studied as a whole[6] (a task which Bidez seems to have contemplated, but left unaccomplished at his death). The present paper does not aim at completeness, still less at finality, but only at (i) clarifying the relationship between Neoplatonism and theurgy in their historical development, and (ii) examining the actual *modus operandi* in what seem to have been the two main branches of theurgy.

I. THE FOUNDER OF THEURGY

So far as we know, the earliest person to be described as θεουργός was one Julianus,[7] who lived under Marcus Aurelius.[8] Probably, as Bidez suggested,[9] he invented the designation, to distinguish himself from mere θεολόγοι: the θεολόγοι talked about the gods, he "acted

These pages are reprinted with a few minor changes from the *Journal of Roman Studies*, Vol. 37 (1947). I must express my gratitude to Professors M. P. Nilsson and A. D. Nock, who read the paper in manuscript and contributed valuable suggestions.

[1] For numbered notes to Appendix II see pages 300–311 below.

upon" them, or even, perhaps, "created" them.[10] Of this personage we know regrettably little. Suidas tells us that he was the son of a "Chaldaean philosopher" of the same name,[11] author of a work on daemons in four books, and that he himself wrote Θεουργικά, Τελεστικά, Λόγια δι' ἐπῶν. That these "hexameter oracles" were (as Lobeck conjectured) none other than the *Oracula Chaldaïca* on which Proclus wrote a vast commentary (Marinus, *vit. Procli* 26) is put beyond reasonable doubt by the reference of a scholiast on Lucian[12] to τὰ τελεστικὰ Ἰουλιανοῦ ἃ Πρόκλος ὑπομνηματίζει, οἷς ὁ Προκόπιος ἀντιφθέγγεται, and Psellus' statement that Proclus "fell in love with the ἔπη, called Λόγια by their admirers, in which Julianus set forth the Chaldaean doctrines."[13] By his own account, Julianus received these oracles from the gods: they were θεοπαράδοτα.[14] Where he in fact got them we do not know. As Kroll pointed out, their manner and content suit the age of the Antonines better than any earlier period.[15] Julianus may of course have forged them; but their diction is so bizarre and bombastic, their thought so obscure and incoherent, as to suggest rather the trance utterances of modern "spirit guides" than the deliberate efforts of a forger. It seems indeed not impossible, in view of what we know about later theurgy, that they had their origin in the "revelations" of some visionary or trance medium, and that Julianus' part consisted, as Psellus (or his source Proclus) asserts,[16] in putting them into verse. This would be in accordance with the established practice of official oracles;[17] and the transposition into hexameters would give an opportunity of introducing some semblance of philosophical meaning and system into the rigmarole. But the pious reader would still stand badly in need of some prose explanation or commentary, and this also Julianus seems to have supplied; for it is certainly he whom Proclus quotes (*in Tim.* III.124.32) as ὁ θεουργὸς ἐν τοῖς ὑφηγητικοῖς. Marinus is probably referring to the same commentary when he speaks of τὰ Λόγια καὶ τὰ σύστοιχα τῶν Χαλδαίων συγγράμματα (*vit. Procli* 26), and Damascius (II.203.27) when he cites οἱ θεοὶ καὶ αὐτὸς ὁ θεουργός. Whether it was identical with the Θεουργικά mentioned by Suidas we do not know. Proclus once (*in Tim.* III.27.10) quotes Julianus ἐν ἑβδόμῃ τῶν Ζωνῶν, which sounds like a section of the Θεουργικά dealing in seven chapters with the seven planetary spheres through which the soul descends and reascends (cf. *in Remp.* II.220.11 ff.). On the probable content of the Τελεστικά, see below, section IV.

Be the origin of the *Chaldaean Oracles* what it may, they certainly included not only prescriptions for a fire and sun cult[18] but prescriptions for the magical evocation of gods (see below, p. 298). And later tradition represents the Juliani as potent magicians. According to Psellus,[19] the elder Julianus "introduced" (συνέστησε) his son to the ghost of Plato; and it seems that they claimed to possess a spell (ἀγωγή) for producing an apparition of the god Χρόνος.[20] They could also cause men's souls to leave and reenter the body.[21] Nor was their fame confined to Neoplatonic circles. The timely thunderstorm which saved the Roman army during Marcus' campaign against the Quadi in 173 A.D. was attributed by some to the magic arts of the younger Julianus;[22] in Psellus' version of the story Julianus makes a human mask of clay which discharges "unendurable thunderbolts" at the enemy.[23] Sozomen has heard of his splitting a stone by magic (*Hist. Eccl.* 1.18); and a picturesque Christian legend shows him competing in a display of magical powers with Apollonius and Apuleius: Rome being stricken with a plague, each magician is assigned the medical superintendence of one sector of the city; Apuleius undertakes to stop the plague in fifteen days, Apollonius in ten, but Julianus stops it instantly by a mere word of command.[24]

II. THEURGY IN THE NEOPLATONIC SCHOOL

The creator of theurgy was a magician, not a Neoplatonist. And the creator of Neoplatonism was neither a magician nor—*pace* certain modern writers—a theurgist.[25] Plotinus is never described by his successors as a θεουργός, nor does he use the term θεουργία or its cognates in his writings. There is in fact no evidence[26] that he had ever heard of Julianus and his *Chaldaean Oracles*. Had he known them he would presumably have subjected them to the same critical treatment as the revelations "of Zoroaster and Zostrianus and Nikotheos and Allogenes and Mesos and others of the sort," which were analysed and exposed in his seminar.[27] For in his great defence of the Greek rationalist tradition, the essay *Against the Gnostics* (*Enn.* 2.9), he makes very clear both his distaste for all such megalomaniac "special revelations"[28] and his contempt for τοῖς πολλοῖς, οἳ τὰς παρὰ τοῖς μάγοις δυνάμεις θαυμάζουσι (c. 14, I.203.32 Volkmann). Not that he denied the efficacy of magic (could any man of the third century deny it?). But it did not interest him. He saw in it merely an application to mean personal ends of "the true magic which is the sum of love and hatred in the universe," the mysterious and truly admirable συμπάθεια which makes the cosmos one; men marvel at human γοητεία more than at the magic of nature only because it is less familiar.[29]

Despite all this, the article "Theurgie" which appeared in a recent volume of Pauly-Wissowa calls Plotinus a theurgist, and Eitrem has lately spoken of "Plotin, dont sans doute dérive la théurgie."[30] The main grounds for this opinion seem to be (1) his alleged[31] Egyptian birth and the fact that he studied at Alexandria under Ammonius Saccas; (2) his allegedly profound[32] knowledge of Egyptian religion; (3) his experience of *unio mystica* (Porph. *vit. Plot.* 23); and (4) the affair at the Iseum in Rome (*ibid.*, 10, quoted and discussed in section III below, p. 289). Of these considerations only the last seems to me to be really relevant. On the first point it must suffice here to say that Plotinus' name is Roman, that his manner of thought and speech is characteristically Greek, and that in the little we know of Ammonius Saccas there is nothing which warrants calling him a theurgist. As to the acquaintance with Egyptian religion displayed in the *Enneads*, I cannot see that it amounts to more than a few casual references to matters of common knowledge: Porphyry learned as much or more by reading Chaeremon.[33] And as to the Plotinian *unio mystica*, it must surely be clear to any careful reader of passages like *Enn.* 1.6.9. or 6.7.34, that it is attained, not by any ritual of evocation or performance of prescribed acts, but by an inward discipline of the mind which involves no compulsive element and has nothing whatever to do with magic.[34] There remains the affair of the Iseum. That is theurgy, or something like it. It rests, however, only on school gossip (see below). And in any case one visit to a séance does not make a man a spiritualist, especially if, like Plotinus, he goes there on someone else's initiative.

Plotinus is a man who, as Wilhelm Kroll put it, "raised himself by a strong intellectual and moral effort above the fog-ridden atmosphere which surrounded him." While he lived, he lifted his pupils with him. But with his death the fog began to close in again, and later Neoplatonism is in many respects a retrogression to the spineless syncretism from which he had tried to escape. The conflict between Plotinus' personal influence and the superstitions of the time appears very plainly in the wavering attitude of his pupil Porphyry[35]—an honest, learned, and lovable man, but no consistent or creative

thinker. Deeply religious by temperament, he had an incurable
weakness for oracles. Before he met Plotinus[36] he had already published a collection under the title Περὶ τῆς ἐκ λογίων φιλοσοφίας.[37]
Some of these refer to mediums, and are themselves clearly what we
should call "séance-room" products (see below, section v). But there
is no trace of his having quoted the *Chaldaean Oracles* (or used the term
theurgy) in this work; probably he was still unaware of their existence
when he wrote it. Later, when Plotinus has taught him to ask questions, he addresses a series of decidedly searching and often ironic-
sounding inquiries on demonology and occultism to the Egyptian
Anebo,[38] and points out, among other things, the folly of attempting
to put magical constraint on gods.[39] It was probably later still,[40]
after the death of Plotinus, that he disinterred the *Chaldaean Oracles*
from the obscurity in which they had survived (as such books do) for
more than a century, wrote a commentary on them,[41] and "made continual mention of them" in his *de regressu animae*.[42] In the latter work
he held that theurgic τελεταί could purify the πνευματικὴ ψυχή and
make it "aptam susceptioni spirituum et angelorum et ad videndos
deos"; but he warned his readers that the practice was perilous and
capable of evil as well as good uses, and denied that it could achieve,
or was a necessary ancillary to, the soul's return to god.[43] He was, in
fact, still a Plotinian at heart.[44] But he had made a dangerous con-
cession to the opposing school.

The answer of that school came in Iamblichus' commentary on the
Chaldaean Oracles[45] and in the extant treatise *de mysteriis*.[46] The *de
mysteriis* is a manifesto of irrationalism, an assertion that the road to
salvation is found not in reason but in ritual. "It is not thought that
links the theurgists with the gods: else what should hinder theoretical
philosophers from enjoying theurgic union with them? The case is
not so. Theurgic union is attained only by the efficacy of the un-
speakable *acts* performed in the appropriate manner, acts which are
beyond all comprehension, and by the potency of the unutterable
symbols which are comprehended only by the gods. . . . Without
intellectual effort on our part the tokens (συνθήματα) by their own
virtue accomplish their proper work" (*de myst.* 96.13 Parthey). To
the discouraged minds of fourth-century pagans such a message
offered a seductive comfort. The "theoretical philosophers" had now
been arguing for some nine centuries, and what had come of it? Only
a visibly declining culture, and the creeping growth of that Christian

ἀθεότης which was too plainly sucking the lifeblood of Hellenism. As vulgar magic is commonly the last resort of the personally desperate, of those whom man and God have alike failed, so theurgy became the refuge of a despairing intelligentsia which already felt *la fascination de l'abîme*.

Nevertheless it would seem that even in the generation after Iamblichus theurgy was not yet fully accepted in the Neoplatonic school. Eunapius in an instructive passage (*vit. soph.* 474 f. Boissonade) shows us Eusebius of Myndus, a pupil of Iamblichus' pupil Aedesius, maintaining in his lectures that magic was an affair of "crazed persons who make a perverted study of certain powers derived from matter," and warning the future emperor Julian against "that stagy miracle-worker" the theurgist Maximus: he concludes, in words which recall Plotinus, σὺ δὲ τούτων μηδὲν θαυμάσῃς, ὥσπερ οὐδὲ ἐγώ, τὴν διὰ τοῦ λόγου κάθαρσιν μέγα τι χρῆμα ὑπολαμβάνων. To which the prince replied: "You can stick to your books: I know now where to go"—and betook himself to Maximus. Shortly afterwards we find the young Julian asking his friend Priscus to get him a good copy of Iamblichus' commentary on his namesake (Julianus the theurgist); for, says he, "I am greedy for Iamblichus in philosophy and my namesake in theosophy [θεοσοφία, i.e. theurgy], and think nothing of the rest in comparison."[47]

Julian's patronage made theurgy temporarily fashionable. When as emperor he set about reforming the pagan clergy, the theurgist Chrysanthius found himself ἀρχιερεύς of Lydia; while Maximus as theurgic consultant to the imperial court became a wealthy and influential *éminence grise*, since ὑπὲρ τῶν παρόντων ἐπὶ τοὺς θεοὺς ἅπαντα ἀνέφερον (Eunap. p. 477 Boiss.; cf. Amm. Marc. 22.7.3 and 25.4.17). But Maximus paid for this in the subsequent Christian reaction, when he was fined, tortured, and eventually in 371 executed on a charge of conspiracy against the Emperors (Eunap. p. 478; Amm. Marc. 29.1.42; Zosimus 4.15). For some time after this event theurgists deemed it prudent to lie low;[48] but the tradition of their art was quietly handed down in certain families.[49] In the fifth century it was again openly taught and practised by the Athenian Neoplatonists: Proclus not only composed a Περὶ ἀγωγῆς and a further commentary on the *Chaldaean Oracles*, but also enjoyed personal visions (αὐτοπτουμένοις) of luminous "Hecatic" phantasms and was, like the founder of the cult, great at rainmaking.[50] After Justinian theurgy went underground again, but did not wholly die. Psellus has described a θεαγωγία conducted by an archbishop on the lines of pagan theurgy (τοῖς Χαλ-δαίων λόγοις ἑπόμενος), which he asserts took place at Byzantium in the eleventh century;[51] and Proclus' commentary on the *Oracles* was still known, directly or indirectly, to Nicephoros Gregoras in the fourteenth.[52]

III. A SÉANCE IN THE ISEUM

Porphyry, *vita Plotini* 10 (16.12 ff. Volk.): Αἰγύπτιος γάρ τις ἱερεὺς ἀνελθὼν εἰς τὴν Ῥώμην καὶ διά τινος φίλου αὐτῷ (sc. Πλωτίνῳ) γνωρισ-θεὶς θέλων τε τῆς ἑαυτοῦ σοφίας ἀπόδειξιν δοῦναι ἠξίωσε τὸν Πλωτῖνον ἐπὶ θέαν ἀφικέσθαι τοῦ συνόντος αὐτῷ οἰκείου δαίμονος καλουμένου. τοῦ δὲ ἑτοίμως ὑπακούσαντος γίνεται μὲν ἐν τῷ Ἰσείῳ ἡ κλῆσις· μόνον γὰρ ἐκεῖνον τὸν τόπον καθαρὸν φασιν εὑρεῖν ἐν τῇ Ῥώμῃ τὸν Αἰγύπτιον. κληθέντα δὲ εἰς αὐτοψίαν τὸν δαίμονα θεὸν ἐλθεῖν καὶ μὴ τοῦ δαιμόνων εἶναι γένους· ὅθεν τὸν Αἰγύπτιον εἰπεῖν· μακάριος εἶ θεὸν ἔχων τὸν δαίμονα καὶ οὐ τοῦ ὑφειμένου γένους τὸν συνόντα. μήτε δὲ ἐρέσθαι τι ἐκγενέσθαι μήτε ἐπιπλέον ἰδεῖν παρόντα, τοῦ συνθεωροῦντος φίλου τὰς ὄρνεις, ἃς κατεῖχε φυλακῆς ἕνεκα, πνίξαντος εἴτε διὰ φθόνον εἴτε καὶ διὰ φόβον τινά.

This curious passage has been discussed by Hopfner, *OZ* II.125, and more fully by Eitrem, *Symb. Oslo.* 22.62 ff. We should not attach too high a historical value to it. Porphyry's use of φασίν[53] shows that his source was neither Plotinus himself nor any of the actual "sitters"; and since he says that the affair prompted the composition of Plotinus' essay, Περὶ τοῦ εἰληχότος ἡμᾶς δαίμονος (*Enn.* 3.4), it must have taken place, like the composition of that essay, before Porphyry's own arrival in Rome, and at least thirty-five years before the publication of the *vita*. The testimony on which his story rests is thus neither first-hand nor (probably) close in time to the event. It cannot, as Eitrem rightly says, "avoir la valeur d'une attestation authentique."[54] Nevertheless, it affords an interesting if tantalizing glimpse of high-class magical procedure in the third century.

Neither the purpose nor the place of the séance need much surprise us. The belief in an indwelling δαίμων is very old and widespread, and was accepted and rationalised, in their respective fashions, by Plato and by the Stoics.[55] That it may have played some part in Greco-Egyptian magic is suggested by *PGM* vii.505 ff., where a recipe, un-fortunately incomplete, is headed Σύστασις ἰδίου δαίμονος.[56] (It should not, however, be confused with the much commoner evocation of a πάρεδρος or "familiar," whose connection with the magician is *created* for the first time by the magical procedure.) For the δαίμων turning out to be a god, cf., besides Plot. *Enn.* 3.4.6 (I.265.4 Volk.) δαίμων τούτῳ θεός (quoted by Eitrem), Olympiodorus *in Alc.* p. 20 Cr., where, after distinguishing θεῖοι δαίμονες from those of lower rank, he tells us that οἱ κατ' οὐσίαν ἑαυτῶν βιοῦντες καὶ ὡς πεφύκασι τὸν θεῖον δαίμονα ἔχουσιν εἰληχότα . . . κατ' οὐσίαν δέ ἐστι ζῆν τὸ πρόσφορον αἱρεῖσθαι βίον τῇ σειρᾷ ὑφ' ἣν ἀνάγεται, οἷον στρατιωτικὸν μέν, ἐὰν ὑπὸ τὴν ἀρεϊκήν, κτλ. As to the choice of place, it is sufficiently explained by the well-known requirement of a τόπος καθαρός for magical operations,[57] together with Chaeremon's statement that Egyptian temples were accessible at ordinary times only to those who had purified themselves and undergone severe fasts.[58]

But what puzzles Eitrem, as it has puzzled me, is the part played by the birds, ἃς κατεῖχε φυλακῆς ἕνεκα, i.e., to protect the operators from attack by evilly disposed spirits (not, surely, to keep the birds themselves from flying away, as MacKenna, Bréhier, and Harder unanimously mistranslate: for then their presence would be wholly unexplained). Protective measures are sometimes prescribed in the papyri.[59] But how did the birds act as a φυλακή? And why did their death banish the apparition? Hopfner says that the impurity of death drove the god away: they were brought there so that their killing should act as an ἀπόλυσις in case of need,[60] but it was done prematurely and needlessly. Eitrem, on the other hand, comparing *PGM* xii.15 ff., where the strangling of birds is part of the ritual for animating a wax figure of Eros, thinks that the real intention must have been sacrifice and that Porphyry or his informant misunderstood what happened: he finds the motives attributed to the φίλος "invraisemblables." In support of this view he might have quoted Porphyry's own statement in the *Letter to Anebo*[61] that διὰ νεκρῶν ζῴων τὰ πολλὰ αἱ θεαγωγίαι ἐπιτελοῦνται, which seems to put Hopfner's explanation out of court. There is, however, another passage of Porphyry which appears to imply that in killing *birds* on *this* occasion the φίλος was breaking a rule of the theurgic μυστήριον: at *de abst.* 4.16 (255.7 N.) he says, ὅστις δὲ φασμάτων φύσιν ἱστόρησεν, οἶδεν καθ' ὃν λόγον ἀπέχεσθαι χρὴ πάντων ὀρνίθων, καὶ μάλιστα ὅταν σπεύδῃ τις ἐκ τῶν χθονίων ἀπαλλαγῆναι καὶ πρὸς τοὺς οὐρανίους θεοὺς ἱδρυνθῆναι. This fits the occasion at the Iseum so aptly (for ἀπέχεσθαι can surely cover abstention from killing as well as from eating) that it is difficult not to feel that Porphyry had it in mind. We may perhaps compare also the Pythagorean rule which specifically forbade the sacrifice of cocks (Iamb. *vit. Pyth.* 147, *Protrept.* 21).

But if so, why were the birds there? Possibly because their presence was in itself a φυλακή. ὄρνιθες without qualifying description are usually domestic fowl, κατοικίδιοι ὄρνιθες (cf. L.-S.⁹, s.v.). And the domestic fowl, as Cumont has pointed out,[62] brought with it from its original home in Persia the name of being a holy bird, a banisher of darkness and therefore of demons:[63] Plutarch, for example, knows that κύνες καὶ ὄρνιθες belong to Oromazes (Ormuzd).[64] Is it not likely that in this matter, as in its fire-cult, the theurgic tradition preserved traces of Iranian religious ideas, and that Porphyry at least, if not the Egyptian priest, thought of the birds' function as apotropaic and of their death as an outrage to the heavenly phantasm? There is, in fact, later evidence to support the guess: for we learn from Proclus not only that cocks are solar creatures, μετέχοντες καὶ αὐτοὶ τοῦ θείου κατὰ τὴν ἑαυτῶν τάξιν, but that ἤδη τινὰ τῶν ἡλιακῶν δαιμόνων λεοντοπρόσωπον φαινόμενον, ἀλεκτρύονος δειχθέντος, ἀφανῆ γενέσθαι φασὶν ὑποστελλόμενον τὰ τῶν κρειττόνων συνθήματα.[65]

IV. The Modus Operandi: τελεστική

Proclus grandiloquently defines theurgy as "a power higher than all human wisdom, embracing the blessings of divination, the purifying powers of initiation, and in a word all the operations of divine possession" (*Theol. Plat.* p. 63). It may be described more simply as magic applied to a religious purpose and resting on a supposed revelation of a religious character. Whereas vulgar magic used names and formulae of religious origin to profane ends, theurgy used the procedures of vulgar magic primarily to a religious end: its τέλος was ἡ πρὸς τὸ νοητὸν πῦρ ἄνοδος (*de myst.* 179.8), which enabled its votaries to escape εἱμαρμένη (οὐ γὰρ ὑφ' εἱμαρτὴν ἀγέλην πίπτουσι θεουργοί, *Or. chald.* p. 59 Kr.; cf. *de myst.* 269.19 ff.), and ensured τῆς ψυχῆς ἀπαθανατισμός (Procl. *in Remp.* I.152.10).[66] But it had also a more immediate utility: Book III of the *de mysteriis* is devoted entirely to techniques of divination, and Proclus claims to have received from the δαίμονες many revelations about the past and future (*in Remp.* I.86.13).

So far as we can judge, the procedures of theurgy were broadly similar to those of vulgar magic. We can distinguish two main types:

(i) those which depended exclusively on the use of σύμβολα or συνθή-ματα; and (ii) those which involved the employment of an entranced "medium."

Of these two branches of theurgy, the first appears to have been known as τελεστική, and to have been concerned mainly with the consecrating (τελεῖν, Procl. *in Tim.* III.6.13) and animating of magic statues in order to obtain oracles from them: Proclus *in Tim.* III.155.18, τὴν τελεστικὴν καὶ χρηστήρια καὶ ἀγάλματα θεῶν ἱδρῦσθαι ἐπὶ γῆς καὶ διά τινων συμβόλων ἐπιτήδεια ποιεῖν τὰ ἐκ μερικῆς ὕλης γενόμενα καὶ φθαρτῆς εἰς τὸ μετέχειν θεοῦ καὶ κινεῖσθαι παρ' αὐτοῦ καὶ προλέγειν τὸ μέλλον: *Theol. Plat.* I.28, p. 70, ἡ τελεστικὴ διακαθήρασα καί τινας χαρακτῆρας καὶ σύμβολα περιτιθεῖσα τῷ ἀγάλματι ἔμψυχον αὐτὸ ἐποίησε: to the same effect *in Tim.* I.51.25, III.6.12 ff.; *in Crat.* 19.12.[67] We may suppose that a part at least of this lore goes back to the Τελεστικά of Julianus; certainly the σύμβολα go back to the *Chaldaean Oracles*.[68]

What were these σύμβολα, and how were they used? The clearest answer is given in a letter of Psellus:[69] ἐκείνη γὰρ (sc. ἡ τελεστικὴ ἐπιστήμη) τὰ κοῖλα τῶν ἀγαλμάτων ὕλης ἐμπιπλῶσα οἰκείας ταῖς ἐφεστηκυίαις δυνάμεσι, ζώων, φυτῶν, λίθων, βοτανῶν, ῥιζῶν, σφραγίδων, ἐγγραμμάτων, ἐνίοτε δὲ καὶ ἀρωμάτων συμπαθῶν, συγκαθιδρύουσα δὲ τούτοις καὶ κρατῆρας καὶ σπονδεῖα καὶ θυμιατήρια, ἔμπνοα ποιεῖ τὰ εἴδωλα καὶ τῇ ἀπορρήτῳ δυνάμει κινεῖ. This is genuine theurgic doctrine, doubtless derived from Proclus' commentary on the *Chaldaean Oracles*. The animals, herbs, stones, and scents figure in the *de myst.* (233.10 ff., cf. Aug. *Civ. D.* 10.11), and Proclus gives a list of magical herbs, stones, etc., good for various purposes.[70] Each god has his "sympathetic" representative in the animal, the vegetable, and the mineral world, which is, or contains, a σύμβολον of its divine cause and is thus *en rapport* with the latter.[71] These σύμβολα were concealed inside the statue,[72] so that they were known only to the τελεστής (Procl. *in Tim.* I.273.11). The σφραγῖδες (engraved gems) and ἐγγράμματα (written formulae) correspond to the χαρακτῆρες καὶ ὀνόματα ζωτικά of Procl. *in Tim.* III.6.13. The χαρακτῆρες (which include such things as the seven vowels symbolic of the seven planetary gods)[73] might be either written down (θέσις) or uttered (ἐκφώνησις).[74] The correct manner of uttering them was a professional secret orally transmitted.[75] The god's attributes might also be named with magical effect in an oral invocation.[76] The "life-giving names" further included certain secret appellations which the gods themselves revealed to the Juliani, thus enabling them to obtain answers to their prayers.[77] These would be among the ὀνόματα βάρβαρα which according to the *Chaldaean Oracles* lose their efficacy if translated into Greek.[78] Some of them have indeed been explained to us by the gods;[79] as to the rest, if a χαρακτήρ is meaningless to us αὐτὸ τοῦτό ἐστιν αὐτοῦ τὸ σεμνότατον (*de myst.* 254.14 ff.).

In all this the theurgic τελεστική was far from original. The ancient herbals and lapidaries are full of the "astrological botany" and "astrological mineralogy" which assigned particular plants and gems to particular planetary gods, and whose beginnings go back at least to Bolus of Mendes (about 200 B.C.).[80] These σύμβολα were already utilized in the invocations of Greco-Egyptian magic; thus Hermes is evoked by naming his plant and his tree, the moon-goddess by reciting a list of animals, etc., ending εἴρηκά σου τὰ σημεῖα καὶ τὰ σύμβολα τοῦ ὀνόματος.[81] χαρακτῆρες, lists of attributes, ὀνόματα βάρβαρα, belong to the standard Greco-Egyptian *materia magica*; the use of the last was familiar to Lucian (*Menipp.* 9 *fin.*), and Celsus, and the theory of their untranslatable efficacy was stoutly maintained by Origen against the latter (*c. Cels.* 1.24 f.). For a god revealing his true name in the course of a magical operation, cf. *PGM* i.161 ff.; for the importance of correct ἐκφώνησις, *PGM* v.24, etc.

Nor was the manufacture of magical statuettes of gods a new industry or a monopoly of the theurgists.[82] It rested ultimately upon the primitive and widespread belief in a natural συμπάθεια linking image with original,[83] the same belief which underlies the magical use of images of human beings for purposes of *envoûtement*. Its centre of diffusion was evidently Egypt, where it was rooted in native religious ideas.[84] The late Hermetic dialogue *Asclepius* knows of "statuas animatas sensu et spiritu plenas" which foretell the future "sorte, vate, somniis, multisque aliis rebus," and both cause and cure disease: the art of producing such statues, by imprisoning in consecrated images, with the help of herbs, gems, and odours, the souls of daemons or of angels, was discovered by the ancient Egyptians: "sic deorum fictor est homo."[85] The magical papyri offer recipes for constructing such images and animating them (ζωπυρεῖν, xii.318), e.g., iv.1841 ff., where the image is to be hollow, like Psellus' statues, and is to enclose a magic name inscribed on gold leaf; 2360 ff., a hollow Hermes enclosing a magic formula, consecrated by a garland and the sacrifice of a cock. From the first century A.D.[86] onwards we begin to hear of the private[87] manufacture and magical use of comparable images outside Egypt. Nero had one, the gift of "plebeius quidam et ignotus," which warned him of conspiracies (Suet. *Nero* 56); Apuleius was accused, probably with justice, of possessing one.[88] Lucian in his *Philopseudes* satirized the belief in them;[89] Philostratus mentions their use as amulets.[90] In the third century Porphyry quoted a Hecate-oracle[91] giving instructions for the confection of an image which will procure the worshipper a vision of the goddess in sleep.[92] But the real vogue of the art came later, and appears to be due to Iamblichus, who doubtless saw in it the most effective defence of the traditional cult of images against the sneers of Christian critics. Whereas Porphyry's Περὶ ἀγαλμάτων seems to have advanced no claim that the gods were in any sense present in the images which symbolised them,[93] Iamblichus in his like-named work set out to prove "that idols are divine and filled with the divine presence," and supported his case by narrating πολλὰ ἀπίθανα.[94] His disciples habitually sought omens from the statues, and were not slow to contribute ἀπίθανα of their own: Maximus makes a statue of Hecate laugh and causes the torches in her hands to light up automatically;[95] Heraiscus has so sensitive an intuition that' he can at once distinguish the "animate" from the "inanimate" statue by the sensations it gives him.[96]

The art of fabricating oracular images passed from the dying pagan world into the repertoire of mediaeval magicians, where it had a long life, though it was never so common as the use of images for *envoûte-ment*. Thus a bull of Pope John XXII, dated 1326 or 1327, denounces persons who by magic imprison demons in images or other objects, interrogate them, and obtain answers.[97] And two further questions suggest themselves in connection with the theurgic τελεστική, though they cannot be pursued here. First, did it contribute something to the belief, familiar alike to mediaeval Italy and mediaeval Byzantium, in τελέσματα (talismans) or "statuae averruncae"—enchanted images whose presence, concealed or visible, had power to avert natural disaster or military defeat?[98] Were some of these τελέσματα (usually attributed to anonymous or legendary magicians) in fact the work of theurgists? We are told by Zosimus (4.18) that the theurgist Nestorius saved Athens from an earthquake in 375 A.D. by dedicating such a τέλεσμα (a statue of Achilles) in the Parthenon, in accordance with instructions received in a dream. Theurgic also, it would seem, was the

statue of Zeus Philios dedicated μαγγανείαις τισὶ καὶ γοητείαις at
Antioch by a contemporary of Iamblichus, the fanatical pagan
Theoteknos, who practised τελεταί, μυήσεις, and καθαρμοί in connection with it (Eus. *Hist. Eccl.* 9.3; 9.11). A like origin may be guessed
for that statue of Jupiter, armed with golden thunderbolts, which in
394 was "consecrated with certain rites" to assist the pagan pretender
Eugenius against the troops of Theodosius (Aug. *Civ. Dei* 5.26): we
may see here the hand of Flavianus, Eugenius' leading supporter and
a man known for his dabbling in pagan occultism. Again, the ἄγαλμα
τετελεσμένον which protected Rhegium both from the fires of Etna
and from invasion by sea seems to have been furnished with στοιχεῖα
in a way that recalls the σύμβολα of theurgy and the papyri: ἐν γὰρ τῷ
ἑνὶ ποδὶ πῦρ ἀκοίμητον ἐτύγχανε, καὶ ἐν τῷ ἑτέρῳ ὕδωρ ἀδιάφθορον.[99]

Secondly, did the theurgic τελεστική suggest to mediaeval alche-
mists the attempt to create artificial human beings ("homunculi") in
which they were constantly engaged? Here the connection of ideas is
less obvious, but curious evidence of some historical linkage has recently been brought forward by the Arabist Paul Kraus,[100] whose
premature death is a serious loss. He points out that the great corpus
of alchemy attributed to Jâbir b. Ḥayyan (Gebir) not only refers in
this connection to a (spurious?) work of Porphyry entitled *The Book
of Generation*,[101] but makes use of Neoplatonic speculations about
images in a way which suggests some knowledge of genuine works of
Porphyry, including perhaps the letter to Anebo.[102]

V. The Modus Operandi: Mediumistic Trance

While τελεστική sought to induce the presence of a god in an inanimate "receptacle" (ὑποδοχή), another branch of theurgy aimed at in-
carnating him temporarily (εἰσκρίνειν) in a human being (κάτοχος or,
a more specific technical term, δοχεύς).[103] As the former art rested on
the wider notion of a natural and spontaneous συμπάθεια between
image and original, so did the latter on the widespread belief that
spontaneous alterations of personality were due to possession by a
god, daemon, or deceased human being.[104] That a technique for
producing such alterations goes back to the Juliani may be inferred
from Proclus' statement that the ability of the soul to leave the body
and return to it is confirmed by ὅσα τοῖς ἐπὶ Μάρκου θεουργοῖς ἐκδέδο-
ται· καὶ γὰρ ἐκεῖνοι διὰ δή τινος τελετῆς τὸ αὐτὸ δρῶσιν εἰς τὸν
τελούμενον.[105] And that such techniques were practised also by others

is shown by the oracle quoted from Porphyry's collection by Firmicus Maternus (*err. prof. rel.* 14) which begins, "Serapis vocatus et intra corpus hominis collocatus talia respondit." A number of Porphyry's oracles appear to be founded, as Frederic Myers saw,[106] on the utterances of mediums who had been thrown into trance for the purpose, not in official shrines but in private circles. To this class belong the directions for terminating the trance (ἀπόλυσις), professedly given by the god through the entranced medium,[107] which have their analogues in the papyri but could hardly form part of an official oracular response. Of the same type is the "oracle" quoted (from Porphyry?) by Proclus *in Remp.*I.111.28, "οὐ φέρει με τοῦ δοχῆος ἡ τάλαινα καρδία," φησί τις θεῶν. Such private εἴσκρισις differed from official oracles in that the god was thought to enter the medium's body not as a spontaneous act of grace but in response to the appeal, even the compulsion,[108] of the operator (κλήτωρ).

This branch of theurgy is especially interesting because of the evident analogy with modern spiritualism: if we were better informed about it, we might hope by a comparison to throw light on the psychological and physiological basis of both superstitions. But our information is tantalisingly incomplete. We know from Proclus that before the "sitting" both operator and medium were purified with fire and water[109] (*in Crat.* 100.21), and that they were dressed in special chitons with special girdles appropriate to the deity to be invoked (*in Remp.* II.246.23); this seems to correspond to the Νειλαίη ὀθόνη or σινδών of the Porphyrian oracle (*Praep. Ev.* 5.9), whose removal was evidently an essential part of the ἀπόλυσις (cf. *PGM* iv.89, σινδονιάσας κατὰ κεφαλῆς μέχρι ποδῶν γυμνόν ... παῖδα, the "lintea indumenta" of the magicians in Amm. Marc. 29.1.29, and the "purum pallium" of Apul. *Apol.* 44). The medium also wore a garland, which had magical efficacy,[110] and carried, or wore on his dress, εἰκονίσματα τῶν κεκλημένων θεῶν[111] or other appropriate σύμβολα.[112] What else was done to induce trance is uncertain. Porphyry knows of persons who try to procure possession (εἰσκρίνειν) by "standing upon χαρακτῆρες" (as mediæval magicians did), but Iamblichus thinks poorly of this procedure (*de myst.* 129.13; 131.3 ff.). Iamblichus recognises the use of ἀτμοί and ἐπικλήσεις (*ibid.*, 157.9 ff.), but denies that they have any effect on the medium's mind; Apuleius, on the other hand (*Apol.* 43), speaks of the medium being put to sleep "seu carminum avocamento sive odorum delenimento." Proclus knows of the practice of smearing the eyes with strychnine and other drugs in order to procure visions,[113] but does not attribute it to the theurgists. Probably the effective agencies in the theurgic operation, as in spiritualism, were in fact psychological, not physiological. Iamblichus says that not everybody is a potential medium; the most suitable are "young and rather simple persons."[114] Herein he agrees with the general ancient opinion;[115] and modern experience tends on the whole to support him, at least as regards the second part of his requirement.

The behaviour and psychological condition of the medium are described at some length, though obscurely, by Iamblichus (*de myst.* 3.4–7), and in clearer terms by Psellus (*orat.* 27, *Scripta Minora* I.248. 1 ff., based on Proclus: cf. also *CMAG* VI.209.15 ff., and *Op. Daem.* xiv, *PG* 122, 851). Psellus distinguishes cases where the medium's personality is completely in abeyance, so that it is absolutely necessary to have a normal person present to look after him, from those where consciousness (παρακολούθησις) persists θαυμαστόν τινα τρόπον, so that the medium knows τίνα τε ἐνεργεῖ καὶ τί φθέγγεται καὶ πόθεν δεῖ ἀπολύειν τὸ κινοῦν. Both these types of trance occur today.[116] The symptoms of trance are said by Iamblichus to vary widely with different "communicators" and on different occasions (111.3 ff.); there may be anaesthesia, including insensibility to fire (110.4 ff.); there may be bodily movement or complete immobility (111.17); there may be changes of voice (112.5 ff.). Psellus mentions the risk of ὑλικὰ πνεύματα causing convulsive movement (κίνησιν μετά τινος βίας γενομένην) which weaker mediums are unable to bear;[117] elsewhere he speaks of κάτοχοι biting their lips and muttering between their teeth (*CMAG* VI.164.18). Most of these symptoms can be illustrated from the classic study of Mrs. Piper's trance phenomena by Mrs. Henry Sidgwick.[118] It is, I think, reasonable to conclude that the states described by the ancient and the modern observers are, if not identical, at least analogous. (One may add the significant observation quoted by Porphyry, *ap.* Eus. *Praep. Ev.* 5.8, from Pythagoras of Rhodes, that "the gods" come at first reluctantly, but more easily when they have formed a habit—i.e., when a trance personality has been established.)

We do not hear that these "gods" furnished any proofs of identity; and it would seem that their identity was often in fact disputed. Porphyry wished to know how the presence of a god was to be distinguished from that of an angel, archangel, δαίμων, ἄρχων, or

human soul (*de myst.* 70.9). Iamblichus admits that impure or in-
expert operators sometimes get the wrong god or, worse still, one
of those evil spirits who are called ἀντίθεοι[119] (*ibid.*, 177.7 ff.). He
himself is said to have unmasked an alleged Apollo who was in reality
only the ghost of a gladiator (Eunap. *vit. soph.* 473). False answers are
attributed by Synesius, *de insomn.* 142A, to such intrusive spirits,
which "jump in and occupy the place prepared for a higher being"; his
commentator, Nicephoros Gregoras (*PG* 149, 540A), ascribes this
view to the Χαλδαῖοι (Julianus?), and quotes (from the *Chaldaean
Oracles?*) a prescription for dealing with such situations. Others
account for false answers by "bad conditions"[120] (πονηρὰ κατάστασις
τοῦ περιέχοντος, Porph. *ap.* Eus. *Praep. Ev.* 6.5 = Philop. *de mundi
creat.* 4.20), or lack of ἐπιτηδειότης;[121] others again, by the medium's
disturbed state of mind or the inopportune intervention of his normal
self (*de myst.* 115.10). All these ways of excusing failure recur in the
literature of spiritualism.

Besides revealing past or future through the medium's lips, the
gods vouchsafed visible (or occasionally audible)[122] signs of their presence. The medium's person might be visibly elongated or dilated,[123]
or even levitated (*de myst.* 112.3).[124] But the manifestations usually
took the form of luminous apparitions: indeed, in the absence of
these "blessed visions," Iamblichus considers that the operators cannot be sure what they are doing (*de myst.* 112.18). It seems that Proclus distinguished two types of séance: the "autoptic," where the
θεατής witnessed the phenomena for himself; and the "epoptic," where
he had to be content with having them described to him by the
κλήτωρ (ὁ τὴν τελετὴν διατιθέμενος).[125] In the latter case the visions were,
of course, exposed to the suspicion of being purely subjective, and
Porphyry seems to have suggested as much; for Iamblichus ener-
getically repudiates the notion that ἐνθουσιασμός or μαντική may be of
subjective origin (*de myst.* 114.16; 166.13), and apparently refers to
objective traces of their visit which the "gods" leave behind.[126] Later
writers are at pains to explain why only certain persons, thanks to a
natural gift or to ἱερατικὴ δύναμις, can enjoy such visions (Procl.
in Remp. II.167.12; Hermeias *in Phaedr.* 69.7 Couvreur).

The luminous apparitions go back to the *Chaldaean Oracles*, which
promised that by pronouncing certain spells the operator should see
"fire shaped like a boy," or "an unshaped (ἀτύπωτον) fire with a voice
proceeding from it," or various other things.[127] Compare the πυραυγῆ

φάσματα which the "Chaldaeans" are said to have exhibited to the Emperor Julian;[128] the φάσματα Ἑκατικὰ φωτοειδῆ which Proclus claimed to have seen (Marin. *vit. Procl.* 28); and Hippolytus' recipe for simulating a fiery apparition of Hecate by natural if somewhat dangerous means (*Ref. Haer.* 4.36). At *de myst* 3.6 (112.10 ff.) these phenomena are clearly associated with mediumship: the spirit may be seen as a fiery or luminous form entering (εἰσκρινόμενον) or leaving the medium's body, by the operator (τῷ θεαγωγοῦντι), by the medium (τῷ δεχομένῳ), and sometimes by all present: the last (Proclus' αὐτοψία) is, we are told, the most satisfactory. The apparent analogy with the so-called "ectoplasm" or "teleplasm," which modern observers claim to have seen emerge from and return to the bodies of certain mediums, has been noted by Hopfner[129] and others. Like "ectoplasm," the appearances might be shapeless (ἀτύπωτα, ἀμόρφωτα) or formed (τετυπωμένα, μεμορφωμένα): one of Porphyry's oracles (*Praep. Ev.* 5.8) speaks of "the pure fire being compressed into sacred forms (τύποι)"; but according to Psellus (*PG* 122, 1136c) the shapeless appearances are the most trustworthy, and Proclus (*in Crat.* 34.28) gives the reason—ἄνω γὰρ ἀμόρφωτος οὖσα διὰ τὴν πρόοδον ἐγένετο μεμορφωμένη. The luminous character which is regularly attributed to them is doubtless connected with the "Chaldaean" (Iranian) fire-cult; but it also recalls the φωταγωγίαι of the papyri[130] as well as the "lights" of the modern séance-room. Proclus seems to have spoken of the shaping process as taking place "in a light":[131] this suggests a λυχνομαντεία, like that prescribed at *PGM* vii.540 ff., where the magician says (561), ἔμβηθι αὐτοῦ (sc. τοῦ παιδός) εἰς τὴν ψυχήν, ἵνα τυπώσηται τὴν ἀθάνατον μορφὴν ἐν φωτὶ κραταιῷ καὶ ἀφθάρτῳ. Eitrem[132] would translate τυπώσηται here as "perceive" (a sense not elsewhere attested); but in view of the passages just referred to I think we should render "give shape to" ("abbilden," Preisendanz) and suppose that a materialization is in question. The "strong immortal light" replaces the mortal light of the lamp, just as at *PGM* iv.1103 ff. the watcher sees the light of the lamp become "vault-shaped," then finds it replaced by "a very great light within a void," and beholds the god. But whether a lamp was ever used in theurgy we do not know. Certainly some types of φωταγωγία were conducted in darkness,[133] others out of doors,[134] while lychnomancy does not figure among the varieties of φωτὸς ἀγωγή listed at *de myst.* 3.14. The similarity of language remains, however, striking.

NOTES TO APPENDIX II

1 W. Kroll, *de Oraculis Chaldaicis* (Breslauer Philologische Abhandlungen, VII.i, 1894).

2 *Catalogue des manuscrits alchimiques grecs* (abbrev. *CMAG*), Vol. VI; *Mélanges Cumont*, 95 ff. Cf. his "Note sur les mystères néoplatoniciens" in *Rev. Belge de Phil. et d'Hist.* 7 (1928) 1477 ff., and his *Vie de l'Emp. Julien*, 73 ff. On Procopius of Gaza as Psellus' proximate source see L. G. Westerink in *Mnemosyne*, 10 (1942) 275 ff.

3 *Griechisch-Aegyptische Offenbarungszauber* (quoted as *OZ*); and in the introduction and commentary to his translation of the *de mysteriis*. Cf. also his articles "Mageia" and "Theurgie" in Pauly-Wissowa, and below, n. 115.

4 Especially "Die σύστασις und der Lichtzauber in der Magie," *Symb. Oslo.* 8 (1929) 49 ff.; and "La Théurgie chez les Néo-Platoniciens et dans les papyrus magiques," *ibid.*, 22 (1942) 49 ff. W. Theiler's essay, *Die chaldaischen Orakel und die Hymnen des Synesios* (Halle, 1942), deals learnedly with the doctrinal influence of the *Oracles* on later Neoplatonism, a topic which I have not attempted to discuss.

5 *Papyri Graecae Magicae*, ed. Preisendanz (abbrev. *PGM*).

6 Cf. Bidez-Cumont, *Les Mages hellénisés*, I.163.

7 τοῦ κληθέντος θεουργοῦ Ἰουλιανοῦ, Suidas, s.v.

8 Suidas, s.v., cf. Proclus *in Crat.* 72.10 Pasq., *in Remp.* II.123.12, etc. Psellus in one place (confusing him with his father?) puts him in Trajan's time (*Scripta Minora* I, p. 241.29 Kurtz-Drexl).

9 *Vie de Julien*, 369, n. 8.

10 See Eitrem, *Symb. Oslo.* 22.49. Psellus seems to have understood the word in the latter sense, *PG* 122, 721D: θεοὺς τοὺς ἀνθρώπους ἐργάζεται. Cf. also the Hermetic "deorum fictor est homo," quoted on p. 293.

11 Proclus' expression οἱ ἐπὶ Μάρκου θεουργοί (*in Crat.* 72.10, *in Remp.* II.123.12) perhaps refers to father and son jointly.

12 ad *Philops.* 12 (IV.224 Jacobitz). On this scholion see Westerink, *op. cit.*, 276.

13 *Script. Min.* I.241.25 ff., cf. *CMAG* VI.163.19 ff. As Westerink points out, the source of these statements seems to be Procopius.

14 Marinus, *vit. Procl.* 26; cf. Procl. *in Crat.* c. 122. On such claims of divine origin, which are frequent in Hellenistic occult literature, see Festugière, *L'Astrologie*, 309 ff.

15 Bousset, *Arch. f. Rel.* 18 (1915) 144, argued for an earlier date on

the ground of coincidences in doctrine with Cornelius Labeo. But Labeo's own date is far from certain; and the coincidences may mean merely that the Juliani moved in Neopythagorean circles, which we know to have been interested in magic.

16 *Script. Min.* I.241.29; cf. *CMAG* VI.163.20. On doctrinal oracles received in vision see Festugière, *op. cit.*, 59 f.

17 See chap. iii, n. 70.

18 Kroll, *op. cit.*, 53 ff. The passages about the divine fire recall the "recipe for immortality" in *PGM* iv.475 ff., which is in many ways the closest analogue to the *Chaldaean Oracles*. Julian, *Or.* V, 172D, attributes to ὁ Χαλδαῖος (i.e., Julianus) a cult of τὸν ἑπτάκτινα θεόν. This solar title has been disguised by corruption in two passages of Psellus: *Script. Min.* I.262.19: Ἐρωτύχην ἢ Κασόθαν ἢ Ἔπτακις (read Ἐπτάκτις), ἢ εἴ τις ἄλλος δαίμων ἀπατηλός, *ibid.*, I.446.26: τὸν Ἔπακτον (Ἐπτάκτιν, Bidez) ὁ Ἀπουλήιος ὅρκοις καταναγκάσας μὴ προσομιλῆσαι τῷ Θεουργῷ (sc. Juliano). Cf. also Procl. *in Tim.* I.34.20: Ἡλίῳ, παρ' ᾧ . . . ὁ Ἐπτάκτις κατὰ τοὺς θεολόγους.

19 Περὶ τῆς χρυσῆς ἁλύσεως, *Ann. Assoc. Ét. Gr.* 1875, 216.24 ff.

20 Proclus, *in Tim.* III.120.22: οἱ θεουργοί . . . ἀγωγὴν αὐτοῦ παρέδοσαν ἡμῖν δι' ἧς εἰς αὐτοφάνειαν κινεῖν αὐτὸν δυνατόν· cf. Simpl. *in Phys.* 795.4, and Damasc. *Princ.* II.235.22. Both σύστασις and ἀγωγή are "terms of art," familiar to us from the magical papyri.

21 Proclus, *in Remp.* II.123.9 ff.

22 Suidas, s.v. Ἰουλιανός. The ascription of the credit to Julianus is perhaps implied also in Claudian, *de VI cons. Honorii*, 348 f., who speaks of "Chaldaean" magic. For other versions of the tale, and a summary of the lengthy modern discussions, see A. B. Cook, *Zeus*, III.324 ff. The attribution to Julianus may have been suggested by a confusion with the Julianus who commanded against the Dacians under Domitian (Dio Cass. 67.10).

23 *Script. Min.* I.446.28.

24 S. Anastasius of Sinai, *Quaestiones* (*PG* 89, col. 525A). For Julianus' supposed rivalry with Apuleius see also Psellus quoted above, n. 18.

25 Cf. Olympiodorus *in Phaed.* 123.3 Norvin: οἱ μὲν τὴν φιλοσοφίαν προτιμῶσιν, ὡς Πορφύριος καὶ Πλωτῖνος καὶ ἄλλοι πολλοὶ φιλόσοφοι· οἱ δὲ τὴν ἱερατικήν (i.e., theurgy), ὡς Ἰάμβλιχος καὶ Συριανὸς καὶ Πρόκλος καὶ οἱ ἱερατικοὶ πάντες.

26 The prose injunction, μὴ ἐξάξῃς ἵνα μὴ ἐξίῃ ἔχουσά τι, which he quotes at *Enn.* I.9 *init.*, is called "Chaldaean" by Psellus (*Expos.*

or. Chald. 1125c ff.) and in a late scholion *ad loc.*, but cannot come from a hexameter poem. The doctrine is Pythagorean.

²⁷ Porph. *vit. Plot.* 16. Cf. Kroll, *Rh. Mus.* 71 (1916) 350; Puech in *Mélanges Cumont*, 935 ff. In a similar list of bogus prophets, Arnob. *adv. gentes* 1.52, Julianus and Zoroaster figure side by side.

²⁸ Cf. esp. c. 9, I.197.8 ff. Volk.: τοῖς δ᾽ ἄλλοις (δεῖ) νομίζειν εἶναι χώραν παρὰ τῷ θεῷ καὶ μὴ αὐτὸν μόνον μετ᾽ ἐκεῖνον τάξαντα ὥσπερ ὀνείρασι πέτεσθαι . . . τὸ δὲ ὑπὲρ νοῦν ἤδη ἐστὶν ἔξω νοῦ πεσεῖν.

²⁹ *Enn.* 4.4.37, 40. Observe that throughout this discussion he uses the contemptuous word γοητεία and introduces none of the theurgic terms of art. On the Stoic and Neoplatonic conception of συμπάθεια see K. Reinhardt, *Kosmos und Sympathie*, and my remarks in *Greek Poetry and Life*, 373 f. To theurgists such explanations appeared entirely inadequate (*de myst.* 164.5 ff. Parthey).

³⁰ *Symb. Oslo.* 22.50. As Eitrem himself notes, Lobeck and Wilamowitz thought otherwise; and he might have added the names of Wilhelm Kroll (*Rh. Mus.* 71 [1916] 313) and Joseph Bidez (*Vie de Julien*, 67; *CAH* XII.635 ff.).

³¹ See on this *CQ* 22 (1928) 129, n. 2.

³² J. Cochez, *Rev. Néo-Scolastique*, 18 (1911) 328 ff., and *Mélanges Ch. Moeller*, 1.85 ff.; Cumont, *Mon. Piot*, 25.77 ff.

³³ *de abst.* 4.6, cf. *de myst.* 265.16, 277.4. See further E. Peterson's convincing reply to Cumont, *Theol. Literaturzeitung*, 50 (1925) 485 ff. I would add that the allusion in *Enn.* 5.5.11 to people who are excluded from certain ἱερά because of their γαστριμαργία probably refers to Eleusis, not Egypt: παραγγέλλεται γὰρ καὶ Ἐλευσῖνι ἀπέχεσθαι κατοικιδίων ὀρνίθων καὶ ἰχθύων καὶ κυάμων ῥοιᾶς τε καὶ μήλων, Porph. *de abst.* 4.16.

³⁴ Cf. *CQ* 22 (1928) 141 f., and E. Peterson, *Philol.* 88 (1933) 30 ff. Conversely, as Eitrem has rightly pointed out (*Symb. Oslo.* 8.50), the magical and theurgic term σύστασις has nothing to do with *unio mystica*.

³⁵ See Bidez's sympathetic, elegant, and scholarly study, *La Vie du Néoplatonicien Porphyre*. A like infection of mysticism by magic has occurred in other cultures. "Instead of the popular religion being spiritualised by the contemplative ideal, there is a tendency for the highest religion to be invaded and contaminated by the subrational forces of the pagan underworld, as in Tantric Buddhism and in some forms of sectarian Hinduism" (Christopher Dawson, *Religion and Culture*, 192 f.).

³⁶ νεὸς δὲ ὢν ἴσως ταῦτα ἔγραφεν, ὡς ἔοικεν, Eun. *vit. soph.* 457 Boissonade; Bidez, *op. cit.*, chap. iii.

37 The fragments were edited by W. Wolff, *Porphyrii de Philosophia ex Oraculis Haurienda* (1856). On the general character of this collection see A. D. Nock, "Oracles théologiques," *REA* 30 (1928) 280 ff.

38 The fragments as reconstructed (not very scientifically) by Gale are reprinted in Parthey's edition of the *de mysteriis*. On the date see Bidez, *op. cit.*, 86.

39 *apud* Eus. *Praep. Ev.* 5.10, 199A (= fr. 4 Gale): μάταιοι αἱ θεῶν κλήσεις ἔσονται . . . καὶ ἔτι μᾶλλον αἱ λεγόμεναι ἀνάγκαι θεῶν· ἀκήλητον γὰρ καὶ ἀβίαστον καὶ ἀκατανάγκαστον τὸ ἀπαθές.

40 It is probable that the letter to Anebo did not quote Julianus or the *Chaldaean Oracles*, since Iamblichus' reply is silent about them. Whether the "theurgy" of the *de mysteriis* is in fact independent of the Julianic tradition remains to be investigated. The writer certainly claims to be acquainted with the "Chaldaean" (p. 4.11) or "Assyrian" (p. 5.8) doctrines as well as the Egyptian, and says he will present both.

41 Marinus, *vit. Procli* 26; Lydus, *mens.* 4.53; Suidas, s.v. Πορφύριος.

42 Aug. *Civ. Dei* 10.32 = *de regressu* fr. 1 Bidez (*Vie de Porphyre*, App. II).

43 *Ibid.*, 10.9 = fr. 2 Bidez. On the function of the πνευματικὴ ψυχή in theurgy see my edition of Proclus' *Elements of Theology*, p. 319.

44 Cf. Olympiodorus' judgement, above, n. 25.

45 Julian, *Epist.* 12 Bidez; Marinus, *vit. Procli* 26; Damasc. I.86.3 ff.

46 The *de mysteriis*, though issued under the name of "Abammon," was attributed to Iamblichus by Proclus and Damascius; and since the publication of Rasche's dissertation in 1911 most scholars have accepted the ascription. Cf. Bidez in *Mélanges Desrousseaux*, 11 ff.

47 *Epist.* 12 Bidez = 71 Hertlein = 2 Wright. The Loeb editor is clearly wrong in maintaining against Bidez that τὸν ὁμώνυμον in this passage means Iamblichus the younger: τὰ Ἰαμβλίχου εἰς τὸν ὁμώνυμον cannot mean "the writings of Iamblichus to his namesake"; nor was the younger Iamblichus θεόσοφος.

48 Cf. what Eunapius says of one Antoninus, who died shortly before 391: ἐπεδείκνυτο οὐδὲν θεουργὸν καὶ παράλογον ἐς τὴν φαινομένην αἴσθησιν, τὰς βασιλικὰς ἴσως ὁρμὰς ὑφορώμενος ἑτέρωσε φερούσας (p. 471).

49 Thus Proclus learned from Asclepigeneia the θεουργικὴ ἀγωγή of "the great Nestorius," of which she was, through her father Plutarchus, the sole inheritress (Marinus, *vit. Procli* 28). On this family transmission of magical secrets see Dieterich, *Abraxas*,

160 ff.; Festugière, *L'Astrologie*, 332 ff. Diodorus calls it a Chaldaean practice, 2.29.4.

50 Marinus, *vit. Procli* 26, 28. The Περὶ ἀγωγῆς is listed by Suidas, s.v. Πρόκλος.

51 *Script. Min.* I.237 f.

52 Migne, *PG* 149, 538в ff., 599в; cf. Bidez, *CMAG* VI.104 f., Westerink, *op. cit.*, 280.

53 Nauck's correction for φησίν, which has no possible subject.

54 Among later writers, Proclus (*in Alc.* p. 73.4 Creuzer) and Ammianus Marcellinus (21.14.5) refer to the incident. But Proclus, who says ὁ Αἰγύπτιος τὸν Πλωτῖνον ἐθαύμασεν ὡς θεῖον ἔχοντα τὸν δαίμονα, is clearly dependent on Porphyry; and so, presumably, is Ammianus, whether directly or through a doxographic source.

55 See chap. ii, pp. 42 f. Ammianus, *loc. cit.*, says that while each man has his "genius," such beings are "admodum paucissimis visa."

56 Since the surviving part of the recipe is an invocation to the sun, Preisendanz and Hopfner think that ἰδίου is a mistake for ἡλίου. But loss of the remainder of the recipe (Eitrem) seems an equally possible explanation. On such losses see Nock, *J. Eg. Arch.* 15 (1929) 221. The ἴδιος δαίμων seems to have played a part in alchemy also; cf. Zosimus, *Comm. in* ω 2 (Scott, *Hermetica*, IV.104).

57 E.g., *PGM* iv.1927. Similarly iv.28 requires a spot recently bared by the Nile flood and still untrodden, and ii.147, a τόπος ἁγνὸς ἀπὸ παντὸς μυσαροῦ. So Thessalus, *CCAG* 8(3).136.26 (οἶκος καθαρός).

58 *apud* Porph. *de abst.* 4.6 (236.21 Nauck). He goes on to speak of ἀγνευτήρια τοῖς μὴ καθαρεύουσιν ἄδυτα καὶ πρὸς ἱερουργίας ἅγια (237.13). On magical practices in Egyptian temples see Cumont, *L'Égypte des Astrologues*, 163 ff.

59 E.g., *PGM* iv.814 ff. For φυλακή cf. Proclus in *CMAG* VI, 151.6: ἀπόχρη γὰρ πρός ... φυλακὴν δάφνη, ῥάμνος, σκύλλα, κτλ; and for spirits turning nasty at séances, Pythagoras of Rhodes in Eus. *Praep. Ev.* 5.8, 193в; Psellus, *Op. Daem.* 22, 869в.

60 Aspersion with blood of a dove occurs in an ἀπόλυσις, *PGM* ii.178.

61 Fr. 29 = *de myst.* 241.4 = Eus. *Praep. Ev.* 5.10, 198а.

62 *CRAI* 1942, 284 ff. Doubt may be felt about the late date which Cumont assigns to the introduction of domestic fowl into Greece; but this does not affect the present argument.

63 "The cock has been created to combat demons and sorcerers along with the dog," Darmesteter (quoted by Cumont, *loc. cit.*). The belief in its apotropaic virtues survives to this day in many countries. On this belief among the Greeks see Orth in P.-W., s.v. "Huhn," 2532 f.

Theurgy 305

⁶⁴ *Is. et Os.* 46, 369ꜰ.

⁶⁵ *CMAG* VI.150.1 ff., 15 ff. (partly based on the traditional antipathy of lion and cock, Pliny, *N.H.* 8.52, etc.). Cf. Bolus, Φυσικά fr. 9 Wellmann (*Abh. Berl. Akad.*, phil.-hist. Kl., 1928, Nr. 7, p. 20).

⁶⁶ Very similar ideas appear in the "recipe for immortality," *PGM* iv.475 ff., e.g. 511: ἵνα θαυμάσω τὸ ἱερὸν πῦρ, and 648: ἐκ τοσούτων μυριάδων ἀπαθανατισθεὶς ἐν ταύτῃ τῇ ὥρᾳ. It, too, culminates in luminous visions (634 ff., 694 ff.). But the theurgic ἀπαθανατισμός may have been connected with a ritual of burial and rebirth, Procl. *Theol. Plat.* 4.9, p. 193: τῶν θεουργῶν θάπτειν τὸ σῶμα κελευόντων πλὴν τῆς κεφαλῆς ἐν τῇ μυστικωτάτῃ τῶν τελετῶν (cf. Dieterich, *Eine Mithrasliturgie*, 163).

⁶⁷ Psellus, though he too connects τελεστική with statues, explains the term otherwise: τελεστικὴ δὲ ἐπιστήμη ἐστὶν ἡ οἷον τελοῦσα (so MSS) τὴν ψυχὴν διὰ τῆς τῶν ἐνταῦθ' ὑλῶν δυνάμεως (*Expos. or. Chald.* 1129ᴅ, in *PG*, Vol. 122). Hierocles, who represents a different tradition, makes τελεστική the art of purifying the pneuma (*in aur. carm.* 482ᴀ Mullach).

⁶⁸ Psellus says that "the Chaldaeans" διαφόροις ὕλαις ἀνδρείκελα πλάττοντες ἀποτρόπαια νοσημάτων ἐργάζονται (*Script. Min.* I.447.8). For σύμβολα cf. the line quoted by Proclus, *in. Crat.* 21.1: σύμβολα γὰρ πατρικὸς νόος ἔσπειρεν κατὰ κόσμον.

⁶⁹ *Epist.* 187 Sathas (*Bibliotheca Graeca Medii Aevi*, V.474).

⁷⁰ *CMAG* VI.151.6; cf. also *in Tim.* I.111.9 ff.

⁷¹ Cf. Proclus in *CMAG* VI.148 ff., with Bidez's introduction, and Hopfner, *OZ* I.382 ff.

⁷² An identical practice is found in modern Tibet, where statues are consecrated by inserting in their hollow interiors written spells and other magically potent objects (Hastings, *Encycl. of Religion and Ethics*, VII.144,160).

⁷³ Cf. R. Wünsch, *Sethianische Verfluchungstafeln*, 98 f.; A. Audollent, *Defixionum Tabellae*, p. lxxiii; Dornseiff, *Das Alphabet in Mystik u. Magie*, 35 ff.

⁷⁴ Proclus, *in Tim.* II.247.25; cf. *in Crat.* 31.27. Porphyry, too, included in his list of theurgic *materia magica* both "figurationes" and "soni certi quidam ac voces" (Aug. *Civ. Dei* 10.11).

⁷⁵ Marinus, *vit. Procl.* 28; Suidas, s.v. Χαλδαϊκοῖς ἐπιτηδεύμασι. Cf. Psellus, *Epist.* 187, where we learn that certain formulae are inoperative εἰ μή τις ταῦτα ἐρεῖ ὑποψέλλῳ τῇ γλώσσῃ ἢ ἑτέρως ὡς ἡ τέχνη διατάττεται.

⁷⁶ Psellus, in *CMAG* VI. 62.4, tells us that Proclus advised invoking

Artemis (= Hecate) as ξιφηφόρος, σπειροδρακοντόζωνος, λεοντοῦχος, τρίμορφος· τούτοις γὰρ αὐτήν φησι τοῖς ὀνόμασιν ἕλκεσθαι καὶ οἷον ἐξαπατᾶσθαι καὶ γοητεύεσθαι.

[77] Proclus, *in Crat.* 72.8. Cf. the divine name which "the prophet Bitys" found carved in hieroglyphs in a temple at Sais and revealed to "King Ammon," *de myst.* 267.14.

[78] Psellus, *expos. or. chald.* 1132c; Nicephoros Gregoras, *in Synes. de insomn.* 541A. Cf. *Corp. Herm.* xvi.2.

[79] Cf. the Greek translations of such magical names given by Clem. Alex. *Strom.* 5.242, and Hesych. s.v. Ἐφέσια γράμματα.

[80] See Wellmann, *Abh. Berl. Akad.*, phil.-hist. Kl., 1928, Nr. 7; Pfister, *Byz. Ztschr.* 37 (1937) 381 ff.; K. W. Wirbelauer, *Antike Lapidarien* (Diss. Berl., 1937); Bidez-Cumont, *Les Mages hellénisés* I.194; Festugière, *L'Astrologie*, 137 ff., 195 ff.

[81] *PGM* viii.13; vii.781. Cf. vii.560: ἧκέ μοι τὸ πνεῦμα τὸ ἀεροπετές, καλούμενον συμβόλοις καὶ ὀνόμασιν ἀφθέγκτοις, and iv.2300 ff.; Hopfner, *P.-W.*, s.v. "Mageia," 311 ff.

[82] Cf. J. Kroll, *Lehren des Hermes Trismegistos*, 91 ff., 409; C. Clerc, *Les Théories relatives au culte des images chez les auteurs grecs du II*e siècle après J.-C.*; J. Geffcken, *Arch. f. Rel.* 19 (1919) 286 ff.; Hopfner, *P.-W.*, s.v. "Mageia," 347 ff., and *OZ* I.808–812; E. Bevan, *Holy Images.*

[83] Cf. Plot. *Enn.* 4.3.11 (II.23.21 Volk.): προσπαθὲς δὲ τὸ ὁπωσοῦν μιμηθέν, ὥσπερ κάτοπτρον ἁρπάσαι εἶδός τι δυνάμενον, where ὁπωσοῦν seems to involve denying any specific virtue to magical rites of consecration.

[84] Erman, *Die ägyptische Religion*, 55; A. Moret, *Ann. Musée Guimet*, 14 (1902) 93 f.; Gadd, *Divine Rule*, 23. Eusebius seems to know this: he lists ξοάνων ἱδρύσεις among the religious and magical practices borrowed by the Greeks from Egypt (*Praep. Ev.* 10.4.4). A simple ritual of dedication by offering χύτραι was in use in classical Greece (texts in G. Hock, *Griech. Weihegebräuche*, 59 ff.); but there is no suggestion that this was thought to induce magical animation.

[85] *Asclep.* III.24ᵃ, 37ᵃ–38ᵃ (*Corp. Herm.* i.338, 358 Scott). Cf. also Preisigke, *Sammelbuch*, no. 4127, ξοάνῳ (so Nock for αοανω) τε σῷ καὶ ναῷ ἔμπνοιαν παρέχων καὶ δύναμιν μεγάλην, of Mandulis-Helios; and Numenius *apud* Orig. *c. Cels.* 5.38.

[86] This is also the period when gems incised with magical figures or formulae begin to appear in large numbers (C. Bonner, "Magical Amulets," *Harv. Theol. Rev.* 39 [1946] 30 ff.). The coincidence is not fortuitous: magic is becoming fashionable.

[87] Legends about the miraculous behaviour of public cult-statues

were, of course, as common in the Hellenistic world as in the mediaeval: Pausanias and Dio Cassius are full of them; Plutarch, *Camillus* 6, is a *locus classicus*. But such behaviour was ordinarily viewed as a spontaneous act of divine grace, not as the result of a magical ἵδρυσις or κατάκλησις. On the classical Greek attitude see Nilsson, *Gesch. der Griech. Rel.* I.71 ff.; down to Alexander's time, rationalism seems to have been in general strong enough to hold in check (at least in the educated class) the tendency to attribute divine powers to images whether public or private. In later days the belief in their animation may sometimes have been sustained by the use of fraudulent contrivances; see F. Poulsen, "Talking, Weeping and Bleeding Sculptures," *Acta Archaeologica*, 16 (1945) 178 ff.

88 Apul. *Apol.* 63. Cf. P. Vallette, *L'Apologie d'Apulée*, 310 ff.; Abt, *Die Apologie des A. u. die antike Zauberei*, 302. Such statuettes, which were permanent possessions, are, of course, somewhat different from the image constructed *ad hoc* for use in a particular πρᾶξις.

89 *Philops.* 42: ἐκ πηλοῦ Ἐρώτιόν τι ἀναπλάσας, "Ἄπιθι, ἔφη, καὶ ἄγε Χρυσίδα. Cf. *ibid.* 47, and *PGM* iv.296 ff., 1840 ff.

90 *vit. Apoll.* 5.20.

91 Animated statues may have played a part in the classical Greek Hecate-magic; see the curious notices in Suidas, s.vv. Θεαγένης and Ἑκάτειον, and cf. Diodorus 4.51, where Medea makes a hollow statue of Artemis (Hecate) containing φάρμακα, quite in the Egyptian manner.

92 Eus. *Praep. Ev.* 5.12 = *de phil. ex orac.*, pp. 129 f. Wolff. So the maker of the image at *PGM* iv.1841 asks it to send him dreams. This explains the reference to "somnia" in the *Asclepius* passage.

93 See the fragments in Bidez, *Vie de Porphyre*, App. I.

94 Photius, *Bibl.* 215. The report is second-hand, but may be accepted as showing the main drift of Iamblichus' argument. Cf. Julian, *epist.* 89b Bidez, 293AB.

95 Eunap. *vit. soph.* 475. Cf. *PGM* xii.12. The πῦρ αὐτόματον is an old piece of Iranian magic (Paus. 5.27.5 f.), of which Julianus may have preserved the tradition. But it was also known to profane conjurers (Athen. 19E; Hipp. *Ref. Haer.* 4.33; Julius Africanus, Κεστοί, p. 62 Vieillefond). It reappears in mediaeval hagiology, e.g., Caesarius of Heisterbach, *Dialogue on Miracles*, 7.46.

96 Suidas, s.v. His "psychic" gifts were further shown by the fact that the mere physical neighbourhood of an impure woman always gave him a headache.

⁹⁷ Th. de Cauzons, *La Magie et la sorcellerie en France*, II.338 (cf. also 331, 408).

⁹⁸ Cf. Wolff's App. III to his edition of Porphyry's *de phil. ex orac.*; H. Diels, *Elementum*, 55 f.; Burckhardt, *Civilisation of the Renaissance in Italy*, 282 f. (Eng. ed.); Weinreich, *Antike Heilungswunder*, 162 ff.; C. Blum, *Eranos*, 44 (1946) 315 ff. Malalas attributed to a τελεσματοποιός the virtues even of the Trojan palladium (Dobschütz, *Christusbilder*, 80* f.).

⁹⁹ Olympiodorus of Thebes in Müller's *FHG* IV.60.15 (= Photius, *Bibl.* 58.22 Bekker). The fire and water were doubtless symbolized by χαρακτῆρες. It may be a coincidence that they are the two elements used in theurgic purifications (Proclus, *in Crat.* 100.21).

¹⁰⁰ *Jâbir et la science grecque* (= *Mém. de l'Inst. d'Égypte*, 45, 1942). I am indebted to Dr. Richard Walzer for my knowledge of this interesting book.

¹⁰¹ Porphyry figures as an alchemist in Berthelot, *Alchim. grecs*, 25, as well as in the Arabic tradition (Kraus, *op. cit.*, 122, n. 3). But no genuine works of his on alchemy are known to have existed. Olympiodorus, however, and other late Neoplatonists dabbled in alchemy.

¹⁰² References to the *ad Aneb.* in Arabic literature are quoted by Kraus, *op. cit.*, 128, n. 5.

¹⁰³ I do not know on what ground Hopfner (*OZ* II.70 ff.) excludes both these types of operation from his definition of "theurgic divination proper." In defining a term like theurgy we should be guided, it seems to me, by the ancient evidence and not by *a priori* theory.

¹⁰⁴ See chap. iii, p. 60. For secondary personalities professing to be pagan gods and accepted as such by Christian exorcists, cf. Min. Felix, *Oct.* 27.6 f.; Sulpicius Severus, *Dial.* 2.6 (*PL* 20, 215c), etc.

¹⁰⁵ *in Remp.* II.123.8 ff. To judge from the context, the aim of this τελετή was probably, like that of the imaginary experiment with the ψυχουλκὸς ῥάβδος which Proclus quotes at 122.22 ff. from Clearchus, to procure a "psychic excursion" rather than possession; but it must in any case have involved the induction of some sort of trance.

¹⁰⁶ "Greek Oracles," in Abbott's *Hellenica*, 478 ff.

¹⁰⁷ Lines 216 ff. Wolff (= Eus. *Praep. Ev.* 5.9). G. Hock, *Griech. Weihegebräuche*, 68, takes the directions as referring to withdrawal of the divine presence from a statue. But such phrases as βροτὸς θεὸν οὐκέτι χωρεῖ, βροτὸν αἰκίζεσθε, ἀνάπαυε δὲ φῶτα, λῦσόν τε δοχῆα, ἄρατε φῶτα γέηθεν ἀναστήσαντες ἑταῖροι, can refer only to

a human medium. ("Controls" at modern séances regularly speak of the medium in this way, in the third person.)

[108] This is stated in several of Porphyry's oracles, e.g., l. 190, θειοδά-μοις Ἑκάτην με θεὴν ἐκάλεσσας ἀνάγκαις, and by Pythagoras of Rhodes whom Porph. quotes in this connection (*Praep. Ev.* 5.8). Compulsion is denied in the *de myst.* (3.18, 145.4 ff.), which also denies that "the Chaldaeans" use threats towards the gods, while admitting that the Egyptians do (6.5–7). On the whole subject cf. B. Olsson in ΔΡΑΓΜΑ *Nilsson*, 374 ff.

[109] In *CMAG* VI.151.10 ff. he mentions purification by brimstone and sea water, both of which come from classical Greek tradition: for brimstone cf. Hom. *Od.* 22.481, Theocr. 24.96, and Eitrem, *Opferritus*, 247 ff.; for sea water, Dittenberger, *Syll.*³ 1218.15, Eur. *IT.* 1193, Theophr. *Char.* 16.12. What is new is the purpose—to prepare the "anima spiritalis" for the reception of a higher bè-ing (Porph. *de regressu* fr. 2). Cf. Hopfner, P.-W., s.v. "Mageia," 359 ff.

[110] Cf. λύσατέ μοι στεφάνους in the Porphyrian oracle (*Praep. Ev.* 5.9), and the boy Aedesius who "had only to put on the garland and look at the sun, when he immediately produced reliable oracles in the best inspirational style" (Eun. *vit. soph.* 504).

[111] Porphyry, *loc. cit.*

[112] Proclus in *CMAG* VI.151.6: ἀποχρὴ γὰρ πρὸς μὲν αὐτοφάνειαν τὸ κνέωρον.

[113] *in Remp.* II.117.3; cf. 186.12. Psellus rightly calls it an Egyptian practice (*Ep.* 187, p. 474 Sathas): cf. *PGM* vᵃ, and the Demotic Magical Papyrus of London and Leiden, verso col. 22.2.

[114] *de myst.* 157.14. Olympiodorus, *in Alc.* p. 8 Cr., says that children and country people are more prone to ἐνθουσιασμός owing to their lack of imagination (!).

[115] Cf. Hopfner's interesting paper, "Die Kindermedien in den Gr.-Aeg. Zauberpapyri," *Festschrift N. P. Kondakov*, 65 ff. The reason usually alleged for preferring children is their sexual purity, but the real cause of their superior effectiveness was doubtless their greater suggestibility (E. M. Butler, *Ritual Magic*, 126). The Pythia of Plutarch's day was a simple country girl (Plut. *Pyth. Orac.* 22, 405c).

[116] Cf. Lord Balfour in *Proc. Soc. for Psychical Research*, 43 (1935) 60: "Mrs. Piper and Mrs. Leonard when in trance seem to lose all sense of their personal identity, whereas, so far as the observer can judge, this is never the case with Mrs. Willett. Her trance sit-tings abound with remarks describing her own experiences, and

occasionally she will make comments . . . on the messages she is asked to transmit." See also chap. iii. nn. 54, 55.

117 οὐ φέρουσιν. This explains the line οὐ φέρει με τοῦ δοχῆος ἡ τάλαινα καρδία quoted by Proclus *in Remp.* I.111.28.

118 *Proc. Soc. Psych. Research*, 28 (1915): changes of voice, convulsive movements, grinding the teeth, pp. 206 ff.; partial anaesthesia, pp. 16 f. Insensibility to fire was attributed to the medium D. D. Home, and is associated with abnormal psychological states in many parts of the world (Oesterreich, *Possession*, 264, 270, Eng. trans.; R. Benedict, *Patterns of Culture*, 176; Brunel, *Aissâoûa*, 109, 158).

119 Cf. *PGM* vii.634: πέμψον τὸν ἀληθινὸν Ἀσκληπιὸν δίχα τινὸς ἀντιθέου πλανοδαίμονος, Arnob. *adv. nat.* 4.12: magi suis in accitionibus memorant antitheos saepius obrepere pro accitis, Heliod. 4.7: ἀντίθεός τις ἔοικεν ἐμποδίζειν τὴν πρᾶξιν, Porph. *de abst.* 2.41 f., Psellus, *Op. Daem.* 22, 869B. The source of the belief is thought to be Iranian (Cumont, *Rel. Orient.*⁴, 278 ff.; Bousset, *Arch. f. Rel.* 18 [1915] 135 ff.).

120 Porphyry, *loc. cit.*, quotes a "god's" request in such circumstances that the sitting be closed: λῦε βίην κάρτος τε λόγων· ψευδήγορα λέξω. Just so will a modern "communicator" close the sitting with "I must stop now or I shall say something silly" (*Proc. Soc. Psych. Research*, 38 [1928] 76).

121 According to Proclus *in Tim.* I.139.23, and *in Remp.* I.40.18, this involves, besides the presence of the appropriate 'σύνθημα, a favourable position of the heavenly bodies (cf. *de myst.* 173.8), a favourable time and place (as often in papyri), and favourable climatic conditions. Cf. Hopfner, P.-W., s.v. "Mageia," 353 ff.

122 Proclus *in Crat.* 36.20 ff. offers a theoretical explanation of what spiritualists would call "the direct voice"; it follows Posidonian lines (cf. *Greek Poetry and Life*, 372 f.). Hippolytus knows how to fake this phenomenon (*Ref. Haer.* 4.28).

123 ἐπαιρόμενον ὁρᾶται ἢ διογκούμενον. Cf. the alleged elongation of a sixteenth-century Italian nun, Veronica Laparelli (*Jour. Soc. Psych. Research*, 19.51 ff.), and of the modern mediums Home and Peters (*ibid.*, 10.104 ff., 238 ff.).

124 This is a traditional mark of magicians or holy men. It is attributed to Simon Magus (ps.-Clem. *Hom.* 2.32); to Indian mystics (Philost. *vit. Apoll.* 3.15); to several Christian saints and Jewish rabbis; and to the medium Home. A magician in a romance lists it in his repertoire (*PGM* xxxiv.8), and Lucian satirizes such

claims (*Philops*. 13, *Asin*. 4). Iamblichus' slaves bragged of their master's being levitated at his devotions (Eunap. *vit. soph.* 458).

[125] See the passages from Psellus and Nicetas of Serrae collected by Bidez, *Mélanges Cumont*, 95 ff. Cf. also Eitrem, *Symb. Oslo.* 8 (1929) 49 ff.

[126] *de myst*. 166.15, where τοὺς καλουμένους seems to be passive (sc. θεούς), not (as Parthey and Hopfner) middle (= τοὺς κλήτορας): it is the "gods," not the operators, who improve the character of the mediums (166.18, cf. 176.3). If so, the "stones and herbs" will be σύμβολα carried by the "gods" and left behind by them, like the "apports" of the spiritualists. Cf. chap. iv, n. 19.

[127] Procl. *in Remp*. I.111.1; cf. *in Crat*. 34.28, and Psellus, *PG* 122, 1136B.

[128] Gregory of Nazianzus, *orat*. 4.55 (*PG* 35, 577C).

[129] "Kindermedien," 73 f.

[130] Cf. *de myst*. 3.14, on various types of φωτὸς ἀγωγή.

[131] Simpl. *in phys*. 613.5, quoting Proclus, who spoke of a light τὰ αὐτοπτικὰ θεάματα ἐν ἑαυτῷ τοῖς ἀξίοις ἐκφαῖνον· ἐν τούτῳ γὰρ τὰ ἀτύπωτα τυποῦσθαί φησι κατὰ τὸ λόγιον. Simplicius, however, denies that the *Oracles* described the apparitions as arising ἐν τῷ φωτί (616.18).

[132] *Greek Magical Papyri in the British Museum*, 14. Reitzenstein, *Hell. Myst.-Rel.*, 31, translated it "damit sie *sich* forme nach."

[133] *de myst*. 133.12: τοτὲ μὲν σκότος σύνεργον λαμβάνουσιν οἱ φωταγωγοῦντες, cf. Eus. *Praep. Ev*. 4.1. Conjurors pretend for their convenience that darkness is necessary, Hipp. *Ref. Haer*. 4.28.

[134] *de myst*. 133.13: τοτὲ δὲ ἡλίου φῶς ἢ σελήνης ἢ ὅλως τὴν ὑπαίθριον αὐγὴν συλλαμβανόμενα ἔχουσι πρὸς τὴν ἔλλαμψιν. Cf. Aedesius, *supra* n. 110, Psellus, *Expos. or. Chald*. 1133B, and Eitrem, *Symb. Oslo*. 22.56 ff.

Index

INDEX

(Figures in parentheses refer to the numbered notes)

Abaris 140, 144
accident, not recognised in early thought 6
Adonis 194
Aeacus 143 f., 165 (57)
Aeschines 41, 57 (71)
Aeschylus, Erinyes in 8
   evil spirits in 40
   inherited guilt in 33
   phthonos in 30 f.
   post-mortem punishment in 137
   Agam. 1497 ff.: 40
   Cho. 534: 123 (24)
   Cho. 807, 953: 91 (66)
   Eum. 104 f.: 157 (3)
   P.V. 794 ff.: 162 (37)
   Supp. 100–104: 197 (20)
   fr. 162: 57 (65)
Aetius, *Placita,* 5.2.3: 124 (28)
Afterlife, antiquity of idea 136
   deification in 144 f., 225 (9)
   epitaphs and 241, 257 (29)
   fear of 158 (13), 233 (77), 253
   reward and punishment in 35, 137 f.,
      150 f., 210, 221
   see also Hades, rebirth
ἅγος 37
ἀγωγή, in magic 301 (20)
aidos 18
aisa 8
αἰσχρόν applied to conduct 26 (109)
Al Ghazali 207
alastor 31, 39 f., 186
alchemy 295, 308 (101)
Alexander, W. H. ix
Alexander Polyhistor 111, 127 (53)
Alföldi, A. 141
ἀμηχανία 29
Ammonius Saccas 286
Amphiaraus, shrine of 110
Amphikleia, oracle of 86 (30)
amulets 253, 268 (103), 294
Anacreon, *psyche* in 138
analgesia 274
ἀνάμνησις, *see* "recollection"
Anaxagoras, and Hermotimus 143
   prosecution of 189 f., 201

angels 293, 297
Anonymus Iamblichi 197 (27)
Antiphon ὁ τερατοσκόπος distinguished
   from Antiphon the sophist 132 (100)
ἀντίθεοι 298, 310 (119)
anxiety 44, 78, 80, 97 (98), 252
anxiety-dreams 106
Apollo, ἀλεξίκακος 75
   Asiatic origin of 69
   Hyperborean 141, 144, 161 (36)
   Nomios 77
   in Plato's *Laws* 221, 223, 234 (85)
   patron of prophetic madness 68–70
   see also Delphi, Pythia
Apollonius of Tyana, as magician 285
apparitions, luminous 298 f.
   see also epiphanies, visions
"apports," in dreams 106, 123 (19)
   in theurgy 298, 311 (126)
Apuleius, as magician 285, 294, 296
"Apulunas" 69, 86 (32)
Archaic Age, definition of 50 (1)
   religious attitudes of 28–35
   social conditions in 44 f., 76 f.
"archetypal images" 121 (4)
Archilochus 31
Ares 10, 77
arete, Protagoras and Socrates on 183 f.
   change in meaning 197 (29)
Argos, oracle at 70, 73
Arimaspians 141
Aristarchus, the astronomer 246
Aristeas 141, 162 (37)
Aristides, Aelius 109 f., 113–116, 125 (32),
   130 (79), 253
Aristides Quintilianus 78
Aristophanes, incubation in 127 (56)
   and "Orphism" 147
   and Socrates 188
   Vesp. 8: 85 (21)
   Vesp. 122: 96 (91)
Aristotle, on catharsis 48, 79
   on dreams 120, 134 (116)
   early opinions of 120, 135
   on passion 185
   on the psyche 135

Aristotle—*Continued*
  psychological insight of 238 f.
  on tragedy 62 (110)
  de anima 410^b 19: 171 (94)
  Div. p. somn. 463^b 14: 134 (112)
  Met. 984^b 19: 143, 164 (50)
  Rhet. 1418^a 24: 143
Arnold, Matthew 243
Artemidorus 107, 124 (24), 133 (107)
Asclepiades 80
Asclepius 79, 110–116
  cult of, "a religion of emergencies"
    203 (83)
  holy dogs of 114, 128 (65)
  epiphany of 203 (86)
  becomes a major god 193
  holy snakes of 114, 128 (64), 193
askesis 150, 154
Assyria, dreams in 109
  oracles in 86 (31)
astral theology 220 f., 232, 240, 246
  and Pythagoreanism 248, 263 (68)
astrology 245 f., 250, 261 f., 267 (91)
astronomy, an indictable offence at
    Athens 189
  disapproval of 201 (64)
  Plato on 235 (88)
ate 2–8, 17 f., 37–41
Athena 15, 35, 54 (38), 111, 126 (50), 243
Attis 194
Auden, W. H. 238, 269 (107)
"Aufklärung," *see* Enlightenment

Bacchus, *see* Dionysus
Bakis 71, 88 (45)
βάκχαι, *see* maenads
βακχεύειν 278 (1)
Beauchamp, Sally 66
"belly-talkers" 71 f.
Bendis 194, 204 (89)
Berossus 245
Bidez, J. 283
Bilocation 140, 144
Bion of Borysthenes 34, 53 (33)
birds, in magic 290 f.
body and soul 138–143, 149, 152, 159 (27)
  in Plato 212–214
σῶμα-σῆμα 148, 152, 169 (87)
Bolus of Mendes 246 f., 248, 263 (69), 293
Bonner, Campbell 116
books, burning of 189
Bowra, Sir Maurice 2

Branchidae, oracle of 69, 73, 93 (70)
Burckhardt, Jacob 192, 212
burial rites, expenditure on 158 (9)
  Heraclitus on 181 f.
  mimic 305 (66)
  Pythagorean 226 (9)
Burnet, John 138 f.

Calhoun, G. M. 47 f.
Cassandra 70 f., 88 (45)
castration-motif 61 (103), 130 (79)
catharsis, in Archaic Age 35–37, 43 f., 48
  Aristotelian 48
  Corybantic 77–79, 231 (59)
  Cretan 162 (41)
  Dionysiac 76–78, 95 (87)
  Heraclitus on 181, 196 (13)
  Homeric 35 f., 54 (39)
  of occult self 153 f.
  Orphic 154
  in other cultures 62 (109)
  Platonic 210, 212, 222
  Posidonius on 239 f.
  Pythagorean 79, 154, 247
  shamanistic 174 (116), 175 (118)
  theurgic 295 f., 309 (109)
caves, sacred 110, 142, 166 (60)
Chalcidius, on dreams 107, 117, 124 (26)
Chaldean Oracles, see oracles
χαρακτῆρες 292, 296
"Charon's Cave" 110
children, as mediums 263 (70), 297, 309
    (115)
  stolen by maenads 275, 281 (38)
China, divine jealousy in 51 (8)
  possession in 53 (70)
  effects of religious breakdown in 203
    (81)
Christianity 249
  opposition to 260 (47)
Chrysanthius 288
Chrysippus 237, 239 f.
Cicero, on astrology 246
  on dreams 121
clairvoyance, in dreams 107, 118 f.
Claros, oracle of 69, 73, 89 (53), 91 (60),
    92 (70)
Cleanthes 237, 241
Clearchus 143
"closed" society 216, 237, 243, 255 (1),
    269 (107)
clubs, Hellenistic 243

cock, apotropaic virtue of 291, 304 (63)
conflict, moral 213, 227 (24), 257 (16)
conscience 37, 42, 55 (46)
Cook, A. B. 70
Corybantes 77–79
  relationship to Cybele cult 96 (90)
cosmopolitanism, Hellenistic 237
cosmos 221, 234 (78), 241, 247 f.
Cratippus, on dreams 121
cremation, supposed significance of 158 (8)
Cumont, F. 291
Cybele 77, 96 (90), 117, 194

daemonion, *see* Socrates
daemonios 12 f.
daemons, in Archaic Age 39–43, 45
  dreams of 57 (70)
  in Empedocles 153, 173 (111)
  evil 12, 23 (77), 31, 39–42
  evolution of term 23 (65)
  of the family 42
  fear of 39, 253, 268 (103)
  in Homer 11–14
  imprisoned in images 293 f.
  of the individual 42 f., 59 (84), 182, 289 f., 304 (55 f.)
  and the insane 68, 97 (98)
  and *moira* 23 (65), 42, 58 (79)
  in Plato 42, 213 f., 218
  and τύχη 58 (80)
Damascius 284
dancing, religious 69, 76–79, 95 (87), 270 f., 273 f.; modern survivals of 279 (9)
  mania 76, 272 f., 279
Dawkins, R. M. 275
dead, the, dreams about 119, 127 (52)
  oracles of 111
  possession by 84 (14), 298
  tendance of 136 f., 158 (8 f.)
  see also Afterlife, rebirth
defixio 194, 204, 206
deification, *see* Afterlife, ruler-worship
δεκατεύειν 56 (50)
Delphi, oracle of 44, 70–75, 222 f.
  belief in 74 f., 93 (71)
  supposed chasm and vapours at 73 f., 90 (59), 91 (66)
  originally Earth-oracle 92 (66), 110
  reasons for decline of 75

verse responses at 92 (70)
  see also Apollo, Pythia
Demetrius of Phaleron 137
Demetrius Poliorcetes 241 f., 258 (32)
Democritus, on dreams 118, 120, 132 (95)
  on poetry 82
Demodocus 80
Diagoras, prosecution of 189
Dicaearchus 134 (117)
Diels, H. 141, 143
Dieterich, A. 276
Dio Cassius 121
Diodorus 4.3: 270 f., 277
Diogenes the Cynic 113
Diogenes Laertius 1.114: 164 (51)
Dionysus 76 f., 82, 270–280
  animal vehicles of 277 f.
  not aristocratic 94 (80)
  equated with Hades 196 (14)
  as god of healing 94 (78)
  Λύσιος 273, 279 (19)
  and "Orphism" 171 (95), 176 (129)
  as god of prophecy 86 (30)
  and Titans 155 f., 176–178, 277
Diopeithes 190
  date of his decree 201 (62)
"direct voice" 310 (122)
divination, in *Iliad* always inductive 70
  Plato on 217, 222
  by shamans 140 f., 144
  theurgic 291
  rejected by Xenophanes 181
  see also dreams, prophecy
diviners, *see* seers
Dodona, oracle of 72, 126 (47)
dogs in Asclepius cult 114, 128 (65)
dreambooks 109 f., 119, 121, 132 (100), 133 (107)
dreamers, privileged 125 (35)
dreams 102–134
  anxiety- 106
  "apports" in 106
  clairvoyant or telepathic 107, 118 f., 134 (116)
  ancient classifications of 107
  influence of culture-pattern on 103, 108 f., 112, 114, 127 (52)
  "daemonic" 120, 134 (112)
  about daemons 57 (70)
  about the dead 119, 127 (52)
  from the dead 111
  dedications prescribed in 108, 294

dreams—*Continued*
 "divine" or godsent 107–110, 118–120, 125 (37)
 father-image in 109
 fear of 253, 269 (105)
 interpretation of 132 (99). *See also* dreambooks
 in Homer 104–107
 and myth 104, 128 (58)
 objective 104–106
 Oedipus- 47, 61 (105)
 Oriental 109
 prescriptions given in 115 f.
 techniques for provoking 110, 294
 as psychic excursions 104, 135, 172 (97)
 surgery in 115, 129 (72)
 symbolic 104, 106 f., 109, 119 f.
 as symptoms 119, 133 (102)
 as wish-fulfilment 106 f., 119
dualism, Platonic and Mazdean 228 (33)
 revived in first century B.C. 247
 and monism in late Greek thought 264 (72)
 see also body and soul
Dunne, J. W. 107

ecstasis, meaning of 77, 94 (84)
 see also "frenzy," possession
"ectoplasm" 299
Edelstein, L. ix, 112, 115
education, and intellectual decline 250, 267 (88)
ἐγγαστρίμυθοι, *see* "belly-talkers"
ego-consciousness 16, 41, 81
Egypt, animation of images in 293, 306 (84)
 dreams in 109 f.
 no theory of rebirth in 160 (29)
Egyptian religion, Plotinus' knowledge of 286
Ehnmark, E. 12
Eitrem, S. 283, 286, 289 f., 299
Eleusis 137, 172 (102), 258 (29), 302 (33)
 Plato's attitude to 234 (82)
Eliot, T. S. 42, 215
elongation 298, 310 (123)
Empedocles 145 f.
 on madness 65
 and "Orphism" 145, 147, 169 (81)
 psyche and daemon in 153, 173 (111)
 bodily translation of 167 (65)

frs. 15, 23: 146
fr. 111: 145 f.
fr. 129: 143, 165 (55)
ἔνθεος, meaning of 87 (41)
ἐνθύμιον 55 (46)
"enthusiasm," *see* inspiration, possession
Enlightenment, older than Sophistic Movement 180–182
 reaction against 188–192
 effects of 191–195, 203 (81)
 Plato and 208
Ἐφέσια γράμματα 204 (95)
Epicureans 240
Epicurus 237–238, 241, 246
 as a god 259 (36)
 alleged scientific spirit of 265 (77)
Epidaurus, Temple Record of 112
Epigenes 149, 171 (96)
epilepsy, confused with possession 66, 83 (10)
 ancient medical opinion on 84 (20)
 musical treatment of 99 (109), 179 (17)
 why called "sacred" 83 (11)
Epimenides 110, 141–146, 163, 175 (121), 234 (81)
epiphanies 24 (91), 116 f., 126 (50), 131 (83 f.), 203 (86), 277
epitaphs 241, 257 (29)
ἐπῳδαί 175 (119), 212, 226 (20)
Erinyes 6–8, 18, 38 f., 42
 not the vengeful dead 21 (37)
Eros 41, 218, 231
Eudoxus 245
Euripides 186–188
 and Anaxagoras 182
 Dionysiac rites in 270–278
 Erinyes in 42
 and Heraclitus 182, 197 (21)
 and "Orphism" 147 f.
 prosecution of (?) 189
 on *phthonos* 31
 and the Sophists 182
 and Xenophanes 182, 197 (21)
 Med. 1078–80: 186, 199 (46)
 Hipp. 375 ff.: 186 f., 200 (49)
 Hyps. fr. 31 Hunt: 169 (82)
 Tro. 1171 ff.: 159 (22)
 fr. 472: 169 (82)
Eurycles 71
Eusebius of Myndus 288
exorcism 99 (103)

family, patriarchal 45 f.
　solidarity of 33 f., 46 f., 76, 109, 150
　tensions in 46–48
fasting 110, 140
Fate, see moira
father, image of, in dreams 109
　king as 259 (36)
　offences against 46 f.
　Zeus as 47 f.
Festugière, A. J., 147 f., 240, 249, 251
fey 24 (88)
finger-sacrifice 116, 130 (79)
fire, insensibility to 274, 297, 310 (118)
　spontaneous 307 (95)
Flavianus 295
flute 78, 97 (95), 273
foreign cults at Athens 193 f.
Forster, E. M. 64
Frankfort, H. and H. A. 41
freedom, fear of 246, 252, 254
　loss of political, effects of 250
　of thought, limitations on, at Athens
　　201 (63), 202 (68), in Plato's
　　Laws 223 f.
free will in Homer 7, 20 (31)
"frenzy," of the poet 82
　of the Pythia 87 (41)
Freud, S. 42, 49, 59 (84), 106, 114, 116,
　119 f., 151 f., 213, 218
Fry, Roger 1

Galen, believes in dreams 121, 133 (104)
Gebir 295
ghost, consubstantial with corpse 136–
　138, 172 (102)
Ghost Dance 279 (11)
Glotz, G. 34, 40
gods, astral 220 f., 232, 240
　cause ate 4–5
　compulsion of 309 (108)
　disguised 25 (93)
　Epicurean 240
　famine and pestilence as 41, 84 (14)
　love and fear of 35, 54 (38)
　communicate menos 8–10
　send monitions 11 f.
　mythological, in Plato 220, 231 (66)
　physical intervention of 14, 24 (90)
　representation of, in art 63 (112)
　inspire song 10
　tempt men 38–41, 57 (65), 63 (112)

Xenophanes on 181
see also epiphanies, phthonos
gold plates 147 f., 154
griffons 141
Gruppe, O. 277
guilt, inherited 31 f., 34, 53, 150, 221
guilt-culture 17 f., 26 (106), 28, 43
　divine jealousy in 62 (108)
　emphasis on justice in 54 (34)
　and puritanism 152
　needs supernatural authority 75
guilt-feelings, in Archaic Age 36 f., 47,
　151, 156
　in Greco-Roman world 130 (79), 252 f.
　abreaction of 63 (110)
Guthrie, W. K. C. ix

Hades, in the air 111
　Dionysus equated with 196 (14)
　mud in 172 (102)
　as state of mind 221, 233 (77)
　this world as 115, 174 (114), 225 (5)
　see also Afterlife
hallucinations, see visions
head, ecstatic carriage of 273 f.
　mantic 147, 168 (78)
healing, religious 69, 77–79, 98 (100, 102),
　111–116, 140, 144–146, 193, 272
Heaven, see Afterlife
Hecataeus of Miletus 180, 195 (5)
Hecate, cult at Aegina 96 (91)
　apparition of 299
　magical images of 294, 307 (91)
　and mental disturbance 77–79
　shrines of 200 (61)
Heinimann, F. 182
heliocentric hypothesis, rejection of 246,
　262 (58)
Helios, see sun-cult
Hell, see Afterlife, Hades
Hellenistic Age 235–243
Heraclides Ponticus 143
Heraclitus 8, 42, 93 (71), 94 (80), 113
　on dreams 118, 131 (91)
　influence of 182
　rationalism of 181 f., 196 f.
　on the soul 150, 152, 173 (109)
　frs. 14, 15: 196 (14)
　fr. 92: 85 (27)
Heraiscus 294
Hermae, mutilation of 191, 202 (78)
Hermocles 241, 258 (32)

Hermotimus 141, 143 f.
Herodas 4.90 f.: 129 (66)
Herodotus, on dreams 118
    fatalism of 42, 56 (55)
    inherited guilt in 33
    causes of madness in 65
    phthonos in 30 f.
    2.81: 169 (80), 171 (96)
    4.36: 161 (33)
    4.95: 144, 165 (60)
    5.92: 111
    6.105: 117
    6.135: 40
"heroes" 77, 243
heroisation 259 (34)
Herophilus, on dreams 107, 124 (28)
Herzog, R. 112
Hesiod 33, 38, 42, 45, 81
    Theog. 22 ff.: 81, 117, 131 (86)
    Theog. 188 ff.: 61 (103)
High Priest, in Plato's *Laws* 233 (71)
Hippocrates, *de morbo sacro* 67 f., 77 f.
    On Regimen 119, 133
    Int. 48: 117, 131 (90)
    Progn. 1: 84 (20)
history, irrational elements in 269 (108)
Hittites 46, 61 (103), 69, 86 (32), 109
Holiness Church 275
Homer 2–27
    catharsis in 35 f., 54 (39)
    Dionysus in 94 (80)
    divine justice in 32
    divine machinery in 9, 12, 14, 105
    dreams in 104–107
    ego-consciousness in 16, 25 (98)
    free will in 7, 20 (31)
    attitude to gods 29, 35
    Hades in 136 f.
    late elements in 5, 6, 52 (16), 60 (102), 99 (115)
    madness in 67
    appeals to Muses 80 f.
    alleged Orphic interpolation in 137
    silence of 43 f., 70, 110
    virtue in 45
    Iliad 1.63: 123 (22)
        1.198: 14
        2.484 ff.: 80 f., 100 (116)
        3.278 f.: 158 (10)
        9.512: 6
        10.391: 19 (20)
        11.403–410: 25 (98)
        13.61 ff.: 9
        15.461 ff.: 12
        19.86 ff.: 3, 6
        19.259 f.: 158 (10)
        22.199 ff.: 123 (20)
        24.480: 19 (17)
    Odyssey 1.32 ff.: 32, 52 (21)
        8.487 ff.: 100 (116)
        9.410 ff.: 67
        18.327: 67
        20.351 ff.: 87 (38)
        20.377: 67
        22.347 f.: 10
homunculi 295
Hopfner, T. 283, 289 f., 299
Hosioi at Delphi 73 f.
Hrozný, B. 69
hubris 31, 38 f., 48, 52 (13)
Hugo, Victor 102
Huxley, Aldous 271
Huxley, T. H. 236
hydromancy 264 (70)

Iamblichus 287 f., 294, 296–298, 303
    de myst. 166.15: 311 (126)
    vit. Pyth. 240: 178
images, Chrysippus on cult of 240
    Heraclitus on cult of 182
    magical animation of 292–295, 307 (91)
    used for magical attack 194, 205 (96)
    miraculous 306 (87)
immortality, *see* Afterlife
impurity, *see miasma*
incest 61 (105), 187, 200 (57)
incubation 110–116, 203 (83)
    see also dreams
India, pollution and purification in 62 (109), 156
    rebirth in 156, 160 (29), 172 (97)
    "recollection" in 173 (107)
Indian dreambooks 133 (107)
individual, emancipation of 34, 142, 150, 191, 237, 242 f.
insanity, *see* madness
Inscriptiones Graecae II², 4962: 128 (65)
    IV², i.121–124: 112
inspiration, of minstrels in Homer 10, 22 (63), 80 f.
    of poets 81 f.
    of Pythia 70–74, 87 (41)
intellectualism, Greek 16 f., 26 (105), 184, 239 f.

intellectuals and masses, cleavage between 180, 185, 192 f., 221, 244 f.
prosecutions of 189–191, 223 f.
Ion of Chios 149
Irrational, Greek awareness of the 1, 254
return of the 244–253
irrational soul, *see* soul
Isocrates 4.29: 54 (37)
Italy, pollution and purification in 62 (109)

Jaeger, W. 146
James, William 1
jealousy, divine, *see phthonos*
John XXII, Pope 294
Julian, the Emperor 288, 299
Epist. 12: 303 (47)
Julianus, the theurgist 283–285, 288, 292–295, 301
Julianus, the "Chaldaean philosopher" 284 f.
Jung, C. G. 121 (4), 125 (37)
justice, divine 31–35, 45, 150 f., 221
guilt-culture and 54 (34)

κάθαρσις, *see* catharsis
Κακοδαιμονισταί 188
καλόν applied to conduct 26 (109)
Kardiner, A. 37
κατάθεσις, *see defixio*
kettledrum 78, 273
Kinesias 188 f., 200 (61)
Koestler, A. 216
koros 31, 51 (8)
Kraus, P. 295
Kroll, W. 283 f., 286
Kronos 46, 61 (103)
Κυανέαι, oracle of 87 (40)
Kumarbi, Epic of 61 (103)

Labeo, Cornelius 301 (15)
Latte, K. 70, 117
laurel 73
levitation 298, 310 (124)
Lévy-Bruhl, L. viii, 40
libido 213, 218
Liddell and Scott's *Lexicon*, mistakes in 5, 19 (17), 54 (37), 89 (49), 159 (19)
"lights" at séances 299
Linforth, I. M. ix, 75, 78 f., 147 f.
Locrian Tribute 37
Long Sleep 142, 164 (46), 210

Lourdes 113, 115, 128 (60)
luck 42
lychnomancy 299
Lycurgus, the orator 39
Lysias, fr. 73: 188 f.

Macrobius, on dreams 107, 109, 124 (24)
madness, Greek attitude to 65–68, 85 (23)
daemonic origin of, 5, 39, 66 f.
in Homer 67
special language in 85 (24)
poetic 80–82
prophetic 68–75
ritual 75–79, 270–280
supernatural power in 68
maenads 270–280
magic, biological function of 45
birds in 290 f.
family transmission of 303 (49)
in fifth-century literature 205 (99)
fourth-century revival of 194 f., 206
of the Juliani 285
and mysticism 302 (35)
Neopythagorean 263 (70)
Plotinus on 285 f.
purity required in 290, 304 (57)
ritual 223
see also defixio, ἐπῳδαί, theurgy
magical papyri 110, 283, 289, 292 f., 299
PGM vii.505 ff.: 304 (56)
PGM vii.540 ff.: 299
Malinowski, B. 45, 59 (92)
Malraux, A. 254
mana, royal 259 (36)
μαντική, *see* divination, prophecy
μάντις, derivation of 70
see also seers
Marcus Aurelius 121, 215, 248
Marinus 284
Marxism 49, 251
masks 94 (82)
Maximus, the theurgist 288, 294
Mazon, P. 2
Medea 186, 199 (44, 46), 257 (16)
medical clairvoyance 119
medicine, profane, and religious healing 115 f., 129 (74), 130 (77)
mediums, spirit 70, 73
may break down during trance 90 (59)
stertorous breathing of 72, 89 (52)
not "frenzied" 87 (41)

mediums—*Continued*
  see also children, possession, spiritual-
    ism, trance
Melampus 77, 95 (85)
Melville, Herman 135
Menecrates 66
menos, communication of 8–10
  of kings 22 (47)
Mesopotamia, incubation in 126 (48)
  see also Assyria
Meuli, K. 140
miasma, 35–37, 44, 48, 56 (47), 223, 235
  (86 f.)
  infectiousness of 36, 55 (43 f.), 191,
    205 (98)
  of spilt blood 154
microcosm, man as 119
Milet VI.22: 276
Miltiades 40
Minoan religion, survivals of, *see* religion
Minoans, incubation known to (?) 110,
  126 (48)
minstrels 10, 23 (63), 80 f.
moira 6–8, 20 (30), 34, 38, 42
  and daemon 23 (65), 42, 58 (79)
Moirai 7, 20 (29 f.)
Murray, G. 2, 45, 179, 192
Muses 80–82, 99 (111), 117
music, as means of healing 78–80, 99
  (108 f.), 272
  orgiastic 273
  Pythagorean 79, 154, 175 (119)
  of shamans 147, 175 (119)
Myers, Frederic 296
Mysteries, Heraclitus on 181
  see also Eleusis
myth, and dream 104, 128 (58)

natural theology, rejection of 248, 264
  (71)
Nechepso, Revelations of 245
necromancy 264 (70), 285
nemesis 26 (109), 31
Neoplatonism, and theurgy 285–289
Neopythagoreanism 247 f., 263, 301 (15)
Nero 294
Nestorius, the theurgist 294
Nicephoros Gregoras 289, 298
Nietzsche, F. 68
Nilsson, M. P. viii, 13–15, 69, 150, 190,
  242, 249, 251, 283
Nock, A. D. ix, 249, 252, 270, 283

Nomos and *Physis* 182 f., 187 f.
nous, separability of 143

occult properties 246 f.
occult self 139 f., 146 f., 155, 156 (1), 247
  called "daemon" by Empedocles 153,
    173 (111)
  identified by Plato with rational *psyche*
    210
occultism 248
  distinguished from magic 265 (76)
Oedipus dream 47, 61 (105)
  myth of 36
Oesterreich, T. K. 73
Old Testament, divine jealousy in 51 (8)
  inherited guilt in 53 (26)
Olympiodorus, *in Phaed.* 87.1 ff.: 178
Omophagia 76, 155, 276–278
  ὠμοφάγιον ἐμβαλεῖν 276, 281 (49)
ὀνειροπόλος 123 (22)
oneiros, meaning in Homer 104
  see also dreams
Onomacritus 143, 155
"open" society 237, 252, 254, 255 (1),
  269 (107)
oracles, Assyrian 86 (31)
  Chaldaean 283–285, 287 f., 292 f.
  dream- 110 f., 126 (49)
  from magic images 292–295
  of the Muse 82
  of Orpheus 147
  Porphyrian 287, 294, 296, 299
  in late Roman times 94 (75)
  see also Amphikleia, Argos, Branchidae,
    Claros, Delphi, Dodona, Κυανέαι,
    Patara, Ptoon
ὀρειβασία 76, 270 f.
Oriental influence on Greek thought 61
  (103), 133 (107), 140, 228 (133), 249,
  257 (20), 266 (86)
Original Sin 156
Orpheus 147 f.
Orphic influence on Aeschylus, alleged 137
  catharsis 154
  theory of dreams 118 f.
  reform at Eleusis, alleged 137
  interpolation in Homer, alleged 137
  poems 143, 148 f., 154
  Titan myth 155 f.
"Orphism," alleged Asiatic origin of
  160 (29)
  unproved assertions about 147 f.

as historical mirage 170 (88)
and Empedocles 145, 147, 169 (81)
and Heraclitus 196 (14)
and Plato 148, 234 (82)
and Pythagoras 143, 149
and Pythagoreanism 149, 171 (95 f.)
Ouranos 46, 61 (103)
"overdetermination" 7, 16, 30 f., 51 (10)

Pan, causes mental disturbance 77, 95 (89)
  vision of 117
Panaetius 246, 256 (14)
parents, offences against 32, 46 f., 60 (101)
Parke, H. W. 74
"participation" 40
passion, Greek view of 185 f.
  Plato on 213
  Stoics on 239, 256 (11, 16)
Patara, oracle of 69 f.
πατραλοίας 61 (104)
patria potestas 45
Pausanias 8.37.5: 155
Pearce, Nathaniel 274
Pentheus, myth of 278
Peregrinus 253, 267 (100)
Periander 111
personality, secondary 66
Pfeiffer, R. 270
Pfister, F. 37, 44
Phaedra 186 f., 199 (44, 47)
Phemius 10, 99 (115)
Pherecydes, two souls in 153
Philippides 117
Phocylides 42
Phoenicians, prophecy among 69
phthonos, divine 29–31, 41, 44, 221
  origin of belief in 62 (108)
  parallels from other cultures 51 (8)
Physis, see Nomos
Pindar, 33, 42, 104
  on Afterlife 135, 137 f.
  and the Muse 81 f.
  vision experienced by 117
  fr. 127: 155 f.
Piper, Mrs. 89 (52), 91 (61), 297, 309 (116)
Plato, and astrology 245, 261 (52 f.)
  on Corybantic rites 79, 217 f.
  daemon of the individual in 42, 213 f.
  on Delphi 222 f.
  on dreams 108, 120
  and the Enlightenment 208

Epinomis, authorship of 233 (70)
  on Evil 212 f.
  and family jurisdiction 46
  "Guardians" in 210 f., 216
  on inherited guilt 34, 53 (32), 221
  hedonism in 211
  influence on Hellenistic religion 240
  on love 218, 231
  on magic 194, 205 (97)
  Mazdean influence on (?) 228 (33), 232 (70)
  and "Orphism" 148, 234 (82)
  on poetry 82, 217 f., 230
  post-mortem cult of 226 (9)
  on prophecy 71, 88 (46), 217 f., 230
  on the psyche 135, 210, 212–215
  and the Pythagoreans 209 f., 225 (5), 226 (9), 227 (30)
  on rebirth 151
  on religious reform 219–224
  on sacrifice 222
  and shamanism 209 f.
  and Socrates 198 (33), 208 f., 212, 216 f., 226 (19), 230 (48)
  Crat. 400C: 169 (87)
  Euthyd. 277D: 79, 99 (104)
  Gorg. 493A–C: 209, 225 (5)
  Ion 536C: 79, 98 (102)
  Laws 701C: 156, 176 (132)
  Laws 791A: 98 (102), 231 (59)
  Laws 854B: 156, 177 (133)
  Laws 887D: 232 (70)
  Laws 896E: 227 (24)
  Laws 904D: 233 (77)
  Laws 909B: 222, 234
  Meno 81BC: 155 f.
  Phaedo 62B: 171 (95)
  Phdr. 244AB: 64, 87 (41)
  Phdr. 251B, 255CD: 231 (59)
  Prot. 319A–320C: 198 (33)
  Prot. 352B: 199 (47)
  Rep. 364B–365A: 149, 170 (92), 222, 234
  Rep. 468E–469B: 225 (9)
  Soph. 252C: 89 (49)
  Symp. 215C: 98 (102)
Platonism 247, 249
Pliny, N.H. 11.147: 96 (94)
Plotinus, rationalism of 246, 265 (78), 285 f.
  evocation of his daemon 289–291
  Enn. 1.9: 301 (26)
  Enn. 5.5.11: 302 (33)

Plutarch 34, 121, 253
  on Delphi 72–74
  def. orac. 438BC: 72 f., 90
poets, inspiration of 80–82, 101, 217 f.
  and seers 100 (118)
polarisation of Greek mind 193, 203 (87)
pollution, *see miasma*
Porphyry 286 f., 294 f., 298
  vit. Plot. 10: 289–291
  de abst. 4.16: 290
  de phil. ex orac. 216 ff.: 308 (107)
Poseidon 77
Posidonius 111, 228 (30), 239, 247, 256,
  263 (65), 310 (122)
possession, origin of belief in 66 f.
  Corybantic 78
  by the dead 84 (14), 298
  Dionysiac 77, 271 f.
  fear of 253
  by Muses 80, 82
  passion as 186
  prophetic 70–75
  dist. shamanism 71, 88 (43), 140
  somnambulistic dist. lucid 72, 89 (54)
  un-Homeric 10, 67
  see also mediums, trance
power, communication of 8–10
Prince, Morton 66
Proclus, on the *Chaldaean Oracles* 284, 289
  theurgy of 288, 291 f., 298 f.
Procopius of Gaza 283
progress, idea of 183
prophecy, Dionysiac 86 (30)
  older than divination 86 (31)
  ecstatic, in western Asia 69 f., 86 (31)
  oracular 70–75
  Plato's view of 217 f.
  spontaneous 70
  in verse form 92 (70)
Prophetes, at Claros 93 (70)
  at Delphi 72 f., 74
Protagoras 183–185
  prosecution of 189, 201 (63, 66)
Psellus, Michael 283–285, 289, 292, 297
  Script. Min. I.262.19, 446.26: 301 (18)
psyche, in Homer 15 f., 136–138
  in Ionian poets 138
  in fifth-century Attic writers 138 f.
  in Empedocles 153
  in Plato 212–215
  as appetitive self 138 f., 159 (26)
  sometimes resides in blood 159 (27)

  as dog's name 159 (26)
  as occult self of divine origin 139 f.,
    209 f., 212
  occult powers of 118–120, 133 (104), 135
  returns to fiery aether 174 (112)
  unitary and tripartite 213 f., 227 (24,
    30), 228
  see also Afterlife, rebirth, soul
psychiatry, ancient 79 f.
  philosophy as 265 (79)
psychic excursion, dream as 104, 135,
  172 (97)
  in trance 140–143, 149, 285
psychic intervention in Homer 2–18
Ptoon, oracle of 91 (60)
puppet, man as 214
purification, *see* catharsis
puritanism, Greek 139 f., 149 f., 154–156,
  175, 212 f.
  and guilt-culture 152
purity, ritual and moral 37, 55 (47), 243
  as means to salvation 154
Pythagoras 110, 143–146, 154, 166 f., 168
  (75), 247
  and "Orphism" 143, 149, 172 (96)
  as magician 167 (64), 264 (70)
Pythagoras of Rhodes 297
Pythagorean catharsis 79, 154
  community 144
  silence 154, 175 (122)
  "recollection" 152
  vegetarianism 154, 171 (95)
Pythagoreanism, Alexander Polyhistor's
  account of 127 (53)
  and astral religion 248, 263 (68)
  Empedocles and 145
  and "Orphism" 149, 171 (95 f.)
  "scientific" and "religious" 167 (68)
  and shamanism 167 (63)
  unity of soul in 227 (30)
  status of women in 165 (59)
  see also Neopythagoreanism
Pythia, inspiration of 70–74, 87 (41)
  bribery of 92 (68)
  see also Delphi
pythons, *see* "belly-talkers"

racial memory, alleged 121 (4)
rationalism, Greek 1, 254
  achievements of 34, 116, 117–120, 180–
    185, 236–238
  of Plato 208 f., 212, 216–218

of Hellenistic philosophy 238–241
decline of 247–253
see also Enlightenment
rebirth, in animal form 154, 215, 229 (43)
of Epimenides and Pythagoras 143 f.
absent from epitaphs 258 (29)
not of Egyptian origin 160 (29)
relation of Greek to Indian belief in
160 (29), 172 (97)
taught in Orphic poems 149
as privilege of shamans 144, 151, 165
(58)
Thracian belief in 166 (60)
why some Greeks accepted 150–152
"recollection," Pythagorean dist. Platonic 152, 173 (107), 210
religion, Apolline dist. Dionysiac 68 f.,
76, 156
in Archaic Age 28–50
Hellenistic 240–243
Homeric 2–18, 35, 43 f.
Minoan, survivals of 14 f., 59 (91),
91 (62), 142, 146
and moral paradoxes 63 (112)
moralisation of 32–35
and morals 31
rationalist critique of 180–182
regression of, in late fifth century 192–
195
proposals for stabilising 219–224
see also daemons, gods, "Orphism"
responsibility, fear of 77, 97 (98), 246,
252, 254
Rohde, E. 7, 65, 68, 139, 150
Rose, H. J. 104, 106
ruler-worship 242, 258 (32), 259

Sabazius 194, 276, 281 (42, 44), 282 (58)
sacrifice 222
Sarapis 108
scapegoats 43
Sceptics 240
science, Greek, achievements of 236 f.
alleged overspecialisation in 250
lack of experiment in 251, 267 (94)
contempt of Hellenistic philosophers for
265 (77)
second-sight 70
seers, attack intellectuals 190
in Plato 88 (46), 217, 222, 230 (56)
and poets 81 f., 100 (118)
ridicule of 182, 190

Semonides of Amorgos 30, 138
Seneca 249
sex, Greek puritanism and 154 f., 175
(122 f.), 199 (43)
change of 140, 161 (32)
Shackleton, Sir Ernest 117
shamanism, definition of 140
dist. Dionysiac religion 142
dist. possession 71, 88 (43), 140
Thraco-Scythian 140 f.
Greek 141–147, 149 f., 152, 161 (32)
Plato's transposition of 209 f.
bibliography of 160 (30)
shamanistic use of arrows 161 (34)
bilocation 140 f., 144
power over birds and beasts 147, 168
(75)
change of sex 140, 161 (32)
divination 140 f., 144
fasting 140–142
food-taboos 175 (121)
healing 140 f., 144–146
journey to spirit world 140, 144, 147,
151, 210
use of music 147, 175 (119)
psychic excursion 140–143, 149, 160
(31)
purifications 174 (116), 175 (118)
reincarnation 144, 153, 165 (56)
"retreat" 140, 142, 149, 210
tattooing 142
trance 140–142, 160 (31), 164 (46), 210
shame-culture 17 f., 28, 43
Sibyl, the 71
Sidgwick, Mrs. Henry 297
sin, sense of 36 f.
slavery, and intellectual decline 251
sleepwalking 66, 84 (14)
Small, H. A. ix
snake-handling in Kentucky 275
in the Abruzzi 281 (43)
snakes in Asclepius cult 114, 128 (64)
in Dionysiac cult 275–277, 281
sneezing 24 (87)
Snell, B. 15
Socrates, on *arete* 183 f.
takes part in Corybantic rites 79
daemonion of 117, 185, 190, 202 (74)
dreams of 107, 185
believes in oracles 93 (71), 185, 198 (36)
paradoxes of 17
prosecution of 189 f., 192, 202 (74), 209

Socrates—*Continued*
  in what sense rationalist 184 f.
  practises mental withdrawal 225 (6)
  see also Plato
solidarity of the city-state 191, 235 (87)
  of the family 33 f., 46 f., 76, 109, 150
Solon, poems of 30, 33
  legislation of 46, 137
Sophistic Movement 180, 182–185, 187–189
Sophocles, exponent of archaic world-view 49
  entertains Asclepius 193
  body and soul in 138
  Erinyes in 42
  Eros in 41
  status of man in 51 (6)
  phthonos in 52 (12)
  Ajax 243 f.: 85 (24)
  Ant. 176: 139
  Ant. 583 ff.: 49 f.
  Ant. 1075: 21 (37)
  El. 62 ff.: 141, 162 (39)
  O.C. 964 ff.: 53 (25)
  O.T. 1258: 85 (25)
Soranus 80
soul, in bird form 141, 162 (38)
  inconsistent views of 179 f.
  irrational, in Plato 120, 213 f., 228 (30),
    denied by Stoics 239
  plurality of souls 153, 174 (111)
  shadow- 122 (10)
  stolen 147
  see also Afterlife, body, *psyche*, rebirth
Sparagmos 155, 276–278
Spengler, O. 269 (106)
spirit language 85 (24)
spirits, "dumb" 90 (57)
  see also daemons
spiritualism, modern 74, 206, 250
  and theurgy 296–299
  see also mediums
spitting, apotropaic 98
springs, sacred 73, 91 (64)
στάσις, *see* conflict
statues, *see* images
Stoic acceptance of astrology 246, 262 (57)
  view of dreams 121
  view of inspiration 93 (71)
  intellectualism 239 f.
  religion 240 f.
  doctrine of "sympathy" 247

στοιχεῖα 295
sublimation 218, 227 (26)
σύμβολα 292 f., 295 f.
sun-cult, in Plato's *Laws* 221, 223
  in *Chaldaean Oracles* 285, 301 (18)
Super-ego 42
superstition, Theophrastus and Plutarch
  on 253
survival, *see* Afterlife
σύστασις, in magic 301 (20), 302 (34)
swan-maidens 162 (37)
"sympathies," occult 247, 292 f.
Synesius 298

Taghairm 126 (43)
talismans 294
ταπεινός 215, 229 (39)
ταράσσειν 51 (3)
tattooing, sacral 142, 163 (43 f.)
telepathy, in dreams 118, 120, 134 (116)
τελεστική 292–295, 305 (67)
Tennyson, Lord 184
Theoclymenus 70
Theognis 30, 33, 39, 41 f.
θεόπεμπτος, meaning of 132 (97)
Theophrastus 80, 237, 253
Theoris 204 (95), 205 (98)
Theoteknos 295
Thesiger, Ernest 276
theurgy, 283–311
  bibliography of 283
  Iranian elements in 291, 299
  origin of 282–285
  and magic 285, 288, 291
  and Neoplatonism 285–289
  modus operandi of 291–299
Thomas, H. W. 147
thumos 16, 138 f., 186, 228 (32)
Tibet, animation of images in 305 (72)
time 17 f., 32, 174 (113)
Timo 40
Titan myth, antiquity of 155 f., 176–178
tradition, and the individual 237 f., 242 f.
trance, Corybantic 78, 96 (94)
  induction of 73 f., 89 (52), 295–297
  of Pythia 72, 87 (41), 89 (53), 90 (55)
  shamanistic 140–142, 160 (31), 164
    (46), 210
  theurgic 295–299

voice heard in 113
  change of voice in 91 (61), 297
  see also mediums, possession, psychic
    excursion
transmigration of souls, *see* rebirth
τριετηρίδες 270, 278 (2)
τύχη 58 (80)
  cult of 242, 259 (37)
Tylor, E. B. 112

unio mystica, dist. theurgy 286
Upanishads 156
Uranus, *see* Ouranos

vegetarianism, origin of 154, 175 (121)
virtue, *see* arete
  visions, hypnopompic 124 (24), 128 (62)
  waking 108, 116 f., 128 (62), 130 (82),
    131
Viza mummers 275

war, social effects of 190 f., 250
wealth, Homeric and Archaic attitudes
  to 45, 60 (95)
Weinreich, O. 66, 112
Whitehead, A. N. 179, 243

Wilamowitz, U. von 73, 147, 155, 182
  191, 193
will, concept lacking in early Greece 7,
  26 (105)
  see also free will
wine, *ate* caused by 5, 38
  and poetry 101 (124)
  religious use of 69

Xenocrates, and Titan myth 156, 177
  (133), 178 (134)
Xenophanes, rationalism of 118, 180 f.
  influence of 182
  fr. 7: 143, 165 (55)
  fr. 23: 196 (9)
Xenophon, on the *psyche* 135
  Anab. 7.8.1: 132 (99)
  Mem. 1.6.13: 133 (100)

Zalmoxis 144, 165 (60), 166 (61), 175
  (119)
Zeno of Citium 237–240
Zeus 3 f., 6, 18, 29, 42, 108, 241
  as heavenly Father 47 f.
  as agent of justice 31–33
  capable of pity in Homer 35